THE CONQUERING NINTH

The Ninth U.S. Army in World War II

NATHAN N. PREFER

CASEMATE

Philadelphia & Oxford

Published in the United States of America and Great Britain in 2020 by
CASEMATE PUBLISHERS
1950 Lawrence Road, Havertown, PA 19083, USA
and
The Old Music Hall, 106–108 Cowley Road, Oxford OX4 1JE, UK

Hardback Edition: ISBN 978-1-61200-828-8
Digital Edition: ISBN 978-1-61200-829-5

A CIP record for this book is available from the British Library

Printed and bound in the United States of America by Sheridan

Typeset by Versatile PreMedia Services (P) Ltd

For a complete list of Casemate titles, please contact:

CASEMATE PUBLISHERS (US)
Telephone (610) 853-9131
Fax (610) 853-9146
Email: casemate@casematepublishers.com
www.casematepublishers.com

CASEMATE PUBLISHERS (UK)
Telephone (01865) 241249
Email: casemate-uk@casematepublishers.co.uk
www.casematepublishers.co.uk

"There is a soul to an army as well as to the individual man, and no general can accomplish the full work of his army unless he commands the soul of his men as well as their bodies and legs."

William T. Sherman: *Memoirs*, 1875

"The qualities which commonly make an army formidable are long habits of regularity, great exactness of discipline, and great confidence in the commander."

Samuel Johnson, 1709–1784

"A Crackerjack Army"

Remark made by General Omar N. Bradley describing the Ninth U.S. Army, as recorded in the diary of his senior aide, Major Chester ("Chet") Hanson, MHRC

Contents

Maps

Introduction

They have been called the "Greatest Generation." Books have been written about their lives and the way they changed the world we now live in but, as always, there is much left overlooked and uncovered. This book tells one of those many stories which has yet to be presented to students of that era. It covers the period 1944–1945 and relates the achievements of the Ninth U.S. Army, one of five armies which participated in the Northwest European campaign.

Much has been written of the American participation in that campaign. But concentration has remained on the more "flamboyant" leaders and their armies, such as Lieutenant General George S. Patton's Third U.S. Army, or the First U.S. Army, which was first ashore and which carried a major share of that campaign. But the others, the Seventh U.S. Army under Lieutenant General Alexander ("Sandy") Patch and the Ninth U.S. Army under Lieutenant General William H. Simpson, are often neglected or mentioned in passing. These armies, and the latter arriving Fifteenth U.S. Army under Lieutenant General Leonard Gerow, made major contributions to the victory of the "Greatest Generation" in this campaign.

The purpose of this book is to bring to light the workings of an American field army in World War II, how it operated, what it accomplished and where it stood in the hierarchy of the American military organization of the period. Field armies are often overlooked in the history of the war, seen as headquarters sinecure for high-ranking officers to collect their pay and add to their medals, preparing for post-war billets. This story also tells of the importance of personalities in the way the war was conducted in Western Europe in 1944–1945.

But most importantly it tells the tale of the soldiers who fought the war, often without newspaper headlines to cheer the folks at home, in battles that never made headlines. It tells of the choices, compromises, and judgements made by the senior commanders, often based on needs other than purely military.

There has been no published history of the Ninth U.S. Army since immediately after the war, when the Army itself published a history of its own, largely facts, figures, dates, and places. But for eight months the Ninth U.S. Army fought its way across Western Europe alongside better-known commands, accomplishing important victories, and becoming a vital link in inter-allied cooperation and success. For nearly half of that time, it was under the command of Field Marshal Bernard L. Montgomery's Twenty-First Army Group, the only American Army to serve under foreign command for so long a period. Given the well-known inter-allied bickering during these campaigns, it is a tribute to the Ninth U.S. Army, and particularly its commander, General Simpson, that this unusual arrangement worked so well for so long. Yet by its very attachment to a foreign command, little has been related about that army. It is past time for its story to be told.

As with any literary work, no author stands alone. There are many whose contributions to this book need to be mentioned, but space and time for only a few. Chief among these are my publisher, Ruth Sheppard, and her staff at Casemate Publishers, including the hard-working editors Isobel Fulton, David Smith, and Felicity Goldsack. These individuals encouraged and worked with me to produce the first modern history of a remarkable military command with energy and dedication that is much appreciated.

Equally important are Jo Ellen Chizmar and her staff at Real War Photos who not only produced many of the photos included in this book but had to do it twice through no fault of their own. This they did with a grace and charm that deserves gratitude. Similarly, the staff at the National Archives and Records Administration at College Park, Maryland, with their untiring dedication and knowledgeable expertise were of immense assistance throughout the process of research and illustration. Nevertheless, any errors remain mine alone.

Finally, without the encouragement, assistance and critiques of my wife, Barbara Ann, the history of this all but forgotten army would have never seen the light of day. And to my mother, Jeannette Florence, herself a member of the "Greatest Generation," who also served without recognition, eternal gratitude is given.

This book is respectfully dedicated to all those who have worn the uniform, past, present and future.

CHAPTER I

A New Field Army

The United States Army is often described as being unprepared for its role in World War II. In part this is because, until the appointment of General George C. Marshall to the post of Chief of Staff of the United States Army in 1939, much of the planning and preparation had been based on the unwarranted assumption that this new war would be much like the previous one. The American Army had acquitted itself well during that earlier conflict, and with some changes to absorb modern weapons and techniques it was felt in some quarters that it would do so again with little organizational change.

Between 1939 and 1941, the Army made a series of these organizational changes, intended to better prepare it for the coming conflict. Along with his chief staff officers (Brigadier General Harry J. Malony, Deputy Chief of Staff, and Brigadier General Mark W. Clark, Operations Officer), Lieutenant General Lesley J. McNair developed what would become the organizational structure of the United States Army in World War II.[1] Nothing was exempt from the review or immune to potentially significant changes in organization, tasks, and armament. Not all the changes were for the better, however. Some, such as the Specialized Field Army and Corps, were eventually discarded in favor of more generalized types of ground forces.

Spurred on by President Franklin D. Roosevelt, who was concerned about growing threats in both the Pacific and in Europe, a number of steps were taken to ready the American military forces for conflict. Naval rearmament in particular was a topic of considerable debate in Congress in the late 1930s. In 1939 the U.S. Navy conducted a review that resulted in a special report entitled "Are We Ready Now?" which concluded that both the Navy and Marine Corps were significantly under-strength and underequipped. The Navy also lacked sufficient bases from which to project power deep enough to provide adequate defense for the United States. Also in 1939, the War Department, which oversaw the Army and fledgling Army Air Corps, presented what it termed a "balanced approach" to the President. However, Congress reduced the President's subsequent budget request to $300 million and authorized the Army Air Corps only 3,251 new aircraft. Even the Army's highly regarded leader, Chief of Staff General George C. Marshall, did not favor a major manpower mobilization at this time. It was not until the following year, 1940, that the National Guard was called into Federal service to begin additional training and absorb modifications that had been developed between the wars. By and large, the ideas and improvements theorized by Army leaders between the wars did not bear fruit until the outbreak of war in Europe.

Many of these ideas involved changing the basic structure of the Army. Ponderous, World War I-style four-regiment infantry divisions had been shown to be obsolete by the early battles of World War II. Speed and power were the new mantras of modern armies, and the American Army, led by General Marshall and his assistant for Army Ground Forces, Lieutenant General McNair, was quick to implement a new design. There was one aspect, however, that remained basically unchanged—the field army (except for a brief testing of a "specialized field army").

From July 1943, to the end of the war, a field army was composed of a head-quarters, which commanded one or more army corps and one or more independent combat units under its direction and administration. General McNair would describe it as both a combat and administrative agency. It included supporting services and combat units, to add strength to the combat divisions within its assigned corps as needed. It directly supplied the fighting divisions, answering their supply needs without reference to the corps unless in an emergency. The field army directly supplied food, fuel and ammunition, which it in turn received from the services of supply. The field army also established and controlled "supply points" in forward areas, which were accessible to the supply services of the units under its command and control. Army level personnel sorted supplies into unit lots and loaded the trucks arriving at the supply points. In order to facilitate these duties, the Army was assigned a number of units that could readily be assigned to subordinate corps or divisions, as needed. These included quartermaster truck, railhead and gasoline supply companies. Ordnance ammunition companies and depot companies were also assigned. Field armies provided what was termed "third-echelon maintenance" for both the divisional and non-divisional units under its control. These included engineer battalions, ordnance maintenance and signal repair service units. Medical services, including hospitals, medical collecting and clearing companies (for needs that exceeded the organic medical units of the assigned divisions) were also the field army's responsibility. Bridge-building, water supply, map-making and photography, along with engineer and signal functions, were additional responsibilities.

Clearly, the field army performed a great number of administrative tasks beyond the capabilities of the tactical units—the corps and divisions under its command.[2] It also directed the tactical operations of its subordinate units and assigned them objectives. The size and variety of the units normally assigned to a field army varied from a squad of military historians assigned to record the army's history, to a rein-forced combat division numbering more than 17,000 officers and men. The corps remained primarily a fighting organization. Corps commanders were responsible for training and employing all units assigned to them, as well as all non-divisional units (i.e. independent tank, tank destroyer, engineer, artillery, antiaircraft and others) that fell under their command. In combat, the corps was to be a balanced force with units assigned by the field army to accomplish the currently assigned tactical mission.

During World War II the United States Army created 11 field armies. Of these, three operated in the Pacific Theater of Operations, one in the Mediterranean and five in Europe. The remaining two field armies remained as training commands within the United States.[3] Some of these, such as "Patton's Third Army" or "Mark Clark's Fifth Army", achieved significant notoriety due to the flamboyance of their commanders. Others, which fought just as hard and as long (like the Sixth U.S. Army of General Walter Krueger), were largely unknown.[4] Another such overlooked field army was the Ninth.

*   *   *

Officially, Ninth Army came into existence at Fort Sam Houston, Texas, on May 22, 1944. However, its roots lay further to the west. When war broke out in December 1941, the United States activated the Western Defense Command to protect the West Coast and Alaska. Included in its command structure was Fourth Army. By September of 1943, with Japan now on the defensive in the Pacific, it became clear that an active defense of the West Coast was less necessary than it had been earlier. As a result, Fourth Army was separated from the Western Defense Command and headquartered at the Presidio of San Francisco, California. It was designated as a training command under the umbrella organization of the Army Ground Forces, and given a new commander, Major General William Hood Simpson, who assumed command on October 13, 1943.

The Western Defense Command furnished the new staff for the fledgling army. Most came from California and were personally approved by General Simpson before being accepted on the new army staff. Simpson assembled his new command at San Jose, California, and set about unifying and training a staff that would basically stay together for two full years of training and combat, until the need for them no longer existed. Throughout October, the staff made plans to operate as a training army. Soon the mantra of the staff (to ensure effectiveness and training quality) was reduced to the single question: "Would it work effectively in combat?"[5]

It was not long before the growing headquarters needed more room. By November 1, having outgrown its shared facilities at the Presidio of San Francisco, Fourth Army moved to the Presidio of Monterey, California. On this same date the army became operational, responsible for the training of all ground forces troops on the West Coast. It was also to process units designated for overseas shipment. However, the army had no subordinate corps, and so the work was done largely and directly by the army staff. The many training tests and field exercises consistent with training a combat unit were performed under direct army control and supervision. This, it would turn out, would also be of great benefit to the new staff, as it gave them a much greater familiarity with the workings of combat units from division to battalion size, as well as their needs, problems and quirks of operation.

The new army command also began preparation for its own deployment abroad. Although it was the newest army formed at the time, the hope was that it would eventually be sent overseas. Although no orders or indications had yet arrived to substantiate this hope, the experience with sending other units overseas would be of considerable assistance to the army staff if and when its turn came.

The call didn't come right away. Instead, Fourth Army was ordered to Fort Sam Houston, Texas. There it was to assume the training duties of Third Army while the latter prepared to move to Europe. For the first time, Fourth Army was assigned three subordinate corps and additional army troops to accomplish its new mission. Additionally, it was given responsibility for the Louisiana Maneuver Area, where units preparing for overseas shipment were tested against each other in army-wide maneuvers. To cover both responsibilities, Fourth Army rotated its staff officers between Texas and Louisiana.

By early spring of 1944, the staff began receiving additional personnel for the purpose of enabling it to split itself in two. Orders were received to form a new field army, under the command of Simpson, which would eventually be sent to Europe. On May 5, 1944, sufficient additional staff had been integrated to allow the new Eighth Army to be activated at Fort Sam Houston, Texas. The additional staff formed the "new" Fourth Army at the same location and continued with its training duties as before.

The new Eighth Army began its own training with a map exercise designed to acclimate it to combat operations in a war zone. Designed to work out a standard operating procedure for the new army, it was directed by Major General William H. H. Morris, then commander of XVIII Corps and a recent graduate of the Louisiana Maneuver Area.[6] Results of the exercise were evaluated and necessary changes made to army staff procedures.

*   *   *

William Hood Simpson was born on May 19, 1888, in Weatherford, Texas, the son of a Confederate cavalry veteran from Tennessee. He graduated from the United States Military Academy at West Point, New York, as the 101st of 103 graduates in the class of 1909, and was commissioned into the infantry.[7] Carrying his West Point nickname of "Texas Bill," he served in the 6th Infantry Regiment in the Philippines between graduation and 1912. There he had his first combat experience while fighting the Moros in the Philippine jungles. Simpson served on the Panama-Pacific Exposition in 1915 before accompanying General John J. Pershing's Mexican

Punitive Expedition in search of revolutionaries. When the United States entered World War I, he was assigned to the 33rd Division in the American Expeditionary Force. By then a first lieutenant, he served as an aide to the division commander (Major General George Bell, Jr.) before becoming the Assistant Chief of Staff as a lieutenant colonel. He saw action in the Saint-Mihiel offensive in September 1918, and the Meuse-Argonne offensive later that same month. Awards included the Distinguished Service Medal and the Silver Star. By the end of the war, at the age of 30, he was a temporary lieutenant colonel and the divisional Chief of Staff.

Inter war assignments included duty as Chief of Staff of the 6th Division in Illinois and a permanent promotion to major in 1920. He then served in the Office of the Chief of Infantry in Washington. He took time out of his career to marry an old acquaintance from West Point, Mrs. Ruth (Webber) Krakauer. Simpson then attended the Infantry School Advanced Course at Fort Benning, Georgia, graduating in 1924.

As did most of the senior officers of the American Army in World War II, Simpson attended the Command and General Staff School, graduating as a Distinguished Graduate in 1925. After two years commanding the 3rd Battalion, 12th Infantry Regiment in Maryland, he graduated from the Army War College in 1928, after which he returned to be an instructor (as a lieutenant colonel, a rank he had first held more than 10 years earlier) from 1936 to 1940. Between graduating and teaching at the Army War College, he served from 1932 to 1936 as a professor of military science at Pomona College in Claremont, California.

It was at the War College that he became acquainted with future Chief of Staff of the Army, then-Colonel George C. Marshall. Another acquaintance, a fellow classmate, was Lieutenant Colonel Dwight D. Eisenhower. The newly promoted Colonel Simpson, now known by the nickname "Big Simp" to differentiate him from another officer of the same name, took command of the 9th Infantry Regiment at Fort Sam Houston, Texas, in 1938. He was promoted to brigadier general and assistant division commander of the 2nd Infantry Division in October 1940. Promotion to major general the following year found him commanding the Army's largest Infantry Replacement Center at Camp Wolters, Mineral Wells, Texas. By October 1941, he was in command of the 35th and then the 30th Infantry Divisions. His next posting was as commander of XII Corps, and he was promoted to lieutenant general in October 1943 when he took command of Fourth Army. He would retire as a lieutenant general in November 1946, and be promoted to full general on the retired list in July 1955, by a special Act of Congress.[8]

Simpson was regarded as "good-natured and affable," a leader who encouraged the confidence of his officers and enlisted men alike.[9] Major General Ernest N. Harmon, who served under many of the top American commanders of the war and a not-uncritical commentator, recorded that he considered that Simpson "… though little known outside military circles, was one of the truly great leaders of the European theater, a real general's general …. He was a pleasure to fight under."[10] He was also regarded as possessing a good sense of humor and a quick wit, as well as being a sincere and friendly person. At six feet two inches tall, and topping out at about 170 pounds at the age of 56, he always dressed impeccably and reminded some of the biblical kings with his closely shaven head. One of his long-serving corps commanders, Major General Alvan C. Gillem, Jr., described Simpson as "pleasant, very personal, understanding and cooperative."[11]

Simpson was also conscious of giving his subordinates credit for their achievements. Unlike some generals (for example, Douglas MacArthur in the Pacific), Simpson had his subordinate commanders accept the surrender of German generals, giving them the credit and the newspaper publicity, and enhancing their future careers.

Another officer who knew Simpson well, Lieutenant Colonel Thomas Stone (who often briefed the General on military situations), later described him in the following terms: "Even-tempered and composed, he refrained from interrupting and allowed the briefer to complete his presentation before questions were asked."[12] Other commanders, who served in multiple armies during the war, remarked on the differences between Ninth Army and other armies in Northwest Europe. In Ninth Army they received their orders early enough to have time to plan and reconnoiter their assignments, which did not often happen in other outfits. Finally, as one journalist would later note, "… what is most striking about Simpson may be that, in a doctoral dissertation and a book about him and the Ninth Army, there was almost nothing to relate about him—no stormy meetings, few revealing anecdotes, almost no memorable phrases. There is just an efficient, low-key headquarters operating under an undemonstrative steady leader."[13]

One of the most senior generals in the European Theater, Lieutenant General Jacob Devers, who commanded Sixth Army Group, remarked that "Simpson could think ahead of time, and he didn't talk too much, either; that's what I liked about him."[14] This is especially worthy of comment if one remembers that throughout most of the combat career of Ninth Army, it was subordinated to the multi-national Twenty-First Army Group, commanded by British Field Marshal Sir Bernard Law Montgomery, who was famously difficult to get along with during operations. Although Simpson personally found Montgomery "a very pompous guy" and much too cautious for his taste, he nevertheless made it a point to get along with the Field Marshal and did not openly complain about him, in contrast to General Omar N. Bradley of Twelfth Army Group, General Courtney Hicks Hodges of First Army and Patton of Third Army. He was, therefore, a rarity among American generals in Europe, in that he was an optimistic team player with a small ego and a great ability to work with others. Even Montgomery, known for his criticism of most American generals, supported this when he wrote to Eisenhower on January 11, 1945, commenting that he found Simpson "a great pleasure to work with."[15]

Simpson's team spirit went beyond that of many of his fellow Army commanders in Northwest Europe. When, during the ammunition shortage of late 1944, an inspector was sent from Washington to find out the cause of that shortage, only Ninth Army was fully transparent with him. Major General Henry Aurand was repeatedly snubbed by officers in First and Third Armies during his inspections, and many supply sites were hidden from him. In Third Army, for example, Patton was never available to discuss the problem, and both his Chief of Staff and supply officers were equally unavailable. The situation was the same at Twelfth Army Group and First Army. However, when Aurand reached Ninth Army, matters were quite different. Simpson and Aurand had taught together at the War College, and Aurand remembered that Simpson had given the lecture on supply in a theater of operations. Simpson claimed the "supply of ammunition in the 9th Army to be no problem" and he and his staff retained "complete confidence in Lee and his ComZ."[16] Much of the other army commanders' attitude had to do with a simmering feud between them and the commander of the Communications Zone Services of Supply, whom they both disliked and distrusted. Again, Ninth Army was like another world, and Aurand would report that Simpson was "a very tolerant understanding type" who harbored "no serious complaints and trusts ComZ to support him."[17]

After the war, Eisenhower, who had acted as commander of Supreme Headquarters Allied Expeditionary Force (SHAEF), would write, "If Simpson ever made a mistake as an army commander, it never came to my attention. After the war I learned that he had for some years suffered from a serious stomach disorder, but this I never would have suspected during hostilities. Alert, intelligent and professionally capable, he was the type of leader that American soldiers deserve. In view of his brilliant service, it was unfortunate that shortly after the war ill-health forced his retirement before he was promoted to four-star grade, which he had so clearly earned."[18] That this was not merely post-war hyperbole is evidenced by the fact that while the war was still raging, in March 1945, Eisenhower had written to Simpson that, "your Army has performed magnificently and your leadership has been outstanding." Eisenhower closed the letter by remarking that he was "truly delighted with the combat record you have made."[19] Just a month before, Eisenhower had written a memorandum in which he listed all of his senior commanders and arranged them by the "value of services each officer has rendered in this war and only secondarily upon my opinion as to his qualifications for future usefulness."[20] Of the 38 senior American officers listed, Simpson was listed as 12th with the comments "clear thinker, energetic, balanced"[21] next to his name. After observing in person Ninth Army's Rhine crossings, Eisenhower would write to Marshal, the Army's Chief of Staff that, "Simpson performed in his usual outstanding style."[22]

*　　*　　*

On May 6, 1944, Simpson and a cadre from his army staff flew to England to learn first-hand what they would be doing once overseas. He attended the final briefing for the Normandy invasion, where he first met Montgomery, who would play a prominent role in the future of Ninth Army. He also met with Eisenhower, whom he had first met at the War College as a classmate. They had met again during the

Louisiana maneuvers of 1941, when Simpson commanded the Infantry Training Center and Eisenhower was Third Army's Chief of Staff. In 1943, when Simpson (then commander of XII Corps) had visited the North African front to observe the operations then under Eisenhower's command, they had spent some time together. It was during this later meeting (1944), that Eisenhower expressed concern that there would be confusion between Simpson's Eighth Army and the British Eighth Army, already under SHAEF's command. As a result, at Eisenhower's recommendation the War Department renumbered Simpson's army as the Ninth.[23]

During his sojourn in England, Simpson became acquainted with Generals Bradley and Patton. He had been in the same West Point graduating class as Patton, but this was his first meeting with Bradley, his new boss. He and Bradley knew of each other by reputation in the "old army" but had never actually met before. Ninth Army's first duty was to play a role in the grand deception of German intelligence known as Operation *Fortitude*. Designed to deceive the enemy as to where, when and how powerful the obviously approaching cross-channel invasion was to be, both Third and Ninth Armies were to play on the German fears of a landing in the Pas de Calais area of France.

Simpson set up his headquarters at Clifton College, Bristol, and when the rest of his headquarters arrived in June, he immediately began the task of receiving, training and equipping units destined for France. He made his first visit to the battlefield on July 18, 1944, where he met with General Courtney H. Hodges (soon to command First Army) on a tour of the battlefield. During this visit he also met several of the corps commanders who would soon be serving under him.[24] Back in England, he continued with his role in the ruse to convince the Germans that a second invasion was planned by the Allies elsewhere on the French Atlantic coast.

During one visit to the front, Simpson joined a party of high-ranking officers to observe the Allies attempt to breakout out of the Normandy beachhead. A key element of the plan (Operation *Cobra*) was a massive aerial bombardment, which was designed to open a hole in the German defenses and allow the Americans to thrust into central France. On this day the bombing fell short, causing numerous friendly casualties, and the party of visiting dignitaries was caught in the bombing. As he hugged the ground, Bradley's senior aide, Major Chester Hanson, recalled: "We dove to the ground. I looked up and found myself face to face with General Simpson, who looked at me with a grin on his face. One of the most friendly and companionable men in the Army, easy going and soft-spoken, never excited or angry and horribly considerate of everyone."[25] Fortunately, none of the generals were injured. Later, General McNair, who was with the party, would invite Simpson to return the next day, when a new bombing attack was scheduled. Simpson declined, anxious to get his new army ready for combat. It was only several days later that he learned McNair had been killed in the second day's bombing.

Probably unknown to Simpson at this time, was the discussion about what to do with him and his army. Plans called for four American field armies to deploy in France.

In August, the invasion of southern France brought the experienced Seventh Army ashore, making three American field armies already fighting in France. Eisenhower suggested that Seventh Army[26] be detached from Sixth Army Group, to which it belonged, under Lieutenant General Jacob L. Devers, and be added to his main forces. There was also discussion about promoting an experienced field commander already in France to army command.[27] Eisenhower favored one of his corps commanders and an old friend, Major General Leonard T. ("Gee") Gerow, then commanding V Corps in France. But in the end General Marshall ruled that he had agreed senior commanders who had spent the time in training and organizing an army would be allowed to lead it in action. Thus, Simpson and his Ninth Army would fight in France and Germany.[28] Eisenhower, who later had nothing bad to say about Simpson, would remark that, "If I had been able to foresee two or three months ago the actual developments in command arrangements, I would probably have advanced a corps commander to take over this army." He would also conclude that Simpson would remain in command of Ninth Army because "it is best to follow through."[29]

Operation *Fortitude* covered several deceptions, designed to deceive the Germans and to divide their reserve forces among a number of possible invasion points. It involved a wide variety of measures, from using enemy agents to creating false friendly forces. One of the most important measures was the creation of an entirely fictitious American Army Group, the First United States Army Group (FUSAG). The first "commander" of FUSAG was Patton, whose reputation had been made against the Germans in North Africa and Sicily. This worked well for a time, but when Patton and his Third Army entered combat at the end of August 1944, a new commander for FUSAG was needed. General McNair had been sent to England for this purpose, but when he was killed in Normandy a replacement needed to be found. Intelligence officers wanted to maintain the deception that FUSAG was ready to conduct another landing against the German Atlantic Wall, thereby tying up German reserves that might otherwise have been deployed to Normandy. Eisenhower immediately thought of Simpson but felt, "that his name will not be of sufficient significance to the enemy."[30] Nevertheless, Simpson was temporarily appointed to be the acting commander of FUSAG while Eisenhower sent to Marshall for a more widely known officer of high enough rank. Coincidently, that officer turned out to be Lieutenant General John L. DeWitt, who had preceded Simpson as commander of Fourth Army before Ninth Army left for England.[31] At the time of his summons to command FUSAG, DeWitt was the commander of the Army and Navy Staff College. Simpson was therefore released from his "duties" with FUSAG and returned to full-time command of Ninth Army.

*   *   *

One of the first things Ninth Army had to do was design a new shoulder patch. This was the shoulder sleeve insignia used to identify troops belonging to a unit of the American Army. Begun in World War I by the 81st ("Wildcat") Division, it had become traditional Army procedure. It was decided that because the headquarters of Ninth Army was basically the headquarters of Fourth Army under a new designation, the shoulder sleeve insignia should reflect that origin. The result was a white heraldic rosette, placed vividly on the red nonagon of the Ninth Army emblem, similar visually to Fourth Army's patch.

The main body of Ninth Army headquarters arrived at Gourock, near Glasgow, on June 28, after a fast journey on the ocean liner *Queen Elizabeth*. They quickly moved to Bristol where the headquarters was once again united. They immediately began the processing and training assignment they had been given. Some of the staff were assigned the task of keeping in touch with ongoing operations on the continent, as a learning and preparation process. Additional members were added to equate Ninth Army with those already in combat. Among these additions were the 4th Information and Historical Service and two Army Air Force units (the 125th Liaison Squadron and the 50th Mobile Reclamation and Repair Squadron), with which they would be working once ashore in France. Both contained light aircraft for communications with army headquarters.

Staff officers also visited the continent to see how procedures were working under actual combat conditions. Units of all sizes were visited to ensure that a full and complete picture of battle was understood and integrated into Ninth Army operations. Officers from Eisenhower's theater headquarters came to Ninth Army to discuss and initiate the existing methods of operation, while Ninth Army's Chief of Staff conducted numerous map exercises to acclimate the staff to planning for battle. By late August it was judged that the army was ready to join the ongoing campaign in Europe. They were now under the leadership of the Commanding General of Twelfth Army Group, Bradley. General Gillem's XIII Corps was made the executor for the Army's troop-processing mission in the United Kingdom.[32] Ninth Army was going to war.

Its headquarters departed England in two echelons from Southampton and landed at Utah Beach on August 28 and 29. Known by the radio call sign "Conquer," it set up shop in Normandy at Saint-Sauveur-Lendelin. This tent camp was for the forward group, while the rear headquarters established itself in a school building at Périers, a few miles north. Soon orders were received assigning Simpson's command to take over the ongoing battle in the Brittany Peninsula. Headquarters moved closer to the operational area, around the hamlet of Mi-Forêt, northeast of Rennes. Set up in tent camps, Conquer was now ready for its first combat assignment.

CHAPTER 2

Brittany

The first combat operation for the new Ninth Army was the conquest of the Brittany Peninsula in western France. On September 5, 1944, the army officially became operational and was ordered to take over the area, formerly the responsibility of Third Army. It was also tasked with the protection of Twelfth Army Group's south flank, along the Loire River, as far east as Orléans.

The Battle for Brittany was all about ports. After American, British and Canadian forces had established their lodgment in Normandy in June 1944, the most important factor in their continued success was the uninterrupted flow of supplies to keep the armies fed, mobile and sufficiently armed. The only way to accomplish this in a permanent manner was to seize a port, or several ports, that would be able to handle the required tonnage to keep the Allied armies moving. When Ninth Army arrived on the continent, only the major port of Cherbourg, on the Normandy coast, had been seized, but it needed considerable rehabilitation before it could become a part of the supply chain. Even when it did, its maximum capacity was sufficient to provide only a portion of the projected supply levels the Allies would require.

It had always been a part of the plan for the cross-Channel invasion to seize the Brittany Peninsula and make use of the several ports along its coast. After two months of bloody fighting in Normandy, the newly committed Third Army (under Patton) turned the corner from Normandy into Brittany during a planned breakout operation. Operation *Cobra* was so successful that the Allied forces found themselves far ahead of projections in pushing the Germans out of France. Rather than delay their advances by laying siege to the several port "fortresses," it was decided that pursuing the retreating Germans took priority. Eisenhower, while acknowledging that supply ports remained a necessity, modified the plan because he believed the Germans in France had been struck such a severe blow that pursuit across the Seine River would quite possibly open the way to Germany. On August 17 he ordered a pursuit to and across that river. Meanwhile, the German Chancellor, Adolf Hitler, had decreed a policy that every port along the Atlantic coast would be held by the Germans as a fortress, with orders to hold "to the last man." He did this in the knowledge that the Achilles heel of the Allies was logistics. Until they had a strong supply operation, they were vulnerable, and he intended to keep them from establishing such a logistical base by holding on to the ports.

In Brittany, the ports were St. Malo, Brest, Lorient and Saint-Nazaire. These cities were provided with all the troops the Germans could find to act as garrisons. When Third Army turned into Brittany, Patton decided to send only one corps down the peninsula, turning the rest of his army east and north towards Germany. He selected VIII Corps under Major General Troy H. Middleton.[1] The first port to fall was St. Malo, which was captured after a fierce house-to-house battle by Major General Robert C. Macon's 83rd Infantry Division, reinforced with the 121st Infantry Regiment of the 8th Infantry Division. The port, although captured, was in serious disrepair and would need months of rehabilitation before it could be put to use by the Americans.

The biggest port in Brittany was Brest. During World War I, most American troops sent to France, including then-Captain William H. Simpson, had landed at Brest and then moved on to training bases deeper in France. Now it not only promised to return to that role, but its capture would remove a significant portion of the German Navy's submarine bases. A city of some 80,000 inhabitants on a peninsula that juts out into the Atlantic Ocean like a finger pointing west, Brest had also been the largest port of the French Navy and the second largest port in France. Allied logisticians estimated that their armies could survive on the supplies brought over the open Normandy beaches and through Cherbourg until early September, by which point Brest needed to be in their hands to ensure an uninterrupted flow of supplies. Middleton's VIII Corps besieged the city and began operations to capture it in mid-August 1944. The battle, expected to last a week, dragged on for a month.

In order to ease Third Army's burden of attacking east while trying to seize a port in its distant rear, Ninth Army was given orders in Twelfth Army Group's Letter of Instructions Number 7, dated September 5. The orders were to assume responsibility for the conquest of Brittany and its ports. Ninth Army took command of the 50,000 troops of VIII Corps at noon on September 5 and began combat operations. In a meeting between Generals Bradley (commanding Twelfth Army Group) and Simpson, the latter was urged to do whatever was necessary to speed the conquest of the port city and end the Brittany campaign.

VIII Corps brought into Ninth Army Major General Walter M. Robertson's veteran 2nd Infantry Division, Major General Donald A. Stroh's 8th Infantry Division, the Maryland-Virginia-District of Columbia National Guard 29th Infantry Division (veterans of Omaha Beach) and General Macon's 83rd Infantry Division. The VIII Corps Artillery, under Brigadier General John E. McMahon, Jr., included 17 battalions of medium and heavy artillery. Also attached was Brigadier General John F. Uncles' 34th Field Artillery Brigade, which was soon to become Ninth Army's own artillery brigade.

Three of the newly added divisions of Ninth Army (the 2nd, 8th and 29th) were already engaged in the reduction of Brest, while two task forces were clearing the rest of the peninsula of German troops. The siege was 12 days old when Ninth Army took command. The 6th Armored Division, under Major General Robert Grow, was containing other German pockets at Lorient and Quiberon Bay. The 83rd Infantry Division was providing flank protection and containing the enemy pockets at Saint-Nazaire and Nantes. Of considerable assistance was the help of significant numbers of fighters from the French Forces of the Interior (the FFI) or French Underground.

Upon arrival, Simpson found that the port of Brest is divided in two by the Penfield River. The actual city of Brest lies to the east of the river while on the west side lies the city of Recouvrance. The old portion of the city had a massive stone wall surrounding it, built in ancient times and solidly constructed. The Bay of Brest, which led to the port itself, was formed by the Crozon Peninsula coming up from the south. A narrow inlet led into the bay and was known as the Channel of Brest.

The port had long been a military objective and was accordingly protected by forts old and new. The main fortifications had been built by the noted French military engineer Sébastien Le Prestre de Vauban in the 17th century. Earlier attacks on Brest by the British and Dutch fleets in 1694 had failed utterly, but in 1794 the British had returned and had succeeded in destroying the French fleet based there, although they did not capture the port itself. By 1944 there were over 75 major defensive fortifications protecting the old city, and since the French surrender in 1940, Brest had been developed into a major submarine base by the German Navy.

This was the situation when Ninth Army arrived on the scene. The city of Brest was held by elements of three German divisions. Under the command of Major General Hermann Bernhard Ramcke, an experienced and dedicated German parachute officer, the 266th and 343rd Infantry and 2nd Parachute Divisions had dug themselves in to defend the city in accordance with Hitler's directive. Reinforcing these regular troops was a heterogeneous mix of German units that had been cut off and moved into Brest to add to its defense. These latter units included static coastal garrisons, naval and marine units, submarine mechanics, German Navy Meteorological Service members and even 21 Italian soldiers. All together, some 30,000 German troops garrisoned Brittany, of which about 3,400 defended Brest itself.

General der Fallschirmtruppe (Paratroops) Ramcke was born on January 24, 1889, to a family of German farmers. During World War I he enlisted in the German Navy and then transferred to the Naval Infantry. He served in a Marine Assault Battalion in Flanders, where he earned the First and Second-Class Iron Cross. He went on to receive the Military Cross in Gold and was promoted from the ranks to Ensign, a rarity for a German enlisted man at the time. After the war he transferred to the German Army, served in the Baltic and received his fifth wound. By 1937 he was a colonel, but spent the Polish and French campaigns as an observer for higher headquarters. Determined to command troops in combat, he approached an old acquaintance of his, General Kurt Student, who was in command of a new organization, the German Paratroopers. This required a transfer to the German Air Force (*Luftwaffe*) which he achieved in July 1940. He went through jump school training at the advanced age of 51 and soon found himself leading a regiment of paratroops during the invasion of Crete. For his outstanding leadership in that battle he was promoted to major general, awarded the Knight's Cross, and given command of the 1st Parachute Assault Regiment.

Ramcke's next task was to organize the Italian Army's *Folgore* Parachute Division, which he did in 1942. He was then sent to North Africa, where he organized an *ad hoc* "Paratroop Brigade Ramcke," which fought within the German *Afrika Korps* at the critical battle of El Alamein. Cut off by the advancing British, he managed to lead his men to safety after capturing an enemy supply convoy and using its vehicles to transport his otherwise foot-borne force to safety. For these actions he received the Oak Leaves to his Knight's Cross. Appreciated by his men, he had quickly earned the nickname "Papa Ramcke," despite also being known as a tough and disciplined leader. He received command of the 2nd Parachute Division in Italy, but was soon injured when an Allied fighter plane attacked his car and forced it off the road. After recovery he resumed command and took his division to Brittany, where they arrived on August 8, 1944. In order to limit civilian casualties and to better prepare his defenses at Brest, he ordered the French population to leave the city on August 21.

The attack on Brest had stalled due to determined resistance, terrain that favored the defenders and skillfully built German defenses (including antiaircraft guns and ship's guns). The defense was aided by a critical shortage of ammunition for the American artillery battalions. Although on paper there was an overwhelming amount of artillery available to General Simpson, in fact this advantage was severely curtailed by a shortage of transport to bring ammunition forward. Simpson immediately placed a request for an expedited resupply while ordering a temporary halt in operations to allow the artillery to build up a supply for a planned ground attack. Simpson's staff worked with the Communications Zone staff to expedite artillery resupply by using nearby beaches at Morlaix, where eventually some 40,000 tons of ammunition would arrive. Using small boats and landing craft, ammunition was shipped from England and Normandy to build up to the required levels. French civilians were employed to help unload the ships as they arrived—these civilians were paid not with money (which had little value at the time), but with food, which only aggravated another supply problem.

Ninth Army also operated under a further disadvantage when it first entered combat. All other American field armies in France had an assigned tactical air command for air support. For the Brittany Campaign, Ninth Army was forced to rely on XIX Tactical Air Command, which belonged to Third Army. Since Ninth Army was protecting the southern flank of Third Army, this made sense in the short term, but the assignment did not provide full support. As XIX TAC followed Third

Army east, and as its airfields moved accordingly, less and less support was available to Ninth Army back in Brittany.

It wasn't until September 12 that the situation was dealt with, when XXIX Tactical Air Command (under Brigadier General Richard E. Nugent) was activated and assigned to support Ninth Army.[2] This would prove to be one of the best Army-TAC relationships. Using the 84th and 303rd Fighter Wings as a basis and adding four fighter-bomber groups, the new command began operations. XXIX TAC was not fully operational, however, until early October. Meanwhile, Ninth Army got down to the business of taking Brest.

*   *   *

Ninth Army's Battle for Brest began mid-morning on September 8. Major General Charles H. Gerhardt's 29th ("Blue and Gray") Infantry Division was four miles west of the city. Across the Penfeld, the 2nd and 8th Infantry Divisions were within two to three miles of the city. The river divided the approach to Brest and, as a result, the 29th Infantry Division would clear the Conquet Peninsula and take Recouvrance, a suburb of Brest that had formerly held the French naval base. The 2nd and 8th Infantry Divisions, meanwhile, would strike directly for Brest itself. Plans called for Stroh's 8th Infantry Division to be pinched out of the line as the Americans entered Brest, which was to be left to Robertson's 2nd Infantry Division to clear. The situation left no room for maneuver, indirect approaches or other tactics that might have prevented the necessity of a direct frontal assault. With the city's back to the sea, and heavy coastal defense guns precluding an amphibious assault, the only choice was a head-on approach.

The attacks faced a strong defense. Pillboxes and minefields covered every advance, while strong points and booby traps slowed progress. The Germans used radio-controlled miniature tanks, carrying high explosives, to halt attacks by the American infantry. Fortunately, only two small air attacks from the German Air Force were recorded during the battle. However, one German Air Force resupply mission did mis-drop hundreds of Iron Crosses, rocket ammunition, ciphers and codes on the attacking Americans. As if to make up for this, American planes later dropped surrender leaflets on General Robertson's headquarters.

As expected, the fighting was fierce. The 2nd Infantry Division, which had first landed in France at Brest in 1917, attacked on the east, or left side, of the American line in WWI. The troops, used to the blasted and broken countryside of Normandy, were pleasantly surprised at the "green fields and blue late-summer skies"[3] they found around Brest. As was becoming common throughout western France, the Americans were welcomed by a French population beaming with gratitude. The only missing segment in that population were the men of military age, who had either been drafted into labor units or were away with the French Resistance. The division faced the original defenses of the "Old City," which included the 17th-century fortress defenses created by Vauban, to which the Germans had added their own touches. The obvious first task was to clear the Daoulas Peninsula, which jutted out to the southeast of the port of Brest and looked down upon the city. Enemy observation and fire from this area had to be eliminated as a preliminary to the main attack.

Colonel Ralph W. Zwicker's 38th Regimental Combat Team, led by the Assistant Division Commander, Brigadier General James A. Van Fleet, was assigned the task.[4] Supported by the 323rd Field Artillery Battalion, the 3rd Battalion, 330th Infantry Regiment (attached from the 83rd Infantry Division) and two companies of the 705th Tank Destroyer Battalion, this grouping, known as Task Force B, first moved against Daoulas in late August.[5] It soon found itself facing numerous coastal defense and antiaircraft guns, which were able to traverse through 360 degrees, allowing them to be used against a land attack.

Van Fleet divided his task force into two groups. To the south he sent the bulk of his force, now reinforced with the 50th Armored Infantry Battalion and the 83rd Armored Field Artillery Battalion of the 6th Armored Division. The 38th Infantry Regiment, supported by the 3rd Battalion, 330th Infantry Regiment, Companies B and C of the 705th Tank Destroyer Battalion, Company A of the 68th Tank Battalion and Company A of the 603rd Tank Destroyer Battalion, were sent to the northern side of the peninsula. To screen the flanks of the main force attacking Brest, mobile patrols were sent up and down the coast to prevent enemy interference or any reinforcements from gaining entrance to the Brest fortifications.

The first obstacle was Hill 154. This was assigned to Lieutenant Colonel Olinto M. Barsanti's 3rd Battalion, 38th Infantry. A massive volume of fire from positions on Hill 154, as well as unobserved artillery fire from positions north of the hill, opposed the advance. German soldiers from the 266th Infantry Division, reinforced with naval troops and elements of the 2nd Parachute Division, defended the area.[6] They were well dug-in, including a network of trenches around the crest of the hill, eight steel and reinforced concrete pillboxes and barbed wire entanglements. There were more than 25 machine guns, several antitank weapons and mortars strengthening the defense.

Although the Germans knew the enemy was coming, they couldn't see the advancing Americans, despite the otherwise excellent visibility from Hill 154. One German non-commissioned officer, later captured and interrogated, reported that he could see for miles from his observation post of the 811th Naval Antiaircraft Battalion, but he never saw troops, vehicles or movement of any kind before the attack. As the Americans approached, the Germans could hear them coming, but even then they saw no targets to shoot at, nor any vehicles approaching. They did not open fire until the Americans actually launched their attack. The 3rd Battalion, 38th Infantry's stealthy advance toward Hill 154 was a key to its seizure by the 2nd Infantry Division.

The attack began with Companies I (Captain Robert L. Utley) and L (Captain George Van Hoorebeke) moving forward by platoons, infiltrating single-file toward the enemy. Taking advantage of every bit of cover the terrain provided, the Americans surrounded and surprised the Germans atop the hill, which turned out to be the key enemy position on the peninsula. The Germans, however, put up a fight. A hail of fire from small arms, automatic weapons and mortars fell upon the Americans as they tried to clear the hill. Staff Sergeant Alvin P. Casey led his men against a pillbox holding up the advance. The young man from Lycippus, Pennsylvania, was leading a machine gun section when automatic weapons fire from the pillbox halted the advance. Although it was 200 yards away over open ground, Carey deployed his guns to cover the enemy and then, loading up with grenades, started up the hill toward the pillbox. Along the way he killed a German rifleman who tried to stop his advance, then kept moving. He reached grenade-throwing distance and began throwing grenades at the enemy. Machine gun fire from the pillbox was aimed directly at him, but despite being mortally wounded he continued to throw his grenades until one entered the pillbox, knocking it out before he fell. His Medal of Honor was awarded posthumously.[7]

The reverse slope defenses of the hill were protected by thick barbed wire. Privates Clifford Nolan and Leo Bose from L Company grabbed a bazooka and crawled forward to destroy a 75mm self-propelled weapon just outside the wire.[8] This gun had prevented Company L from reaching its objective and once the gun was knocked out, the advance continued. Technical Sergeant Hubert D. Deatherage took a large-bore German gun and fired continuously at eight German pillboxes, adding confusion in the German ranks.[9] Three teams using M1A1 flamethrowers moved forward to eliminate the pillboxes. One operator was killed, and his fuel tanks destroyed, while the second team moved forward only to find that the hoses connecting their oxygen tanks to the nozzles of their flamethrowers had been cut by enemy fire. Only the third team managed to fire into a pillbox, after which supporting infantrymen were able to capture it. It was well after midnight before the Americans were able to consolidate their gains.

There was yet another defense position at the base of the hill on the reverse side. More machine guns, small arms and mortars had to be overcome. Van Fleet scheduled an attack to clear this section of the hill the next morning, but the Germans didn't wait. They had noticed a gap opening between the two American assault companies as they maneuvered around Hill 154 and, with reinforcements arriving, they launched their own counterattack just as dawn broke, infiltrating between Companies I and L. The apparent aim was to capture the battalion command post. Some 40 Americans of the headquarters group grabbed their weapons and moved forward to tackle the advancing German infantrymen. Company I's heavy weapons platoon soon realized what was going on and opened fire with machine guns and mortars at the advancing enemy. Then a platoon each from Company L and Company K moved against the German force.

The result was a defeat for the enemy. A dozen German dead were counted in the area and 35 prisoners taken when it was over. Once again, the Americans began moving across the hill, singly and in small groups, taking advantage of what cover was available. Nevertheless, enemy resistance remained firm. Tank destroyers from the 705th Tank Destroyer Battalion were called forward and directed their fire at pillboxes some 450 yards away. While the enemy was reeling from this new threat, a platoon of Company K hit them on their flank. Outmaneuvered and outflanked, the Germans withdrew, blowing up the bridge at Point St. Barbe (which had connected the tip of the Daoulas Peninsula with the mainland) as they went.

One enemy force estimated at 125 men was seen retreating to a new line of defense at the town of Plougastel. Artillery rained down on them but they refused to surrender. They were finally overcome by the advancing American infantry. At a cost of seven killed and 28 wounded, the last enemy force had been overwhelmed and with the fall of Hill 154 the rest of the German positions on the peninsula were rendered useless—the rest of the fighting was anticlimactic. The Americans accounted for 100 enemy dead and 2,700 prisoners were sent back to prisoner-of-war cages. Its gallant struggle to seize Hill 154 and clear the Daoulas Peninsula earned the 3rd Battalion, 38th Infantry Regiment, a Presidential Unit Citation.[10]

Although the town of Loperhet and the area around it had been seized against light opposition, sources from the FFI reported that there were at least 10,000 German troops dug in on the peninsula. The American advance continued until August 27, when they came up against Hill 63. Entrenched atop the hill were 18 French heavy machine guns, captured in 1940 and issued to German rear-area troops. Initial advances were quickly halted by heavy automatic weapons fire. American artillery was then used on the hill while Task Force B turned over the job to the much stronger Task Force A.

General Middleton immediately sent artillery battalions to take advantage of the observation opportunities provided by the Daoulas Perninsula. This group was able to fire upon the rear of the landward defenses around Brest as well as on the Crozon Peninsula. To further trouble the enemy, Middleton organized another provisional battalion group of 57 machine guns, 12 tank destroyers and eight 40mm Bofors guns to provide security for the artillery group and to engage "targets of opportunity" within Brest.[11] He also set up another Task Force, called Task Force S, under the command of Colonel Leroy H. Watson (the Assistant Division Commander of the 29th Infantry Division), and assigned it the mission of clearing the tip of the Brittany Peninsula between Brest and le Conquet.[12] These actions resulted in the capture of a German radar station and several heavy German artillery batteries at Lochrist. The entire episode was brought to an end when First Lieutenant Robert T. Edlin of the 2nd Ranger Infantry Battalion pierced the enemy lines and entered their main headquarters with his four-man patrol, pulling the pin on a hand grenade and demanding the commandant's surrender. All the outlying forts and more than 1,000 German soldiers immediately surrendered. Edlin received a Distinguished Service Cross for his actions.[13]

*   *   *

Task Force A had been created on July 31, 1944, during Third Army's race past Brittany. To try a *coup de main* and prevent widespread destruction of vital bridges, roads and communications, the task force was created using the headquarters of the 1st Tank Destroyer Brigade. The brigade commander, Brigadier General Herbert L. Earnest, took over leadership of the 15th Cavalry Group, the 705th Tank Destroyer Battalion, the 159th Engineer (Combat) Battalion and the 509th Engineer Light Pontoon Company. Originally, because the task assigned was predicted to last only a few days, no infantry or medical support was attached to the force. However, it in fact lasted for nearly two months during the conquest of the Brittany Peninsula.

The rush into Brittany was led by Colonel John B. Reybold's 15th Cavalry Group, with Company C, 705th Tank Destroyer Battalion and Company B, 159th Combat Engineers attached. Despite attacks by German aircraft as they crossed into Brittany, the advance group made good initial progress. In the rush to get behind German lines, the lead elements ran into an ambush near the town of Baguer-Pican, in which Reybold and several of his men in the leading vehicles were captured and sent to the German-occupied Channel Islands. Colonel Logan Berry, commander of the 6th Tank Destroyer Group, assumed command of the 15th Cavalry Group, the ambush point was bypassed, and Task Force A continued forward.

As it moved, however, supplies were quickly exhausted. In a little recognized epic of courage, fortitude and ingenuity, the quartermaster vehicles assigned to the task force ran several supply trips through German lines, risking ambushes, aerial attack, friendly fire and other obstacles to keep the force supplied as it rolled deeper and deeper into Brittany.

Meanwhile, Task Force A encircled St. Malo until relieved by infantry units of the 83rd Infantry Division. A roadblock at Chateauneuf, built of steel bars set in concrete and concrete blocks, halted the advance and an infantry unit from the 329th Infantry, 83rd Infantry Division, was called up to knock it out. The attack failed with heavy casualties. Then the reconnaissance company of the 15th Cavalry attacked and, although also suffering heavy casualties, kept the Germans busy long enough to allow engineers to place explosive charges on the steel rails. The tank destroyers then fired point blank at the charges on the rails, but the resulting blasts seemed to cause little damage. Finally, an M32 tank retriever was sent forward and managed to drag the damaged roadblock out of the way.

Next, Task Force A moved to Dinan. With increasing German presence as they moved deeper into Brittany, the 3rd Battalion, 330th Infantry, and C Battery, 323rd Field Artillery Battalion, were attached to the task force to give it more power. Delayed by the occasional blown bridge, the task force, in cooperation with the FFI, managed to seize several others intact, and it soon became clear that the Germans were far more interested in reaching one of the fortresses along the coast than delaying the Americans' advance. Soon, only infrequent ambushes and scattered mines delayed the advance. The 17th Cavalry Reconnaissance Squadron was detached and ordered to rush ahead to seize the critical (and largest) railroad bridge at Morlaix. After encountering several ambushes, minefields and similar obstacles, the mission was accomplished.

By late August, Task Force A had exchanged the 3rd Battalion, 330th Infantry, for the 50th Armored Infantry Battalion of the 6th Armored Division. The 159th Engineer (Combat) Battalion had also been exchanged for the 35th Engineer (Combat) Battalion. Artillery support was now provided by the 83rd Armored Field Artillery Battalion and the force continued moving along the southern flank of the Crozon Peninsula against light opposition. The town of Loperhet was easily captured and it was then that reports began to come in from the French Underground stating that there were some 10,000 German troops dug-in further down the peninsula. The Americans continued their advance, but as the lead troops came up to Hill 63, heavy automatic weapons fire from the hill halted them. The 18 German-manned French Hotchkiss machine guns entrenched atop and around Hill 63 prevented the Americans from continuing. Fearing additional German attacks, Task Force A was pulled out and sent further south to prevent any reinforcements from reaching the hill. Task Force B took over and, after a fierce struggle, captured 3,000 prisoners and 50 large antiaircraft and naval guns. For its actions during this fight, the 50th Armored Infantry Battalion was awarded the French Croix De Guerre with Palm.[14]

The German commander, General Ramcke, was displeased with the rapid fall of the Daoulas Peninsula. He laid blame on a senior officer of the 343rd Division, whom he believed had become soft during long occupation duty and had not sufficiently inspired the defense. As a result, most of his sector commanders from this point on would be trusted officers of his 2nd Parachute Division. With the Daoulas Peninsula in the hands of the Americans, who were heavily supplied with artillery, mortars and aerial observers, the Germans around and within Brest had to be careful not to be caught out in the open during daylight hours. As an example of what now faced the Germans within Brest, the 2nd Infantry Division organized a group of fifty-caliber machine guns (normally used for antiaircraft defense), 12 tank destroyers and eight 40mm antiaircraft guns into a group known as "Ivory X" (after the division's radio call sign) and set them up to fire together on specific targets within Brest. Targets as small as motorcycles and other vehicles were now struck by this combined fire whenever they revealed themselves. Some 72,000 rounds of fifty-caliber ammunition was fired in one afternoon, with a total of half a million rounds expended during the battle.

* * *

The 8th Infantry Division called itself the "Golden Arrow Division" after the design on its shoulder sleeve insignia. It was a regular Army division activated at Camp Jackson, South Carolina on July 1, 1940. It went through the usual training and army-wide maneuvers during its time in the United States. For a while it was designated and trained as a motorized division, before the Army decided that such special designations were unnecessary. In June 1943 it lost one of its regular regiments, the 34th Infantry, but received one from the National Guard. Joining the regulars of the 13th and 28th Infantry Regiments was the 121st Infantry Regiment of the Georgia National Guard. Originally a part of the 30th Infantry Division, this regiment had become separate when the army reduced its infantry divisions from four regiments to three. It was assigned to the 8th Infantry Division on November 21, 1941. As a result, for a brief while the division had four infantry regiments assigned to it.

The 8th Infantry Division landed at Utah Beach on July 3–4, 1944. As it did, it received its eighth commander since June 1940. Brigadier General Donald A. Stroh took command just as the division entered combat.[15] It was placed between the 79th and 90th Infantry Divisions in the difficult hedgerow country of Normandy and slowly forced its way forward, the 13th Infantry Regiment seizing the town of Rennes. After the breakout, the 121st Infantry Regiment assisted the 83rd Infantry Division in its attack on St. Malo and Dinard, where its 3rd Battalion would be cut off behind German lines for four days and earn the title "Lost Battalion." The 28th Infantry regiment led the 6th Armored Division in the attack on Brest's Guipavas airport, but lack of support forced a withdrawal. Another battalion of the 121st Infantry cleared the Cap Fréhel area and captured 300 Germans. The division's next battle would be at Brest itself.

The bulk of the 8th Infantry Division reached the outskirts of Brest during the night of August 17–18. It relieved the 6th Armored Division, which went off to lay siege to the port of Lorient. Patrols were immediately sent out to reconnoiter the German defenses and, three days later, the 2nd Infantry Division came up on its left and took over that sector. In the following days the 29th Infantry Division moved in on the right. By August 21, Stroh felt he was ready to begin the main assault on Brest and small-scale attacks were immediately launched to test the German defenses and improve starting positions for the coming main attack. These small-scale attacks soon revealed that the Germans had the terrain well covered by their mortars, which were deadly accurate. Every hill, lane, and hedgerow was zeroed in by the enemy.

Nor were the Germans simply sitting behind their defenses awaiting the attack. Their patrols were as active as the Americans'. First Lieutenant John O. Gawne was made aware of this unexpectedly when he was walking back to his company command post one day and encountered a German soldier armed with an automatic weapon. The German opened fire but somehow the bullets missed the American entirely. Gawne then rushed the German and knocked the weapon from his hands, capturing him.[16]

The Golden Arrow Division began its attack during the night of August 23–24, when the 13th and 28th Infantry Regiments began an infiltration of the German lines. The idea was to bypass the enemy's outer defenses and reach a line along a creek for the main assault. That assault had to be postponed for a day due to a shortage of artillery ammunition, but it was launched on August 25, supported not only by American artillery but also by the British warship HMS *Warspite*, which fired 300 rounds of 15in. naval ordnance in support (several direct hits knocked out some of the German fortifications). A total of 150 heavy bombers and dozens of medium bombers struck both Brest and Recouvrance, starting fires, and several enemy ships sheltering in the harbor were also sunk.

The attack quickly identified two German strong points blocking the American advance. The 1st Battalion, 13th Infantry, found itself in a life-and-death struggle for the town of Bohars. Nearby the 2nd Battalion, 13th Infantry, came up against Hill 88, another of the keys to the German defense of Brest. Hill 88 was named by American soldiers who believed, probably erroneously, that there were dozens of heavy German antiaircraft (88mm) guns defending the hill. Later, four 105mm antiaircraft guns were, in fact, found on the hill, and these were just as deadly against ground targets as the dreaded 88mm weapons. In addition to facing these heavy guns, the assault force had to cross 600 yards of open ground against heavy automatic weapons and mortar fire just to get close enough to engage the defending German paratroopers. For the next 30 hours, the 13th Infantry struggled to take Hill 88. The contest quickly became a hand-to-hand struggle, with Americans cut off by Germans, and Germans surrounded by Americans. One American platoon managed to cross the Penfield River, shallow at this point, and hit the exposed flank of the Germans atop the hill.

It was on August 26 that Lieutenant Colonel Edmund Fry, commanding the division's 12th Engineer (Combat) Battalion, was captured while trying to reconnoiter enemy defenses. He managed to escape by sea several days later and rejoined his battalion on the Crozon Peninsula 19 days after being captured. It was on the same day that Fry was captured that Second Lieutenant Earl O. Hall, of the 13th Infantry, led his men forward in a series of vicious battles for the trenches and concrete emplacements from which the Germans defended Hill 88. Over two days, his men knocked out several of these critical positions before he was killed by enemy artillery fire. His Distinguished Service Cross was posthumously awarded.[17]

The following day saw a great personal tragedy for General Stroh, the 8th Division commander. His son, Major Harry R. Stroh, was a pilot with the 378th Fighter Squadron. On August 27, the squadron was flying its P-47 fighter-bombers over the 8th Infantry Division in support of the continuing attack. After successfully hitting their assigned target, the pilots still had ordnance and were seeking more targets. General Stroh was present with the air controller and personally directed the planes to strike a wooded area that was holding up a battalion of his division. Exactly what happened next is disputed. One version has it that Major Stroh was shot down by German antiaircraft fire from those woods. The other version, from his fellow pilots, was that he flew too low during his strafing run and was hit by a friendly artillery shell. In any case, Major Stroh was killed in the crash. It would be several days before the general learned that the crash that he had witnessed had killed his son.[18]

Meanwhile, the fight for Hill 88 continued. The first men to get to the top were led by Staff Sergeant Needham Morris and numerous German counterattacks failed to drive the Golden Arrow men off the hill. By the end of August 27, all of the 13th Infantry Regiment's objectives had been taken, but the German defenses had not been broken. Casualties had been heavy, and both sides needed a respite. In front of the 2nd Battalion, 28th Infantry, the Germans asked for a truce to evacuate their wounded. The truce was granted on the morning of August 29 and both sides cared for the wounded. But when the truce was ended, two companies of the 2nd Battalion had disappeared. Both had been somewhat in advance of the main American line, and were suddenly out of communication. It wouldn't be until after the capture of Brest that these American soldiers would be found (in a German prisoner-of-war camp on the Crozon peninsula) and returned to duty. The Germans had used the cover of the truce to surround and cut off the two advanced companies, which had been forced to surrender.

*   *   *

As Ninth Army moved in to take over operations, it was clear that the massive advances of all divisions at the same time was not working. The continuing shortage of artillery ammunition prevented the usual bombardment that American infantry had come to rely on for their attacks. Further, the strength of the enemy had been underestimated, as had the strength of the German fortifications. The closer the Americans came to Brest, the stronger these fortifications became.

General Middleton changed tactics. Instead of the grand, sweeping infantry advance, he now turned to widespread individual attacks, knocking out one enemy post at a time, all across the American front line. The infantry now began to probe each individual pillbox and trench, and then systematically destroy each one. Surprise attacks were launched to take advantage of any carelessness on the part of the Germans. Weak spots were located and attacked, the use of flamethrowers and demolitions was more widespread and time was taken for clearing the many minefields protecting the enemy's positions. Finally, smoke screens were employed to get American infantry closer to their objectives before receiving enemy fire.

*   *   *

Major General Walter Melville Robertson was born June 15, 1888, in Nelson County, Virginia. He was commissioned into the infantry from West Point in 1912 and served in Hawaii and France during World War I. After the usual interwar assignments, including graduation from both the Command and General Staff School and Army War College, he was promoted to colonel and took command of the 9th Infantry Regiment in November 1940, succeeding the then-Colonel Simpson. During the next two years, Robertson moved up to Assistant Division Commander, and then Division Commander, of the 2nd Infantry Division. He would command the division throughout its combat career.

The 2nd Infantry Division, nicknamed "Indian head" after its shoulder sleeve insignia, was another regular Army division. It was stationed at Fort Sam Houston, Texas, before going on maneuvers in Texas and Louisiana as a part of the Army's training program. The division left New York on October 3, 1943 and arrived in England later that month. It spent the rest of that year training until it shipped out for France, landing at Omaha Beach on June 7, 1944. It fought in the bitter campaign for Normandy, seizing the critical Hill 192 on the approaches to St. Lo. It went on to cross the Vire River and advanced into Brittany on August 17, 1944.

Like the Golden Arrow Division next to it, the Indian head Division found the fighting as tough as any it had yet encountered. It wasn't long before some rifle companies were seriously below authorized strength. In the 9th Infantry Regiment, Lieutenant Colonel H. K. Wesson found that one of his rifle companies, Company B, had only 46 men left of the 200 it was authorized. Despite this, when attacked by a captured American tank painted with a swastika, he organized the company for an attack. He personally led an assault to seize a group of defended hedgerows, knocking out a machine gun post and capturing 14 German paratroopers, before he was killed in action.[19]

It was about this time, on September 1, that the ammunition problem appeared to be improving. Middleton, with his artillery now well stocked and his infantry well into the enemy defenses, therefore decided upon another coordinated attack. After a 45-minute artillery preparation and a strike by medium bombers, the infantry moved forward, but only the 8th Infantry Division was able to report progress and even that one small victory was partially lost to a German counterattack.

Middleton was discouraged. He reported to General Bradley that his troops were "none too good," that replacements for losses were behind schedule, that ammunition was in short supply and that air support "left much to be desired." He requested more heavy mortar support, more artillery, and more air support. He also requested amphibious landing craft for a possible attempt at assaulting Brest from the sea, but none were available. Yet, even as Middleton's letter was reaching higher headquarters, the 2nd Infantry Division was providing the breakthrough he was seeking.

The division had been attacking through country covered with hedgerows, much the same as in Normandy. Originally the attack was expected to be easy and additional flamethrowers and an extra supply of Thompson sub-machine guns were issued in expectation of street fighting.[20] On August 24, the division attacked with the 9th Infantry Regiment on the right and the 23rd Infantry Regiment on the left. Intelligence sources reported that they were facing the 7th *Fallschirmjäger* Regiment, supported by the 2nd *Fallschirmjäger* Engineer Battalion. In addition, there were the usual additions of naval and antiaircraft troops. The immediate objectives were the village of Kervern and Hill 100 for the 9th Infantry, while the 23rd Infantry advanced on the villages of Lavallot and Toralan, and Hill 105.

The advance began slowly, and tank destroyers had to be called forward to knock out individual pillboxes holding things up. Colonel Chester J. Hirschfelder's 9th Infantry faced strong resistance, which knocked out three tanks from Company D, 709th Tank Battalion, operating in support of the regiment. One of the crews found themselves trapped inside their vehicle when the Germans set up a machine gun position immediately outside the disabled tank. The crew was forced to stay put, keeping quiet for two days, before they again heard American voices outside.

The attack made slow progress, despite tank and artillery support. Mutually supporting defensive positions prevented the Americans from knocking out one position at a time, and difficulties also arose when it was found that many of the new troop replacements had no training on Bangalore torpedoes or demolition charges. In one instance, Company Commander Captain Cameron A. Clough found that none of the men in his company knew how to operate a flamethrower. He took one himself and led the advance into Kervao, where they were counter attacked by Germans manning a captured Sherman tank. Once again, Clough led some of his men in manning a captured German 37mm antitank gun to drive off the tank. During this engagement Clough was severely injured and lost an eye, but despite his wounds, he refused to leave his command until he was sure that they had secured their objective. For his outstanding leadership, Clough received a Distinguished Service Cross.[21]

A German position known as Battery *Domaine* contained a group of 105mm antiaircraft guns in heavily constructed concrete positions. It had excellent fields of fire in the direction the Americans were attacking from and threatened to halt the advance. It took the 3rd Battalion, 23rd Infantry, three days of constant attacks, several P-47 air strikes, the assistance of Companies A and C, 5th Ranger Infantry Battalion, and the capture of the nearby village of Keramo before the Germans finally abandoned the position. For its actions in the battle to seize the approach to Hill 105, the 3rd Battalion, 23rd Infantry, would receive a Presidential Unit Citation.[22]

As the Americans moved up to take over their hard-won prize, sudden explosions rocked the area. Apparently, the Germans had primed six of their pillboxes, loaded with munitions, to explode at the time the Americans moved into the position. The blasts sent large pieces of concrete several feet into the air and the night sky was lit up. Numerous casualties resulted and it was later determined that 48 Americans had been killed in the blasts.

The next major obstacle was the village of Fourneuf. Once again, paratroopers of the 7th *Fallschirmjäger* Regiment stiffened the defense. Major William F. Kernan led his 3rd Battalion, 9th Infantry, against the town. For the next four days, from August 29 to September 1, the battle raged. Forced to attack across a minefield and open fields, the battalion suffered horrendous casualties—a platoon of Company I was wiped out in one attack and it took another platoon five tries before they could cross the open fields. Once in the town, the fighting became hand-to-hand and lasted well into the night. Every house was defended and the cost to the Americans was 45 killed and 110 wounded, but during the evening of September 1, the Germans withdrew. So complete was the German defeat that the 9th Infantry Regiment was able to advance 1,000 yards without opposition and more than 1,000 prisoners were taken. For its actions between August 29 and September 1, the 3rd Battalion, 9th Infantry Regiment, received a Presidential Unit Citation.[23] So depleted was the regiment that it was then pulled out of the line and replaced by the 38th Infantry Regiment, fresh from its conquest of the Daoulas Peninsula.

It was on August 29 that a young man from Philadelphia made a major contribution to the battle. Sergeant John J. McVeigh was a member of Company H, 23rd Infantry Regiment, 2nd Infantry Division. Company H was the 2nd Battalion's heavy weapons company and McVeigh's machine gun squad had been attached to Company G when it began to build defensive positions for the night. One of the platoons had not yet begun its digging when a platoon of Germans counter attacked, supported by automatic weapons and antiaircraft guns. The result was that much of the American platoon was pushed back, leaving only McVeigh's machine gun fighting off the enemy. So swiftly did the attack come that within moments the German infantrymen were almost upon McVeigh's position. Without hesitation, he stood erect in the face of intense enemy fire and directed the fire of his squad in halting the attack. Still the Germans came on, and soon they were at the machine gun position itself. Pulling his trench knife, his rifle already empty, McVeigh personally charged the oncoming enemy and engaged in hand-to-hand combat. Armed only with his knife, he killed one of the Germans and then attacked three more before he was cut down by small-arms fire, but the delay he had provided allowed his men to turn their gun on the Germans and kill the remaining attackers. McVeigh was almost solely responsible for stopping this counter attack which, if successful, could have had serious consequences. For his self-sacrifice he was awarded a posthumous Medal of Honor.[24]

* * *

Still the Germans resisted. Indeed, if anything their defense became more diabolical. With the vast German and French naval supplies at hand, they began to use naval artillery shells, torpedo warheads and French 75mm shells as mines and booby traps. Some roads were found to have 2,000 pounds of high explosives buried under them. Doorknobs to houses were booby-trapped, trip wires were laid to explosives and teller mines (used to destroy tanks) were set to trigger at the weight of a man, rather than that of a tank, and buried on likely routes of approach. Rumors circulated of poisoned bottles of wine and booby-trapped German pistols, a sought after prize for American souvenir hunters.

In return, the Americans bombed Brest every day of the battle but one. By the end of the first week in September, the Germans were using their last reserves (the Parachute Division's band and its military postmen) to shore up the front lines. But the 2nd Infantry Division was approaching Hill 92 (the last major obstacle before the city itself), the 8th Infantry Division was approaching the village of Lambézellec, while the 29th Infantry Division faced Hill 103 and Fort de Mengant. By this point, the remaining area under German control was so small that bombing had to be stopped to avoid friendly casualties. With General Simpson now in charge and providing an increased ammunition supply, Middleton felt confident enough to launch another major attack. He ordered a coordinated effort for September 8, after a strong artillery barrage and with constant air cover.

The attack made good progress. The 2nd Infantry Division captured Hill 92. During the fight Sergeant Mike S. Rambago was leading his squad forward when a German concussion grenade came flying at his men. Without hesitation and without regard for his own life, Rambago leaped to one side and tried to knock down the grenade before it reached his friend, Sergeant Vernon Woody, the squad leader. Unable to reach the grenade, Rambago blocked it with his chest and let it fall to the ground. Instantly, he dropped to the ground, threw his steel helmet over the grenade, and smothered it, saving his men from death or injury. For his courage, Rambago received a Distinguished Service Cross.[25]

In the 8th Infantry Division's sector, the advance moved close to Lambézellec, largely thanks to the efforts of Private First Class Ernest W. Prussman, who led the attack. The young soldier, from Brighton, Massachusetts, led his company of the 13th Infantry Regiment forward when the other battalions had been halted by intense mortar, machine gun and sniper fire at Les Coates. Seeing that the main enemy fire was coming from a fortified position to his left, Prussman led his squad in the assault. He jumped over a hedgerow and captured two German soldiers. Then he led his squad across an open field to the next hedgerow, where he placed them in covering positions as he went forward alone. He advanced to an enemy machine gun and knocked it out, capturing the crew and supporting riflemen. Prussman once again led the way forward, only to be mortally wounded. As he fell to enemy fire, he tossed a grenade that killed the enemy facing him. This sudden and unexpected attack disrupted the German defenses and the two trapped battalions quickly advanced and overran the enemy position. For his gallant self-sacrifice Prussman received a posthumous Medal of Honor.[26]

Still the struggle went on. Staff Sergeant George T. Scanlon of the 121st Infantry Regiment single-handedly attacked a German dugout and knocked it out, earning his Distinguished Service Cross.[27] Across the river, the 29th Infantry Division moved closer to the key village of Penfield. Although the fighting had been intense, the results were clearly in the Americans' favor, with 1,000 prisoners being taken against American losses of 250. It was also on September 8 that the first fruits of Simpson's assumption of command bore fruit. Eight large landing craft (LSTs) and two train loads of artillery ammunition arrived. General Middleton was optimistic for the first time since the battle for Brest began.

Supported by heavy artillery fire, both the 2nd and 8th Infantry Divisions reached the streets of Brest on September 9. Prisoners taken that day totaled 2,500. Clearly the battle was going in favor of the Americans, but both divisions then became bogged down in vicious street fighting. Every street and every square was contested. Machine gun and antitank fire came from cleverly hidden positions throughout the city. To move forward, the Americans had to blast holes in the walls between buildings—to venture out on the street was to invite death or injury. General Robertson would describe this phase of the attack as "a corporal's war."[28] All fighting was done at the squad or perhaps platoon level. One example was the taking of a concrete reinforced dugout that protruded no more than 10 inches above ground level on a street corner. Inside was a heavy machine gun and its crew. It took eight Americans, armed with two flamethrowers, a bazooka and two Browning automatic rifles, all day to knock this position out, by circling the dugout, eliminating the supporting positions, and then capturing the 13 Germans hidden within the dugout itself.

General Stroh's 8th Infantry Division came up against Fort Bougen, protecting the fortified wall around the city. An infantry assault supported by artillery failed to gain any ground. Stroh then turned his heavy artillery directly on the fort's wall, some 55 feet high and behind a moat 25 feet deep. This merely blew some holes in the upper portion of the wall, the lower sections remaining intact. It was then that Middleton ordered the 8th Infantry Division to move over to the Crozon Peninsula and clear that area. The rest of Brest fell to the 2nd Infantry Division to clear. After more days of bitter house-to-house fighting, and the addition of British flamethrower tanks, Major William F. Kernan of the 3rd Battalion, 9th Infantry, received an offer to surrender from Colonel Erich Pietzonka of the German 7th Parachute Regiment. The fight for Brest ended on September 18. It had cost the 2nd Infantry Division 2,314 casualties, while the surrendering Germans had lost 3,307 officers and men.

*   *   *

The 29th Infantry Division was inducted into Federal service on February 3, 1941 and had undergone the usual training and maneuvers before leaving the United States on October 5, 1942. It continued to train in England and was selected to be an assault division on D-Day, at Omaha Beach. After securing that beachhead at a terrific cost, it fought at the Vire River and at St. Lo. It had moved into Brittany and began its attack there on August 25, 1944.

The commander of the division throughout its combat career was Major General Charles Hunter Gerhardt, Jr., born in Tennessee on June 6, 1895. He was commissioned into the cavalry from West Point in 1917 and fought in two World War I campaigns before graduating from the Command and General Staff School. He was promoted to major general in June 1942 and given command of the 91st Infantry Division before being transferred to the 29th.

The 29th Infantry Division had been fighting across the Penfield River from Brest since August 23. Reinforced with the 2nd and 5th Ranger Infantry Battalions and Task Force A, it had a large area to cover and an open flank, which Task Force A was assigned to protect. Weeks of fighting, like that experienced by the 2nd and 8th Infantry Divisions across the river, followed. As the division moved closer to Brest, one of its main obstacles was Fort Keranroux. This strongly defended position had blocked progress for three days. Another attack was launched by the 2nd Battalion, 175th Infantry, on September 12. Company F managed to move to within several hundred yards of the enemy position but was halted there by strong defenses. Realizing that no further delay could be allowed, Staff Sergeant Sherwood H. Hallman, an original member of the division from Spring City, Pennsylvania, ordered his squad to cover his movements with fire while he advanced alone to a point where he could make an attack on the position. Without hesitation, Hallman leaped over a hedgerow into a sunken road, which was the central point of the enemy defenses and which was known to contain machine guns and a strong enemy garrison. Firing his Browning automatic rifle and hurling grenades at the enemy, he killed or wounded four of them and ordered the 12 others to surrender. Then, waving his company forward, he led them in clearing out the rest of the enemy stronghold. Seeing the Americans force a breach in their defenses, another 75 enemy soldiers immediately surrendered. This one act advanced the front of the 175th Infantry by over 2,500 yards and led to the capture of Fort Keranroux later that day. For his gallantry and intrepid leadership, Hallman (who was killed in action two days later) was awarded a posthumous Medal of Honor.[29]

Hill 103 was taken after fierce fighting by the 3rd Battalion, 115th Infantry, earning Major Randolph Millholland promotion to lieutenant colonel. The heavy mortars of the attached 86th Chemical Mortar Battalion were liberally used to keep the Germans pinned down while the American infantry advanced. The 5th Ranger Infantry Battalion, acting as regular infantry, seized Forts Toulbroch, Mengant and Dellec along the Bay of Brest. Fort Kerrognant fell to the 115th Infantry Regiment. With the aid of British flamethrower tanks of the 141st Regiment, Royal Tank Corps, Fort Montbarey fell to the 2nd Battalion, 115th Infantry and 1st Battalion, 116th Infantry.

With these outlying defenses in their hands, General Gerhardt's men moved into Recouvrance where, like their comrades in Brest proper, they engaged in vicious street fighting. A man-made hill, used by the French Navy as a backstop for their naval gunnery range and known as Sugar Loaf hill to the Americans, fell to Company C, 175th Infantry. The old city wall was reached on September 16. Company E of the 175th Infantry was the first to scale the wall and the first to actually enter the city of Brest. Over 600 prisoners were taken and the advance moved further into the city. The 115th Infantrymen soon reached the vast submarine pens, defended by numerous pillboxes made of 14in. thick steel. A 155mm gun brought up to knock them out failed, as its shells merely bounced off the thick steel. Undaunted, the 5th Ranger Infantry Battalion tried a new tactic, pouring gasoline down the ventilator shaft and detonating the fuel with demolition charges, but just as this method was being employed, the Germans suddenly surrendered. All firing west of the Penfield River ceased on September 18.

General Ramcke was not among the prisoners assembled in Brest. The German commander had moved to the Crozon Peninsula when it became obvious that Brest was falling. The Crozon Peninsula forms the southern side of the Bay of Brest. It, too, was heavily fortified with defenses dating back to the 17th century. When the 6th Armored Division had first arrived at Brest, it had cut off the German forces there and kept them bottled up by use of cavalry patrols and Task Force A. French Forces of the Interior reported that there were at least 10,000 German troops defending the area.

Early attempts to clear the peninsula by Task Force A were halted by German defenses at Hill 330. The presence of the Americans, however, emboldened several groups of impressed Russian Army men to turn on their captors. Dozens of Germans were turned over to the Americans by these Russians, who also engaged in combat against their former masters. One American, a Private Bodlak, was captured during these maneuvers. As an interpreter for the 15th Cavalry Squadron, he spoke fluent German, and when there were no German officers around, he managed to talk some 300 German soldiers into surrendering. The German defenses at Hill 330 soon collapsed and Task Force A moved forward.

The next German line was at the airfield near Saint Efflez. With the town and the airfield at Lanvéoc strongly held, Task Force A was once again stymied. In addition to the usual infantry weapons and artillery, the airfield provided numerous antiair-craft guns to strengthen the defense. There was no way the lightly armed cavalry and reconnaissance units could successfully attack such a position, so Task Force A settled down to await reinforcements, meanwhile identifying German positions for air attacks.

The 8th Infantry Division, pinched out of the line at Brest, had been moved to the Crozon Peninsula. It sent its 28th Infantry (on the right) and the 121st Infantry (on the left) down the peninsula. Assisted by the 34th Artillery Brigade and the 174th Artillery Group, firing from the Daoulas Peninsula, the division attacked on September 14. Here the fighting was much like the earlier action in front of Brest. Germans were well dug-in, hedgerows limited vision and maneuver and the Germans, realizing that this was the end, used their artillery in abundance. A break came when Company L, 28th Infantry, captured some Germans, including an officer. Private First Class Jacob Reif, a German-speaking interpreter, searched this officer and discovered papers showing the entire German defensive position on the peninsula. Despite orders to get back to his unit, Reif refused until he could deliver this important intelligence to a staff officer.[30] The information allowed General Stroh to pound the German defenses with all guns available to him, lowering casualties and speeding up the clearing of the peninsula.

The next two days saw the Americans break the German line, and more and more enemy troops surrendered voluntarily—the fight was clearly ending. On September 16, the town of Crozon was captured. The 13th Infantry Regiment came forward and faced the last serious obstacle, the defenses at the tip of the peninsula. These consisted of a stone wall and a moat filled with water. It was heavily defended with minefields and barbed wire. Plans were made to use the 2nd Ranger Infantry Battalion in an amphibious assault to bypass these defenses, but General Ramcke had other ideas. Having inspected what remained of his defenses, ammunition supply and the troop's morale, he finally admitted to himself that the situation was hopeless. He ordered his men to destroy their code books and began surrender negotiations, but not before the 13th Infantry attacked on September 19, supported by 14 battalions of artillery.

If Ramcke needed any further convincing, this was it. As the infantrymen of the 13th Infantry came over the wall, Ramcke sent out a request to discuss surrender. First Lieutenant James M. Dunham, a platoon leader in the 13th Infantry, was led to the general's headquarters. He was soon followed by Brigadier General Canham, the Assistant Division Commander, Colonel Robert A. Griffin, commanding the 13th Infantry and Lieutenant Colonel Earl L. Lerette, commanding the 3rd Battalion.

Ramcke, arrogant as ever, demanded to see the Americans' credentials before he would discuss surrender. General Canham is said to have replied, pointing to his combat-weary infantrymen, "These are my credentials." It would become the motto of the 8th Infantry Division from that point on.[31] Ramcke surrendered his 873 remaining men and was sent off to a prisoner-of-war camp in the United States.[32]

The Brittany campaign was over, although there remained some mopping up to do. American casualties totaled 9,831 and prisoners taken numbered 38,000, of which more than 20,000 were combat troops. The campaign had cost the 2nd Infantry Division 2,314 casualties, the 8th Infantry Division 1,500, and the 29th Infantry Division 329 killed and 2,317 wounded, but Ninth Army had completed what Patton had begun.

CHAPTER 3

Geilenkirchen

The surrender of General Ramcke did not end the Brittany Campaign for Simpson's Ninth Army. The formal surrender, on September 19, merely set off a new chain of responsibilities for the Ninth Army staff. First, they had to process some 28,000 German prisoners of war, including Ramcke, Brigadier General Hans von der Mosel, the Brest Garrison Chief of Staff, Colonel Hans Kroh (who commanded the 2nd Parachute Division when Ramcke became garrison commander), and Rear Admiral Kahler of the German Navy. Total prisoners captured, including those taken by VIII Corps prior to coming under Ninth Army's command, numbered 37,888. Ninth Army casualties, from September 5 through September 20, included 436 killed in action and 2,286 wounded in action, with a total casualty list of 2,952.

Simpson now had to evaluate the port of Brest for use by the Allies, the purpose for the campaign. The decision was that the port was "entirely useless."[1] It had been completely destroyed and remained unavailable to the Allies for the remainder of the war in Europe. Eventually the new French government would have to decide if it was even worth repairing the port for civilian use after the war.

For the first time, Ninth Army had to address the issue of handling German wounded, of which some 5,982 were captured in Brest and 1,900 in Recouvrance. The Ninth Army Surgeon, Colonel William E. Shambora, reviewed the situation and learned that the conditions under which German medical facilities were operating were deplorable, due to lack of supplies, ventilation, lighting, and being housed in underground facilities. The "hospitals" were over crowded, damp and had a critical shortage of qualified medical personnel. Colonel Shambora utilized a Ninth Army medical clearing company at Morlaix and a Communications Zone field hospital at Plestin, using landing craft to transport the enemy wounded from St. Michel-en-Gréve. Patients who were able to be transported were then shipped to the United Kingdom via one of these units. The occasional hospital train was also utilized when available, taking the casualties to Cherbourg. Every available medical unit and all personnel were gathered for the huge task of clearing Brest and its environs of both friendly and enemy wounded. So efficient was the system developed by Colonel Shambora that within 24 hours one German field hospital had its population reduced from 1,184 to 620. Most of the latter were critical and could not be immediately moved. By September 24, just four days after the formal surrender, only 40 non-mobile patients remained within Brest.

Another unpleasant and sad duty that fell to Ninth Army was the care of the American and enemy dead. For much of September four cemeteries, two for American dead and two for the Germans, were operated by Ninth Army. When it relocated east, it turned over the responsibility for these cemeteries to the Normandy Base Section of the Communications Zone.

Ninth Army also discovered that planning had not provided for a casualty-reporting section within a field army headquarters. Simpson had decided (while Ninth Army was in England) that such a need existed, but War Department tables of organization failed to provide for such a unit. Simpson therefore appointed Colonel John A. Klein, the army's Adjutant General, to organize an unofficial section within Ninth Army headquarters. Taking a few men from several sections of the HQ staff, Klein organized a casualty-reporting section and constantly expanded it as the need arose throughout Ninth Army's combat career. Under Klein's direction, subordinate units including corps and divisions organized a similar reporting system. This proved critical when Ninth Army casualties needed to be confirmed in order to request necessary replacement personnel in a timely manner.

Nor had this ended the actual fighting for Ninth Army. When Simpson had taken over from Patton's Third Army, part of the reason was that Third Army was fighting a war on two fronts far apart. Patton had not only left Middleton and his VIII Corps headquarters in charge of the conquest of Brittany, he had also assigned it the protection of Third Army's right (southern) flank, which ran some 310 miles in length. On September 10 Simpson had decided that this unwieldy arrangement was not good military procedure, and transferred the two VIII Corps divisions, which were guarding the flank, to direct Ninth Army control. Both Major General Robert W. Grow's 6th Armored Division and Major General Macon's 83rd Infantry Division thus came directly under Ninth Army command. The arrangement allowed Middleton to concentrate on Brittany, while the flanks of both Third and Ninth Army were under the direct command of Simpson.

Barely a day after this new command arrangement went into effect, Twelfth Army Group headquarters ordered Simpson to forward more troops to Patton as soon as possible. It was believed that the rapid progress Allied forces were making towards Germany, and the arrival of General Patch's Seventh Army to the south of Third Army, would remove any threats to Third Army's flank.

Simpson therefore released Combat Command B of the 6th Armored Division on September 11. That same day, Twelfth Army Group increased Ninth Army's responsibilities by placing an additional 80 miles of open Third Army flank in Ninth Army's zone of responsibility. This greatly lengthened the line that Simpson's army was expected to hold. In order to stiffen the line, Twelfth Army Group assigned the newly arrived 94th Infantry Division, under the command of Major Harry J. Malony, to Ninth Army.[2] Malony was ordered to expedite his division's movement to Brittany, where it would take over the containment of the German enclaves at Lorient and Saint-Nazaire.

Simpson also learned from Twelfth Army Group that the German garrisons at Lorient, Saint-Nazaire and south of the Loire River would not be aggressively attacked. They were to be contained and allowed to sit idle while the main American forces raced east to Germany itself. There were believed to be some 15,000 enemy troops in the Lorient area and an additional 10,000 in the Saint-Nazaire zone. A third pocket, near Pointe de Grave, northwest of Bordeaux, would also remain dormant until the war's end. As was the case at Brest, these garrisons were made up of seasoned combat troops, naval, antiaircraft and air corps personnel. There were, as the Americans would soon learn from deserters, many impressed Russian and Polish troops who were eager to surrender, and did so at the first opportunity.[3]

As elements of the 94th Infantry Division arrived in Brittany, elements of the 6th Armored Division departed for Third Army. By September 16, General Malony's troops had taken over responsibility for Lorient and were patrolling between Quimper and Redon. That same day the 6th Armored Division officially rejoined Third Army. Malony's men then expanded their zone towards the 83rd Infantry Division.

General Macon's troops had been busy while awaiting release back to Third Army. The invasion of southern France on August 15 had prompted the German forces occupying that area to withdraw to the north and east. A group of largely noncombatant military personnel, under the command of *Generalmajor* Botho H. Elster, had lost contact with its screening force escort and had come under increasing attack by Allied aircraft and French Forces of the Interior. By September 5 the column was in distress, stretched out over more than thirty miles of road between Poitiers and Châteauroux. It was discovered by the Intelligence and Reconnaissance Platoon of the 329th Infantry Regiment, led by 1st Lieutenant Samuel W. Magill. Magill and his 24 soldiers took the initiative and crossed the Loire to make contact with the German commander. General Elster and Lieutenant Magill met on September 8 and arranged surrender terms. Elster insisted that a mock battle be staged in order to "save face" before he would surrender. He also insisted that he would not surrender to less than two battalions of American troops. At the time, Magill and his platoon were the only American troops south of the Loire—Magill therefore rushed to report to Colonel E. B. "Buckshot" Crabill, his regimental commander. At the top of the chain of command, General Macon refused the request and demanded a face-to-face meeting. Two days later, Elster surrendered his entire command to Macon without a shot being fired, after observing a fly-over by XIX Tactical Air Command (requested by Macon). The 83rd Infantry Division added 754 officers, 18,850 enlisted men and 10 women to the prisoner-of-war cages. The surrender included 400 civilian automobiles, 500 enemy trucks and over 1,000 horse-drawn wagons.[4]

Yet even this episode was not without consequences for Ninth Army. Lieutenant Colonel William M. Spinrad, of the army's ordnance section, drove to Beaugency to supervise the collection of weapons and ammunition by the surrendering Germans. As he was having dinner in the hotel dining room on September 22, seven shots were fired through a glass window, killing the colonel. The assailant was never identified.

* * *

On September 22, the 94th Infantry Division had completely relieved the 83rd Infantry Division. General Malony now had the responsibility for guarding almost 400 miles of the flank of Twelfth Army Group, reporting to Simpson at Ninth Army. Knowing that he did not have nearly enough men to cover this vast territory, Malony made excellent use of the numerous FFI personnel available to him. Armed with a variety of German, French, Russian, Czech and American weapons, thousands of local patriots were quite willing to keep their former oppressors cooped up in their own "fortresses." Having served in France during World War I, Malony was fluent in French and as a result developed close cooperation with his allies. He agreed to furnish them a major portion of their supply needs and integrated their forces into those of his own 94th Infantry Division. Many of the FFI men were soon seen wearing the shoulder sleeve insignia of the division as they went about their duties. As a result, there was soon no need for further American troops to hold down the German garrisons remaining in Brittany.[5]

Malony also made good use of American air support to discourage German sorties from the ports. In order to provide that support, Ninth Army made an arrangement with a French Air Force squadron of medium bombers. Under Major Jean Lagoir, they had fought earlier in the North African campaign and were eager to fight on their home soil. The attendant difficulties of locating suitable airfields, spare parts and supplies were another obstacle overcome by Ninth Army staff. By the time Ninth Army departed, the French force, known as "*Groupe Patrie,*" was fully operational. Its targets were usually ferry boats supplying the isolated German garrisons, landing sites, railroad tracks, command posts, troop barracks and military installations. These were most often identified by members of the FFI who had penetrated German lines and even observed the attacks to report on the damage inflicted.

On September 29, 1944, Simpson visited Malony at his headquarters at Châteaubriant and discussed the situation of the Channel ports. Simpson informed Malony that his division had not originally been intended for assignment to the Brittany mission and believed that at some point in the not-too-distant future it would be moved to the active front line. Malony in reply asked for more equipment and supplies for distribution to the FFI, and Simpson replied that he would do all he could, but that First and Third Armies had priority. He also informed

Malony that when Ninth Army moved east, as was expected momentarily, the 94th Infantry Division would remain holding Brittany, under Twelfth Army Group control.[6]

The task of keeping the Germans bottled up at Lorient and Saint-Nazaire was not as easy as it first appeared. Even as the 301st Infantry Regiment moved into position, two men were killed in an enemy probe and the first German prisoners were taken. When Company K, 301st Infantry, came under a heavy enemy artillery attack, Private First Class Dale Proctor remained exposed with his telephone at his observation post. Despite being mortally wounded, he remained at his post and gave accurate directions to the division artillery that was responding to the attack. Even as medics attempted to treat his wounds, he insisted on remaining at his post until it became necessary to literally pry the phone from his hands and force him to submit to medical treatment. His Distinguished Service Cross was posthumously awarded.[7]

Meanwhile, Ninth Army remained responsible for the reception, processing and training of all units arriving in France that would eventually be assigned to any one of the field armies of Twelfth Army Group. To accomplish this task, III Corps, under the command of Major General John Millikin, established itself on the Cherbourg Peninsula on September 5, under Ninth Army direction.[8] Over the month of September and into October, III Corps would process XIX Corps, the 26th, 44th, 84th, 95th, 99th, 102nd, and 104th Infantry Divisions, plus the 9th, 10th, 11th and 12th Armored Divisions. This was in addition to a large number of support and service units that passed through Ninth Army's command. In addition, Ninth Army's XIII Corps was still processing units arriving in England from the United States.

As it had since its time in England, Ninth Army stressed physical training for soldiers about to enter combat for the first time. Among the requirements was the ability to run a mile bearing a combat pack, and an eight-mile march with full combat pack, plus leadership classes, small-unit training, tank-infantry cooperation in the attack, marksmanship with all weapons, map reading, camouflage and supply discipline. As General Gillem would later write of Simpson's policies, the army commander believed strongly that "the battle is won by the trained and resourceful soldier who has complete confidence in his weapons and in the skill and ability of his leaders."[9]

The rapid advance of the Allied Forces towards Germany in August and September created another logistical problem. With most railroads destroyed and roads in poor shape, there was a need to find a way to get critical supplies to the distant armies. The Communications Zone developed a single-route truck system, which soon became famous as the "Red Ball Express," to which Ninth Army contributed by stripping its field artillery, tank destroyer and antiaircraft units of their cargo vehicles.[10] In addition to this, several divisions (including the 26th, 95th and 104th Infantry Divisions) were likewise stripped while processing under Ninth Army.

Meanwhile, Ninth Army continued its work in Brittany. Civil Affairs detachments were sent to the various French government officials to assist in re-establishing those communities after years of occupation and recent military operations. Food, soap and diesel oil to operate power plants were distributed. Outbreaks of typhoid, paratyphoid and diphtheria were discovered and treated, and medical supplies were made available to French public health authorities. Rehabilitation of public utilities, restoration of a free press and radio, and assistance in the establishment of local governments were also undertaken.

*   *   *

It was on September 24 that Ninth Army learned of its next mission. Twelfth Army Group issued a new letter of instructions in which Ninth Army and VIII Corps were ordered to move to positions in Belgium-Luxembourg, between First and Third Armies, along the Siegfried Line. The 29th Infantry Division was transferred to First Army and was to move immediately, before Ninth Army or VIII Corps. Earlier orders to expect a move to the south of Third Army were rescinded. Ninth Army was to move to an area bounded on the north by St. Vith and on the south by Metz.

General Simpson promptly began addressing the issues attendant to moving a field army across France. There were some 80,000 American troops in Brittany at the time—16 battalions of artillery, service troops and tank destroyer units needed to move in a coordinated manner to the new area of operations. There was a serious lack of railroads and tank transporters. Without these, the tracks on all tracked vehicles would quickly wear out, requiring replacements as well as time to conduct the repairs. The large stock of ammunition left over after the surrender of Brest was another problem. Once the flow of ammunition had begun, it proved difficult to curtail. By September 24, there was 25,000 tons of ammunition in and around Brest awaiting use. Ninth Army managed to increase the allotment of ammunition that each artillery battalion carried, and took 12,000 tons to its new area. Vehicles had to make two or three trips of up to 1,200 miles just to accommodate this transfer, and ordnance companies serviced 600 trucks in three days as a result of this move.

The 29th Infantry Division left first, on the day of the new orders, September 24. They were soon followed by VIII Corps headquarters and troops, which moved directly to Bastogne. Ninth Army headquarters moved, beginning on September 29, to Arlon, Belgium. The new headquarters location was opened on October 2, the command post being established in a large building known as *L'Ecole Normale*, originally a teachers college. Previously it had been used as a hospital by the Germans.

Ninth Army was now ready for its next assignment. Actually there were several assignments. Within a few weeks, the army had units operating in five different countries—France, Belgium, Luxembourg, the Netherlands and Germany. This widespread distribution of forces caused some problems, mostly communications between the far-flung units. Half of Ninth Army headquarters remained in France at Rennes to finish up duties there. Because of the still-moving communications equipment and personnel, much of Ninth Army's communications between its units had to be passed through either Twelfth Army Group or Communications Zone. This resulted in delays when other communications were given a higher priority by those headquarters. A daily messenger service was therefore arranged, whereby the messengers met half way, in Paris, and exchanged messages. Use of a Very High Frequency (VHF) radio also alleviated the situation somewhat, but messages sent by this method were open to interception by the enemy.

VIII Corps, with its 2nd and 8th Infantry Divisions, immediately began relieving units of First Army. By October 4, Ninth Army had assumed responsibility for the front-line sector between Bollendorf and St. Vith. With but one corps and two divisions, it was by far the smallest American army on the front line. On October 9, the 94th Infantry Division was transferred to Twelfth Army Group, and Ninth Army's Brittany responsibilities went with it.

The main task for Ninth Army now was to build itself up so to be able to assume a larger section of First Army's front to the north, and also relieve a sector of Third Army to the south. Ninth Army's XIII Corps, under General Gillem, was ordered up from Normandy to take over a portion of the front line. It was expected to take over a section covered by VIII Corps, thereby reducing Third Army's front. Ninth Army also awaited the assignment of additional combat divisions to allow it to expand its front. In England, III Corps continued its mission of receiving incoming units from the United States. One of these was the new XVI Corps under Major General John B. Anderson, which was destined for Ninth Army.

John Benjamin Anderson was born on March 10, 1891, in Waxabachie, Iowa. He was commissioned into the infantry from West Point in 1914 and served in France during World War I. Between the wars he graduated from the Command and General Staff School in 1925 and the Army War College in 1928. As a colonel, Anderson served on the War Department General Staff from 1928–32 before being assigned to the office of the Chief of Field Artillery, from 1938–41. He was promoted to brigadier general on October 1, 1941, and to major general in August of 1942. He commanded the 102nd Infantry Division from 1942–43, before being promoted to command of XVI Corps in December 1943 and bringing that headquarters to England. On October 10, 1944, XVI Corps took over the duties of III Corps, after which III Corps was transferred to Third Army.

The build-up of Ninth Army began slowly. First to join was the 83rd Infantry Division, which had been temporarily with Third Army. A boundary change returned it to Ninth Army effective October 12. A portion of the newly arrived 9th Armored Division joined VIII Corps and by the end of October, Ninth Army, with three infantry divisions on line and one armored division in reserve, was holding a nine-ty-mile front. Once again, further growth was delayed by the still critical shortage of transportation and supplies. The railroads of France were still being repaired and trucks were in short supply and limited by a shortage of gasoline. At this point, Ninth Army had only 250 operational trucks. Of these, nearly 50 were in serious need of repair.

Artillery was another concern. The heavy artillery barrages used in Brittany had worn down the artillery gun tubes—they needed repair, rehabilitation and, in some cases, replacement. Once again transportation slowed the calibration of these guns. Armored vehicles, tanks, half-tracks, and self-propelled guns were in need of track replacement. These could only be obtained through Cherbourg, and First and Third Armies had higher priorities. With all these problems facing it, Twelfth Army Group decided to establish a policy by which the armies bid for a daily tonnage of supplies. Ninth Army's tonnage was allocated at 350 tons of supplies per division per day. This basically put the army on a starvation diet, precluding any thought of a supply reserve or possible offensive actions.

Forced to remain on the defensive, Simpson planned ahead. A supply point was created in the Bastogne area, in preparation for an eventual offensive. Road and rail repairs were given priority and artillery missions were kept to a minimum. This was in accordance with Ninth Army's current orders, which were to contain enemy forces along its front lines but keep an active front in the event an offensive was decided upon. This resulted in much patrolling, which the Germans opposed strongly. The Germans, snugly ensconced in their Siegfried Line defenses, fought off any patrol they discovered—both sides conducted the occasional small-scale raid of the other's positions, but no major offensive by either side developed. Artillery and mortar fire remained limited. Individual German soldiers were occasionally captured behind American lines, and under questioning they reported that their assignment was to harass Allied lines of communication and that they were being supplied by parachute drops.

The fear of paratroop attacks created trouble in the rear of the 83rd Infantry Division around October 17. Late that evening, Twelfth Army Group informed Ninth Army headquarters that reliable sources of information had reported German para-chutists dropping in the vicinity of Differdange, a small town only a dozen miles from Ninth Army HQ in Arlon. The drop area was actually even closer to Twelfth Army Group's headquarters location at Luxembourg. Even the Communications Zone felt threatened, as a key steel plant was located at Differdange. Ninth Army alerted the 2nd and 5th Ranger Infantry Battalions, which were reorganizing, re-equipping and retraining after the difficult Brittany campaign. The 83rd Infantry Division, in whose area the drops had been reported, was also alerted. Reconnaissance patrols, however, soon proved the inaccuracy of the reported paratroop drops. It was later determined that a farmer's report that some of his cattle had been butchered had been magnified by language difficulties and imagination.

Orders came from Twelfth Army Group that Ninth Army was to be prepared to remain on the defensive but to plan for an offensive that would extend its front down to Metz, currently in Third Army's zone. Simpson immediately put his staff to work planning the extension south. He also had them plan for eventualities including an advance east to Germany, a crossing of the Rhine River, and an attack to take or bypass Metz, depending upon how the situation developed. Simpson even had his staff study terrain between the Rhine, Mannheim and Cologne, all east of the Rhine. The result was four different plans for the Ninth Army to launch attacks, each envisioning an attack to the east, through the Siegfried Line, to the Rhine and beyond.

Just as these plans were beginning to take shape, however, new orders from Twelfth Army Group arrived, changing the entire situation. Instead of remaining between First and Third Armies, Ninth Army was to move, without troops, to take over the northern (or left) flank of Twelfth Army Group. Once in place, the lineup from left to right would be Ninth, First, Third and Seventh Armies.

* * *

The new orders were highly unusual. No American army had been, or would again be, told to move around behind another and assume a new position. Generally speaking, each army remained in a relatively stable position relative to the others. Ninth Army was the only one to be ordered to move from the center to the far left flank.

Exactly why Eisenhower took this unusual step of moving an army from the center to the end of his front line has not been explored. As early as December 23, 1943, six months prior to the Normandy invasion, Eisenhower had written to Marshall, the U.S. Army Chief of Staff, and recommended Simpson for one of the future American field armies to be established after the invasion. In this same cable, however, he clearly expressed that his preference for an American army group commander was Omar Bradley, with whom he was personally familiar.[11] He also felt that Bradley had the complete confidence of Field Marshall Montgomery, whom he expected to lead the British and Commonwealth forces on the continent. Nevertheless, it was clear that well before his arrival in Europe, Eisenhower had a high opinion of Simpson.

Yet that opinion was tempered by Simpson's lack of combat experience, as borne out when Simpson was considered as a replacement for Patton as the nominal head of the deception army used as part of Operation *Fortitude*. Simpson was never a part of Eisenhower's "inner circle," as were Bradley and Patton. Nor was he an intimate of Bradley, who now ordered Simpson to assume the position between Bradley's Twelfth Army Group and Montgomery's Twenty-First Army Group.

It is no secret that Bradley and Patton disparaged Montgomery and had a low regard for his abilities as an army group commander. When Bradley began to be convinced that Eisenhower would surrender to intense pressure to attach an American army to Montgomery's army group, he decided that if and when that happened, it would be best if the Army he "lost" was the newest and least experienced he had. The choice naturally fell on Ninth Army.

Not that Bradley, any more than Eisenhower, had a poor opinion of Simpson or his army. Later he would write of a visit with Eisenhower to Ninth Army, saying: "We were immensely impressed with Simpson and his staff and the planning they had done. Simpson's Chief of Staff, James E. Moore, was one of the least-known yet ablest officers in the ETO. I had taught him math at West Point, remembered him well and determined to keep an eye on him in the future." He went on to comment, "Owing to Moore's intelligence and talent for administration, Ninth Army's staff, although least experienced in battle, was in some respects superior to any in my command. Moreover both Simpson and Moore got along remarkable well with Monty and the British staffs. Ike and I left Simpson's headquarters convinced that the Ninth Army was destined for outstanding performance, and we were not disappointed."[12]

Bradley was a practical man, and he wanted his closest and most experienced commanders within his own army group. Ninth Army was thus chosen to fill the position of being closest to Montgomery's Twenty-First Army Group. It was to take over a sector north of the German city of Aachen, which placed it on the north flank of Lieutenant General Courtney Hicks Hodge's First Army and between that army and the British-Canadian Twenty-First Army Group. Simpson left behind VIII Corps and its three divisions and upon arrival at its new position, Ninth Army assumed command of XIX Corps. Interestingly, Simpson was heard to comment upon leaving the sector facing the Ardennes Forest, "Thank God we're getting out of this mess."[13] Perhaps he had a more perceptive understanding of the situation facing VIII Corps in the Ardennes than did Bradley.

XIX Corps was under the command of Major General Raymond Stallings McLain. Born April 4, 1890, in Washington County, Kentucky, he was a rarity in the World War II U.S. Army in that he was not a professional soldier—instead, he came from the National Guard. After attending Hills Business College in 1909, he attended the three-month National Guard course given by the Army for National Guard officer candidates. He accepted a commission in the infantry of the Oklahoma National Guard in 1916. Between the wars he graduated from the Command and General Staff School and was promoted to brigadier general in 1938. He remained with the Oklahoma National Guard and was recalled to active duty in September 1940. McLain commanded the 45th Infantry Division's artillery and then the 30th Infantry Division's artillery between 1940 and 1944. Now a major general, he was given command of the troubled 90th Infantry Division in 1944, and its performance under his command earned him promotion to command of XIX Corps, which he led in France and Germany from 1944–45. The former banker from Oklahoma was the only non-regular Army officer to be given a corps command in Europe. (He would be promoted to lieutenant general in June 1945).

*   *   *

The move north brought with it new challenges. Eisenhower had decided upon a "broad front" sweep of all Allied armies to the Rhine, and then into Germany. Ninth Army was to be built up in its new area in preparation for a drive to the Rhine and then north alongside Twenty-First Army Group. To its south, Twelfth Army Group would also advance east. Beginning on October 11, 1944, Ninth Army's Assistant Chief of Staff for Operations, Colonel Armistead D. Mead, Jr., submitted plans for operations in the new zone to Simpson, who gave them his approval. Later it would be remarked that despite several unexpected events and assignments, the plans approved by Simpson in October 1944 would be largely those used by Ninth Army once the New Year dawned.

Once again, Ninth Army was fully occupied in moving its location. The staff left in Brittany was ordered to move directly to Maastricht in the Netherlands. Stocks of ammunition and other supplies were left in place and exchanged for those of First Army in the new zone of operations. Similarly, most artillery units and other supporting groups were exchanged in place. XIII Corps headquarters, still *en route* to Ninth Army, was diverted to the area of Tongres, Belgium. A major renovation of the local railway system was begun.

Ninth Army headquarters opened at Maastricht on October 22, 1944. Command of VIII Corps passed to First Army the same date and Ninth Army assumed command of XIX Corps. Simpson's headquarters now occupied a former Netherlands Army post and a Catholic school on the outskirts of the city. Unknown to anyone at the time was the fact that they would occupy these quarters for the next five months. The army signal center was finally fully established and a teletype room set up. Soon thereafter, Simpson received Twelfth Army Group's Letter of Instructions Number 10, which outlined three new missions.

First, Ninth Army was to continue with the in-progress mission of XIX Corps, which was to protect First Army's flank during the battle for Aachen. It also covered the buildup for the coming major attack against the Siegfried Line. The cavalry of XIX Corps was to continue to operate as before, providing the link between Twenty-First Army Group and Twelfth Army Group, since Lieutenant General Sir Miles C. Dempsey's British Second Army did not have sufficient troops to provide that link.[14] The American 113th Cavalry Group would therefore continue to provide that connection.[15]

Ninth Army's second mission under the new instructions was "to attack in zone to the Rhine in close conjunction with First Army, protecting its left flank."[16] This attack was tentatively scheduled for November 5, with conditions that it not occur

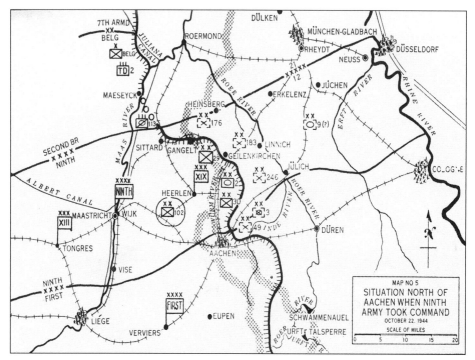

Situation north of Aachen when Ninth Army took command. (*Conquer. The Story of the Ninth Army, 1944–1945*, Infantry Journal Press)

more than two days before the British Second Army attacked on the left. Later, the attack date would be changed. The key to the attack was the success that the First Canadian Army was having in clearing the port of Antwerp, essential for continued Allied success. Once Antwerp had fallen, the British would transfer troops to the east and be ready to continue the attack into Germany. Ninth Army's responsibility for the Antwerp operation was to provide administrative, logistical and personnel reinforcements to Major General Terry de la M. Allen's 104th Infantry Division, which was under British tactical control for the Antwerp battle.

The third assignment for Ninth Army stated that "after the attack of the First Army has reached the Rhine, Ninth Army will attack northward between the Rhine and the Meuse [Maas] Rivers and gain contact [later modified to read 'in conjunction with'] British Second Army. It will then take over the area west of the Rhine to Rees, inclusive."[17] In practice, this meant that Ninth Army would attack east to the Rhine, then turn sharply north and attack towards the British, clearing the west bank of the Rhine as it moved.

Major General McLain's XIX Corps held a 25-mile long stretch of the front from Aachen to Geilenkirchen, and then to Maeseyck on the Maas. The Siegfried Line had been breached to a width of 11 miles and a depth of six miles. XIX Corps had Major

General Leland S. Hobbs' veteran 30th Infantry Division, Major General Ernest N. Harmon's veteran 2nd Armored Division, and (an old friend) General Gerhardt's 29th Infantry Division.[18] The 113th Cavalry Group, reinforced, held Ninth Army's left flank. Further north, the 7th Armored Division under Major General Lindsay McDonald Silvester was, like the 104th Infantry Division, assigned to Ninth Army but under the tactical control of the British Second Army. Another small group, consisting of a Belgian Brigade, a task force of XIX Corps troops and the 2nd Tank Destroyer Group, were also operating under Ninth Army control. Behind the front lines, General Gillem's XIII Corps HQ was assembling and soon the newly arrived 102nd Infantry Division, under Brigadier General Frank A. Keating, would join it.[19]

Like the other armies, Ninth Army used the time before the planned attack to stock up on supplies and give as much rest as possible to the veteran units now under its command. To expedite this rest, Simpson ordered that individual regiments of the new 102nd Infantry Division be used by General McLain to permit a rotation of the front line units of all three divisions, allowing them each a few days of rest and relaxation. As a result, the three infantry regiments of the 102nd Infantry Division entered the front lines beginning October 27.

Intelligence reports reaching Simpson stated that Ninth Army faced five German divisions, one less than Ninth Army would deploy in its attack.[20] It was believed that one unidentified armored division was behind the German front. The Germans in front of Ninth Army showed little aggressive spirit. They attacked only to improve their positions and often did not launch their traditional counterattacks against American incursions. However, in the British sector the 7th Armored Division suffered a serious setback from a local German counterattack, which would result in the relief of the division commander, General Silvester. That German intelligence was equally aware of their opposition was proven when the Germans dropped thousands of leaflets over American lines announcing the arrival of the Ninth Army in the sector.

* * *

Ninth Army was still suffering from logistical problems as it tried to get ready for its first offensive towards Germany. It was short of vehicles, combat units and engineer supplies. Even the placing of Ninth Army staff officers at rear area shipping points could not completely eliminate shipping delays or errors, such as the shipment of hundreds of anvils when the army requested engineer supplies.

Combat troops were another matter. Ninth Army had two corps headquarters assigned to it, along with six combat divisions. Yet only one corps, XIX Corps, and three divisions were ready for combat. General Gillem's XIII Corps had no troops yet assigned. Of those available for it, the 104th Infantry Division was being sent to First Army, the 7th Armored Division was still with the British and the 102nd Infantry Division lacked transport and artillery organic to the division. Only XIX

Corps, with the 2nd Armored, and the 29th and 30th Infantry Divisions, could be said to be ready for an offensive. The pending offensive, labeled Operation *Queen*, only allocated Ninth Army 11 miles of front on which to attack, but it would need more men on the ground, and as the attack progressedits left flank would grow in length, requiring even more troops to defend it.

General Simpson looked earnestly for at least one more division with which he could protect his left flank, along with the 113th Cavalry Group. He had in his area the 104th and 102nd Infantry Divisions, but neither was readily available. Neither was the 7th Armored Division. A new unit, the 84th Infantry Division, was on its way from the beaches, but there was doubt that it would arrive in time. This contributed to the delay in the start date for Operation *Queen*, which was postponed until November 10. It was hoped that either the British would clear the area of the Peel Marshes, which threatened Ninth Army's flank, or that additional combat units would become available to strengthen Ninth Army. Perhaps the 7th Armored Division and/or the 102nd Infantry Division would become available by then. It could be that even the 84th Infantry Division would have arrived.

There was also the question of why Ninth Army was assigned a subsidiary role in the offensive. The terrain in front of it was far more inviting than that facing First Army, designated as making the main effort and reinforced accordingly. General Bradley would later state that "you don't make your main effort with your 'exterior force.'"[21] Bradley had little confidence that the British, busy with other priorities such as Antwerp and Arnhem, could sufficiently cover the American flank should the attack move rapidly forward. That, plus Bradley's confidence in First Army as both his former command and his most experienced army, decreed that Ninth Army became the "exterior force."

Simpson was left to deal with the situation as best he could. He assigned Gillem to command the 113th Cavalry Group and 102nd Infantry Division and had him occupy the 17-mile-long left flank of Ninth Army until relieved by British forces. As soon as they arrived, both 7th Armored Division and 84th Infantry Division were to go straight to XIII Corps. Once relieved by the British, Gillem was to lead his corps northeast along the left flank of XIX Corps, expanding Ninth Army's front.

As expected, it fell to General McLain's XIX Corps to make Ninth Army's main effort. One problem that became quickly obvious was the fortified village of Geilenkirchen. This strongly held town threatened Ninth Army's flank and, even worse, forced it to attack along a narrow corridor barely 10 miles wide between Würselenand Geilenkirchen. To assault and take the village would present problems, because plans placed the entire area within the British zone. Determined to negate this potential threat to progress, Simpson approached the British command. As if there weren't enough concerns, it began to rain, roads broke down and trucks and troops became mired in the mud.

Ninth Army's luck then suddenly turned. Barely two days before the offensive was scheduled to begin, things began to go right. On November 9, Lieutenant General Sir Brian G. Horrocks brought his XXX Corps and the 43rd (Wessex) British Infantry Division to relieve XIII Corps.[22] On the same date, most of the 84th Infantry Division arrived within Ninth Army's zone, as did the 7th Armored Division, having been released by the British. Finally, the 104th Infantry Division, moving behind Ninth Army to join First Army, was halted within Ninth Army's zone. To cap off a fortunate day, Ninth Army staff learned that the attack had been postponed again, until November 11.

CHAPTER 4

Operation *Queen*

Operation *Queen* began with a massive air and artillery bombardment in front of First and Ninth Armies. Some 3,000 Allied heavy, medium and fighter-bombers struck the Germans facing the two American armies. Concerns about the weather had led to the creation of three different air support plans, depending upon the actual conditions. To ensure troop safety in the light of past "friendly fire" tragedies, the bomb line was placed more than 3,000 yards ahead of the most forward friendly troops. Targets in front of Ninth Army included the towns of Linnich and Aldenhoven. Four groups of the XXIX Tactical Air Force, some 300 aircraft, were supporting Ninth Army.[1] Likely sites for enemy command posts or locations for assembling reserves were also targeted.

The terrain differences facing First and Ninth Armies were instrumental in determining how each army progressed. First Army was faced with forests, including the forbidding Hürtgen Forest, while Ninth Army faced a series of village strong points along a fertile plain. The Roerplain lies between the Würm and Roer Rivers. To reach its objective of the Roer, Ninth Army had to cross this plain. Bounded on the south by the Hürtgen Forest and the two rivers, the plain extends about 12 miles wide and includes some 200 square miles of area, which could appear as a right-angle triangle on a map. This area was low and open, with few obstacles to either a defender or attacker. A network of improved and secondary roads crossed the plain in several directions. Villages, of which there were more than a hundred, were close together, usually some three miles apart. To the southwest was a small urban enclave around coal deposits from which the residents gained their livelihood. Portions of the urban area were already in American hands from previous attacks.

General Simpson's plan was based on circumstances. It was a basic frontal assault to break out past the Siegfried Line, using the bridgehead Ninth Army had inherited. A crossing of the Roer in the southeast, near the town of Jülich, was an intermediate objective. This was assigned to General McLain. Unlike First Army's carpet bombing, Ninth Army used XXIX Tactical Air Command to hit targeted villages believed to be fortified or hiding German headquarters or supply dumps.

McLain was concerned that the urban areas near Würselen would delay his advance and separate his corps from First Army, a link with which was his responsibility. Therefore, he charged General Gerhardt's 29th Infantry Division to make its main effort in the center of the corps front, rather than on the right where the urban area lay. To the 30th Infantry Division fell the onerous task of clearing the urban areas, alongside First Army's 104th Infantry Division. The 2nd Armored Division would spearhead the attack.

Concerned lest the 30th Infantry Division become delayed in clearing the urban area, (a role it had taken on in earlier attacks), Simpson gave one regiment from the 84th Infantry Division to McLain, providing a reserve in case one was needed and also allowing McLain to put the full power of the 30th Infantry Division in the forefront of the attack. Just when the last detail seemed to have been arranged, the weather took a hand in events. Since both armies relied on air support to launch their attacks, weather was an important factor, but it did not cooperate. Postponement after postponement came down from Twelfth Army Group, and the days passed until the morning of November 16, when the weather cleared sufficiently for the air attacks to be launched.

General Hobbs, commanding the 30th Infantry Division, had attacked Würselen earlier, during the battle for Aachen, and he was worried, as were Simpson and McLain, that the fortified buildings would significantly delay his attack. In order to obviate this possibility, he ordered all three of his regiments to attack the town in a concentrated pivot attack, whereby each would swing around the other so that all parts of the town were under attack simultaneously. Leading the attack was Colonel Edwin M. Sutherland's 119th Infantry Regiment. Swinging around to the southeast to gain the center of the town was Colonel Banner P. Perdue's 120th Infantry Regiment. Travelling the farthest was Colonel Walter M. Johnson's 117th Infantry Regiment, which would have to cover three times the ground to gain its objective. When McLain passed on the order to attack on November 16, Hobbs initiated his plan.

Each regiment attacked with two battalions, holding the third in reserve. The time spent waiting had been put to good use, and the troops and their leaders were familiar with the terrain and obstacles they would encounter. About the only surprise for the men was the widespread use of mines by the Germans, including a new non-metallic mine, which mine detectors could not locate. Another hidden and undetectable mine was the *Topf,* or antitank, mine. Company F, 117th Infantry, had the worst experience, running into one of these minefields while attacking the village of Mariadorf. The company had progressed well, with enemy artillery coming down late and missing the assault waves. But as it moved on Mariadorf, it was fired on by an enemy machine gun. In attempting to outflank this gun, the company walked into the minefield—losses were immediate and heavy, and German shelling around the area prevented any attempt to extricate the company until darkness fell. Company F lost 60 men during the day.

The thick minefields kept supporting tanks and tank destroyers on the edge of the town, providing static fire support whenever possible. Nevertheless, American infantrymen maneuvered around enemy gun positions and were soon within the main line of defense. Company A of the division's 105th Engineer (Combat) Battalion moved with the front line infantry and managed to save the vital bridge at Mariagube, reaching it before the enemy could blow it up. They removed 400 pounds of explosives from the bridge, all the while fighting off enemy attacks. By nightfall the initial objectives had been reached.

That night, efforts to rescue Company F continued. Although some men had managed to get out during the day, most remained trapped. Tanks of the 743rd Tank Battalion came up to provide covering fire while engineers tried to clear a path through the field with a bulldozer, which was soon knocked out by a mine. A heavier bulldozer was brought forward and, using a boom extension that could reach soldiers 10 yards from the vehicle, Company F was finally extricated. The surviving 40 men of the company moved back up to the front line.

Colonel Purdue's 120th Infantry had better luck. The enemy in its zone was surprised and initially overwhelmed. Descriptions of the attack state that it was like a "Field Manual writer's dream."[2] Some prisoners from the 29th Panzer Grenadier Regiment were even taken while still in their bed clothes. Although a later counter-attack recovered some ground, the Americans clearly had the upper hand.

As expected, the 119th Infantry Regiment drew the hardest assignment. The frontal attack on Würselen faced German infantry dug in amongst the rubble of the town. German machine guns and mortars were well concealed and difficult to outflank. Two battalions of the 3rd Panzer Grenadier Division held the town, determined to prevent the hole in the Siegfried Line from being widened. Once again, American tanks and tank destroyers could not gain access to the front line because of the many minefields. One tank fell to the mines, and another to a German hand-held anti-tank rocket team. The fighting became one of patrols seeking to find an advantage and exploit it. Incidents like that of Private Alexander Mastrobattista of Company L, who lost a foot to a Schü mine and lay exposed to enemy fire, were common. Private First Class Herbert A. McKitrick, a company aid man, risked his life to drag Mastrobattista to safety where he could be treated. Even then, the wounded man had to wait for darkness before he could be evacuated.

Company K, 119th Infantry, was fighting its way through Würselen when machine gun fire from nearby houses pinned the men down in the open flat ground more than 100 yards from their objective. Enemy observers began to direct artillery fire at them, causing several serious casualties. Staff Sergeant Freeman V. Horner, from Shamokin, Pennsylvania, realized that something had to be done or the company would be wiped out. He voluntarily stood up with his Thompson sub-machine gun and rushed forward into the very teeth of the concentrated fire coming at Company K. Slowed by a heavy weapon, spare ammunition and a supply of hand grenades, he reached what he thought was a position of relative safety. Just as he did so, however, a previously silent enemy machine gun opened fire at him. He fired on the newly discovered enemy gun, killing the crew. Without a moment's hesitation he turned again and ran towards the two guns pinning down his company. Dodging enemy fire, he ran the 50 yards to the two enemy machine gun posts. So demoralized were the Germans by his courage and their inability to stop him that the two crews abandoned their guns and took cover in the basement of a nearby house. Horner burst into the building, hurled grenades down into the cellar, and demanded the enemy's surrender. Four men surrendered to him. For destroying three enemy machine guns and knocking out seven enemy soldiers, while saving his company from certain annihilation, Staff Sergeant Horner received the Medal of Honor.[3]

By the end of the day, significant progress had been made except in the area of the 119th Infantry Regiment. Surprisingly, for all the heavy combat encountered, the division suffered just 137 casualties, most of them in Company F, 117th Infantry. But General Hobbs' plan was working. That evening the German command, Fifteenth Army, fearing its line was being outflanked, authorized a withdrawal from Würselen to a second line of villages.

November 17 was an even better day. Two battalions of the 3rd Panzer Grenadier Division were overrun by the 120th Infantry before they could fully establish themselves in the next line of villages (one battalion was captured nearly intact). A German counterattack was beaten off despite being supported by tanks and assault guns. In Würselen it took longer, largely due to the extensive minefields, but a map captured from German engineers showed the placement of all the fields, allowing the Americans to fully occupy the town before nightfall. By the end of the second day, therefore, the Americans had broken the enemy hold on the urban area within Ninth Army's zone and were advancing east. General McLain now ordered Hobbs to clear the remaining six miles to the Roer.

*   *   *

Major General Ernest Nason Harmon was born February 26, 1894, in Lowell, Massachusetts. He was commissioned into the cavalry from West Point in 1917 and served in France with the American Expeditionary Force. He taught at West Point and at Norwich University before graduating from the Command and General Staff School in 1933 and the Army War College in 1934. He was then chief of staff to the new Armored Force from 1939–41, and was promoted to brigadier general in March 1942. Five months later, in August, he was promoted again to major general and assumed command of the 2nd Armored ("Hell on Wheels") Division. Due to a crisis in command, he was transferred to command of the 1st Armored ("Old Ironsides") Division, from 1943–44, which he led in the North African, Sicilian and Italian campaigns, before returning once again to the 2nd Armored Division. He would later command XXI Corps in Germany before the end of the war.

The 2nd Armored Division had been activated at Fort Benning, Georgia, on July 15, 1940, and trained at various locations until it departed New York on December 11, 1942. It participated in the Algeria-French Morocco, Sicilian, Normandy and Northern France campaigns before being assigned to Ninth Army as part of XIX Corps. During its career it had a distinguished series of commanders, including a future army commander (Patton) and three future corps commanders.[4] For the men of the 2nd Armored Division, Operation *Queen* is remembered as a "slow and savage struggle through mud, rain and snow."[5] Considering the history of the division, it is worth noting that it is also described as being "the most determined resistance faced by the 2d Armored Division in the European Theater of Operations."[6]

General Harmon had early concerns about his role in Operation *Queen*. The constant rain and mud would slow his tanks and other armored vehicles down considerably, perhaps even to the point of immobility. To decide for himself, Harmon did what was typical for him—he mounted a tank and ordered it forward, finding that it could make only about three miles per hour. Still doubtful, he queried the driver and asked if he thought the tanks could cross the Roerplain under such conditions. Harmon was finally convinced when the driver replied in the affirmative—the 2nd Armored would attack. Not long after, it began to snow.

Since the ground was not frozen, despite the snow, the tankers fitted "duckbills" to their tracks. These track extensions increased traction in mud and snow conditions. A short supply forced Ninth Army to use locally manufactured duckbills, which, while of poorer quality than American-made versions, nevertheless served the purpose for which they were intended. The light tanks, for which no duckbills were available, carried logs nine feet long and six inches in diameter, which were expected to also increase their flotation. As it turned out, these were not needed as drivers in first or second gear were able to negotiate the mud flats. The division's 17th Armored Engineer Battalion also built bridges (which were carried forward on special tanks), for negotiating the antitank ditches known to be awaiting the division behind the German lines. The presence of the 2nd Armored Division was known to the Germans, who kept their 9th Panzer Division, 15th Panzer Grenadier Division, and several independent tanks battalions in readiness near the Roer.[7]

Harmon set his sights on a bridgehead over the Roer and so issued his operations order. His responsibilities were to protect the left flank of XIX Corps while attacking towards the Roer. Combat Command B (led by Brigadier General Isaac D. White) was directed on the town of Linnich. The attached 2nd Battalion, 406th Infantry Regiment, 102nd Infantry Division, was to capture Immendorf and the high ground, then to defend the area against counterattacks. Harmon also tried to have the rest of the 102nd Infantry Division attack to cover his flank, but this was denied. General Simpson increased Harmon's concerns when he remarked that he expected "one hell of a fight."[8]

The Germans also played on American concerns. One night, Company F, 41st Armored Infantry Regiment, heard a team of horses pulling a wagon through their lines. Thinking the wagon might contain explosives, the Americans allowed the wagon to pass and then captured it from behind. The wagon was empty. The scenario was repeated on the next night, and then the next. Now believing that the Germans were infiltrating patrols using the wagon, on the fourth and fifth night the GIs tossed grenades into the wagons, destroying them, but searches failed to find anything. The Germans had been playing on the Americans' nerves, sending empty wagons forward simply to keep them awake and edgy.

On the other hand, the repeated postponements of the attack because of weather worked to the Americans' advantage. Each time they were alerted to attack, Combat Command B moved into forward positions in preparation.[9] Each time, they were shelled by German artillery and mortar fire. Finally, after several such incidents, the Germans apparently believed the Americans were playing some kind of game and ceased shelling CCB when it moved up. As a result, on the actual day of the attack, the command suffered little from German fire until after the attack had begun. Meanwhile, Harmon's efforts to move his division's boundaries to their advantage bore fruit, as both the 29th Infantry Division and the 102nd Infantry Division agreed to the changes.

Combat Command B led the armored attack. Limited to a two-mile front due to the constricted space allocated to XIX Corps, only one combat command could attack, but initially it went well. The tanks and armored infantry raced ahead behind an artillery barrage, which rolled forward with the speed of the ground forces. Often the Germans were still sheltering from the barrage when the tanks and armored infantry were upon them. Company D, 67th Armored Regiment, raced into Loverich, suppressing the German defenders so that within 20 minutes the accompanying armored infantry had secured the town. Colonel Paul A. Disney's task force then bypassed the town while Lieutenant Colonel Lemuel Pope led his forces on to Puffendorf. Town after town began to fall to the rampaging tankers.

Losses remained lower than feared. Four tanks became mired in the mud, and six others lost their tracks to mines. In the late afternoon, Puffendorf fell to the armored infantry, as did nearby Floverich. Encouraged by the rapidity of the advance, Harmon kept urging greater speed in the attack. The next objective was Hill 102.6, north of Puffendorf. Here the mud slowed the tanks, as did the antitank ditches protecting the German positions, but as one platoon leader was pulling a tank out of a ditch, he noticed a gap. He immediately called up a tank with a bulldozer blade attached and built a crossing. The attack resumed, and although the hill did not fall during the day, the Americans had it surrounded on three sides, making the results of the next attack all but foretold.

Near Apweiler, several tanks ran into an ambush, and three were soon burning, with four others immobilized. Unable to proceed further, the Americans pulled back and set up defensive positions. During the night they heard sounds of armored vehicles approaching behind the German lines. Despite this setback, the 2nd Armored Division had captured all of its first-day objectives and was prepared to continue the attack in the morning. The division had driven a salient into the German defenses and held a dangerously exposed position. Heavy enemy fire from three directions fell into the salient all night long.

The noise the Americans had heard was that of the German reserve forces in the area. These were under the command of *General der Panzertruppen* Heinrich Freiherr von Luettwitz. Luettwitz's XLVII Panzer Corps had recently returned from an attack in the Peel Marshes, where it had dealt the 7th Armored Division such a blow that its commander was relieved of command. It now constituted the Fifteenth Army reserve and was moving into position to take a hand in the battle.

Harmon was upset. He was displeased with the progress of the 29th Infantry Division on his flank—it had not come up as planned, leaving 2nd Armored Division exposed to enemy fire and possible counterattacks. Harmon requested permission to expand his zone and protect his own flank, but permission was denied (General Gerhardt had insisted that his men would clear that area the next day). Division Intelligence reported to Harmon that it believed the German 350th Infantry Regiment, 183rd Infantry Division, had been destroyed during the day. During the night, Harmon brought up Combat Command A, expecting to expand his front the following day.

Ominous signs began to appear as dawn of November 18 approached. Heavy German artillery fire began to fall on Puffendorf, blocking all entrances and exits from the town. Company D, 67th Armored Regiment, began reporting receiving small-arms fire from sources it could not see. Nevertheless, the 1st and 2nd Battalions, 67th Armored Regiment, began to assemble for the day's attack on Geronsweiler. As they waited in line, fully exposed, at least 20 German tanks, supported by infantry, attacked. The LXVII Panzer Corps had arrived. The German tanks were more maneuverable in the thick mud, and more heavily armed than the American Sherman M4 tank, and a fierce tank battle soon developed, with the infantry of both sides pinned down by heavy artillery fire. Soon the Germans began to gain the advantage, as more and more American tanks were knocked out. With little option, the American tanks withdrew into Puffendorf, hoping to use the thick concrete buildings to protect them against the heavier German guns.

First Lieutenant Robert E. Lee, commander of D Company, 67th Armored Regiment, went from foxhole to foxhole to advise the infantry that the American tanks were pulling back. Then he held his forward position, giving the men an opportunity to withdraw to the relative safety of the town. The plan worked, as the Germans refused to expose themselves in the open while the Americans sheltered behind the houses of Puffendorf. As the stalemate continued, the lead elements of Combat Command A appeared.

By now the battle had raged for at least six hours. It was later considered one of the worst defeats the 2nd Armored Division had suffered in its long combat career. Two medium tank companies and a light tank company were lost in action—effectively the loss of an entire tank battalion. In a more positive vein, a prisoner taken later from the 9th Panzer Division reported that the German attack had been intended to retake Immendorf. Two regiments of infantry, tanks, artillery, and reconnaissance elements had been devoted to the attack, which had failed to gain its objective.

The Germans were only getting started, however. An attack on Apweiler failed against strong German resistance. Progress over the open ground covered by German guns was all but impossible. With the Americans stalled in front of the town, the 10th Panzer Grenadier Regiment and 10 tanks from the 9th Panzer Division attacked. Only artillery fire and the guns of the 771st Tank Destroyer Battalion halted the attack, and the fight continued all morning, until the Germans finally withdrew. General White now put Colonel Bernard F. Hurless, commander of the 406th Infantry Regiment, in charge, and added two infantry battalions to his force. A second German counter attack was beaten off after mines, placed by the infantry, knocked out two enemy tanks, while a third was destroyed by Company H, 67th Armored Regiment.

General McLain now authorized the use of Combat Command A, commanded by Brigadier General John H. Collier, to break the German front. Harmon ordered Collier to take CCA to the right flank of CCB and seize the town of Ederen. CCA had originally planned to launch its attack from Setterich, but it had not been secured by the 29th Infantry Division, so a new approach had to be found. A tank ditch blocked the way, and across the ditch the Germans had around 15 tanks lined up. Harmon saw no other solution than to try to outflank the new defenses, but to do this he had to move his tanks through the town of Setterich, which was in the 29th Infantry Division's zone. His offer to send tanks to help the infantry complete the town's seizure was denied by General Gerhardt. A report then came in that more German tanks had been observed moving against the 2nd Armored Division's flank.

The day ended with the 2nd Armored Division stalled, having gained not one yard during an otherwise bloody day. A total of 18 medium tanks and seven light tanks had been totally destroyed, while another 16 medium tanks and 12 light tanks had been severely damaged. Casualty reports showed 56 men killed, 281 wounded and 29 missing in action.

*   *   *

Meanwhile, Ninth Army headquarters struggled with maintaining the impetus of the attack. It had not had sufficient time to amass a stockpile of supplies after moving north and it remained last on the priority list for the four American field armies then on the continent. Once again, artillery ammunition was of particular concern, especially as the assault divisions had been reinforced with corps and army artillery units as well as the artillery of the reserve 7th Armored Division. General Simpson had foreseen the problem and had limited artillery ammunition expenditure before the attack so as to build a small reserve, but even so, certain types of ammunition (including white phosphorus shells and 81mm mortar ammunition) remained in short supply. Thanks to Simpson's foresight, however, there was never a complete absence of shells for the combat units.

Another issue was the supply of replacement tanks, particularly for the armored divisions. Recently the allocation of tanks for the armored divisions had been reduced, but even under the new table of organization, Ninth Army found it difficult to keep the tankers mobile. As a result, the tank battalions operating under Ninth Army in November usually found themselves at 75 percent of authorized strength in terms of tanks, whether in armored divisions or independent tank battalions.

Ninth Army also found itself crowded into a narrow sector with a sudden plethora of troops trying to fit into it. From a one-corps, three-division army, Ninth Army quickly found itself hosting two corps and six divisions, plus 33 non-divisional field artillery battalions and numerous smaller units, yet its operations zone had not expanded accordingly. It was a unique situation along the Western Front during the winter of 1944–45, in that no other army had to crowd so much into so little space. Ninth Army had to find shelter and storage facilities for all these soldiers and their equipment. An expedient solution was simply to store many supplies alongside the roads, allowing easy and quick access while maintaining security as best as possible.

While the arrival of the British XXX Corps on the flank was welcomed by Simpson as relief for his hard-pressed left flank, it also brought problems to Ninth Army. The number of bridges across the Albert Canal and Maas River were few, and later in the month the Maas rose to flood stage, washing away some of the British bridges. As a result, much of the supplies and equipment destined for the British XXX Corps had to cross over Ninth Army bridges, creating a traffic nightmare and threatening to collapse the already strained bridges.

One bright spot, if it can be called that, was that Ninth Army soon learned that the American press had labeled it "The Phantom Army," because it had already moved so fast and so often. Taken as a compliment, it acknowledged that Ninth Army had fought in Brittany, moved to Luxembourg and was now in Germany, ready for battle once again, all in less than two months.

*   *   *

On November 19, Combat Command A moved east from Puffendorf, crossed the antitank ditch blocking its way, and captured the town of Ederen. As it moved forward, a German force of four tanks and 100 infantry attacked its left flank. The Germans, however, had apparently forgotten that the Americans still held Puffendorf. CCB caught the Germans off guard and unprepared, knocking out three of their tanks and sending the infantry racing for cover. Nevertheless, CCA found itself slowed by strong opposition and by the end of the day had reached but not crossed another antitank ditch.

It was on this day that Company F, 116th Infantry, 29th Infantry Division, crossed the antitank ditch at Setterich. General Harmon wasted no time in rushing the remainder of CCA across the ditch to attack Freialdenhoven. With the attached 2nd Battalion, 119th Infantry, the armored task force fought its way forward to within 1,000 yards of the town. Seeing progress, Harmon now ordered his division to strike out for all of his objectives (Freialdenhoven, Ederen and Geronsweiler) the next day. To ensure success, he added the flamethrower tanks of B Squadron, Fife and Forfar Yeomanry, on loan from the British. These would accompany the attack the next day.

November 20 saw one of the largest tank battles fought on the Western Front. An estimated 80 German tanks, identified as Panthers and Tigers, counterattacked the 2nd Armored Division. Using every weapon at their disposal, Harmon's men halted the attacks. One particularly innovative method was employed by Lieutenant Colonel John A. Beall, commanding the 702nd Tank Destroyer Battalion. The battalion had recently received new M-36 Tank Destroyers, armed with a 90mm gun (larger than anything the Germans possessed). To get the Germans to come to him on his terms, Beall had a few American Sherman tanks reveal themselves and then withdraw to where the 702nd Tank Destroyer Battalion was waiting. Firing heavy guns from a position of advantage, Beall and his men knocked out the pursuing German tanks with relative ease.

Meanwhile, other elements of the attacking force, supported by the British flamethrower tanks, moved forward, hindered only by mines. German infantry quickly surrendered when faced with the flamethrowers, and although three of the British tanks fell to mines or ditches, the Americans had made good progress during the day. The defeat of the counterattack and the presence of flamethrowers and heavygunned tank destroyers seemed to have turned the tide of the battle. Slowly but surely, the villages began to fall.

On November 21, Harmon finally had most of his division in action, but the battle remained fierce. Germans defended each town and hill. In one case, three companies of the 11th Panzer Grenadier Regiment raised white flags and came forward to surrender, only to throw hand grenades into Company A, 406th Infantry Regiment, destroying two platoons. Company A was reduced to only 54 men fit for action, and tanks of the 67th Armored Regiment and the 702nd Tank Destroyer Battalion had to restore the gap in the line. Nevertheless, by Thanksgiving Day, November 23, 2nd Armored Division assumed the defensive, all initial missions having been achieved. It would attack again, a day later, to achieve its final objectives. Over the 13 days of battle it had advanced 10 miles against brutal opposition, designed to protect the secret of the coming German Ardennes counter offensive. The cost to the 2nd Armored Division was 203 killed, 1,104 wounded and 198 missing, for a total of 1,505. The division lost 80 tanks, of which 41 could be repaired.

*   *   *

General Gerhardt's 29th Infantry Division, veterans of Normandy and Brittany, got off to a slow start. It was to carry the center of the attack to the Roer, and in particular capture the key town of Setterich, which blocked not only the division's advance, but that of the 2nd Armored Division as well. Gerhardt also had a wider sector in which to maneuver. His review of the situation facing his division convinced him that the German weak points were not the defended villages, but the open ground in between them. He ordered his regimental commanders to keep to the open ground and to isolate the fortified villages. After they had been bypassed, individual infantry companies would attack them and reduce the defenses.

The division's line of departure was between the villages of Baesweiler and Oidtweiler. The first objective was a road center at Aldenhoven, about four miles east, and then the Roer at Jülich, three miles further east. In keeping with his theory of bypassing German towns, Gerhardt planned to uncover the southern flank of Setterich by bypassing it on the south and then attacking it directly. He would use his reserve force, attacking along the Aschen-Linnich highway, to reduce the town. Like General McLain, Gerhardt seems to have been overly optimistic about the coming attack—but then, neither knew that the Germans were determined to hold the area to protect their coming counter offensive.

Supported by dozens of artillery, tank and tank destroyer battalions, the optimism seemed well founded. In fact, Gerhardt made a last-minute cancellation of the planned bombing of Aldenhoven, fearing that the rubble would impede his progress. After XXIX Tactical Air Command's P-47s and P-38s dropped 46.5 tons of bombs in front of Gerhardt's leading regiments, the 5th Infantry reported that results were particularly effective on Setterich, while the 175th Infantry reported that the bombing was "fine."[10]

A battalion each from the two assault regiments attacked as planned on November 16, aiming as directed for the open areas between the fortified villages. The 115th Infantry targeted a line of high ground at a coal mine, some 400 yards north of the town of Siersdorf. Attacking through a smoke screen, the infantry soon came under small arms fire barely 600 yards from the line of departure. Advancing by squad rushes, progress was slowed, but continued. A company commander was killed but another 200 yards were gained. Then a severe crossfire hit both advance companies from four directions, including from Setterich. A platoon leader of Company C, 1st Lieutenant Joseph D. Blalock, would describe it as "the most intense and accurate small arms fire … I have ever encountered."[11] Forced to take cover in the open beet fields, the Americans soon came under mortar and artillery fire. Men threw away their combat packs, as they protruded above the beets and identified them for German snipers and machine guns. Leaders could not see their men or give orders, as they were unable to see anything beyond the foot or two of dirt right before their faces. This was what was meant by being "pinned down." Eventually, Company B succeeded in withdrawing, but Company C was tightly pinned by the German fire and could only hide and pray.

Supporting artillery and the battalion's reserve company tried to help. But nothing diminished the enemy fire. After darkness only about 20 men of Company C managed to escape back to friendly lines. Nearby, the leading companies of the 175th Infantry Regiment met a similar fate. Small-arms fire pinned the men to the ground and then German artillery and mortars, supported by snipers and automatic weapons, hit them as they lay trapped. Fortunately for some, the companies had reached a large drainage ditch just as the enemy opened fire, and many men found cover there, but every attempt to advance beyond the ditch was stopped. Fire from the town of Bettendorf and a nearby railroad embankment pinned the men down and halted movement. As night fell, the men of the 175th Infantry had advanced less than 600 yards for the day.

Gerhardt's plan to advance over the open fields instead of attacking the fortified villages had not worked. He had failed to realize that the villages could be mutually supporting, and each covered the open areas in between them. Worse, he was now under pressure from General McLain and his neighboring division commander, General Harmon, to do something about Setterich, which was holding up the advance of the rest of XIX Corps. McLain, more patient than Harmon, advised Gerhardt that he expected things to "loosen up" the next day. Harmon was less patient and wanted to take over the Setterich sector for his own division.

The sole bright spot on November 16 for the 29th Infantry Division came after dark, when Colonel Edward H. McDaniel, commander of the 115th Infantry, sent the remnants of his First Battalion to take one of the four enemy areas, a windmill, which had halted the daylight advance. When the Americans arrived, the Germans had gone. The first day, with only a few hours of combat by only two of the division's nine infantry battalions, had not gone well. Both of the other XIX Corps divisions had done much better during their first day. Acknowledging that the 29th Infantry Division had drawn the more difficult task, McLain told Gerhardt "I think you'll bust on through there tomorrow."[12]

However, dawn on November 17 brought more disappointment for Gerhardt. Having said that he expected to have Setterich in his control by noon that day, his latest review of the situation had dampened that optimism. A delay caused by the need to reorganize the two assault regiments after the debacle of the previous day held up the start of the attack until after noon. McLain was less patient than the day before, telling Gerhardt that the reorganization should have been done the night before and adding, "It will slow us up another day."[13] Ordering Gerhardt to get the Setterich issue settled quickly, McLain also ordered the advance to move in the center. General Harmon once again renewed his request to take over that part of the 29th Infantry Division's zone, so as to allow his CCA to get forward, but again Gerhardt demurred.

Gerhardt now accepted the fact that the fortified villages needed to be directly attacked, but again he failed to provide any armored support for his infantry and still insisted on attacking east before tackling Setterich directly. The attack on November 17 accomplished no more than it had the previous day. Finally, late in the day, Gerhardt acknowledged that his main obstacle was Setterich. He brought up Major James S. Morris' 1st Battalion, 116th Infantry Regiment, and ordered it to attack Setterich along the Baesweiler-Setterich highway. Without tanks, the result was predictable, and the infantry was soon pinned down in front of the town. Some brave souls managed to crawl forward and gain a toehold on the trenches fronting the town, but that was as far as anyone could go.

Ironically, Gerhardt now called on General Harmon for assistance. He wanted a battalion of the 29th Infantry Division to pass through Harmon's sector and hit Setterich from the north, using the room that Harmon's division had secured in its advance. Harmon agreed, reminding Gerhardt that he in turn needed the antitank ditch at Setterich (which was holding up his CCA) cleared. He offered to send 75 of his tanks to Setterich if the 29th Infantry Division could get him across that ditch.

Gerhardt now gave the job of taking Setterich to Lieutenant Colonel Harold A. Cassell, commander of the 116th Infantry. Major Morris (1st Battalion, 116th Infantry Regiment) was to hit Setterich from the southwest and the west in a two-pronged attack. Another battalion of the 116th would pass through Harmon's area and attack from the direction of Loverich. Gerhardt, who had earlier thought the mud would make his supporting tanks useless, now changed his mind and borrowed a platoon of tanks from the 66th Armored Regiment to reinforce his attached 747th Tank Battalion in supporting the attacks.

The tanks made a difference for Company A, when they knocked out an entrenched German strong point. With one chain of the defense eliminated, Company A was able to outflank the next chain, and so forth. By nightfall, Company A, supported by two tanks, had worked its way into the outskirts of Setterich. Major Morris' battalion attack, however, quickly lost its three tanks to mines, German antitank teams and damage from enemy fire. The other battalion of the 116th Infantry Regiment, attacking from Loverich with the attached platoon of tanks from 2nd Armored Division, had success as well. Again, the tanks knocked out enemy defenses, cleared paths through antipersonnel minefields, and supported the infantry as they entered Setterich. By the end of November 18, Setterich was about to fall.

The next day, while the 116th Infantry mopped up Setterich, the 115th Infantry resumed the advance east. A clear sky provided unobstructed observation for both artillery and air support. Bettendorf fell at a cost of two tanks, while a battalion of the 175th Infantry supported by the 747th Tank Battalion cleared Siersdorf. The Americans had found the right formula to clear the Roerplain—a tank-infantry-artillery coordination that kept the enemy pinned down while the ground troops closed in and finished the job. Now flushed with victory, Gerhardt began to push his regimental commanders forward, urging more speed and refusing to listen to reasons for any delay. By the end of November 18, the German 246th Division had been broken and the 29th Infantry Division was moving swiftly east, reaching the outskirts of Jülich.

On November 20, Colonel William C. Purnell, commanding the 175th Infantry Regiment, launched a two-pronged attack on the division's objective, Aldenhoven. The town was secured the same day. The division was now less than two miles from the Roer. The 3rd Battalion, 175th Infantry, came up against Schleiden during its advance. Lieutenant Colonel William O. Blanford had every heavy machine gun and mortar open fire until his men were within 300 yards of the town, then halted the supporting fire and attacked. Up to that point, not a single incoming bullet had been felt. Supported by a platoon of the 747th Tank Battalion, which moved at an angle to the infantry so as to divert enemy artillery fire away from them, the infantry moved into the town. The soldiers mopped up the defenders in their trenches and houses and by mid-afternoon Schleiden was in American hands.

General der Infanterie Friedrich J. Köchling tried to stem the flood. Pulling troops from the 3rd Panzer Grenadier and 12th Divisions in other sectors of his LXXXI Corps, he rushed them to face the 29th Infantry Division. These moves were too little, too late. Despite increasing pressure from *General der Infanterie* Gustav von Zangen, his superior at Fifteenth Army, to eliminate the gains of the 29th Infantry Division, there were no more reserves available. Köchling's only solace, and a fleeting one at that, was that a volks grenadier division meant for the coming Ardennes counteroffensive would be diverted to LXXXI Corps.

As it turned out, Köchling was able to manage only two real counterattacks against the onrushing 29th Infantry Division. At the town of Dueroslar on November 19, he launched a dozen assault guns to stop the 115th Infantry's advance. Four were knocked out by American bazooka teams and the others chased off by fighters from XXIX Tactical Air Command. The next day, November 20, he sent between six and nine tanks, supported by 100 infantrymen, against the 175th Infantry at Aldenhoven. The American artillery annihilated the German infantry and the tanks, unsupported, withdrew.

The advance took the 29th Infantry Division to within a mile and a half of the Roer, the final objective. It had cost them 1,100 casualties, but they had captured more than that in prisoners of war alone. Only a defensive arc around Jülich remained to be cleared.

* * *

General Harmon's division had only two villages barring its way to the banks of the Roer by November 21. The 29th Infantry Division had three such villages in front of it. The 30th Infantry Division, which had deliberately been delayed by clearing the urban areas during its attack, was within four miles of the river. Most of the American commanders, including Gerhardt, believed that the Germans would now withdraw behind the Roer, giving the Americans a relatively easy stroll to the east bank of that river. Intelligence reports supported this contention, identifying mostly rear-area troops among the prisoners taken in the last days.

But it was not to be. Although under different circumstances the logical military solution would have been to pull back and use the river as the new front line, the German commanders had no such option. They were protecting the coming Ardennes winter counteroffensive (although they did not know of its existence), and had orders not to withdraw under any circumstances. So the ferocity of the Roer battles would continue unabated. Calling for help from Fifteenth Army, the Germans dug in again. Fifteenth Army replied by diverting one of the divisions earmarked for the counteroffensive to the Jülich and Linnich sectors along the west bank of the Roer. General von Zangen had hoped to hold the division east of the river, and perhaps return it for the coming offensive, but the rapid advance of Ninth Army's XIX Corps forced him to commit the division west of the river. In fact, the only reason the 340th Volks Grenadier Division was available at all was that Hitler, who had originally forbidden any diversions of his assembled counteroffensive force, had been forced by circumstances to compromise.

Upon arrival at Jülich, a regiment of the 340th Volks Grenadier Division relieved the remnants of the 246th Infantry Division. Two recently raised artillery corps were added to the defense as well. A battalion of assault guns and a fresh replacement battalion rounded out the defense, and their presence was quickly felt by the attacking Americans.

The 120th Infantry of General Hobbs' division attacked Erberich and gained a foothold, but the German assault guns drove off the supporting tanks and tank destroyers and, without them, the infantry could not clear the village. Under fire, the 120th Infantry infiltrated back to friendly lines. Nearby, two platoons of the 175th Infantry managed to get into Bourheim but were thrown out by a German counterattack. A two-battalion attack on the afternoon of November 22 did no better. At Koslar, the 116th Infantry could not get into the town at all. These two villages, along with a third, Kirchberg, were the final defensive line before Jülich and the Roer.

In the 2nd Armored Division's zone, the last obstacle was the town of Merzenhausen. The British flamethrower tanks got the infantry into the town but were soon knocked out by German tanks. Then the going became even more difficult. The German tanks, supported by infantry from the 246th Infantry Division, halted all further advances. Like the neighboring infantry divisions, the 2nd Armored was stuck.

Being within sight of the Roer, Simpson and McLain now believed there was no hurry to push the Germans into the river. Their positions served no purpose other than to delay a river crossing, which the Americans were not yet prepared to launch anyway. While preparations were underway, and while waiting for First Army to come up on their right, they would take a more leisurely approach toward clearing the west bank of the river. And so McLain allowed all his division commanders to slow operations until all three divisions were on the same line and ready to launch a full-power attack.

November 23 saw half of Merzenhausen fall to the 41st Armored Infantry and a battalion of tanks. Harmon then ordered a halt for reorganization. After straightening out his lines, Hobbs halted for reorganization as well, but Gerhardt was allowed no such respite. The presence of the new 340th Volks Grenadier Division was a threat that could not be ignored. A day of bloody, muddy and generally fruitless attacks finally put a battalion of the 175th Infantry in Bourheim. The Germans strongly resisted with repeated counterattacks, and for the next three days German artillery and counterattacks kept the 175th Infantry busy holding the town. In one day alone, the Americans counted more than 2,000 artillery shells falling in Bourheim. In effect, the battle for the town had become an artillery duel.

When the 116th Infantry forced it way into Koslar, a similar situation developed. Supported by 14 battalions of artillery and 28 armored vehicles, the regiments of the 340th Volks Grenadier Division attacked both villages. The Americans countered by rushing reinforcements forward and calling on XXIX Tactical Air Command for help. While this fight was going on, Gerhardt pushed his last regiment, the 115th Infantry, into Kirchberg, the last of the three villages protecting Jülich in the division's zone. Despite the ongoing battles, for all practical purposes the 29th Infantry Division had closed up to the Roer in its sector.

Both Harmon and Hobbs wanted to renew their attacks at night, but McLain bowed to requests from the neighboring First Army to coordinate with an attack by the 104th Infantry Division at Inden. As a result, XIX Corps renewed its advance to the Roer at midday on November 27. Initially, the 30th Infantry Division's attack stalled in the face of heavy enemy resistance, but Colonel Purdue of the 120th Infantry decided to launch a night attack, which was almost compromised by artillery fire from the neighboring 104th Infantry Division. Due to precautions planned by Lieutenant Colonel Ellis V. Williamson, commanding the assault battalion, the advance continued and had soon secured Altdorf. The 30th Infantry Division had reached the Roer.[14]

The 2nd Armored Division renewed its attack on Merzenhausen on November 27, using a three-pronged attack. General Collier sent a battalion each to two dominating hills, while a third infantry battalion attacked the second half of the town itself. Hill 98.1 was taken by the 41st Armored Infantry, but they could not push on from there against strong enemy opposition. Within Merzenhausen itself, the attached 2nd Battalion, 119th Infantry, engaged in vicious house-to-house fighting supported by tanks and tank destroyers. At the end of the day the town was cleared and the enemy battalion commander was made a prisoner of war.

Hill 100.3 was attacked by the attached 1st Battalion, 119th Infantry. Although he acknowledged that tanks would be needed to clear the hill, Collier saw no way they could be employed due to antitank ditches, an escarpment and a stream that blocked access. He told the battalion commander, Lieutenant Colonel Robert H. Herlong, that if he could find a route for tanks, they would be provided. Herlong's men got to within 400 yards of the crest of Hill 100.3 before the Germans opened fire. He called immediately for an artillery barrage to suppress the heavy small-arms fire his men faced. Although the artillery fire seemed accurate, it failed to stop the incoming fire—in minutes five men were killed and another fifteen wounded. Barely 50 yards had been gained.

It was then that an unidentified soldier reported to Herlong that he had found a railroad embankment that would accommodate tanks. From this they could reach a covered draw that led to the top of the hill. Herlong notified Collier, who dispatched a company of the 66th Armored Regiment up the hill. Ninety minutes later, the tanks appeared at the hill crest and the surprised Germans surrendered. A total of 40 Germans had been killed, with an equal number surrendering. Turning back to Hill 98.1, Collier dispatched a second battalion of the 41st Armored Infantry for a night attack and the hill was taken. The following day, the 2nd Armored Division mopped up in its zone and rested on the west bank of the Roer. All thoughts in XIX Corps now turned to a crossing of that river.

CHAPTER 5

Operation *Clipper*

In a discussion with Eisenhower in May of 1944 about whom his three corps commanders should be, Simpson's first choice had been Major General Alvan C. Gillem.[1] Gillem was born in Nashville, Tennessee, on August 8, 1888, to a military family. Unable to get into West Point, he first attended the University of Arizona between 1908 and 1909. Then he decided to join the Army and did so as an enlisted man between 1910 and 1911. In 1911, he was commissioned into the infantry and sent off to the Philippines for a year. He returned to teach military science and tactics at the University of Montana until 1919. Gillem served with the 27th Infantry Regiment (during the Siberian expedition), for eight months between 1919 and 1920, before returning to the Philippines. He attended the Command and General Staff School from 1922–23. A tour of duty in Hawaii preceded his graduation from the Army War College in 1936, and subsequent assignments included teaching duties at the University of Maryland and at the Infantry School. He was promoted to brigadier general in January 1941. Originally reluctant to embrace the new armored warfare, Gillem soon changed his mind. Before Pearl Harbor, he had commanded an armored brigade and the 3rd Armored Division. Six months later, Major General Gillem was in command of II Armored Corps. A tour as commander of the Desert Training Center in 1942 followed and he became commander of XIII Corps in November 1943. He was described as "dignified, upright and well-mannered, Gillem's calm demeanor and level-headedness reassured superiors and subordinates alike."[2] After fighting with Ninth Army throughout the European campaign, Gillem would be promoted to lieutenant general in June 1945.[3]

Gillem's first combat mission came on what was known as the "Geilenkirchen Salient." Geilenkirchen was a town on Ninth Army's extreme left flank, which restricted its space to maneuver. The salient generally followed the course of the Würm River northeast from Geilenkirchen and the Roer. As such, it formed a wedge between the British Second Army's XXX Corps west of the Würm and the American XIX Corps, which lay between the Würm and the Roer.

General Simpson had addressed this problem by speaking with the British commanders. He wanted a two-pronged attack on the town but was concerned that two different national armies might have difficulties in performing such a complex maneuver. To alleviate this danger, he offered to General Dempsey (commanding the British Second Army) the 84th Infantry Division. Simpson was also aware that the British had greater stocks of artillery ammunition, something that Ninth Army still lacked, and so they could better support such an attack. This would leave Simpson's smaller stock available for the assault by XIX Corps. XIII Corps was scheduled to begin its offensive after XIX Corps attacked, in the hope that some of the forces within the salient would be drawn off to XIX Corps' front.

No German troops were pulled out of the Geilenkirchen Salient to face XIX Corps, but a major German reserve force, the 15th Panzer Grenadier Division, was in fact moved away from the salient and closer to XIX Corps. Although it could still reinforce Geilenkirchen, it was farther away and would take longer to make its presence felt there.

The area around Geilenkirchen was filled with Siegfried Line pillboxes on a relatively flat plain. In appearance, the terrain was much like that of the adjacent Roer plain. The same villages and farms dotted the area, as did mining villages, and beet and cabbage fields. Occasional small wooded areas appeared. As one visitor in 1944 later put it, "At best, the Geilenkirchen area was not one of Germany's more attractive places."[4] Two highways crossed the planned direction of attack. Secondary roads connected the villages, but as everywhere in November 1944, these were muddy tracks unsuitable for military traffic. A railroad followed the valley past Geilenkirchen for a while before veering off to the east.

General Horrocks had placed his 43rd (Wessex) Infantry Division (commanded by Major General Gwilym I. Thomas) to the north west of Geilenkirchen.[5] Between the town to the south and southeast, protecting the flank of XIX Corps, the 405th Infantry Regiment, 102nd Infantry Division, held a narrow sector that was the only portion of the front held at the time by Gillem's XIII Corps.

*   *   *

The plan to eliminate the Geilenkirchen Salient was labeled Operation *Clipper*. It involved XIII Corps with the 84th and 102nd Infantry Divisions under command. The 84th Infantry Division would be under British tactical command, but administration, supply and personnel were the responsibility of XIII Corps and Ninth Army. The attack was divided into four phases.

Phase one had the 84th Division attacking through the 405th Infantry Regiment's lines and seizing the high ground east of Geilenkirchen and Prummern, two miles northeast. Phase two assigned the British 43rd (Wessex) Infantry Division to take the high ground near Bauchem and Tripsrath, two villages west and north of Geilenkirchen. These two phases were intended to surround the town of Geilenkirchen. Phase three was an attack by the 84th Division directly on Geilenkirchen. Phase four involved the 43rd (Wessex) Division clearing the west bank of the Würm as far as Hoven, while the 84th Division cleared the area around Sueggrath and Prummern. The result was to be the elimination of the wedge the Germans held between the British and American armies. It would straighten out the Allied front line from the Maas to the Würm and then south to Gereonsweiler. The new boundary was to be the course of the Würm, northeast along the Aachen-München-Gladbach railroad. A successful Operation *Clipper* would also extend Ninth Army's front by another five to six miles, allowing better distribution of its forces.

Gillem prepared for the attack, and established a task force for a planned crossing of the Roer at Linnich. This force, based upon the 113th Cavalry Group (commanded by Colonel William S. Biddle) was called Task Force Biddle. In addition to his two cavalry squadrons, Biddle was given additional tanks and artillery to perform his planned mission.[6] In the meantime, it was to protect XIII Corps' left, or north, flank. Gillem also planned for the recuperated 7th Armored Division to join his XIII Corps with the 84th and 102nd Infantry Divisions for a push to and across the Roer, and a subsequent drive on the Rhine.

The 84th Infantry Division had been activated at Camp Howze, Texas, on October 15, 1942, and after the usual training and maneuvers it departed from New York on September 20, 1944. It arrived in England on October 4, and made it to France on November 1. They called themselves the "Railsplitters," after their shoulder sleeve insignia, which showed an axe and the number "84" below. By November 17, it was in place ready to take part in Operation *Clipper*. Its commander was Brigadier General Alexander R. Bolling.[7]

Gillem, however, had problems meeting the schedule for Operation *Clipper*. General Keating's 102nd Infantry Division was spread out all over Ninth Army's area and took days to get ready. One of its regiments was attached to the 84th Infantry Division, and a second had been fighting with the 2nd Armored Division. Both were tired and needed reorganization before being ready for a new mission.

By the evening of November 24, Gillem's XIII Corps had assumed responsibility for six miles of the Ninth Army front. Holding this line was the 84th Infantry Division and a regiment of the 102nd Infantry Division. Behind the lines, the 7th Armored Division was still reorganizing after its defeat at the Peel Marshes earlier in the month. Intelligence reports that the Sixth Panzer Army was mustering behind the German front for a possible counterattack against XIII Corps' north flank made haste more urgent.[8]

Initially, Gillem had believed the salient might fall easily and had planned to send Task Force Biddle, supported by a regiment of the 102nd Infantry Division, to seize it. But a study of intelligence and prisoner-of-war interrogations convinced him that

Operation *Clipper*. (84th Infantry Division History)

it would take a full-scale, corps-size attack to overrun the triangle. He dissolved Task Force Biddle and attached the 113th Cavalry Group to the 84th Infantry Division, which was to make the corps' main effort. The 102nd Infantry Division was to make limited objective attacks to protect the 84th's right flank and the corps' boundary. XIII Corps would encounter the usual extensive field fortifications and pillboxes of the Siegfried Line (one antitank ditch ran more than a mile between Beck and Lindern).

Although it would not be facing the might of the Sixth Panzer Army, it did face XII SS Corps, consisting of the 10th SS Panzer Division, fresh from the battle at Arnhem, and elements of the 9th Panzer Division, 407th Volks Artillery Corps, and 183rd Volks Grenadier Division. The 15th Panzer Grenadier Division was also nearby.

Faced with the intelligence that *General der Infanterie* Guenther Blumentritt's XII SS Corps was holding the salient, Ninth Army decided to strengthen XIII Corps for the coming offensive. Several artillery batteries were moved from XIX Corps, either directly to XIII Corps or placed under Ninth Army control for use on either front. Gillem's artillery base was increased to 13 battalions, and British artillery was coordinated with the 84th Division's attack. Both attacking battalions received a full tank destroyer battalion and the 102nd Infantry Division also received a tank battalion. The 7th Armored Division attached one of its tank battalions to the 84th.

The 84th was to take five villages—Muellendorf, Würm, Beeck, Leiffarth and Lindern—and then secure Toad Hill (87.9), which overlooked the area. The division had been facing this area since arriving at the front earlier in November. The infantrymen had been briefed on November 17, the day before the first battalion-sized attack, and were told that they faced an antitank mine belt 25 yards wide. Behind this were German dugouts holding infantry and automatic weapons. British special armored vehicles ("flails" for beating a path through minefields and an "artificial moonlight" troop with massive searchlights, which reflected off the clouds and brightened up the night) would accompany the attack. The 309th Engineer (Combat) Battalion would have men forward to clear any mines missed by the flail tanks of the Sherwood Rangers Yeomanry Regiment. Direct artillery support was provided by the 326th Field Artillery Battalion.

*   *   *

Unlike with other American armies fighting in Europe, Ninth Army's command staff not only expressed confidence in their plans and combat leaders, but displayed such confidence by watching a movie the night before the attack was to begin. Instead of sweating out the coming bombardment and assault, Ninth Army relaxed, since whatever they could do had already been done, and what they would need to do was not yet apparent. As General Simpson would later write to one of his subordinates, Gillem, "I wish to assure you that I have never regretted my choice of you and always considered myself most fortunate to have you with me in my Ninth Army. I have always appreciated the splendid and outstanding job that you did and will always appreciate it. I want you to know that I do have the highest regard for you professionally."[9] Simpson praised his other corps commanders similarly.

The town of Prummern fell after a day's fighting. The 334th Infantry Regiment attacked with two battalions and that evening the Germans counterattacked in force. As morning dawned, the 3rd Battalion, 334th Infantry, was thrown into the battle to clear the town. Just outside the town the Germans had made a strong point of a hill the Americans called "Mahogany Hill." Company I and tanks from the Sherwood Rangers struck the hill and its five pillboxes before noon and battled for an hour, hand-to-hand, before the Germans conceded the hill and the town. The British flamethrower tanks decided the fight. "It was one of those terrible and beautiful sights which the machines of war create so often almost in spite of themselves, which seem all the more unreal against the ugly realities of war. Once the Crocodiles had worked them over, those pillboxes were black, shrunken coffins."[10] The 334th Infantry Regiment now prepared to move deeper into the salient. The fall of Prummern narrowed the German salient from the original 4,000 yards to barely 1,400. The battle for Prummern had made holding the Geilenkirchen Salient much, much harder for the Germans.

The 1st Battalion, 333rd Infantry Regiment, continued the attack with Companies A and B leading. The plan called for a coordinated attack, but the radios soon went out, and the terrain made physical contact difficult if not impossible. As one participant remarked, "In reality, nothing is harder to maintain in combat than contact. It is a lucky day when radios are working, when messengers go where they are supposed to go, and come back, or when you can see anything more than some more mud, a patch of trees, or another hill wherever you turn."[11] Nevertheless, the men of Company B made good progress, despite losses from mines. By 0900 hours on the morning of November 19, they were in the center of Geilenkirchen. They had not seen or heard from Company A, but had the impression that their buddies were in serious trouble somewhere else. Company B began to clear Geilenkirchen as quickly as possible and by midday they were on their way to the next town, Suggerath. Here, enemy fire slowed the attack.

Lieutenant Colonel Thomas W. Woodyard, Jr., the battalion commander, up front with Company B, ordered Company C to take over the attack on Suggerath. British tanks were called up and joined the American infantrymen. It took two difficult hours, but Suggerath was cleared of the enemy. Looking forward to a night time defense, Woodyard and six men patrolled forward to seek out the enemy and terrain. They were ambushed and Woodyard was severely wounded by an enemy grenade. The patrol pulled back to Suggerath and the advance was over for the day.

Meanwhile, Company A was having problems of its own. It faced a stronger defense, including a wider and thicker minefield, protected by barbed wire and small-arms fire. A sports plaza stood before a series of high walls protecting a group of orchards, and a gravel pit blocked part of the way. Having a larger section of Geilenkirchen to clear than Company B, Company A was soon involved in house-to-house fighting. Some Germans tried to surrender, waving white flags, but as soon as an American soldier showed himself to accept their surrender, other Germans fired on the surrender party. German mortars began to fall on the houses already cleared by Company A, and the battle went on for over an hour.

Then a British Lieutenant appeared and asked if he could be of assistance. Two of the Sherwood Ranger tanks drove up and began to blast away at targets pointed out by the American soldiers. One tank even pulled up to a pillbox, stuck its gun in the enemy's gun port, and blasted it away. The town was cleared by mid-afternoon, and Company A led the tanks out of town towards Suggerath. Here again Company A drew the more difficult assignment. Three machine guns halted the advance on Suggerath until the tanks came up and cleared the way. Woods off to the side contained two companies of German infantry, and these were cleared, again with help from the tanks. The infantry moved up the nearby hill and, just as darkness arrived, contacted a British patrol. The British, who had been under a counterattack by German tanks and infantry, had been having a hard time until the entirely oblivious Americans attacked the Germans from behind. This unusual mating of American soldiers and British tankers had succeeded in taking Geilenkirchen with unexpected ease. First Lieutenant Kenneth L. Ayers, of Company A, later said, "I was sold on the British. Those boys were good. There's not a man in my company who will say there's anything wrong with a British soldier because of the support we got from those tankers."[12]

General Bolling now decided to use flank attacks to achieve the remaining objectives. Instead of attacking the villages directly, he decided to strike for Toad Hill first, then Lindern, both of which offered height advantages over the other villages. They were also to the rear of the remaining objectives, meaning the "Railsplitters" would be attacking them from behind. Bolling assigned his 335th Infantry Regiment to make the attack, while the 333rd Infantry and 113th Cavalry staged a demonstration against Beeck. Because there was little or no cover on the approach to Toad Hill or Lindern, Colonel Hugh C. Parker, the regimental commander, elected to employ a night attack. Major Robert W. Kennedy's 2nd Battalion would attack Toad Hill while Major Robert W. Wallace moved against Lindern. There would be no artillery preparation before the attack, to preserve the element of surprise. A company of the 40th Tank Battalion, 7th Armored Division, was attached to each battalion and the attacks were set for November 29.

Parker had impressed upon his men the need for speed. With that in mind, the men of Companies I and K moved quickly in the darkness to cross the open ground in front of Lindern. Carrying only weapons, ammunition, gas masks, and emergency rations, the men at first faced only light enemy fire and the occasional mortar shell exploding nearby. But one of these explosions disabled the equipment of a Company K radioman, and he fell out to obtain a replacement.

The men came to a ditch. The leaders crossed it quickly—again they had been told that to remain in a ditch meant certain death, as the German artillery and mortars no doubt had it zeroed in and would pound them once they realized they were there. Three platoons crossed the ditch, but as the rest of the two companies tried to do so, the enemy did in fact open up with artillery, mortars and automatic weapons fire. The remainder of Companies K and I were stopped at the antitank ditch. 1st Lieutenant Leonard R. Carpenter (commanding Company K), and1st Lieutenant Creswell Garlington, Jr., (commanding Company I) pushed forward, unaware that between them they had just three platoons. Neither group had any communication with the other. Moving forward in the darkness, unable to see how many men remained with them, the two lieutenants pushed on to Lindern.

The two groups, still out of communication with each other or anyone else, attacked. Ordered to move swiftly and leave mopping up to those who followed, they raced through the town, throwing grenades and killing sentries as they went. Despite the sudden incursion, Lindern remained relatively quiet. As dawn rose the three platoons were digging defensive positions north of the town. It was only then that Carpenter and Garlington realized that they were all alone, well behind German lines, with barely a hundred men. Without radios, they could not even alert the 84th Infantry Division as to their position.[13]

If the American command didn't know where they were, the Germans soon did—three large German tanks came at them. A bazooka was fired and the tanks withdrew to the cover of some pillboxes 400 yards away. Then several truckloads of German infantrymen dismounted at those pillboxes, and one tank rolled up to the American position, seemingly uncertain of the situation. The tank commander opened his hatch to look around. An American shot him, and he fell back onto the tank turret. The tank withdrew to the others, but the Germans did not attack, perhaps uncertain as to the strength of the American force. The Americans were well dug in and partially screened by a rise in the ground and a nearby railroad embankment. Still, the two lieutenants were not overly concerned. They expected the rest of their battalion to be coming along at any moment.

Hours passed, and Lieutenant Carpenter started to become concerned. He sent volunteers back along his route to find out what the situation was. They discovered the discarded radio and after some effort managed to get it partially working—they could listen, but not transmit. Four men decided to go back on foot to see what was going on behind them. As it would turn out, communications throughout the 3rd Battalion, 335th Infantry, had ceased to function. Not only were Carpenter and Garlington out of touch, but Colonel Wallace could not contact the rest of Companies K or I. With no information coming to him, Colonel Parker had sent his remaining battalion, the First, to try and outflank Lindern, unaware that Carpenter and Garlington were already past it. But this battalion also lost communications, leaving Parker and his senior officers completely in the dark. A company of the 40th Tank Battalion, waiting for word to proceed into Lindern to assist the infantry, waited without any information.

Becoming increasingly desperate as the hours rolled by and no other Americans appeared, the men in Lindern continued to try and repair their radio. Someone tried to attach a telephone wire to a fence, hoping this would improve reception. They broadcast the coded message that they had achieved their objective. Surprisingly, a tank from the 40th Tank Battalion picked up this message shortly after noon. Lieutenant Colonel John C. Brown, commanding the battalion, acted immediately. He sent his Company A into Lindern under cover of a smoke screen, and six Sherman tanks made it into town. The infantrymen were elated. "When we saw those tanks, we figured the whole German Army couldn't drive us out of here."[14] Soon thereafter, the rest of the tank company arrived, as well as a reserve company of infantry.

The Germans had missed their chance to regain Lindern, but they refused to accept that. Despite the fact that a reinforced battalion of American infantry and two tank companies now held the town, they moved against it. For the next two days they pounded Lindern with artillery, mortars and repeated attacks by elements of the 10th SS Panzer Division, the 9th Panzer Division, the 506th Tank Battalion, and other units they cobbled together. Fighting again was house-to-house and street-to-street. American soldiers, armed in large part with captured German bazookas, roamed the streets knocking out the individual German tanks that had managed to penetrate the outer defenses. The Germans made their last effort on December 1, attacking from three sides. So heavy was the attack that one American soldier remarked of the incoming German artillery: "If there had been any more shells, they would have been colliding in the air."[15] For its part in the Battle of Lindern, Company K, 335th Infantry, received a Presidential Unit Citation.[16]

In order to supply the "Railsplitters" in Lindern along the only road (the Gereonsweiler–Lindern Road, which ran for 4,000 yards under German observation), vehicles had to run a gauntlet. In the beginning, most were knocked out by German artillery. Mud affected both their speed and maneuverability, making them easier targets. Only armored vehicles, like tanks and half-tracks, had a chance of getting through, but eventually the attacks ceased. Demonstrations by the 113th Cavalry Group and units of the 84th Infantry Division at Beeck attracted some German attention, while nearby the 102nd Infantry Division attacked, also drawing off German resources.

For their first combat, the 84th Infantry Division received the compliments of General Horrocks, commanding British XXX Corps, under whose tactical command they were operating. Even more pleasing to the GIs, however, was the issue of their first ever rum ration, as they were part of the British Army for the operation.

* * *

Even as the first Americans were entering Lindern, General Gillem had changed his mind about his attack. Rather than having the 84th Infantry Division attack alone, he decided that the 102nd Infantry Division would be included to add power and speed to the offensive. Anxious to get a chance to seize bridges over the Roer, and thereby deny them to German reinforcements, he ordered the 102nd to begin its attack. Its mission was to reach the Roer in the south eastern sector of XIII Corps' area, near the villages of Roerdorf (sometimes spelled Rürdorf) and Flossdorf. The division was to secure the high ground along the Lindern–Linnich highway and to occupy Linnich itself. Gillem believed this would protect the flank of General Bolling's attack and at the same time ensure that Lindern remained in American hands.

General Keating had originally thought to use only two regiments in the attack, keeping the 406th Infantry in reserve. Upon reflection, he ordered the 406th, recently returned from fighting with the 2nd Armored Division, to seize Linnich. The 405th Infantry was to seize the Lindern–Linnich Highway, while the 407th was directed on Roerdorf and Flossdorf, via Welz. Facing the 102nd Infantry Division were elements of the 10th SS Panzer Division and the 340th Volks Grenadier Division, holding the bridgehead at Linnich.

Again the battle involved open terrain covered with artillery, mortars and automatic weapons fire. Enemy tanks were well dug-in as pillboxes, while villages were full of interconnected trenches and field fortifications in addition to fortified houses. Rain, mud and cold aided the German defense, and each and every village had to be taken individually, usually house by house. In order to deter German artillery firing from across the Roer, Ninth Army guns had prepared a detailed counter-battery program to fend them off. On some days, as many as 20,000 artillery rounds were fired across the Roer. XXIX Tactical Air Command also struck repeatedly at identified targets, dropping 97 tons of bombs in 143 sorties, while Ninth Army artillery and chemical mortar units used smoke shells to distress the Germans.

The first objective was the village of Welz, a mile before the Roer and the target of the 407th Infantry. Lieutenant Colonel William J. Danskin, the regimental Executive Officer, described the attack as a long rush. By mid-morning, the village was in the hands of the Americans and casualties were being suffered from incoming artillery. Tanks from the 771st Tank Battalion supported the attack and lost one tank to mines, but then German artillery took a hand and the continuation of the attack was put off until more tanks and infantry could come up.

During the attack, Captain William A. Rhodey, commanding Company K, 407th Infantry, found his men pinned down by heavy enemy automatic weapons fire and repeatedly exposed himself to lead attacks to knock out these weapons. During a heavy artillery barrage, he disregarded his personal safety and went through the barrage to contact supporting tanks that were firing unknowingly at his men, stopping the fire and saving his men's lives. For his actions he received the Distinguished Service Cross.[17]

Roerdorf and Flossdorf were the next targets. The 2nd Battalion, 407th Infantry, attacked Flossdorf and advanced 600 yards, at which point they were halted by intense fire. Supporting machine guns could not reach many of the enemy positions, so mortars tried unsuccessfully to knock out the German guns. In early afternoon, tanks of the 771st Tank Battalion came up to lend a hand, but six of the eight were soon knocked out by hidden antitank guns. So heavy was the enemy fire that the crews of the disabled tanks were forced to remain in their vehicles until darkness covered their withdrawal. Heavy artillery barrages were called down on the town, and the American infantry moved forward until they were within 800 yards, where they stopped for the night.

The 405th Infantry, fighting along the Lindern–Gereonsweiler road, was also hit with heavy enemy fire and its attack stalled. A nearby attack by the 334th Infantry of the 84th Infantry Division also stalled, and little progress was made on November 30. The 405th Infantry, supported by Company A, 771st Tank Battalion, did manage to reduce several enemy positions in Gereonsweiler. During the fight, Private First Class Curtis F. Behler of Company B, 405th Infantry, made six trips across fire-swept ground to give instructions to supporting tank destroyers. Mortally wounded, he insisted on giving a buddy his last message before succumbing to his wounds. He received a posthumous Silver Star.[18] That evening, General Keating requested additional tank support, and Gillem allocated the 17th Tank Battalion of the 7th Armored Division. Still hoping for a dash to the Rhine, Gillem stipulated it was not to be used unless absolutely necessary.

On December 1, the 407th Infantry was to finish clearing Welz and then move on Flossdorf and Roerdorf. With its 2nd Battalion supported by only the five tanks left in Company C, 771st Tank Battalion, no progress was made, though not for want of trying. Second Lieutenant Kenneth P. Peyton, an artillery forward observer from Battery A, 380th Field Artillery Battalion, grabbed an ignited fragmentation grenade and carried it to the outside of a German command post pillbox, saving many lives. His actions earned him a Silver Star.[19] Keating, who observed the attack from the 407th Infantry's command post in Ederen, decided to send in his reserve regiment, the 406th. The plan was for the 1st and 2nd Battalions to attack together, along with the 17th Tank Battalion. Further support was provided by a company of the 92nd Chemical Mortar Battalion firing smoke, and XXIX Tactical Air Command was to send over fighter-bombers to assist. However, German planes suddenly appeared and the XXIX TAC planes were diverted into dogfights, jettisoning their loads.

The 2nd Battalion, 406th Infantry, began its attack quietly. Limited German fire greeted the men as they marched across the open plain. Following a rolling barrage, keeping pace ahead of them, it seemed as if the Germans had been suppressed. Occasionally an antitank gun would open fire at one of the supporting tanks, and the infantry would halt while the tanks knocked it out. However, antitank fire from across the river could not be silenced, and continued to oppose the American advance. Still, the infantry advanced into Linnich and began to clear the town of its 200 or so defenders. Three combat engineers, Lieutenant William P. O'Brien, Private First Class Mark W. Fullam and Private First Class Charles W. Kirk, of Company A, 327th Engineer (Combat) Battalion, earned Silver Star awards for leading infantrymen and other engineers through heavy fire and then destroying strong enemy fortifications that threatened to hold up the advance.[20] The mopping up continued all night, and at dawn the battalion commander, Major Isaac Gatlin, learned that his command post in Linnich had been directly across the street from that of his German counterpart.[21]

The 1st Battalion, 407th Infantry, delayed its attack due to an enemy counterattack from Roerdorf. Aided by two 406th Infantry battalions, the counterattack was repulsed. That afternoon, the 113th Cavalry Group seized Beeck and 84th Infantry Division troops took the nearby high ground. The subsequent fall of Lindern to the "Railsplitters" also eased the situation in the 102nd Infantry Division's zone. As the 405th and 406th Infantry Regiments advanced, German opposition seemed reduced. That night, indications were that the Germans were withdrawing.

The next day, December 2, proved the indications of the previous night had been correct. Against slight opposition, the 406th Infantry and tanks of Company B, 17th Tank Battalion, cleared Linnich while the 405th Infantry captured the high ground beyond the town. The 407th attacked Roerdorf and Flossdorf again, and despite automatic weapons fire and tank fire from across the river, the attack went forward. When the battalion commander fell, Major John H. Wohner assumed command of the 2nd Battalion and led the attack at the head of his troops, encouraging them to move into Flossdorf. For his leadership and gallantry, Major Wohner received a Distinguished Service Cross.[22]

Supported by tanks, which suppressed the enemy fire from over the river, the attack moved along slowly, but steadily. First Lieutenant Joseph L. Barkley of the 927th Field Artillery Battalion earned his Silver Star by riding atop the advancing tanks, fully exposed to enemy fire, and directing artillery fire as the troops advanced. Another Silver Star went to Private First Class Michael Strizak of Company F, who, after his weapon jammed, rushed an enemy position and seized the gun, turning it on the enemy and routing them.[23] The mopping up captured over 200 German troops, while many others were observed swimming the icy river to the German side. By the end of December 3, the west bank of the Roer was securely in the hands of XIII Corps.

By December 4, XIII Corps had advanced a mile and a half, during which the two divisions had incurred about a thousand battle casualties each. In the 84th Infantry Division, 176 men had been killed while the 102nd lost 142. The "Railsplitters" lost 209 missing in action while the 102nd lost 104, with the remainder of the total casualties being wounded. In addition, a combined 1,000 men were lost to combat fatigue and exposure.

* * *

There remained two more small obstacles to clear possession of the Roer River plain. These were a small group of farm buildings at the Roer (across from Jülich and known as Gut Hasenfeld) and a sports complex consisting of a concrete stadium and a covered swimming pool. Both fell within the zone of the 29th Infantry Division.

The reduction of these last remaining German holds on the west bank of the Roer looked like a relatively easy task, and because General Gerhardt wanted to keep the bulk of his division intact for a possible river crossing, he assigned only the 116th Infantry Regiment to the job.

The attack began on December 1 and it was soon apparent that it would be no easy task. As usual on the Roer plain, the ground was open and attackers were fully exposed to entrenched enemy guns from higher ground along the east bank. The only cover was a small patch of woods near the sports complex, but these woods were thick with antipersonnel mines. Making matters even more difficult, fresh German troops from the 363rd Volks Grenadier Division, recently arrived from Holland, garrisoned the sports complex.

For the next six days, the 116th Infantry would struggle with these objectives. A frustrating and deadly pattern developed, whereby, covered by smoke from the 92nd Chemical Mortar Battalion, the infantry would get within a few hundred yards of the objective, only to run into a minefield. Second Lieutenant Sears G. Sutton, of Company I, commented: "A man would hit a trip wire and there would be a click, then the mine would spring out of the ground and explode five or six feet in the air, spraying metal splinters."[24] As soon as the mine exploded, German automatic weapons, artillery and mortars, previously sited along logical routes of approach, would open fire, inflicting additional casualties. Falling to the ground to avoid this fire might result in more mine explosions, while standing still invited death or injury from shrapnel and bullets.

This kind of frustrating battle went on for days. An attempt at a night attack failed when a bright moon suddenly appeared and exposed the advancing infantry to the enemy, who immediately opened fire. Artillery and air support bombarded the town and sports complex without any noticeable reduction in enemy strength. Soon the entire corps artillery of XIX Corps was pounding the two objectives, now that all other activity within the corps' zone had temporarily ceased, but little result was noticed. It would later be learned that while the bombardment did considerable physical damage to the buildings, the Germans had strong underground shelters that spared them major losses. During the nights, they ferried their wounded across the Roer and brought reinforcements over to the west bank. An attempt by tanks of the 747th Tank Battalion to reinforce an infantry company that had moved close to Gut Hasenfeld failed when German artillery pounced on them and knocked one tank out.

So frustrated did Gerhardt become that he relieved the regimental commander of his post and promoted one of the battalion commanders, Lieutenant Colonel Sidney V. Bingham, Jr., in his place. Still no progress could be made. Finally, Colonel Bingham reported that further attacks by his regiment alone would be pointless. There was no real hope of success with the forces on hand. The 116th Infantry had lost 15 killed, 64 missing and 171 wounded in just the past six days, and others had been lost to illness and disease. The survivors were simply too exhausted to continue.

With no other choice, Gerhardt replaced the 116th Infantry with the 115th Infantry, and ordered them to secure the two outstanding objectives.

The six days of attacks by the 116th Infantry had achieved something, and that was the exhaustion and depletion of the enemy forces and their defenses. As a result, the fresh 115th Infantry looked over the situation and noticed that there was one area that was not covered by German artillery. One infantry company moved through that area, under the protection of a 92nd Chemical Mortar Battalion smoke screen, and approached Gut Hasenfeld unseen. The Germans opened up with their usual "final protective fires," but they were firing blind and the infantry was approaching from an uncovered area. Minefields still took their toll, however, and alerted the defenders to the incoming attack. Nevertheless, 18 men of Company I managed to break through a hole in the wall surrounding the farm, and in a rage cleared out the defenders who were awaiting the end of a barrage deep in the farm's cellars. A total of 85 prisoners were taken.

The "luck" of the 115th Infantry continued. Two platoons of Company B walked right up to the sports complex without setting off a single mine. Beginning with the dressing rooms on the west side of the complex, they began to knock out enemy positions, guns and infantry as they went. Before noon they had cleared the entire complex except for one corner of the arena, where a couple of machine guns could only be reached across an open playing field. Undeterred, Staff Sergeant Floyd Haviland and Sergeant Noah Carter charged across the field and took the guns, while under fire, with rifle grenades. By mid-afternoon the sports complex itself was secured.

Not so the swimming pool area. Here again the only approach was across an open field that was covered by enemy fire. In effect, the swimming pool was being used as one large concrete covered foxhole. Despite German artillery fire from across the river, two 105mm assault guns were brought forward and pounded the pool area. A platoon under Staff Sergeant Daniel Menkovitz then ran across the open ground and accepted the surrender of the now-subdued German garrison. Patrols pushed on to the actual river bank later that night.

*   *   *

In 23 days of November and December 1944, Ninth Army advanced from six to twelve miles against a German defense that never broke and never wavered. Determined to protect the soon-to-be-launched Ardennes counteroffensive, the Germans committed some of their best units to keep Ninth Army away from their staging areas, including the 10th SS Panzer Division and the 15th Panzer Grenadier Division. Unusually for this stage of the war, allied air superiority was even challenged during the battle. Despite XXIX TAC dropping 1,500 tons of bombs and 22,200 gallons of napalm during the offensive, the German line remained firm until tank-supported infantry confronted it toe to toe. Nor did the 90,000 rounds of artillery ammunition determine the outcome, although no doubt it was essential to the victory.

The cost to Ninth Army was 10,000 casualties, including 1,133 killed, 6,864 wounded and 2,059 missing in action. A total of 84 medium tanks and 15 light tanks had been knocked out during the fight, and many others were out of action for various periods as they received repairs due to battle damage. In turn, Ninth Army captured 8,321 German prisoners and buried another 1,264 enemy dead. Estimates were that another 5,000 had been killed during the battle. An estimated 110 German tanks had been destroyed.

Behind the lines, Ninth Army had other battles. Heavy rains had raised the Maas River to a 10-year record level. The main bridge at Maastricht had to be closed and for a while it was feared that it would be washed away. Ninth Army engineers stacked sandbags atop the bridge to weigh it down and prevent its loss, and a nearby pontoon bridge had to be lengthened from 470 feet to 670 feet due to the increased width of the river. British bridges downstream were washed away, and so the Ninth Army bridges had to do double duty, carrying supplies for the British Second Army as well as their own and civilian traffic. In order to prevent traffic jams and preserve the vulnerable roads, only light vehicles were permitted forward of the corps rear areas. The 505th, 510th and 795th Military Police Battalions were kept busy ensuring that traffic flowed with a minimum of disruption.

Road repair was a constant factor within the Ninth Army, and other, zones. Mud not only slowed or stopped vehicles, but it was often carried by the vehicles onto the hard-surfaced roads, where it became slippery, causing more traffic headaches. Ninth Army Ordnance Company trucks were placed at strategic points along the roads to repair breakdowns and recover wrecks. Space remained at a premium, as did shelter, since the area had been fought over and most buildings were destroyed or damaged. Locations for hospitals and service installations had to be found, some built, and others improvised. Captured engineer supplies were put to use and the lumber and electrical equipment was made available to those units that needed them to operate efficiently. Ninth Army sawmills produced as much as 60,000 board feet per day.

Due to a shortage within Ninth Army of a heavy signal construction battalion, use was made of the existing commercial cables in Maastricht, Liége, Aachen, Heerlen and Sittard. By the end of November, 90 per cent of Ninth Army's telephone net was carried on these cables. Still another shortage was the lack of a topographic battalion. General Simpson created an *ad hoc* battalion using an engineer map depot detachment and a corps topographic company. They were soon very busy planning for the Roer crossing and the advance to the Rhine. A shortage of military police units was made up for by the use of Netherlands and Belgian troops.

Like all the American field armies in Germany at this time, reinforcements for depleted combat units remained in short supply. Even those received were found by Ninth Army officers to need refresher training and combat orientation prior to assignment to a combat unit. The Ninth Army Assistant Chief of Staff, G-1, Colonel Daniel H. Hundley, organized a program to give these new men the necessary training. Combat demonstrations were presented and the new men were trained in day-to-day combat conditions. Small-arms instruction, using German as well as American weapons, was conducted. Methods of detection against mines and booby traps were another class in the instruction cycle.

To alleviate the personnel shortage, Ninth Army gave close attention to the prompt return of discharged casualties back to their units. In order to expedite their return, for example, hospitals were allowed to stock new uniforms, equipment and weapons for the returning men to draw upon, thereby losing less time than requisitioning them after a return to the front. Once again, Ninth Army had the unpleasant task of establishing a cemetery for the American dead. One was set up at Margraten, in the Netherlands (Simpson did not want an American military cemetery established in Germany). This would remain Ninth Army's main cemetery, even after the Roer crossing and despite the longer journey required, due to the American soldier's natural aversion to being buried on enemy soil. The Ninth Army Chaplain, Colonel W. Roy Bradley, took charge of all cemetery matters.

Ninth Army also established rest centers in the Netherlands. Due to the non-frat-ernization order from Supreme Headquarters, Allied Expeditionary Forces, it was thought better to have the rest centers off German ground to further ease those rules. Quartermaster fumigation and bathing companies were established, as were laundry facilities. Special Services provided what entertainment could be found at the rest centers.

Since 1944 was an election year, Colonel Frederick J. de Rohan, Ninth Army's Special Service Officer, was responsible for ensuring that each soldier knew what his voting rights and duties were, as well as explaining the qualifications for voting. With winter fast approaching, new sleeping bags, overshoes, additional blankets and shelter tents were acquired and issued by supply services.

With Ninth Army responsible for an area in Belgium, southern Netherlands and Germany, civil affairs and military government took on added duties. The Assistant Chief of Staff, G-5, Colonel Carl A. Kraege, had to provide considerable amounts of supplies, especially food, to the civilians within Ninth Army's zone of responsi-bility. Rehabilitation of local industry, provision of clothing and storage of many items needed for civilian care fell to Colonel Kraege. Even seed for agriculture was an army responsibility. One of the main problems was coal. Many coal mines had been overrun by Ninth Army during its advance and these had to be returned to operation to provide power for warmth in the coming winter and electrical power for industry. It was a problem because many of the workers were not interested in returning to work—money was no inducement because they had nothing on which to spend it. The retreating Germans had also evacuated most skilled miners when they left the area. Those left preferred to remain at home to protect family and property. Civil affairs officers worked long and hard to eventually get the coal mines back to a reasonable production level.

Ninth Army's headquarters location in Maastricht brought it to the attention of the latest German "wonder weapon," the flying bomb, or V-2 rocket. These were launched from an area near the Rhine, south of Cologne. The rocket then traveled some 200 miles to a target. Many of them passed over Maastricht and Liége *en route* to their targets. As soon as Ninth Army established itself, Colonel John G. Murphy, the Army Antiaircraft officer, made plans to defend the area against a rocket attack. Because Ninth Army had been squeezed into a relatively small area, it now made a much better target for the rockets than it normally would have in a more dispersed deployment. As a result, Brigadier General Samuel L. McCroskey and his 55th Antiaircraft Artillery Brigade set up a defensive belt of eight heavy batteries southeast of Maastricht to meet this possible threat. They were prepared, as sometimes a hundred rockets a day passed over Ninth Army headquarters. Many of them passed over the city and exploded nearby, but none ever landed in the city directly. Despite German claims that Maastricht was being destroyed by the rockets because Ninth Army had its headquarters there, no bombs exploded within city limits. A few explosions that did erupt within the city were traced to long-range experimental German artillery.

For Ninth Army, the next step was a river crossing and then a push to the Rhine, the traditional German border and the entry point into the Germany interior. Before this could begin, it had to wait for the adjacent First Army to come up to the Roer. And before that could happen, the offensive that the Germans had fought so hard to protect would strike.

CHAPTER 6

Plans and Preparations

By early December 1944, Ninth Army was closing up to the west bank of the Roer and looking east. The combat divisions holding the front lines along the river were allowed to leave a holding force there while the bulk of each division pulled back to prepare for the next operation. The entire 7th Armored Division was placed in an assembly area to the rear of XIII Corps in preparation for future operations. The overall objective still remained the crossing of the Roer and Rhine (thus outflanking the Siegfried Line), and the capture of the German city of Cologne. Ultimately, Ninth Army's objective was the German industrial heartland known as the Ruhr.

Planning and preparing for future operations usually fell to the chief of staff in an American field army. Helped by a wide variety of experts in differing fields, he was the coordinator, director and filter by which the army commander planned ahead. In the case of Ninth Army, the working relationship between Simpson and his chief of staff, Brigadier General James Edward Moore, was so well established that many compared it to the World War I partnership between the German generals Paul von Hindenburg and Erich Ludendorff.

Born November 29, 1902, in Bedford, Massachusetts, Moore was commissioned in the infantry from West Point in 1924. He served in the Philippines and China before graduating from the Command and General Staff School in 1938. Moore had his first experience with Simpson when he served as his aide between November 1940 and April 1941. After serving in the budget and legislative branches of the War Department General Staff, Moore became chief of staff to Simpson in the 35th Infantry Division in 1942. He then went on to hold the same post with the 30th Infantry Division, XII Corps, Fourth Army and finally with Ninth Army. Promoted to brigadier general in January 1944, at Eisenhower's recommendation, he would achieve the rank of major general in March 1945. He would eventually retire in 1963 as a full general after a long and successful post-war career.[1]

Moore would later explain the Ninth Army's staff working relationship. Unlike Patton and Montgomery, Simpson was "not his own G-3."[2] When Simpson received a mission he would call in Moore with his intelligence, operations and supply officers and tell them generally what the mission was. He would then leave them to develop three different plans to achieve the mission, including maps and overlays. Once completed, Simpson would review each plan in turn and then select the one that he favored best. Usually he would then request that aspects of the other plans that he liked be incorporated into the selected plan, in effect creating a fourth combined plan for operations. While the staff, led by Moore, worked to come up with these plans, Simpson would be out viewing his troops, ensuring their welfare, and satisfying himself that Ninth Army was ready for future operations. Moore would go on to explain that the only reason this system worked was because of Simpson's complete confidence in him. Moore was even authorized to commit Ninth Army's reserve force without first consulting with Simpson, so confident were they in each other's abilities.

Simpson's approach did not only apply to his staff, but often to the combat commanders under his command. Once a plan had been completed, Simpson, Moore and the Ninth Army staff would meet with the combat commanders and go over it with them. Questions, concerns and ideas were welcomed, but in the end Simpson decided upon the final plan. When General Harmon learned that his combat veterans of the 2nd Armored Division were to be transferred to Ninth Army, he wrote, "This was a switch much to my liking."[3]

*   *   *

The final plan adopted by Simpson was called Operation *Grenade*. The overall plan was for a drive from the Roer to the Rhine by all Allied armies, moving abreast— Operation *Grenade* was the name for Ninth Army's part in this new offensive. In many ways, it was a continuation of the November offensive in which the American armies were driving due east to enter central Germany. After Ninth Army crossed the Rhine north of Cologne, having outflanked the Siegfried Line (Germany's much vaunted defensive belt, which was intended to halt any invasion from the west), it was to advance into the German industrial area in the Ruhr. The bulk of the effort was to be made in First Army's sector, while Ninth Army protected the left flank of the entire Twelfth Army Group.

But First Army became stuck in a bitter struggle at Aachen and within the Hürtgen Forest, and the planned breakthrough never came. Strong German resistance slowed the advance and the threat of the German Sixth SS Panzer Army, known to be in the area but whose exact position and plans remained elusive, also slowed the American movements. Finally, the threat of a major flood from the Roer dams kept the American leaders looking ahead with concern. Such a flood would not only halt operations, but would make any significant movement impossible for weeks, leaving the American armies exposed and vulnerable to a German counterattack. Eisenhower particularly feared having one American army exposed across the Rhine while the others were halted west of it by major flooding. He ordered that until the Roer dams were secured, there would be no attempt to cross the river.

As a result of all these factors, General Bradley decreed that only a concerted attack across the Roer would be attempted, once all of his armies were prepared. He rejected the idea of piecemeal assaults across the river, fearing, like Eisenhower, that it could lead to significant portions of American troops becoming isolated on the east bank without the possibility of aid from the rest of Twelfth Army Group. First of all, however, Twelfth Army Group had to close up to the Roer. Although Ninth Army and Seventh Army (to the south) had already done so, neither First nor Third Army were yet at the river. Also, before any crossing was attempted, the Roer dams had to be seized by the Allies.

For Ninth Army the first days of December 1944 were used to clear the several enclaves held by the Germans in its sector on the west bank of the Roer. Hasenfeld Gut and the Jülich Sportsplatz were just two of the more difficult enclaves that were eliminated during the lull. To the south of Ninth Army, First Army prepared to launch an offensive to seize the two key dams along the Roer, the Schwammenauel and Urfttalsperredams. Repeated air attacks on the dams, made in an effort to eliminate the threat of flooding before the Americans reached the flood zone, failed. A ground attack would be required.

*   *   *

What happened next had its origins back on September 16. During a conference in Hitler's East Prussian headquarters, the German Chancellor's senior staff officers outlined the situation on all fronts of the German war effort. As the discussion turned to events in France, where German forces were in full retreat after the Allies' breakout from the Normandy bridgehead, Hitler suddenly cut off the discussion with an entirely unexpected announcement. He said that he had reached a great decision. He would prepare a counteroffensive. It would be on the Western Front. It would be launched from the great Ardennes Forest and the objective would be Antwerp, a key Allied port. It would also separate the American and British armies and hopefully force them to accept a negotiated peace. It would be known to history as the Battle of the Bulge.

From the five options drawn up by the German General Staff in accordance with Hitler's directive, a plan was formed. Dozens of German divisions were to be pulled from the front lines, and reinforced and refurbished for the coming offensive. This was why Ninth Army couldn't determine the location or the objectives of the newly created Sixth SS Panzer Army, which was one of the main forces designated to lead the coming attack.[4] Everything was held in the greatest secrecy—many leading German officers destined to conduct the attack were not informed until the last possible moment.

The attack by First and Ninth Armies at Aachen, known to the Germans as the Third Battle of Aachen but called the Battle of Hürtgen Forest by the Americans, had forced the Germans to commit some of their precious reserves to halt that advance. Fears that the offensive by First and Ninth Armies would achieve a breakthrough and drive to the Rhine in the area between Cologne and Bonn caused Hitler to order the assembly of a force to counterattack should such a breakthrough be made. This counterattack force was stationed north west of Cologne while a second force, mostly exhausted and weak divisions, gathered at the area of the Eifel to strike the right flank of any such penetration. Ninth Army was aware of this grouping and believed it to be Sixth SS Panzer Army.

The lessening of available divisions for the Germans' counteroffensive resulted in more discussions. The gradual eroding of reserves had created fears that the "Big Solution," the capture of Antwerp, was now unrealistic. When Patton's Third Army struck at Metz, fears that more reserves would be drawn away from the main effort intensified the discussion, yet Hitler refused to be swayed and Antwerp remained the ultimate objective. The initial planning had envisioned November 25, 1944, as the date for the offensive to begin. The moves by First, Third and Ninth Armies in November to seize Aachen, Metz and reach the Roer had forced a postponement of this target date. Indeed, there were several postponements due to demands on the reserves by other collapsing fronts. Finally, despite continuing demands for troops elsewhere, the assault was scheduled for December 16.

Across the front lines, the Allies were largely unaware of the coming crisis. Other than a few intelligence officers, who were dismissed as suffering from fatigue, none of the American leaders anticipated a major counteroffensive. Most of the force within First Army was concentrated to the northern end of its front, preparing to seize the Roer dams. Along the center of First Army, only a weak VIII Corps, with two exhausted and two brand new divisions, held the front along the Ardennes Forest. To its south, Patton's Third Army was just reaching the Saar River and below that General Patch's Seventh Army was already at the Rhine.[5]

To the north, Ninth Army had reached the Roer and was preparing a crossing. Further north, Montgomery's Twenty-First Army Group, consisting of the British Second and First Canadian Armies, had just crossed the Waal River (an extension of the lower Rhine), and was preparing to enter Germany. On December 7, 1944, Eisenhower called a meeting of his most senior leaders to plan for future operations. Together with Air Chief Marshal Sir Arthur W. Tedder, Montgomery and General Bradley, the decision was taken to conduct a major offensive early in 1945. A long-standing dispute between Eisenhower and Montgomery on exactly how such an offensive was to be conducted, either on a broad front or as a strong single thrust into Germany, resulted in a tentative agreement that once the offensive began, Montgomery would be given Ninth Army to push north of the Ruhr while to the south Patton's Third Army would strike for the Frankfurt Gate.

In order to support the coming offensive, and to whittle down German reserves, Eisenhower directed that First Army strike for the Roer dams while Third and Seventh Armies mounted an offensive on the Saar front. Ninth Army would cross the Roer once the dams had been secured and push to the Rhine. Montgomery's British Second Army was to "clear up" the remaining concerns around Arnhem and eliminate a major German salient at Heinsberg. Few of these plans were implemented before the Germans changed the entire picture along the Western Front.

*   *   *

While planning at the highest levels on both sides of the front continued, Ninth Army had concerns of its own. It was in the process of completing Operation *Dagger*, the clearing of the Roer's west bank within the army's sector. Planning for Operation *Grenade* was progressing and the expectation was that a crossing of the Roer would take place as soon as First Army seized the dams. The newly arrived XVI Corps, under General Anderson, was headquartered at Heerlen with the 102nd Infantry Division under command. To the south was XIII Corps, headquartered at Kerkrade with the 29th Infantry Division under command. General McLain's XIX Corps connected to First Army with the 8th, 78th and 104th Infantry Divisions under command. Several divisions were held in Ninth Army reserve in anticipation of a thrust across the Roer. These included the 2nd and 7th Armored Divisions, and the 30th, 84th and 75th Infantry Divisions, the latter having only just arrived in Europe.

When the German counteroffensive struck VIII Corps on December 16, 1944, it was at first dismissed as a "spoiling attack." But the rapid and continued success of the German effort soon concerned Bradley, commander of Twelfth Army Group. As more and more German units were identified, including the formerly elusive Sixth SS Panzer Army, that concern turned to alarm. When the attack struck, Bradley was in conference with Eisenhower in Paris. Both he and Eisenhower agreed that it would be prudent to move the 7th Armored Division down from Ninth Army to First Army as a precaution. They also decided to move the 10th Armored Division up from Third Army. The difference in just how these requests were received in their respective army headquarters is revealing.

Upon receiving the request to transfer his 10th Armored Division to General Hodges' First Army, Patton "demurred," claiming that his own army was preparing for an attack on December 19, which would give Third Army its place in leading the Allied offensive into Germany. Bradley rejected Patton's pleas for his own army's aggrandizement and ordered the transfer to be made immediately.[6]

In contrast, when Bradley called Simpson, after hanging up with Patton, his request was acted upon "promptly and generously."[7] Simpson had served with Hodges in World War I and they were well acquainted with each other. Indeed, Simpson's cooperative and generous nature continued to prevail—on the following day he offered to also send to First Army the 30th Infantry Division and the newly received 5th Armored Division. Ninth Army eventually sent the 7th Armored Division and the 30th Infantry Division to First Army on December 17, the second day of the enemy offensive. On December 20, Ninth Army sent the 84th Infantry Division south as well. The next day General Harmon's 2nd Armored Division was sent, and later that same day the new 75th Infantry Division joined the trek south. Finally, the 113th Cavalry Group joined the southern pilgrimage. In all Ninth Army sent five divisions and numerous support troops to First Army to help it in repelling the major German counteroffensive. All of these units played key roles in stopping that attack. In addition, with fewer troops available, Ninth Army took over the sector of First Army's VII Corps front, to allow that corps headquarters to prepare a counteroffensive from the north, which would also be decisive in repelling the German attack. Ninth Army's role in stopping the German counteroffensive, little recognized, was in fact critical.

Simpson had first learned the details of the counteroffensive from his old friend, General Hodges. After trying unsuccessfully to reach Bradley, who was in Paris, Hodges had telephoned Simpson and arranged for a face-to-face meeting. Driving to First Army in a jeep with an armored car escort, Simpson found Hodges in poor spirits. Hodges explained that his troops were falling back and that he considered the situation critical. Captured orders and prisoner interrogations had revealed that a major enemy attack was underway against First Army. To reinforce this intelligence, a German staff officer had been captured with a map of the entire German plan. Simpson tried to calm his friend's fears, remarking, "Well, from what I see here, I don't feel too much alarmed. We are going to have to do some hard fighting, but I think eventually we'll stop this thing."[8] When Hodges continued to bemoan the fact that he could not get in touch with Bradley, Simpson replied, "Hell, you don't have to! I've got the 30th Infantry Division in reserve here. If you need it, I'll turn it over to you right now."[9] Clearly, Simpson's reputation for cooperation and loyalty was well deserved.[10]

Having loaned a significant portion of its troop strength to First Army, Ninth soon found itself on loan. On December 20, it was assigned to the operational control of the Twenty-First Army Group of Montgomery. For the next week, Ninth Army improved defensive positions and regrouped its depleted forces, which allowed it to send still more combat units south to First Army. The 5th Armored Division and the 83rd Infantry Division went to VII Corps to strengthen its scheduled counterattack.[11] The British 51st Infantry (Highland) Division, commanded by Major General T. G. Rennie (which had been placed under Ninth Army's operational control as a reserve), was also passed on to First Army. Much of the flying done in December by XXIX Tactical Air Command, Ninth Army's assigned tactical air support force, was also in support of First Army. Altogether, Ninth Army sent eight combat divisions, a cavalry group and much of its air support to First Army as soon as possible after the German attack was deemed a major offensive.

Ninth Army's contribution to crushing Hitler's last major offensive in the west did not end there. With VII Corps turning south to attack the flank of the German penetration of First Army, Ninth Army had to take over a considerable portion of the front which had formerly been covered by VII Corps and First Army. When all the regrouping had been completed, Ninth Army held a front running from Simmerath to Linnich, a distance of 40 miles. To hold this extended front, Ninth Army had two corps headquarters, XIII and XIX Corps, with five divisions. General McLain's XIX Corps had the 78th Infantry Division, commanded by Major General Edwin P. Parker, and an old friend, the 8th Infantry Division, now under the command of Brigadier General William G. Weaver. XIX Corps' front was rounded out by Major General Terry de la Mesa's veteran 104th Infantry Division.

The northern portion of Ninth Army's front was held by General Gillem's XIII Corps, with the veteran 29th and 102nd Infantry Divisions. Ninth Army's plans for an offensive of its own were shelved and all attention turned to defensive measures. Placed on a starvation diet of ammunition and other supplies, Ninth Army could do little but hold its position and protect the flank of the embattled First Army. Orders were issued that Ninth Army was to ensure that no northern arm of the German offensive could reach Aachen or the Sittard area, which would allow it to link up with the main drive through the Ardennes.

Simpson issued a Letter of Instructions, dated December 19, 1944, in which priority was given to defensive lines to be held by Ninth Army. Engineer units were issued specific instructions with regard to mining the front lines, installing barbed wire, and preparing bridges and other vital installations for demolition should that become necessary. Ninth Army also issued a counterattack plan should any German attack develop on its front. The 5th Armored Division, in Twenty-First Army Group reserve, would be made available for such a counterattack, as would several British and Commonwealth units, which would come under Ninth Army's operational control over the next month.

Simpson also saw to it that his troops dug in deeply. Most of his units had been on the offensive so long that they had neglected to dig defensive positions of sufficient strength to halt a determined attack. His constant visits to the front lines ensured that this deficiency was soon corrected. He also saw to it, in cooperation with representatives of Twenty-First Army Group, that the flanks of his Ninth Army and the British Second Army were well connected, so that no gaps existed for the Germans to exploit.

Ninth Army headquarters was soon joined by a group of liaison officers from Montgomery's headquarters, a standard practice within Twenty-First Army Group. Montgomery himself was a frequent visitor to Ninth Army headquarters, as was Prince Bernhard of the Netherlands. Indeed, the smooth working relationship that Simpson quickly developed with Montgomery came as a surprise to many other leading American commanders. The British commander was not well regarded among the high command of most of the American forces in Europe. Even his own political leader, Prime Minister Winston Churchill, described him as "indomitable in retreat; invincible in advance; insufferable in victory."[12]

The assignment to Twenty-First Army Group was not unexpected. From the time of the Normandy breakout in early August, Bradley feared that at some point in the not-too-distant future he would be required by Eisenhower to turn over at least one American army to Montgomery, whose British and Canadian armies were growing increasingly weaker in manpower due to casualties and shrinking civilian populations at home. His personal ties to the First Army, his first army-level command, and the fact that he worried that Hodges, commanding First Army, and his staff would not be compatible with the Field Marshall's methods, had prompted him to move Ninth Army to the north of First Army, thereby placing it closest to Twenty-First Army Group. Since Eisenhower continued to insist that the main effort should be directed north of the Ardennes Forest, placing Ninth Army in the north fitted his strategic concept. Simpson had in fact been informed that once he reached the Rhine, his army would be turned north to assist the British, although apparently no mention was made of being assigned operationally to Twenty-First Army Group.[13]

*   *   *

Bernard Law Montgomery was born on November 17, 1887, in London, the fourth of nine children. His father was a bishop and his upbringing was strict. He would later attribute his interest in the military in this strict upbringing and his constant duties around the church. Whatever the reason, he entered the Royal Military Academy at Sandhurst with the class of 1908, ranking 36th among the 170 graduates. With no money of his own, he requested assignment to the Royal Warwickshire Regiment because it had a battalion assigned to India, where living expenses were known to be lower than in Great Britain. Montgomery soon formed very firm opinions of his fellow military leaders, most of which were negative. His battalion arrived back in England just in time to participate in the opening months of World War I. Within two months he had been seriously wounded and earned a Distinguished Service Order.

After a year in hospitals he returned to the battalion as a brigade major, and was soon a lieutenant colonel and Chief of Staff of the 47th (London) Division. After the war he suffered the routine of a peacetime officer, illuminated only when he married a widow and had a son of his own. The death of his wife from an insect bite 10 years later appeared to seriously affect his life, making him even more of a determined career officer. By 1938, he was a major general, serving in Palestine. The following year he took command of the 3rd British Infantry Division and led it in France and through Dunkirk. During the retreat, Montgomery moved up to command the II British Corps, with a promotion to lieutenant general.

After returning to England, he again assumed command of the 3rd British Infantry Division. Montgomery's assignment was now to protect the southern coast of England from an expected German invasion. Over the next two years he remained in England, rising steadily in command of first V Corps, then XII Corps, and finally South-Eastern Army. In late 1942, the designated commander of the British Eighth Army in North Africa was killed while *en route* to assume his duties. A hurried call went out to Montgomery to fly to North Africa and take over, and it was here that he made his military reputation. He defeated the highly regarded German Field Marshal Erwin Rommel at Alam Halfa, and then again at El Alamein, where Rommel's forces were shattered. For these feats, Montgomery was promoted to full general and knighted.

Montgomery relied on loyalty. As he had done in the 3rd Infantry Division years earlier, he remade the army in his own image. If he had the slightest doubts about a subordinate's capabilities or loyalties, that individual was quickly "sacked." Many who suffered from his decisions called it a "ruthless purge." In one case a veteran corps commander, Major General W. H. Ramsden, asked for four days leave in Cairo. Montgomery was reportedly quite gracious and encouraged Ramsden to get some much needed rest. The following day Montgomery sent for Ramsden to inform him that he was relieved of his command and would be replaced by Lieutenant General Oliver Leese, a Montgomery favorite.[14] Montgomery, a strict non-drinker and non-smoker, imposed a strict physical fitness regime on his subordinates. His determination to eliminate what he believed was any inefficiency within his command made him both friends and enemies. He was described by fellow officers as "ruthless" and an "unspeakable cad." None of this altered the fact that with the victory in North Africa, and subsequent successful campaigns in Sicily and southern Italy, he was Great Britain's premier soldier. Quick to criticize others, he never admitted to any mistakes of his own.

If Montgomery's reputation varied among the British officer corps, it was nearly universally negative among the Americans in Europe. Bradley, who once threatened to resign if he was placed under Montgomery's command, believed him to be too cautious, losing many opportunities by refusing to take acceptable risks to eliminate the enemy. He believed him to come across as "pompous, abrasive, demanding and almost insufferably vain."[15] Eisenhower agreed, although more circumspectly. In a letter to General Marshall he wrote of Montgomery, "He is unquestionably able, but very conceited."[16] Eisenhower went on to say that, "He is so proud of his successes to date that he will never willingly make a single move until he is absolutely certain of success—in other words, until he has concentrated enough resources so that anybody could practically guarantee the outcome …."[17] Probably the most outspoken critic of "Monty" among American leaders was Patton. Not known for his tactful remarks, Patton wrote in his diary during the Battle of the Bulge that the Field Marshal was "tired" and that he wouldn't take risks that would, in Patton's opinion, move the battle more swiftly to a satisfactory conclusion.[18] Even the naming of Ninth Army was the result of Eisenhower not wanting to "duplicate the famous British Eighth Army" and thereby insult Montgomery.[19]

Not surprisingly, if one was familiar with Simpson, the relationship between him and Montgomery was, and remained throughout their relationship, cordial. This was the word Simpson himself used to describe it. Understanding that the British commander would be skeptical of him at first, Simpson found that Monty visited him quite often, something that neither Eisenhower nor Bradley did. Simpson found that he respected Montgomery for his self-possession during the Battle of the Bulge. Both men were conscious of casualties and worked to keep them low. They both preferred to use artillery or air power instead of risking the lives of their infantrymen and both men liked an orderly battlefield. As their relationship progressed, Simpson became increasingly appreciative of the fact that the Field Marshal pretty much left him alone and didn't interfere, giving Simpson considerable freedom of action.[20] Simpson's chief of staff, General Moore, felt similarly, and both got along well with their new British commander. Unfortunately, neither the Field Marshal nor his chief of staff, Major General Sir Francis De Guingand, mentioned Simpson in their memoirs except in passing.

*   *   *

Ninth Army spent the rest of December supporting the efforts of both First Army and Twenty-First Army Group in repelling the German counteroffensive. More than 100,000 tons of supplies had to be moved to the rear to avoid possible seizure by German forces. Since the port of Antwerp had recently been opened, more and more supplies and equipment were being made available to the combat armies, and so Ninth Army began to stockpile supplies including ammunition, gasoline, signal equipment and other essential items. All shipments to the front were halted to avoid them possibly falling into enemy hands. Meanwhile tons of telephone cables, field telephone wire, radio sets, flash lights and batteries were forwarded to First Army. Mines and defensive supplies were also forwarded, despite the fact that Ninth Army, now on the defensive itself, was still short of such supplies. Ammunition was also sent south. To contribute as much as possible, Ninth Army had one of its supporting artillery battalions use captured German 105mm howitzers until all of the ammunition captured with them was exhausted. Two other battalions used British 25-pounder guns with ammunition supplied by the British.[21] Ordnance parties circulated throughout the army to ensure that all weapons were in the best operating condition, thereby avoiding weapons being put out of service. Requests were placed for winter equipment such as shoe pacs, arctic socks and ponchos, but despite promises for quick delivery, these did not arrive promptly, and then only in small packets, until late January. With heavy snowfalls beginning in late December,

Ninth Army turned to a novel method to cloak itself from the enemy. Finding that no snow suits were available anywhere in Europe, Ninth Army had its Military Government Personnel drive around in trucks with public address systems attached. They called upon the German civilians to bring to the trucks all suitable white cloth in their homes. Tablecloths, bed sheets and even underwear were contributed. Each civilian was given a receipt for what they contributed. More than 41,000 bed sheets alone were collected and a factory was established using Netherlands civilians to turn these items into clothing for the front-line troops.

There was also a shortage of mine detectors. Again, Ninth Army came up with a temporary solution. Since the wooden German Schü mine was not detectable by the usual magnetic mine detectors, Ninth Army found that pitchforks were suitable for removing them. With pitchforks not available through normal supply channels, Ninth Army staff visited all the supply stores in Belgium and soon had 3,000 new "mine detectors" in use. Other, more routine, problems struck Ninth Army as they did all others fighting in the increasingly cold, wet and muddy terrain. Brakes froze, wheel axles failed, tanks slid because tracks were not wide enough. Some problems would have been comical, were they not so serious. In one instance, road-clearing crews had piled up tons of snow alongside a major road. In doing so they had inadvertently covered up a supply of 240mm artillery shells. A considerable distance of the road verges had to be probed before they could be found and recovered.

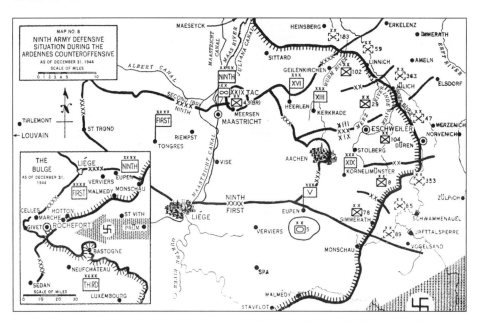

Ninth Army defensive situation during the Ardennes Offensive. (*Conquer. The Story of the Ninth Army, 1944–1945*, Infantry Journal Press)

Combat operations in Ninth Army did not cease during the Battle of the Bulge. Although it was on the defensive, the army still had a considerable front to guard, and a rear area that was increasingly critical to the continued success of the Allied counterattack. Bridges had to be protected, especially in view of previous German attempts to destroy them and disrupt Allied supply lines. In one case, a Ninth Army guard at a bridge observed a water-borne object bobbing its way past a couple of booms protecting a bridge over the Maas at Visé. The soldier fired eleven shots at the object. As his last shot hit the target it exploded with such force that it sprayed the guard with water and shook several nearby houses. Between December 17 and 18, more than 400 enemy planes were counted over Ninth Army's area and antiaircraft crews were kept busy day and night protecting roads, bridges, and rear area bases. They would claim 24 enemy aircraft destroyed.

On New Year's Day, 1945, the Germans launched a major air attack all along the Allied front. It was designed to smash the Allied air effort supporting the armies fighting in the Battle of the Bulge. Ninth Army's command post was strafed while the staff was attending a briefing. American antiaircraft battalions responded quickly to the challenge, and at one point five separate columns of smoke, each marking a downed German aircraft, could be seen from XIX Corps headquarters. Of the estimated 200 enemy planes that struck the Ninth Army areas, 70 were counted as shot down.

But the most constant threat was at the front. There the 102nd Infantry Division placed two regiments on the front lines with the third in reserve. This arrangement lasted only until the neighboring 84th Infantry Division was sent south to aid First Army, and then the reserve regiment also went into the line, to cover the former sector of the "Railsplitters." By December 20, the division was covering a front-line sector in excess of 10,500 yards. Taking advantage of the lull in offensive operations, the division began to rotate units from the front to a rest and training area set up behind the lines around Eigelshoven, Holland. To help the division cover the expanded front line, it received as a temporary attachment the 48th Armored Infantry Battalion of the 7th Armored Division. Once the armored infantrymen departed, the 11th Cavalry Group was attached to assist in covering the front lines.[22] Intended as a temporary attachment, the cavalry group would remain with the division for the next two months.

The division faced the 340th Volks Grenadier Division, which still held a small bridgehead on the western bank of the Roer. Other than regular bombardments from artillery and mortars, little in the way of activity was occurring. On other parts of the division's front across the Roer, the Germans could be observed forcing civilians to dig antitank ditches and foxholes. Enemy strong points were established on hill crests and knobs between the towns of Korrenzig and Boslar, across the river. Prisoners of war reported that they were allowed "rest periods," during which they were made to lay minefields and string wire under the watchful eyes of SS troops.

The Germans also had the advantage of observation, the eastern bank of the Roer being higher than the western bank. North of Linnich, for example, the Germans had a clear view for several miles into the rear areas of XIII Corps' front.

The combat divisions of Ninth Army had no information as to when or how they would resume the offensive. The combat infantrymen knew only that there was a constant demand for patrols to obtain information, capture prisoners, and destroy enemy positions. Ninth Army needed to identify possible crossing points, the location of enemy defenses, what troops opposed the army, where the enemy's supply routes were located and where they had major installations.

Initially, patrol attempts to cross the river had used small, three-man rubber boats. These attempts had all failed due to the rapid current of the Roer in December. It wasn't until the night of December 7–8 that a patrol succeeded in crossing the river. The patrol leader was 2nd Lieutenant Albert L. Doherty, of Company I, 407th Infantry Regiment. After receiving his orders from the 3rd Battalion commander, Doherty chose five men from Company I to accompany him. After a detailed briefing at battalion headquarters, in which the route to be taken, clothes to be worn and equipment to be carried were all explained, the objectives of the patrol were discussed. The patrol was to determine the firmness of the ground and its suitability to hold armored vehicles, the use being made of the enemy trenches and what types of guns were within those defenses, what type of wire the enemy had posted and any other obstacles the enemy had placed to oppose a river crossing. The briefing also included nine combat engineers from the division's 327th Engineer (Combat) Battalion's Company A, under the command of 1st Lieutenant A. B. Robertson, Jr., whose task was to ferry the infantrymen across the river. The group then went down to the river to observe the chosen routes and launching site, and determine landmarks for future reference. Each man studied the enemy shore with binoculars to familiarize himself with obstacles he would meet in the dark of the coming night.

The infantrymen returned to Company I where they ate supper and then prepared for the patrol. Each man carried a Thompson submachine gun and spare ammunition. They also carried four fragmentation and two white phosphorus hand grenades. Cartridge belts were left behind, and first aid kits normally worn on them were carried in trouser pockets. Faces were blackened and helmet chin straps, which might make noise, were removed. The Combat Engineers meanwhile prepared a 15-man, 410-pound assault boat for the crossing. They, too, were stripped of most normal equipment carried by the engineers, and were carrying only the most essential equipment. The two groups met at the old Rocrdorf bridge site, then moved up the river bank some 300 yards, struggling to carry the boat and equipment through the deep mud and thick brush.

At the selected site the engineers tied a half-inch rope to a tree and the remaining 300 feet was placed within the boat. The engineers entered the boat and picked up their oars, followed by the six infantrymen. The group launched at 1830 hours and made it halfway across the Roer before the boat slid sideways to shore. It hit the east bank, beaching itself on the right side instead of head-on as intended. The journey had taken barely five minutes and was without untoward incident. The only difficulty was that the current had carried the patrol party some 75 yards downstream from their intended landing site. The engineers immediately jumped out of the boat, covered by the infantrymen. Once the engineers had determined that there were no land mines in the vicinity, the infantrymen landed. The engineers pulled the rope line (now stretching from one shore to the other) taut. The eastern end of the rope was secured to a tree.

Private First Class Leon J. Stevens, one of the patrol members, remembered, "The first strands of barbed wire were found about five feet from the edge of the water and we cut 'em quickly."[23] The infantrymen then formed a diamond patrol formation and escorted the engineers forward, while the latter probed for mines with their bayonets. After proceeding some 15 yards and finding no mines, the engineers fell back while the infantrymen continued forward. With Lieutenant Doherty and Sergeant Charles A. Bevan in the lead, the patrol moved deeper into enemy territory. Private First Class William T. Patten remembered, "We moved very slowly and without making any noise. Several times we stopped while one or more members of the patrol investigated a foxhole or shell crater. It was very dark and as we moved forward I could barely see the other boys."[24] Patten and Staff Sergeant Robert J. Scott guarded the flanks of the patrol as it moved forward. Guarding the patrol's rear were Privates First Class Louis E. Slogowski and Leon J. Stevens.

After walking cautiously about 250 yards Doherty saw movement ahead and ordered the patrol to the ground. The patrol crawled forward and observed a group of German soldiers grouped together ahead. After a few moments, part of the enemy group dropped into a trench and the others walked away. Doherty decided they had watched a changing of outposts by the Germans. Scott recalled:

> We lay there for a few minutes not more than fifteen yards from the jerries, and then when the Lieutenant motioned we started to crawl to the north, or in the direction of the trench line we knew to be on our left. Just about then we were challenged in what I think was Bavarian, though Lieutenant Doherty later said he thought it was Italian. We were challenged again and of course no one answered. Then I saw a grenade hit Lieutenant Doherty on the backside, roll off into the blackness and explode.[25]

Bevan and Slogowski each threw a grenade in return. Another enemy grenade came sailing in, and Scott replied with one of his own. As the explosions faded away everything became very quiet. The patrol moved back several yards to find that both Doherty and Bevan were seriously injured while Scott and Stevens were slightly hurt. Doherty decided it was time to return to the boat, so he divided the group in two and directed each to take a different route. Patten recalled, "The Lieutenant told me to take Slogowski and follow, swinging to the left, because the first group [Bevan, Stevens and Scott] was told to swing to the right in their return. He said he would cover our withdrawal, but I told Lieutenant Doherty 'no soap'. We all came up together and that's the way we were going back, and that's the way it worked out."[26]

Using luminous buttons they carried with them, both groups returned safely to the boat and the waiting engineers. The return trip was more difficult than the original crossing because the boat had to be pulled back using the rope, which was hanging north to south, forcing the engineers to pull against the river's strong current. Halfway across the river, enough water had entered the boat to threaten to capsize it. Too heavy now, it began to swing around and the engineers were in danger of losing control. Slow progress continued, however, and when the boat came within a few yards of the west bank several engineers jumped into the frigid waters and pulled the boat ashore. Slogowski was rushed through knee-deep mud to a company aid station while Doherty was treated in a nearby engineer aid station. As he was undergoing treatment the Germans opened up with mortars, wounding Doherty once again (this time in the head), as well as several of the aid men. "Of the six-man patrol, three were evacuated and two others injured," Sergeant Scott stated, "but we learned a lot."[27]

Thanks to Lieutenant Doherty's patrol, the 102nd Infantry Division, and Ninth Army, now knew that the enemy trenches and foxholes were filled with water and mud and that only an outpost system of guards manned the forward line. It was also learned that the ground on the east side of the river was muddy but nevertheless could support the weight of armor. It was also learned that the ground across the river was not mined, booby-trapped or blocked by antitank obstacles. Several follow-up patrols substantiated the findings of Doherty's patrol and came back with increased intelligence of the enemy and their defenses.

*   *   *

The reduction of the forces available to Ninth Army as a result of the Battle of the Bulge was made more serious by the need to increase the area of the front covered in order to permit First Army to concentrate a counterattack force. Ninth Army's front, now extended southward to include the Hürtgen Forest and the Roer dams sector, was thinly held and reminded some of the weak front held by VIII Corps, which had invited the German offensive. The 102nd Infantry Division held the entire XIII Corps front. Where a regiment had held a section of the front at the beginning of December, by New Year's Day a battalion held the same frontage. Where the entire 113th Cavalry Group had covered a sector of the front, now only one Cavalry Reconnaissance Squadron, the 17th Cavalry, covered that same front.[28] The situation was similar within General McLain's XIX Corps front, where the 29th Infantry Division held the front lines. Ninth Army inherited the veteran 8th Infantry Division (which had fought with it in Brittany) from VII Corps when that organization turned south to aid in the Ardennes. Exhausted and depleted from intense fighting in the Hürtgen Forest and at Obermaubach, it was in need of rest and replenishment. Assigned to XIX Corps on December 22, it was of limited immediate use. Major General Edwin P. Parker Jr.'s 78th Infantry Division also joined XIX Corps on December 22, and took over a sector of the line. The 104th Infantry Division of Major General Terry de la Mesa Allen, veterans of the Peel Marshes campaign, similarly came under XIX Corps control on December 22. Like the 8th Infantry Division, these two latter divisions were left behind when VII Corps went to aid First Army. In reserve but under the control of Twenty-First Army Group, Ninth Army had assigned the 51st (British) Highland Infantry Division.

With five combat divisions on the front line and only a distant reserve available, Ninth Army remained vulnerable to an expanded German counteroffensive. This was a constant concern to the Ninth Army staff throughout the last days of December and the first weeks of January 1945. The 40-mile long front was especially vulnerable in the north, in XIII Corps' zone, which contained a road net favorable to the enemy if he chose to attack from the Heinsberg area. Intelligence officers were constantly probing for information on the strength and intentions of the enemy. With most of the normally assigned XXIX Tactical Air Command's resources diverted to First Army, the Ninth turned to the British for assistance. The British did in fact fly numerous daylight observation missions over the Ninth Army front to gather needed intelligence. They also flew night photographic and visual reconnaissance missions as planes and weather permitted, but the German New Year's Day attack on British airfields seriously curtailed this service due to the heavy losses sustained by the British Royal Air Force.

In addition to patrols such as the one described earlier, Ninth Army intelligence officers used agents to cross behind enemy lines and return with information. Several of these agents were caught or killed, but others did return with valuable information. It soon became clear from all these various sources that there was no German build up opposite Ninth Army, and therefore the likelihood of a major attack was remote, at least for the near future. The enemy forces facing Ninth Army across the Roer remained basically static. A brief scare caused by enemy infiltrators wearing American uniforms resulted in a much more security-conscious rear area, with vehicles being stopped and asking for much more than just a password. Even identity discs were insufficient. Instead, one had to know who actress Betty Grable was married to, or how the Brooklyn Dodgers had fared in the previous season.

Ninth Army continued to fortify villages behind the front. Dummy tanks were placed where enemy observers or aircraft could see them. Undeterred by the enemy infiltrators, Ninth Army Publicity and Psychological Warfare Officer Colonel Kern C. Crandall had propaganda leaflets fired into German lines and set up loudspeakers to discourage enemy soldiers, and perhaps induce them to surrender. Because hospitals in the Ardennes sector were being bombed or in one case surrounded by the enemy, Ninth Army began absorbing casualties from First Army through its own evacuation system. The welfare of the troops assigned to Ninth Army remained a primary concern, and with operations at a temporary standstill, leaves and passes to Paris and Brussels were inaugurated. Recreational facilities were expanded when possible. American Red Cross "Clubmobiles" were allowed close to the front to comfort the soldiers stationed there.

As the Battle of the Bulge wound down, attention returned to the Roer dams. Simpson was convinced that the dams needed to be seized before any crossing of the Roer could be successfully attempted. Although it did not have sufficient forces yet available, Ninth Army's staff was directed to create a plan for seizing those dams. The estimate was that a minimum of three divisions and supporting troops would be needed to accomplish that seizure. The plans were drawn up, approved, and stored for future use. The first indication that this plan might be put into effect came with a Letter of Instruction from Twelfth Army Group, issued January 4, 1945.

The Letter of Instruction ordered that First and Third Armies clear their respective areas of the bulge penetration and link up, after which the recapture of the key town of St. Vith would be accomplished. At that point, First Army would return to the control of Twelfth Army Group, from Twenty-First Army Group, under which it had been since late December. Ninth Army would continue to operate under Twenty-First Army Group. General Simpson had already discussed the possibility of Ninth Army seizing the Roer dams with both Bradley and Montgomery, but no definite plan had been agreed upon. Without definite knowledge of what forces Ninth Army would have available after the Bulge was eliminated, plans were tentative. Nevertheless, Simpson was convinced that they had to be taken, and further that a drive into the German industrial heartland of the Ruhr was essential to taking Germany out of the war. He was also well aware that the "shortest road to Berlin was across the plains of northern Germany."[29] An attack by Ninth Army was, to Simpson, the most economical way of securing jumping-off points for such a future operation, which would outflank the Siegfried Line north of the so-called Aachen Gap.

Ninth Army had long been planning for what was to become Operation *Grenade*. In early October, even as it was moving to the Maastricht area, Simpson had presented the plan to Bradley, who had found it well conceived. But the delays caused by the battles on the Roer plain and the subsequent delays of the Battle of the Bulge had put the plan on hold. By January 12, Simpson decided it was time they were reactivated. Still believing his Ninth Army was best positioned to launch a main thrust into northern Germany, he reported that given a total of twelve divisions and the appropriate supporting troops for three corps, he could launch a strong offensive which he firmly believed would carry Ninth Army all the way to the Rhine. But at Twelfth Army Group, Bradley and his staff had one serious objection. The Ninth Army plan would require the withdrawal of several combat divisions from the Prüm-Monschau front and a rapid concentration of these divisions within Ninth Army's area in order to take advantage of the German disorganization resulting from the defeat at the Ardennes. The planned main effort of Twelfth Army Group would also have to be redirected from an assault in the direction of Bonn to one north of Cologne. There were also questions raised as to exactly from where the main attack should be launched, and whether First Army would have to take over the section of the front that Ninth Army had received from it when the Battle of the Bulge began.

Simpson was determined to implement Operation *Grenade*, and he presented his plans to Montgomery. He stressed the two main advantages of his plan—shorter supply lines from the Allies' main supply port at Antwerp and the shorter route to the enemy's industrial heartland. The area's road net, the absence of large wooded areas and the opportunity to use large armored forces to exploit success were also presented as additional advantages to the plan.

As it happened, Simpson's plan slotted nicely into Montgomery's own ideas for his Twenty-First Army Group's entry into Germany. A planned attack by the First Canadian Army between the Maas and the Rhine would welcome the support of Operation *Grenade*. Montgomery forwarded Simpson's plan to Eisenhower, recommending that it be approved and that the additional forces required by Ninth Army to implement the plan be transferred to it. Eisenhower, who had been thinking along the same lines, quickly approved the plan with the proviso that Twelfth Army Group, First and Third Armies, would continue their offensive into Germany. However, should they be slowed or stopped by enemy resistance, all main efforts would be directed north to Twenty-First Army Group and Ninth Army. As a result, on January 21, Simpson received from Montgomery approval to prepare to implement Operation *Grenade*.

CHAPTER 7

Operation *Grenade*

The approval from Montgomery triggered intense preparation towards implementing the long-prearranged plans. As was the usual Ninth Army practice, Simpson and his staff held meetings with the different corps commanders and their staffs to familiarize them with the plan and the individual corps' role in each aspect of that plan. Ninth Army had a well-deserved reputation for keeping its subordinate units informed of plans and objectives well ahead of any implementation of those plans. Several combat commanders remarked on the difference between Ninth Army and First and Third Armies, where they often had to go into battle with only the sketchiest knowledge of what they were expected to do, and no knowledge of what the units on either side of them were intending. Ninth Army procedure was to inform all unit commanders of what they were to do as early as possible, as well as providing details on what neighboring units were to do, and to welcome all questions, criticisms, and suggestions for improvement.

In turn, each corps commander was required to provide Simpson with a formal estimate of his corps' situation and its own plans based upon the army plans. A final presentation of all planning was made at a meeting of all corps commanders and key army and corps staff. This guaranteed that each corps commander knew exactly what his neighboring corps was expected to do, how they were planning to do it, and on what schedule those plans were to be carried out. Once all plans had been reviewed and agreed upon, Ninth Army's staff and corps commanders "war gamed" those plans to see if they were feasible. These map exercises gave each commander an idea of the way the plan would develop and what, if any, obstacles they would have to take into consideration. Terrain difficulties, enemy troop dispositions and capabilities, and defensive lines were all considered. Since Ninth Army had been studying this ground since November (before the Battle of the Bulge postponed operations) there was little new to add to the information already gathered. Basically the terrain, road net, rail network and mutually supporting fortified villages remained unchanged. What was new, however, were the enemy defenses, which had been strengthened considerably now that the forces tied up for the Ardennes counter offensive were no longer held in reserve.

Things were different within Ninth Army as well. While in November the army was scheduled to attack in a subsidiary effort, protecting the left flank of First Army (which was assigned the main effort), in February Ninth Army was to provide the main effort while First Army would protect Ninth Army's right flank. Ninth Army would now have the shorter route to the Rhine against fewer terrain obstacles. It would attack northeast instead of the former planned direction, east. This gave the army much greater freedom of action, allowing it to maneuver to its best advantage. It would also permit it to change direction as Simpson saw fit, to take advantage of any enemy weakness.

Another important change was the absence of a threat on the northern flank. Earlier, the German forces assembling for the Ardennes counteroffensive had posed a threat to that flank should Ninth Army attempt an advance. Those forces had gone now, used up in the Battle of the Bulge. During December, the British XII Corps, under Lieutenant General Sir Neil M. Ritchie, had cleared the "Heinsberg Pocket," from which German forces had threatened an attack on Ninth Army's rear areas from that bridgehead over the Roer.[1]

A final factor that promised to make Ninth Army's advance easier was the planned attack by Lieutenant General H. D. G. ("Harry") Crerar's First Canadian Army from the north, which was expected to draw off significant German reserves between the Rhine and the Maas.[2] This depletion of the enemy's reserves was expected to make the German Army's defense much more difficult, since they would be facing two major attacks and would have to divide their reserves between them. Twenty-First Army Group would launch Operation *Veritable* (the First Canadian Army's attack), with most of its forces driving southeast along the Rhine, while Ninth Army, attacking to the northeast, could expect to meet the Canadians coming south, thus striking the Germans from two flanks. The plans were complete and ready for implementation, but first there remained the matter of the Roer dams.

*   *   *

Between September and the middle of December 1944, First Army (under General Hodges) had launched three division-sized attacks to secure the Roer dams. First Army had continually tried to reach the dams through some of the most inhospitable terrain along the border, including the Hürtgen Forest and the city of Aachen. The terrain, and sharp German defenses, stopped each attack at considerable cost to the Americans. One division after another went into the forest and came out severely depleted. None got close to the dams. Finally, in mid-December a corps-sized attack was launched. V Corps, with the 2nd and 99th Infantry Divisions, launched an attack on the dams, bypassing the forest, only to be hit by the incoming German counter offensive in the Ardennes. The two divisions turned from attacking the dams to holding the northern shoulder of the major German penetration of Allied lines.

Part of the December attack had been a subsidiary thrust from the northeast, from Monschau, along the west bank of the Roer to the key town of Schmidt, but this had not gone far when the Germans struck in the Ardennes. In February, the new V Corps commander, Major General Clarence R. Huebner, wanted to repeat the two-pronged attack plan. With V Corps' 2nd and 99th Infantry Divisions attacking from the south, Huebner wanted another division to attack from the north. The best unit for this was the southernmost division of Ninth Army, the 78th Infantry Division.

This division was activated at Camp Butner, North Carolina, on August 15, 1942. Originally designated as a Replacement Pool Division, intended to train and forward replacements to units overseas, it was soon taking part in the Carolina and Tennessee Maneuvers of 1943 and 1944. The division was sent to Camp Kilmer, New Jersey, in October 1944, for overseas shipment. Arriving in France on October 22, 1944, it was assigned to Ninth Army on November 9, and to XIX Corps on November 28. During the Ardennes battles, the division had been assigned to V Corps and VII Corps under First Army, where one of its regiments had participated in the Hürtgen Forest battles, but on December 22 the division reverted to XIX Corps. Major General Edwin Pearson Parker, Jr. commanded the division throughout its training and combat career.[3]

During the Ardennes fighting, the 78th ("Lightning") Infantry Division was assigned to hold positions near the town of Monschau, which was the furthest point reached during the early December attacks toward the dams. Still in place when First and Ninth Armies resumed the offensive after the German defeat in the Ardennes, it was the natural choice for a renewed attack to seize the dams.

The position of the 78th Infantry Division during the Ardennes counteroffensive was precarious. It held a position projecting two miles into the German lines. Under XIX Corps, it held a key road center at Konzen and the equally critical Paustenbach knoll. Surrounded on three sides, the division was ordered to hold its position. Plans to renew the attack on the dams, once the German offensive had run its course, remained in place. From December 16 to the end of January, the division fought to hold on to its territory. Like the rest of Ninth Army, the division made adjustments due to the shortage of normally available items. When most air cover went south to cover First Army, the division used its light Piper Cub observation planes to gather intelligence about the enemy facing it. When no photographic aircraft were available, the artillerymen that flew the Cubs over enemy lines took pictures themselves and set up a photographic laboratory to develop them.

The infantrymen suffered in the intense cold and snow of the 1944–45 winter. Long hours in a foxhole, wet with snow and mud, a lack of overshoes and an inability to light a fire due to enemy soldiers being only yards away, resulted in increased cases of trench foot. Despite the regular provision of clean socks, soldiers had to remove boots and socks and massage their feet regularly or suffer the consequences. The division, with the Combat Command Reserve of the 5th Armored Division in support, not only had to hold the front lines but also had to search for reported enemy paratroopers in its rear. The assignment of the 102nd Cavalry Group and the 2nd Ranger Infantry Battalion helped, but conditions remained precarious. Nor was that all. Enemy air attacks struck the 78th Quartermaster Company and 778th Ordnance Company, in the rear area town of Raeren, for three days in a row in December. The division's 303rd Engineer (Combat) Battalion laid mines and strung wire along the front lines. Litters to carry wounded men were placed on skis to facilitate moving them to aid stations. White sheets were fitted to infantrymen to make them blend in with the snow-covered landscape while on patrol. Slowly but steadily, individual enemy positions in surrounding towns were sought out and destroyed by patrols or short, sharp raids.

At the headquarters of the 2nd Battalion, 310th Infantry Regiment, on December 19, two dirty, tired, bearded and haggard-looking men suddenly appeared out of the darkness. They were members of a group of rifle companies of the battalion, which had been surrounded in the fortified town of Kesternich. A German attack had stranded 74 officers and men of Companies F, G and H in the cellar of a wrecked house. Some were wounded, others suffering from trench foot. Besides a few green apples, they had eaten nothing for four days. Trapped by the German attack when the rest of the battalion had been forced to withdraw, the men had sought shelter in the building, maintaining guards and sending out patrols to learn what was happening around them. It soon became apparent that they had been written off by their battalion. So far the Germans hadn't discovered them, and the two bedraggled men had volunteered to try and get help. It had taken them six hours of crawling to reach the battalion headquarters in Simmerath.

A rescue party was quickly organized, but the two men from Kesternich were in no condition to make a return trip. They gave directions to the rescue party, which set out as soon as it was ready. The men reached Kesternich but were unable to find the hiding survivors. Disappointed, they returned to Simmerath, thinking that the stranded men had been captured by the enemy. The next night, two more men from Kesternich showed up at battalion headquarters. Once again a rescue party went out, and this time it found the group. They returned with everyone who was able to walk or crawl (some barefoot or with feet so swollen they could not get their boots on), but 16 men, too ill to move on their own, had to be left behind. The rescue party then returned later that same night with litters to carry the disabled men to safety.

While all this was going on at the front, division headquarters studied the terrain between it and the Schwammenauel Dam. Finally, on January 28, 1945, came the orders to seize the dam. Supported by the 5th Armored Division's Combat Command A and Squadron B, Fife and Forfar Yeomanry (British) tanks, the 309th, 310th and 311th Infantry Regiments struck out for the long-awaited objective. Fortified town after town fell to the advancing "Lightning" Division. Konzen, Imgenbroich, Belgengacher, Eicherscheid, Kesternich and others fell after heavy fighting. Tank losses to mines increased, but still the advance continued. Finally, on February 4, the final attack on Schmidt and the dam commenced. Schmidt fell, for the last time, on February 7 and Schwammenauel Dam was taken on February 9. The way was clear for Operation *Grenade*.

*   *   *

General Simpson's launching of Operation *Grenade* was scheduled to begin a few days after the First Canadian Army launched Operation *Veritable*. The objective was to join hands along the west bank of the Rhine. In order to prepare for the coming offensive, Simpson had planned to narrow his army's front and build its strength up to at least 10 divisions. When the boundary between First and Ninth Army had been moved north after the Ardennes battle, Ninth Army was left with just two corps, XIII and XIX Corps. It also had but two divisions—the 29th Infantry Division holding XIX Corps' front and the 102nd Infantry Division holding that of XIII Corps. Other divisions, including the 2nd Armored, 5th Armored and 8th Armored Divisions, were being held behind the front lines.[4]

Adjustments in planning still had to be made. Originally the British Second Army was to have forced a crossing of the Maas, near Venlo, and seized that town. A key communications center, Venlo was vital for future operations deeper into Germany. But it was realized that the British army did not have sufficient resources for that operation. Furthermore, in the plan for Operation *Grenade*, XVI Corps of Ninth Army would outflank Venlo to the east, thus making a direct attack on the city unnecessary. A new army boundary needed to be set as well. This was eventually decided to be an area from just south of Jülich to the Erft River bend at Harff, and then along the Erft to where it joined the Rhine. This was exactly what Simpson wanted—a narrow base, less than seven miles wide, from which to launch his offensive. The city of Aachen, in the rear of both First and Ninth Armies, then became a matter of some dispute. Both armies desired the road net centered on Aachen for their own supply and administrative services. The matter was relayed to Bradley at Twelfth Army Group. In true Solomon (but decidedly unmilitary) style, Bradley divided the city in half, giving Ninth Army the northern half and First Army the southern half. The launch date for Operation *Grenade* was set as February 15.

As usual in military operations, things changed quickly. The opening of the Canadian attack on February 8 made it necessary for Ninth Army to move up its attack date to February 10—any further delay would lose the advantages of a double-pronged attack against the enemy. Suggestions that a heavy bomber strike begin the offensive were rejected by Simpson for two reasons. First, it would require that the attack begin in daylight, to allow the bombers to see their targets. This was in direct contradiction to the infantry leaders, who desired to begin the attack in darkness as additional protection for their men. Second, such an attack would

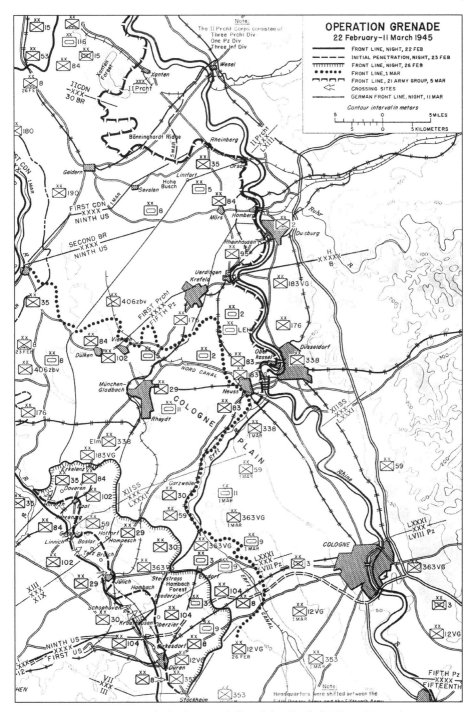

Operation *Grenade*. (U.S. Army, Office of the Chief of Military History)

require the withdrawal of the front line units behind a safety zone 3,000 yards from the banks of the Roer. This, too, was unacceptable to the infantry, as it would leave them exposed as they covered the 3,000 yards of open terrain back to the west bank of the Roer and only then begin to launch their boats. Further, Simpson wanted as much of the element of surprise as he could possibly obtain, and a bombing strike would compromise that for his attacking troops.

The targets of the initial assault were the towns of Linnich and Jülich, each of which controlled a useful road net. An initial bridgehead would include both towns, allowing a buildup before exploitation would begin. This would also place Ninth Army atop a plateau, with all other objectives downhill from there. Simpson was also adamant that the assault force would have no less than one division in reserve, under Ninth Army control. Simpson designated the reserve as an exploitation force should a breakthrough occur during the assault or, secondly, to be available in the event one of the assault divisions became exhausted and needed to be replaced quickly. In such a case the relieved division would become Ninth Army's reserve. With the situation of the Roer dams still uncertain at this point, Simpson also insisted that the assault force assigned to the initial river crossing consist of no less than four infantry divisions. He believed that if a sufficient forcefrom the four assault divisions could be established on the east bank of the Roer, then any counterattack the Germans were likely to launch could be beaten off. Anything less than four divisions risked defeat in detail.

Each corps commander was ordered to provide a plan to deal with such a counterattack. In case Ninth Army found itself flooded by the Germans releasing water from the dams, plans were established for re-supply via airdrop. Bridging equipment, and the troops to use it, were placed on alert for the same contingency. A three-day supply of food, ammunition and other supplies was stockpiled near the front, while amphibious vehicles and landing craft were made available to the assault corps. XXIX Tactical Air Command was informed and included in all of these plans. It was tasked with maintaining air superiority, isolating the battlefield, and providing close air support for the attacking divisions. General Nugent believed that the German Air Force could put up no more than 300 fighters in Ninth Army's zone of action, including perhaps 75 of their new jet fighters. Another 350 night fighters might be used during daylight hours if the Germans were pressed. Against this force, Nugent could provide 300 fighter-bombers of his own XXIX Tactical Air Command and an unknown number of aircraft from the neighboring IX Tactical Air Command of First Army.

The assembling of the strike force began in mid-January. Although only promised 10 of the 12 divisions he had originally asked for, Simpson was pleased that the delays forced upon the execution of Operation *Grenade* had allowed SHAEF to fulfill his original request. XIX Corps would have three infantry and one armored division to begin its attack, while General Gillem's XIII Corps would have two infantry and one armored division. Major General John B. Anderson's new XVI Corps would also contain two infantry and one armored divisions.[5] One infantry division was "on loan" to the British Second Army and another infantry division was in Ninth Army reserve.[6]

Each corps had, in addition to its assigned armored division, the normal complement of tanks assigned by Ninth Army to the American infantry divisions at this stage of the war—a tank battalion and a tank destroyer battalion. A total of 1,394 tanks was therefore available to each of the attacking corps. There were also 130 battalions of field artillery available to support the assault, or one artillery piece for each ten yards of front. There was also the usual assortment of antiaircraft artillery, infantry cannon and supporting mortars. Three million gallons of gasoline were stored in preparation for the rush to the Rhine. After being under severe ammunition restrictions for the winter months, Ninth Army now had some 46,000 tons, about twenty days' supply, stored in preparation for the coming attack. A sudden thaw in the weather turned the roads in Ninth Army's sector to mud, slowing some troop movements and delaying the delivery of supplies, but Ninth Army was ready to strike.

*   *   *

The army faced two river crossings (over the Roer and Erft) and two large forested areas before it would reach the Rhine. Because of some remaining Siegfried Line defenses, which remained intact near Heinsberg, that area was excluded as a crossing site. The second forest, Hambach Forest, was just southeast of one of the main objectives, the city of Jülich. Ninth Army would have to clear that forest to make a successful crossing. The status of the Roer dams was still a question, as when the attack was launched they were still in German hands. To be prepared in case the Germans released a flood in their path, Ninth Army planners chose the narrowest sectors of the Roer to launch their crossings.

The Erft cuts across the Cologne plain, dividing it almost in half, and presenting other problems for Ninth Army. The river was followed in its course by the Erft Canal. Neither was a serious military obstacle, but the muddy terrain surrounding both could delay progress of both front-line and supply forces. It also provided a natural line for whichever side was on the defensive. Simpson looked at it as a natural form of protection for his northern flank.

The biggest city in Ninth Army's path was München-Gladbach, a textile center with the suburban town of Rheydt nearly contiguous to it. The prewar population was about 310,000 but the value to Ninth Army was its road centers, which complemented those at Düren and Jülich. Intelligence reported that the enemy had prepared extensive field fortifications in the area, building three lines of defense. The first ran along the Roer itself. The second was six miles further east, and the third five miles east of that. Once again the defenses were centered on fortified towns and villages. Mines, barbed wire and antitank defenses dotted the plain, but American intelligence officers reported that, while the defenses themselves were strong, there were too few enemy troops to man them adequately. The estimate was that Ninth Army faced 30,000 enemy troops, supported by 70 tanks. Another 23,500 men and 110 tanks were believed to be in reserve near Cologne. A further 17,000 men and 55 tanks were reportedly in distant reserve.

The closer Ninth Army came to the actual attack, the more Simpson believed that the enemy strength facing his Ninth Army was less than reported. He noted, for example, that the Fifth Panzer Army was still tied up in the Eifel region below his area. His estimate of the situation was summed up with the comment, "We will have some tough fighting, but I think we are going right through."[7] His optimism was strengthened when the First Canadian Army launched Operation *Veritable* on February 8. Immediately, intelligence reports indicated that the Germans were rushing reserves to block the Canadians and British. Some of those reserves came from the force based near Cologne. By the end of the first week of the Canadians' crushing attack, an infantry division, two parachute divisions, the 15th Panzer Grenadier Division and the 116th Panzer Division had been drawn to the Canadian front. Later the elite Panzer Lehr Division was also identified fighting the Canadians.

This movement of enemy troops temporarily confused the American intelligence community. With all of the identified enemy armored formations facing the Canadians, was it possible that the enemy had left none to face the obviously imminent attack of Ninth Army? With all those veteran units shifting north, Ninth Army would outnumber its opponents by at least five to one. Unknown to the Americans, however, were the actions of Hitler, who had ordered Field Marshal Gerd von Rundstedt, commanding Army Group B, to assemble the Sixth Panzer Army and send it to the Eastern Front. Against the coming threat of a Roer crossing, Army Group H would have to defend the Roer Plain with the remaining Fifth Panzer Army and Fifteenth Army. Under Fifth Panzer Army, *General der Panzertruppen* Walter Krueger's LVIII Panzer Corps would have three armored divisions positioned immediately behind the Roer. Gasoline shortages, thaws that turned highways to mud and a limited rail net made the concentration of LVIII Panzer Corps slow and difficult. Allied aircraft and bomb-damaged routes added to the misery.

Von Rundstedt understood his situation. As commander of Army Group B, he reported that on average each of his infantry battalions was facing two-thirds of an American division. Reserves could not be moved quickly, nor were enough available. Additional American forces were expected to arrive on the front once the attack began and the artillery ammunition supply was insufficient. The attacks by First Canadian Army south from Nijmegen and First Army's attack into the Eifel had seriously disrupted the attempt to strengthen the Roer line. Even Krueger's LVIII Panzer Corps had to be committed earlier than expected. Facing what was to be Ninth Army were three German corps headquarters, with two infantry divisions each. Army Group B had only the 9th Panzer Division, held near the Roer at Jülich, and the arriving 11th Panzer Division, as reserves. Neither of these units was at full strength. The total of tanks and assault guns in all of Army Group B numbered only 276.

Although Simpson had declined an aerial bombardment to launch Operation *Grenade*, he understood that his attack was expected by the enemy. To further enhance his infantrymen's chance of success, he orchestrated an opening barrage of more than 2,000 artillery guns to announce the launching of his offensive. Still optimistic about the coming attack, Simpson issued orders to his corps commanders that while they were to act as if they expected organized resistance throughout the Cologne plain, "If the violence of our attack should cause disruption of the enemy resistance, each corps will be prepared to conduct relentless pursuit in zone, and phases will be abandoned in favor of taking full advantage of our opportunity."[8]

The scheduled attack date, February 10, was necessarily delayed when the Germans destroyed the discharge valves on the Roer dams, raising the water to prohibitive levels. Not only did the water rise, but the current increased sharply, at some points to more than 10 miles per hour—no Allied amphibious craft could fight such a current. Near Linnich, where the river is normally 30 yards wide, it grew to more than a mile in width. Ninth Army now had a lake facing it.

Simpson quickly conferred with his engineers. Advised that the river would subside when the reservoirs were drained, on or about February 24, he ordered the assault rescheduled to begin on February 23. By that date the river had dropped more than a foot and the current had decreased to no more than six miles per hour. Believing he now had a reasonable chance of crossing successfully, Simpson launched Operation *Grenade*. As was his custom, he "… ordered Operation *Grenade* launched the next morning; he then watched Bing Crosby in *Going My Way*, tossed down a nightcap, and went to bed."[9]

*   *   *

As darkness fell on February 22, the men of Ninth Army began to move forward to the Roer. Engineers brought up boats and bridging equipment to the river's edge. Artillerymen made sure that they only fired the usual harassing night missions. In fact, the Germans knew that an attack was coming but their attention remained focused on the ongoing offensives by the First Canadian Army and Third U.S. Army at Trier.[10] It wasn't until the American artillery began its preliminary barrage, at 0245 hours on the morning of February 23, that their attention turned back to the Ninth Army zone. The huge barrage announced the launching of six American divisions across the Roer.

Major General Bolling's 84th Infantry Division, of XIII Corps, was one of the leading units in the offensive. Following six weeks of bitter fighting in the Ardennes, the division had returned to Ninth Army on February 3. Occupying basically the same sector it had held before heading south, the division was painfully familiar with the area. Tired and in need of rest, the delay in the attack had provided an opportunity to rest, re-equip and plan for the next operation.

Now, in addition to its own 309th Engineer (Combat) Battalion, the division had Ninth Army's 171st Engineer (Combat) Battalion attached for the Roer crossings. The 309th would carry the assault troops across the river in assault boats, while the 171st was responsible for taking and maintaining bridges over the Roer. Because of the swollen state of the river, the crossing point was limited to a former bridge site, which could accommodate only one battalion at a time. The 84th Infantry Division would cross in this fashion—the first battalion would cross in two assault waves, with two infantry companies and 35 boats in each wave. As soon as possible, footbridges were to be installed to speed the arrival of follow-up troops. The first men to cross would be Company B, 334th Infantry Regiment, reinforced with two platoons of Company A, 309th Engineers.

Patrols, prisoners and air reconnaissance had revealed many enemy defenses on the east bank. An engineer platoon was tasked with bringing special equipment (including an R4 tractor, prefabricated Treadway bridge parts, a jeep and a trailer) across the river as soon as possible.[11] Plans called for three footbridges at Linnich, and heavier bridges were to be constructed as soon as the site was secured. Preparations for the bridges, begun before the actual assault, had been dangerous. As Lieutenant John Coester of the 171st Engineers was leading a patrol clearing a minefield at a planned bridge site, he set off a "Schu" mine and was severely wounded. The noise also attracted a storm of enemy fire from across the river, and his patrol was pinned to the ground. First Lieutenant David H. Gibson, of Company B, 309th Engineers, crawled forward, cleared a path through the minefield, treated Lieutenant Coester's injuries and dragged him to safety.

General Bolling set the order for the crossing. The two engineer battalions would be the first across, followed by the 334th Infantry Regiment. The 335th Infantry was next, followed in order by a battalion of the division artillery, the 84th Quartermaster Company (with 50 trucks of supplies), the rest of the division artillery, the 638th Tank Destroyer Battalion, the 771st Tank Battalion and the 333rd Infantry Regiment. The division's military police platoon was responsible for the orderly passage of all these units across the river.

The 334th Infantry and the engineers trained for the crossing on the Würm River. The First battalion would lead the assault, and it drilled in both day and night conditions, as did the Third Battalion, scheduled to cross next. The Second Battalion had only one rehearsal, since it was thought it would be able to cross over footbridges. The delay caused by the flooding of the river allowed additional training, which gave time for a detailed crossing to be ingrained in the troops.

The "Railsplitters" were to seize a bridgehead around the town of Linnich. Supported by the fire of the 333rd Infantry Regiment on the west bank, the two assault regiments would cross and seize a series of towns around which the bridge-head would be formed. A smoke screen would cover the assault. Two feints made on previous nights were hoped to instill a sense of complacency in the enemy. Prisoners later reported that the ruse had worked—with no attack after two scares, the enemy soldiers had relaxed their vigilance by the third night. The engineers and the First Battalion, 334th Infantry, moved down to the river's edge, opposed by only occasional bursts of enemy machine gun fire. The assault boats were picked up and carried to the river. One of the men, Private First Class Leroy Carver of C Company, 334th Infantry, remembered, "I was thinking about home that morning. It was no place for kids there on the river bank. There were too damn many bullets and too much artillery to suit me."[12]

Simpson's massive artillery barrage began, aided by smaller units such as the 557th Antiaircraft Artillery Battalion, which fired more than 275,000 rounds of thirty-caliber ammunition that morning. Crews of the 771st Tank Battalion fired so much and for so long that many crews became sick from the constant fumes within their vehicles. So intense was the barrage that Technical Sergeant George H. Hale of Company C, 334th Infantry, reported that it "was so heavy that as we approached the water to man the boats, we were nearly shocked ourselves."[13] Initially, the only tense moment came when First Lieutenant Eugene R. Giddens, the leading engineer guide, was wounded and a pause for direction occurred. Three engineer officers were quickly sent forward, but by the time they arrived everything had been sorted out and the crossing was well under way.

Companies A and C, 1st Battalion, 334th Infantry, along with the engineers, entered the river at 0330 hours that morning. "I really don't know whether the enemy fired any shots at us or not," remembered 1st Lieutenant Richard Hawkins of Company A. "Our own guns going off all around us… drowned out all other sounds."[14] That the Germans were indeed contesting the attack was noted by Technical Sergeant Hale, who noted, "Going across we received a few 88s and mortars. There were no small arms, except one machine gun which got three men in one of our boats."[15] The strong current pushed the assault boats downstream some 75 yards from their intended landing site. This made the return of these assault boats to the other bank, where they were to pick up the next wave, much more difficult than expected.

Engineers began working on three footbridges as soon as the first wave left the western bank. The first bridge was nearly completed when German troops opened fire with automatic weapons, making it impossible to anchor the bridge on the east bank. Another was knocked out when an assault boat, pushed by the current, smashed into it. The third bridge was also near completion when an enemy artillery shell cut its cable, sending it drifting. As a result, the follow-up battalion had to cross using the few assault boats that had managed to get back across the river. It wasn't until noon that a footbridge was firmly established by the engineers and then follow-up troops were rushed across while the engineers turned to building vehicle bridges.

A light vehicle bridge was in place by mid-afternoon and a heavy Treadway bridge was opened but soon closed when German aircraft bombed and strafed it, causing damage. The "Railsplitters" would get no tank support on D-Day.

Once across, the combat troops dropped their rubber life belts and raced ahead about 400 yards for a railroad track, an intermediate objective. Here the disrupted platoons and companies organized themselves again before pushing forward. "What the boys were most afraid of was the expected minefields across the river,"[16] remembered Technical Sergeant Harry L. Peiffer of Company A. This fear was well founded, for the east bank had several minefields, but as 1st Lieutenant Hawkins soon discovered, most were harmless: "We went right through a field full of stake mines but all the trip wires attached to the mines had been cut by our artillery and mortars, and not one of the mines exploded in spite of the fact that some of the boys even stumbled over the mines themselves."[17]

General Keating's 102nd Infantry Division was on the right of XIII Corps and upstream from Linnich. In this sector two regiments made the assault. Here too, fire from the east bank was slight, in part because Keating had sent a patrol across the river half an hour before H-Hour with orders to knock out any enemy defenses found close to the river. The patrol, known as "Buck Rogers's Night Raiders"[18] and commanded by 1st Lieutenant Roy Rogers, knocked out four enemy machine guns facing the 407th Infantry Regiment. The 405th Infantry Regiment lost several assault boats due to enemy mortar fire, but the rubber life belts prevented any men from drowning. Here again the current was the main opponent. As the second wave arrived on the west bank they found only two assault boats available for the crossing. Others had been swept away. A search turned up a few more, and the follow-up battalion began crossing, one company at a time. Engineers from the 327th and 279th Engineer (Combat) Battalions manned what boats they could find and continued with the crossings.

The division's initial crossings at Roerdorf were completed before dawn. At Linnich, where less opposition was encountered, the initial crossing was completed even earlier. The Infantry advanced easily against sporadic opposition, and soon had 160 enemy prisoners on the way to the rear. German machine gun and mortar fire caused some brief delays, but soon Gevenich was in American hands. Ammunition was brought forward by each regiment's ammunition and pioneer platoon. Battalion aid stations were quickly established along the river bank, but progress was threatened in mid-afternoon when the Germans launched a counterattack on the town of Glimbach, with tanks and infantry. Like the neighboring 84th Infantry Division, the 102nd had not yet received any tank or tank destroyer support because no bridges had yet been built. The only antitank defense was provided by the antitank platoon of 2nd Lieutenant Louis Spitzer, which had already acquired three abandoned German 75mm field guns. These were being used to knock out enemy machine gun positions and other targets of opportunity.

Artillery support was greatly aided by such actions as that of 1st Lieutenant Irving R. Nelson, of the 379th Field Artillery Battalion, who went out alone 500 yards ahead of the infantry to locate and destroy enemy gun positions after his entire observation party became casualties. His Silver Star was matched by that of 1st Lieutenant Hyman Rabinovitz of Company F, 405th Infantry Regiment, who repeatedly exposed himself to aid wounded men in his command and personally evacuated them to waiting boats for medical treatment. He had to personally recover many of those boats, under enemy artillery and mortar fire, in order to bring them to where they could be used to evacuate wounded.[19]

The counterattack on Glimbach was stopped in its tracks by eight battalions of American artillery, called down from across the river. To ensure success, P-47 Thunderbolt fighters of XXIX Tactical Air Command added their weight to the destruction. The 2nd Battalion, 407th Infantry Regiment, spent the rest of a quiet afternoon in Glimbach.

Back at the river, engineers were still struggling to get their bridges placed. The first footbridge was knocked out by German artillery. A second was so heavily shelled that the infantry could not use it and eventually a tree fell on it, severing its cable link to the far shore. It would not be until midday that a useable footbridge was in place. Soon after, a company of the 407th Infantry crossed, towing 57mm antitank guns, before this bridge was also knocked out by enemy artillery.

Concern began to grow that the failure to get a sturdy bridge across the river was delaying antitank and tank support, leaving the infantry exposed on the far bank. The action at Glimbach indicated that the enemy was massing for a counterattack and this was confirmed by prisoner interrogations. Keating ordered every antitank gun rushed across the available bridges while the engineers concentrated on getting a Treadway bridge operational. This they managed to do, and a company of tank destroyers was about to cross it when three low-flying German planes knocked the bridge out. Undeterred, the engineers put in a second bridge just before nightfall, having to haul tons of rubble across the river to build up its eastern bank to accommodate the bridge. It wasn't until after dark that the first American tank destroyers of the 771st Tank Destroyer Battalion reached the far side. Lieutenant Colonel Robert N. Anderson, commanding the 317th Engineer (Combat) Battalion, earned his Silver Star for remaining on the bridges to direct his men despite the heavy enemy fire, and rallying his men time after time to complete the job. Not far away, Colonel William L. Rogers, commanding Ninth Army's 1141st Engineer (Combat) Group also earned a Silver Star for exposing himself time and again under intense artillery, rocket and mortar fire to ensure that the job of the Ninth Army engineers was completed.[20]

Company L, 406th Infantry Regiment, felt the enemy counterattack first. Strong patrols probed its positions around the town of Boslar. The 1st Battalion of Colonel Bernard F. Hurless' 406th Infantry was rushed forward to reinforce the town's defenses. Shortly before midnight, an enemy platoon attacked but was quickly repulsed. Then came a stronger attack, supported by self-propelled guns of the German 341st Assault Gun Brigade, which managed to penetrate into the outskirts of Boslar during the night. Heavily supported by artillery, the Americans defeated the German infantry and, without infantry support, the enemy assault guns withdrew. Nevertheless, probing attacks continued, with such ferocity that at one point American artillery was actually directed on Boslar in order to keep the Germans out. The Americans would later report that seven counterattacks were made against the town before the enemy withdrew for good. Lieutenant Colonel Eric E. Bischoff, of the 405th Infantry, would later describe that evening as one of "indescribable confusion."[21]

Still the struggle went on. Lieutenant Colonel Leroy E. Frazier, commanding the 3rd Battalion, 405th Infantry, led his men through dense minefields and personally directed the movements of his assault units. For his leadership he received a Distinguished Service Cross.[22] When Company F, 405th Infantry, was scattered by a heavy enemy barrage, Technical Sergeant James L. Hansen, leader of the first platoon, reorganized his men and then went personally to knock out the enemy gun crew that had halted his company's advance. Returning to his men, he then led a furious and well-conceived attack that resulted in his unit seizing its objective. He, too, earned a Distinguished Service Cross and promotion to 2nd Lieutenant.[23] At Boslar, Staff Sergeant Kenneth L. Wheatcroft and Private James S. Brown of Company K, 405th Infantry, remained in an exposed position during the enemy counterattack and fought off repeated attacks, repeatedly forcing the enemy infantry to withdraw. They both received Silver Stars.[24] Actions such as these and many others ensured that XIII Corps had crossed the Roer to stay.

*   *   *

Two miles to the south, upstream along the Roer, General McLain's XIX Corps faced many of the same obstacles. Here, General Gerhardt's 29th Infantry Division was to cross around Jülich, while General Hobbs' 30th Infantry Division crossed three miles upstream. Both faced their own problems. In the zone of Gerhardt's 29th Infantry, north of Jülich, where the 115th Infantry Regiment would cross, no bridges were planned because the river had expanded to more than 400 yards in width. Instead, after the far shore was secured, engineers would build bridges at Jülich itself. In the zone of the 175th Infantry Regiment, the other assault team, bridges would be put in as soon as possible, since here the high banks of the river favored bridge installation. Just 30 minutes before the friendly artillery barrage ceased, two patrols of 25 men each were sent across the river in assault boats to secure bases from which the engineers could secure a bridge once the crossings had been completed. Under cover of smoke, the engineers would anchor their bridges on these east bank sites.

The attempt to secure bridge-landing sites in advance of the main attack was only partially successful. One of the two teams made it across despite enemy machine gun fire, while the second team's boat capsized and another was washed downstream by the current. But the one success was enough for the engineers, who completed a footbridge in less than an hour after the main assault began. A brief delay was caused by undetected minefields on the west bank, which knocked out a tank that in turn blocked an access road to the river. A Landing Vehicle, Tracked (LVT) also hit a mine and blocked a column of LVTs behind it. The infantry were ordered to instead use the assault boats to cross, which they did after a 20-minute delay. The LVTs soon found a bypass and joined in the river crossings. Long-range German machine gun fire covered the footbridge throughout the morning, causing some casualties but not stopping the crossings. Enemy artillery strikes on an uncompleted Treadway bridge forced the engineers to move the bridge site a few hundred yards further upstream, where it was blocked from enemy vision by the houses in Jülich. Tanks and bulldozers began crossing the river in mid-afternoon.

Supported by the 90mm guns of the 702nd Tank Destroyer Battalion, the assault companies of the 2nd Battalion, 115th Infantry Regiment, assembled at Koslar for the river crossing. Nearby, the 3rd Battalion did the same at Hasenfeld Gut. German plastic mines caused delays despite the fact that the area had been swept earlier. The leading company, Captain Arthur Lawson's Company L, loaded into LVTs at Koslar while, nearby, Captain Mark Hogan's Company I dragged heavy assault boats down to the water's edge. Captain Robert Armstrong's Company K moved up and waited to use the assault boats when they returned after leaving Company L on the east bank. Tanks from Company A, 747th Tank Battalion, moved up in support. It was one of these tanks that hit a mine and blocked the road for a time. Nevertheless, Company I reported itself across the river and reorganized before dawn.

In fact, Company I was between the Roer and the small canal which ran just east of the river at this point. Attempts to cross the 10 yards were foiled when it was discovered that the waters of the canal were well over the heads of the infantrymen, and felling a nearby tree failed to provide the hoped-for bridge. Determined to force a crossing of the annoying canal, Staff Sergeant Edward Lancione and Private First Class Stanley Dombroski crawled out to the end of the fallen tree, then swam the rest of the way across. Once over, they acquired some more wood and were able to assist the rest of their company to cross the canal.

Meanwhile, Companies K and L crossed and began their own advances. Shortly after daylight, two platoons of Company I under 1st Lieutenants John Westman and Roy Webb reached the main Jülich–Broich road, where they were stopped by strong enemy machine gun and artillery fire. Minefields claimed 13 members of Lieutenant Ralph Harris' 3rd Platoon, but prisoners captured soon revealed the locations of the German minefields and progress became less costly.

Upstream, General Hobbs' veteran 30th Infantry Division had sent a patrol across the river before the artillery barrage began. The patrol, from the 119th Infantry Regiment, landed near the village of Schophoven and provided a screen behind which the engineers began to build their bridge just as the artillery fire began. Using assault boats, the engineers dragged prefabricated duckboard bridges across the river, which were to be used to cross the Muhlenteich Canal beyond the Roer. Under cover of the artillery, the 119th Infantry raced across the river and canal with little difficulty. Covered by the guns of the 531st Antiaircraft Automatic Weapons Battalion, which fought off six or eight enemy air attacks, one wing of the 30th Infantry Division was safely across the river.

A few hundred yards upstream from the 119th Infantry, the other assault force, the 120th Infantry Regiment, was having much more difficulty. During the night preceding the assault, a patrol had discovered that the current in this area was still too swift for the assault boats to make a successful crossing. Instead, the engineers had to come up with a plan to construct two cable ferries in order to get the troops across the river. Physical obstacles allowed only one such ferry to be built before the artillery barrage began. Just before that, Company G had managed, with great difficulty, to pull themselves across the half-mile wide river in small pneumatic boats. Wooden assault boats also were successfully used. When the time came for the full assault to begin, only part of one infantry company was across the river. Mortar fire began to fall, adding to the 120th Infantry's difficulties.

The engineers resorted to their last option. A group of LVTs had been held in reserve for the planned Rhine crossing. They were under restriction that they were not to be used at the Roer unless in case of an emergency. Hobbs recognized an emergency when he saw one and, with Simpson's approval, the LVTs were ordered forward. Company F, which had undergone brief training on using the LVTs, was ordered to use them to cross the river. Joining Company G, they soon found themselves in a "perfect hell"[25] of booby traps and anti-personnel mines. A total of 75 men fell to these defenses and for a moment disorganization threatened to halt the advance.

But it did not. Companies F and G, soon joined by Company E, continued to move east and secured the towns of Krauthausen and Selhausen. The company-sized garrisons in each town put up what the Americans later described as weak resistance. The sole strong point at the railroad station in Krauthausen was overcome by companies E and G by mid-morning. Follow-up battalions began to arrive and cleared German positions behind the first line of river defenses. By mid-afternoon the 3rd Battalion, 120th Infantry, had cleared the initial bridgehead zone within the 30th Infantry Division's area. Using searchlights (aimed at the clouds to reflect light on the ground), the regiment launched a night attack with the 3rd Battalion, 119th Infantry, and 1st Battalion, 120th Infantry, clearing the last of the remaining enemy defenses.

Behind the advancing infantry, the engineers were still struggling with the river. Four attempts to bridge it had failed. Covered by Ninth Army's 83rd Smoke Generator Company, the engineers cleared debris, built approaches for bridges, crossed bogs and worked in the ice-cold water to get the bridges in place. At one point, 150

German prisoners and dozens of American and German wounded were awaiting transportation back across the river. With no bridge, they were stuck under fire on the east bank. The engineers proposed to the unwounded Germans that they help them with the construction. Under the rules of the Geneva Convention, the prisoners could not be forced to work on the bridge, but all of them quickly volunteered and began hauling logs and planks, installing a bridge within 35 minutes of starting. Only 150 yards away, the battle was still raging in Krauthausen.

*   *   *

In XIII Corps' zone, the 84th Infantry Division continued to make good progress on its first day across the Roer. The division's 334th Infantry Regiment had been fortunate in that it had landed at the boundary of a German corps. Hitting the north flank of the 59th Infantry Division of LXXXI Corps, the Americans took the enemy by surprise and seized the key village of Koerrenzig even before daylight. The 1st Battalion turned north to clear the east bank of the Roer facing the waiting XVI Corps of General Anderson. As it did so, it unintentionally began to roll up the flank defenses of the neighboring 183rd Infantry Division of XII SS Corps. Rurich was cleared in under an hour, and so swift was the advance that artillery officers voiced their disappointment when the infantry called to cancel planned artillery strikes on the town, saying, "Don't bother. We're in already."[26] By dark, the advance elements were approaching the crossroads of Baal and its nearby village.

The 3rd Battalion, 334th Infantry, now came up to assist in the drive north. The battalion advanced on Baal, with Company K on the left, Company L on the right and Company I in reserve. As the battalion moved forward, a seemingly innocent haystack some 300 yards from a large chateau on the right suddenly opened up with machine gun fire. The concealed pillbox forced a brief withdrawal by Companies L and K, but mortars soon turned the haystack into a blazing inferno, forcing the defenders out and into retreat. The advance resumed, facing a patch of woods. For the first time that day, the enemy was prepared. The woods contained an enemy force that had been dispatched from Baal to Rurich. Spotting the advancing Americans, they took cover among the trees.

The enemy force consisted of a battalion of infantry from the 183rd Infantry Division, supported by four tanks or assault guns and six armored personnel carriers. As the Americans approached, their scouts spotted the enemy and soon artillery and P-47 Thunderbolts from the XXIX Tactical Air Command were called in to deal with them. The survivors quickly pulled out towards Baal as darkness fell. The 3rd Battalion approached Baal, then called in the usual artillery support for 10 minutes—a relatively easy occupation of the town followed. The 84th Infantry Division was now three and a half miles inland from Linnich and had two full infantry regiments within its bridgehead.

The infantry in Baal was still in the process of organizing a defense when three enemy tanks, which had inadvertently been bypassed in the woods, struck Company L from the rear (a party of 30 German prisoners being escorted to the rear was freed by this attack). Thinking the tanks were friendly, some Company L riflemen tried to warn them, only to be cut down. Then enemy machine guns, until then concealed along a railroad embankment, opened fire. Under cover of this fire, the tanks rolled through Baal and exited towards Granterath. Things quieted down, but the men of the 334th Infantry remained on edge.

Their nervousness proved justified. Shortly before midnight, three enemy infantry battalions and three assault guns launched a counterattack against Baal. The 343rd and 330th Volks Grenadiers, along with the 176th Fusilier Battalion, each attacked the town from different directions. One thrust was halted immediately by artillery fire, but the others struck Companies K and L. Lieutenant William Nelson, commanding Company L's 2nd platoon, recalled:

> Enemy bullets began pounding the rear of the building. Germans seemed to be everywhere but in the dark they could not be spotted. Machine gun and BAR fire held the attackers back but our ammunition ran low. The situation became so critical that there was nothing left to do but to call down artillery on that very spot. I had no radio communications so I sent runners to the company CP, but they never got there. Lucky for us, the company commander had received word from somewhere else that there was trouble and he called for artillery on the underpass. For an hour the underpass was shelled and my platoon sweated it out in our house which was only 25 yards away.[27]

The artillery fire broke the attack. Soon Lieutenant Nelson's men heard Germans calling out to surrender, and small groups began coming into the platoon with raised hands. Soon the 2nd Platoon had some 25 Germans stuffed into the cellar of their house. The rest of Company L and Company K had much the same experience. As dawn approached, three German tanks and some infantry again came down the road from Granterath towards Nelson's 2nd Platoon. The enemy force stopped before the overpass, just 500 yards from Nelson's position. With ammunition nearly exhausted, the Americans were understandably concerned, but the Germans waited there for over an hour, each side watching the other. Just as dawn broke over Baal, the Germans withdrew.[28] Another counterattack against the 3rd Battalion, 335th Infantry, at Rurich, was halted by heavy small-arms fire and dispersed.

The most dangerous counterattack against Ninth Army's Roer bridgehead came against the 407th Infantry, 102nd Infantry Division, on the south wing of XIII Corps' advance at Boslar. With the defeat of this attack, the new German Army Group B commander, Field Marshal Walter Model, began to understand the plan of Ninth Army. He moved quickly to place his reserves into position to counterattack. The 9th and 11th Panzer Divisions were assigned to Fifteenth Army, and he intended to join the two divisions for a counterattack against the flank of the advancing Americans. But the officer assigned to command this force, Lieutenant

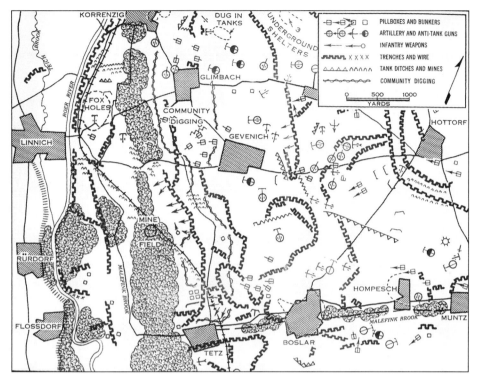

Enemy defenses east of the Roer River in the 102nd Division's Zone. (102nd Infantry Division History)

General Fritz Bayerlein, reported that only parts of both divisions had arrived and that these would be insufficient to make a strong attack. Instead, *General der Infanterie* Gustav von Zangen, commanding Fifteenth Army, sent the detachments to *General der Infanterie* Friedrich Köchling LXXXI Corps, where he believed the main American attack was directed, but their arrival could not be expected until the next day. In the interim, Köchling sent his last remaining reserves (two infantry battalions and two separate tank battalions), along with an assault gun brigade, to halt the American drive.

General Keating was aware of the German moves to counterattack his bridgehead. He placed all three of his infantry regiments on line and formed a defensive arc running through Boslar, Gevenich and Tetz at the river. Although his infantry was in place and ready, Keating still had no armored support. If the Germans fielded armored vehicles, his infantry would be hard pressed to halt them. As described, the American tanks never showed up, but the infantry defended Gevenich and Boslar successfully despite this shortcoming. Total American casualties were surprisingly low, at just 30.

To the south, VII Corps of First Army, under Major General J. Lawton Collins, forced a crossing near Düren to protect the flank of Ninth Army. General de la Mesa's

104th Infantry Division and General Weaver's 8th Infantry Division fought hard for their bridgehead. Düren was another communications hub and the two divisions were to seize it while the 4th Cavalry Group cleared the nearby Hamback Forest. The 3rd Armored Division of Major General Maurice Rose was held in reserve for exploitation. Here conditions were, if anything, worse than in Ninth Army. The Roer was still too swollen to allow bridges to be built, so all crossings were made by assault boat. Like the situation for Ninth Army, resistance facing VII Corps was spotty, in some places non-existent and in others briefly fierce. The most difficult experience was that of the 8th Infantry Division. Many of its boats were swept away, and soldiers separated from their weapons. The motors on many of the boats failed to operate and companies were split between the east and west banks by the strong current. Only one battalion crossed in reasonably good order, and only the fact that the Germans failed to counterattack the disorganized bridgehead allowed the division to pull success from near-disaster.

The river assault crossings of XIII and XIX Corps, meanwhile, had been successful, despite some hard fighting and extremely difficult engineering obstacles. At the end of the first day, Ninth Army was across the Roer to stay. Despite the great difficulties of First Army on its flank, the Ninth had established a firm bridgehead. The deep thrusts of the 84th and 102nd Infantry Divisions of XIII Corps, and the seizure of Hambach and Niederzier by the 30th Infantry Division, made it clear to Simpson that the German defensive line had been significantly breached. Next, according to the plan, was to get XVI Corps across to join the rest of Ninth Army and push north to meet the oncoming British and Canadians. In fact, so confident was Ninth Army of success, Generals Gillem and Anderson agreed that there was no need for XVI Corps to await the clearing of the east bank facing it, but that it could begin crossing on D+1.

CHAPTER 8

The Race to the Rhine

The planning for Operation *Grenade* had set D+1 as a day for consolidation of the gains made on D-Day. Despite German attacks on the vital bridges, by artillery fire and airstrikes (including some from the new jet aircraft), the follow-up plans went forward with ease. Antiaircraft gunners of Ninth Army's 55th Antiaircraft Artillery Brigade had an unusual opportunity to put their gunnery skills to work, knocking down 18 enemy planes. During that day, infantry strength on the east bank rose from 16 battalions to 38 battalions. Armored support, so eagerly sought the day before, reached all of the assault divisions. Three tank destroyer battalions, four tank battalions and eight field artillery battalions had crossed the river during the night and into the early morning hours. Seven Class 40 bridges were in place along with a dozen smaller bridges. Unit supply trains were pouring across these bridges to keep the advancing combat troops supplied. Early casualty returns for D-Day listed 92 killed, 61 missing, 913 wounded and more than 1,100 prisoners taken by the Germans.

General Simpson was anxious to turn his army to the north to begin clearing the east bank of the Roer and to link up with the British and Canadians coming down from the north. The plan called for XIII and XIX Corps to wheel north while swinging their right wings around to that direction. In doing so, each Corps would expose its right flank to the enemy. XIX Corps, which would be farthest on the right, had the most dangerous position. The delays imposed upon it in the crossing and the initial failure of VII Corps to secure the Hambach Forest (threatening XIX Corps' right flank), made these dangers more evident. Nevertheless, Simpson ordered the plan executed. He believed, correctly, that the Germans had no reserves strong enough to seriously threaten the flank of Ninth Army. Progress, particularly by Gillem's XIII Corps, had been "remarkable."

As mentioned earlier, the 9th Panzer Division had been ordered to the German Fifteenth Army as a counterattack force, but it could not concentrate until the evening of D+1. Even as it attempted to assemble for a counterattack, General von Zangen was forced to commit the division piecemeal in an effort to restore his collapsing defensive lines. The under-strength division was soon rendered impotent.

The threat of the Hambach Forest was left to the 30th Infantry Division. This division began the day with a problem at the town of Niederzier, where the Germans had emplaced two strong points with antiaircraft and antitank guns in concrete pillboxes. After the 120th Infantry Regiment cleared the area, the 117th Infantry took up the lead. Its objective was the town of Steinstrass which lay along a road to the Hambach Forest. The taking of this town was the final step before McLain at XIX Corps would have a secure bridgehead at Jülich for reinforcements and supply. Prisoner interrogations had led the Americans to believe that the garrison at Steinstrass was composed of replacement troops and rear-echelon men of the 363rd Infantry Division with little or no combat experience.

As a result of this intelligence, the 117th Infantry Regiment planned a race down the road with a task force of tanks carrying infantry, reinforced with six tank destroyers and six British flail tanks. The 2nd and 3rd Battalions were to move into Hambach Forest and clear it out. But unknown to the 117th Infantry, one of the places to which von Zangen had dispatched portions of the 9th Panzer Division was Steinstrass. Another surprise was the approximately 2,000 mines placed by the engineer battalion of the German 363rd Infantry Division.

The forested areas were cleared by American infantry relatively quickly, and soon the battalions were facing the roadblocks outside Steinstrass. Company L, the infantry element of the task force, moved forward, only to encounter three armored half-tracks carrying 20mm antiaircraft guns and protected by infantrymen. "We threw a paralyzing volume of fire at them with everything we could get our hands on—rifles, machine guns, bazookas and rifle grenades, and then made a bayonet charge," reported the Company L commander.[1] The attack succeeded in knocking out a 75mm antitank gun and three of the antiaircraft guns, but it was then halted. Three Sherman tanks of the 743rd Tank battalion came forward but were disabled by mines. One of the mine-flail tanks was then knocked out by fire from two enemy tanks hidden further up the road. Another attack cleared the roadblock but a further advance was difficult due to the hidden tanks and more antitank guns down the road.

Meanwhile, the adjacent 119th Infantry cleared out the rest of the Hambach Forest. Fears of another Hürtgen Forest were unfounded. There was no enemy artillery or tree bursts to hinder the advance and there was only a handful of German infantry within the forest. A regimental command post and 130 German soldiers, who were wandering around looking for the captured command post, were added to the prisoner-of-war enclosures. The next morning, the 119th Infantry had a "field day" shooting up retreating columns being pushed past them by the 29th Infantry Division.

Despite tanks firing at them from both flanks, the 2nd and 3rd Battalions, 119th Infantry, attacked Höllen and Rotengen, placing them northwest of Steinstrass. Along the way, Company G knocked out four enemy tanks with hand weapons. Light tanks of the newly arrived 744th Tank Battalion came up to assist in the attacks. Back in Steinstrass, the 2nd Battalion, 117th Infantry, attacked the town from the west at noon with a platoon of tanks from the 743rd Tank Battalion. But once again enemy antitank guns knocked out two tanks, forcing the others to withdraw, before the infantry continued with the attack and entered the town. Clearing Steinstrass was expedited by the arrival of the 3rd Battalion, which had raced over 500 yards of open ground from the east to engage in the house-to-house fighting that eventually cleared the town.

The Germans were not content to give up Steinstrass, however. As darkness fell, a battalion of armored infantry in six half-tracks arrived and attacked from the east, supported by tanks. The attack was pressed and American artillery was called down, breaking up the attack. A total of 74 enemy prisoners were taken within the town and two tanks and three half-tracks were knocked out. In the rear, the hidden tanks that had held up the initial advance were dealt with by the 823rd Tank Destroyer Battalion. The capture of Steinstrass opened the main supply route from the south, allowing an unhindered advance north from town to town. General McLain was pleased, and radioed General Hobbs with instructions to keep going. A combat command of the reserve 2nd Armored Division moved up to protect the division's right flank and it soon became clear that there was no longer an organized enemy defense facing XIX Corps. German prisoners soon began complaining that their supporting tanks had pulled out without permission and without notice to the infantry. Captured tank crews complained that they had been left without essential infantry support and were thus unprotected. Clearly the German defense was in disarray.

On Hobbs' right flank, the 29th Infantry Division advanced only its 175th Infantry Regiment on D+1 in order to stay abreast of the 30th Infantry Division, and to await the arrival of a new division into the line to secure the right flank of XIX Corps. That morning, a regiment of the 83rd Infantry Division was attached to the 29th Infantry Division.

*   *   *

Once again the main enemy opposition came against XIII Corps. The rapid advance of General Bolling's 84th Infantry Division, and the inability of XIX Corps to move with it, left the right flank of Keating's 102nd Infantry Division exposed. Because the Germans had expected an attack due east, they were positioned to strike at this exposed flank. This was made evident when two companies of the 701st Tank battalion moved north in advance of the 405th Infantry to the village of Hottorf. The tanks had barely begun to move when hidden antitank guns to the east opened a deadly fire. Four tanks in one company were knocked out, and eight in the other. Eight other tanks, trying to avoid this fire, became stranded in German infantry trenches. Two more failed mechanically. This left only five tanks to assist the infantry at Hottorf. So well hidden were these antitank guns that later, when the tank company commander walked the area, he found them only by stumbling into the gun pits.[2]

The infantry continued its advance. In the town of Kückhoven, 1st Lieutenant John E. Lance, the Executive Officer of Company B, 406th Infantry, led several infantrymen into the town. As they moved, Lance saw a group of Germans arranging an ambush for another column of his company. He immediately charged them, killing two and scattering the rest. When he was walking back to his command, he saw more enemy soldiers threatening the flank of an unsuspecting group of GIs and again charged alone into their midst. After killing four and dispersing the rest, he returned to his administrative duties. For his actions that day he received the Distinguished Service Cross.[3] Also in Kückhoven, Staff Sergeant Abe M. Kuzminsky of Company C deliberately exposed himself to enemy fire to locate the position of machine guns for his buddies to knock out. He succeeded at the cost of his life and was awarded a posthumous Distinguished Service Cross.[4]

When Company I, 406th Infantry, was held up in the town of Hardt by enemy machine guns, Staff Sergeant Ova I. Madsen advanced alone to knock them out. Despite being mortally wounded, he persisted in his mission until both guns were inoperative before succumbing to his wounds. He, too, earned a posthumous Distinguished Service Cross.[5] Another award of the same medal went to 1st Lieutenant Richard H. Scott of Headquarters Battery, 380th Field Artillery Battalion, who, while flying on an observation mission above the battle lines, saw a P-47 Thunderbolt fighter aircraft about to strafe a column of American troops near Glimbach. He dove his tiny liaison plane between the P-47 and the friendly ground troops and thus avoided a tragedy.[6]

In the 84th Infantry Division zone, one regiment remained in Baal while the 335th Infantry Regiment moved on to the next village. The seizure of Doveren would allow General Anderson's XVI Corps to begin its river crossings unopposed. The 84th Division began the morning auspiciously when its attached Battery C, 557th Antiaircraft Automatic Weapons Battalion, shot down two of the new ME 262 jet aircraft, which were trying to bomb the division's Treadway bridge. With this opposition removed, Company A, 771st Tank Battalion, began to cross the Roer and the first full company was across by noon. Company A immediately went to Baal and completed the mopping up at that contested village.

Doveren lay some 2,500 yards northwest of Baal. Just to get out of Baal the 1st Battalion, 335th Infantry, had to fight its way. It ran into opposition from enemy small-arms fire and machine guns and it took all morning before this opposition could be cleared. To speed the subsequent advance, the regiment's second battalion was inserted alongside the first. The 2nd Battalion, 335th Infantry, was ordered to move across county through Rurichand on to Doveren. Here, again, entrenched enemy forces delayed the advance. At mid-afternoon, Company C, 771st Tank

Battalion, arrived to aid in the attack. Firing over the heads of the advanced infantry, the tanks softened opposition and together the force broke through to Doveren. After clearing the town for the balance of the afternoon, the combined force set up a night defense on the northern edge of the village. The "Railsplitters" bridgehead now extended some four miles in length and three miles in width. Flanks remained open until the 102nd Infantry Division could come up on the right and the soon-to-cross 35th Infantry Division on the left. A breakthrough seemed imminent.

That night the 1st Battalion, 351st Volks Grenadier Regiment, 183rd Volks Grenadier Division, launched a counterattack against Doveren. Faced with two full infantry battalions and a full tank company defending the town, the outcome was predictable—the combined infantry-tank-artillery team made quick work of the German offensive. Captain B. C. Mills of Company C, 771st Tank Battalion, acted as a liaison officer when the radio link between the infantry and the artillery failed. With communications to both, Mills spent four hours relaying requests up and down the chain of command. By daybreak, only harassing enemy artillery fire threatened Doveren.

That same afternoon, the last difficulty at the river crossings developed. Enemy artillery fire hit both the infantry footbridge and the Treadway bridge. The footbridge went out of service until repaired, but the Treadway could still handle trucks of up to two and a half tons, although no armored vehicles could cross. A few hours later, a Bailey bridge was completed and opened at Körrenzig, relieving the need for more bridges in XIII Corps.[7] The Treadway bridge was repaired by the next morning and resumed carrying heavy traffic.

On the east bank, advances continued against the occasional lone enemy tank, antitank gun or machine gun. Snipers held up individual platoons until they were eliminated. If one column was halted, the opposition was usually outflanked by the adjacent column. Clearly the Germans had no line of defense and were defending what they could when they could. The advancing American infantry saw the enemy ahead of them manning machine guns, and at the first sign the Americans were beginning an attack, many (although not all) of the crews would flee. After several hours of this, Captain Francis K. Price, the Operations Officer of the 2nd Battalion, 335th Infantry, commented,

> I like to tell myself that it was a perfect operation, the sort of thing they dream of at Fort Benning. We moved northeast from Doveren, Company E with a platoon of heavy machine guns from Company H and Company C of the 771st Tank Battalion. Ahead of us was as neat a set of trench works, anti-tank ditches, and obstacles as I have seen. The doughboys double timed, firing as they ran, while from their flanks the heavy machine guns covered them and over their heads the tanks were spitting lead from their machine guns and 76s. The Jerries in the trenches came out with their hands up and we waved them to the rear.[8]

For the first time, the advancing infantrymen encountered *Volkssturm* elements—home guards with minimal training and equipment—defending their towns. Every sign indicated that the German 183rd Infantry Division was coming apart. Many prisoners had no idea of the unit they were assigned to, so quickly had they been pressed into front-line service. Once the "Railsplitters" moved beyond Baal and Doveren, the entire feeling of the battle began to change.

*   *   *

Generals Simpson and Moore had the same sense as the front-line infantrymen. They were watching two zones in particular. The boundary between XIX Corps and XIII Corps was a danger area due to the rapid advance of the latter, which had exposed its right flank as it pulled ahead of XIX Corps. But this had been foreseen in the planning stages and a regiment of the 83rd Infantry Division was committed by General McLain to protect the exposed flank. Equally aware of the potential danger, General Gillem committed his reserve 5th Armored Division to cover the gap.

The other reason for concern was Simpson's desire to get Anderson's XVI Corps into the battle. In the original plans for Operation *Grenade*, XIII Corps was to secure the triangle of land on the Roer plateau bounded by Huckelhoven-Ratheim-Golkrath, northwest of Baal, after which XVI Corps would have an unobstructed crossing of the river. This crossing would provide a line of departure for the planned XVI Corps attack to the north. But seeing the rapid progress of his forces, Simpson was loath to slow it down by the necessity of clearing a crossing site for XVI Corps. He altered the plans and ordered Anderson to consider the possibilities of XVI Corps forcing a crossing of its own near the town of Hilfarth.

The problem of forcing a crossing at Hilfarth was complicated for Anderson by the presence of several German-held bridgeheads on the west bank, one of which included the area of Hilfarth itself. In order to force a crossing there, XVI Corps would first have to clear this German enclave. Anderson immediately planned a two-pronged attack to accomplish this. Major General Ira T. Wyche's veteran 79th Infantry Division would make a feint a few miles downstream from the town, while Major General Paul W. Baade's 35th Infantry Division attacked Hilfarth directly.[9,10]

The XVI Corps plan called for a direct attack on Hilfarth and a forced crossing by the 35th Infantry Division at that point. Preparations began immediately. The division's engineers (the 60th Engineer (Combat) Battalion) assembled Bailey bridges, heavy pontoon equipment, floating Treadway bridges and miles of road base, along with 50 tons of explosives for destruction of Siegfried Line defenses. Assault boats were assembled at Geilenkirchen, a central point from which these supplies and equipment could be easily distributed. Infantry attended assault schools while the engineers attended special schools set up to learn about enemy mines and booby traps. Baade's initial step was to send his 320th Infantry Regiment across the Würm River over improvised footbridges, before dawn on February 23. His men quickly cleared the 1,500 yards between the Würm and the Roer and set up defenses on the west bank of the Roer.

Meanwhile, the 134th Infantry Regiment sent strong patrols into the town of Hilfarth, on the west bank of the Roer, the same night. This was followed by an attack into Hilfarth by the 1st Battalion, 134th Infantry, on the night of February 25. Despite a vicious defense by automatic weapons, lethal mines and booby traps, the town was cleared by dawn. During the attack, the 134th Infantry captured an intact stone bridge crossing the river to the east of Hilfarth. The bridge had been an objective of the attack and had been saved by constant harassing fire from the division's 161st Field Artillery Battalion. Hundreds of carefully placed air-burst artillery shells had kept German engineers away from the bridge for several days. During the final attack, two combat engineers from the 60th Engineer (Combat) Battalion (Technician Fifth Grade James Stanislau and Private Harold Wright) slipped past enemy defenders, machine guns and mortars and cut demolition wires on the bridge, removing the charges and dropping them into the river. Engineers later constructed two footbridges across this narrow stretch of the Roer. Before noon, tanks and other vehicles were streaming across. XVI Corps had crossed the Roer.

General Baade also sent his 137th Infantry Regiment, reinforced with tank destroyers of the 654th Tank Destroyer Battalion, across the river on bridges of the 84th Infantry Division. The regimental combat team marched to Doveren and launched an attack from there to the northeast. Supported by tanks of the 784th Tank Battalion, the advance seized town after town.

With his 84th Division now freed of the responsibility of moving beyond Baal to obtain a crossing site for XVI Corps, Gillem launched his reserve force, Major General Lunsford E. Oliver's 5th Armored Division, on his right flank.[11,12] Supported by the 102nd Infantry Division, XIII Corps drove hard for the road center at the town of Erkelenz. The 84th was to cut roads leading to the west. Even though the first enemy reinforcements (the 338th Infantry Division) arrived within XII SS Corps during the day, their presence was barely felt by the rampaging American task forces. XIII Corps's drive to Erkelenz was largely unopposed and the 102nd Infantry Division entered the town to find it deserted. So lacking were the German defenses that in one case a unit of the 84th Infantry Division entered a deserted town to find no opposition, but beer on tap at the local *Gasthous*.

*   *   *

XIX Corps had more opposition, due largely to the commitment by General von Zangen of the portions of the 9th and 11th Panzer Divisions, which he had managed to acquire. These had provided the bulk of the forces that had held up the 30th Infantry Division at Steinstrass. Once the 117th and 119th Infantry Regiments broke that resistance, however, the pace of the advance picked up. In attacking Oberembt, the 117th Infantry took 168 prisoners and knocked out a German tank. Prisoners complained that they had only arrived the night before and were busy setting up defenses facing west when the 30th Infantry ("Old Hickory") Division hit them from the south. Most of them had just sat down to breakfast when the Americans arrived.

It was also at Oberembt that Company C, 117th Infantry, came upon a unique prize. This was a huge 380mm (15in.) howitzer mounted on a heavy Royal Tiger tank chassis, the first seen by Allied forces. When captured, the gun was loaded and ready to fire, with a 770-pound shell in the breach, but its crew were swiftly killed or captured. At Lich, the 2nd battalion, 117th Infantry, found itself in a scene of mass confusion. Seven German tanks had defended the town. Five had retreated, one had been knocked out, and the last was still unaccounted for while about a hundred prisoners were being rounded up. Men of Companies B and C were waiting for tanks of the 743rd Tank Battalion to arrive to continue their own advance to Oberembt. Tanks were heard approaching and the GIs waved them forward. Suddenly they realized that these were not American tanks, but heavy German Mark V tanks. The lead German tank commander stuck his head out and shouted to one GI "Move over!" and then opened fire.[13]

"I could have reached out and touched one of the tanks," one officer remembered, "when he swung that 'telephone pole' [an 88mm tank gun] around toward me."[14] But the German tankers were not interested in a fight, they wanted only to get out of town and back to friendly lines. Not all of them made it, with two tanks and several half-tracks being knocked out and 15 prisoners taken.

The "Old Hickory" Division's infantry soon began using a relatively new tactic— night attacks—to make their advances. They found that experienced combat troops were less susceptible at night to enemy machine guns and tanks, which could not see far enough in the darkness to accurately fire on them. They also varied the time of their attacks so as not to fit into a predictable pattern, further confusing the enemy. Although this didn't eliminate casualties, it helped to keep them low.

XIX Corps continued to face the most severe opposition, due to the commitment of the enemy armor on its front. At Grottenherten and Kirchherten, the 1st Battalion, 120th Infantry, ran into 10 tanks, antitank guns used in a ground role, and machine guns. "The Krauts started shooting their machine guns into the ground, then slowly lifted their fire to sweep the ground," one soldier recalled. "They were shooting flares every two minutes and together with the fires we had started the place was as light as day."[15] Eventually, one German tank fell to a bazooka round and two others were knocked out by artillery fire. The defenders, probably from the 11th Panzer Division, soon withdrew. Supported by tanks of the 743rd Tank Battalion and tank destroyers of the 823rd Tank Destroyer Battalion, the advance continued. Soon the "Old Hickory" Division paused to allow the 2nd Armored Division to roll on past, aiming for the Rhine bridges at Düsseldorf. The 30th Infantry Division moved to protect the right flank of XIX Corps while the 83rd Infantry Division and 2nd Armored Division moved north.

While "Old Hickory" cleaned up in its area, the 29th Infantry Division raced ahead some four miles against spotty opposition. It reached the egg-shaped plateau known as the Cologne plain at its southern edge. So swift and unopposed was the advance that the attached 330th Infantry Regiment had not a single fatality and only 59 wounded during the advance. General McLain concluded that the way to the Rhine was clear. Only pockets of antitank guns offered real resistance and the German infantry seemed confused and disorganized, having lost all enthusiasm for a fight.

Although satisfied that the battle was clearly going his way, McLain hesitated to release his armor because of concern over the third enemy defensive line, which his corps had yet to reach. When the 30th Infantry Division reached the town of Garzweiler, McLain would then be confident enough to send the 2nd Armored Division forward. As described, this occurred quicker than anticipated.

On Ninth Army's flank, General Collins and his VII Corps faced opposition from elements of the 9th Panzer Division, but these defenses turned out to be weak, and in many cases the defenders were eager to surrender. The 104th and 8th Infantry Divisions soon pierced this tenuous line of resistance and made good progress until the Germans began to withdraw. During this phase of operations, General Weaver, commanding the 8th Infantry Division, suffered his fourth heart attack and was replaced by Brigadier General Bryant E. Moore, the former Assistant Division Commander of the 104th Infantry Division. With enemy defenses collapsing, Collins released his 3rd Armored Division with orders to strike for the Rhine and any bridges that might be found intact. Reinforced with the 13th Infantry Regiment of the 8th Infantry Division, General Rose began his race for the Rhine. Upon reaching the Erft Canal, progress was halted while another crossing operation was organized.

After February 24, the German command could not fail to understand that Operation *Grenade* was designed to crush Army Group H between the Canadians and Ninth Army. The success of the operation would mean the encirclement and total defeat of the southern wing of Army Group H, along with First Parachute Army and Fifteenth Army. Field Marshal Model soon agreed with the assessment, but there was nothing he could do to prevent it. He had one distant reserve, the veteran Panzer Lehr Division, but it was weakened by recent combat against the British and was several days away from the critical scene of action.

Field Marshal von Rundstedt was also alarmed and sought guidance from Hitler. As Commander-in-Chief West, the Field Marshal had problems both north and south. Besides Operation *Grenade*, the attacks of Third Army at Trier and Bitburg were also of a very dangerous nature.[16] When no immediate response was forthcoming, von Rundstedt asked for permission to withdraw to the north in order to strengthen his defenses. This request brought an immediate and predictable answer from Hitler. No withdrawal was permitted. Desperate, von Rundstedt asked again. This time, aided by a factual briefing by the operations staff of the Army High Command, Hitler reluctantly agreed to a limited withdrawal.

* * *

Hitler's approval came not a moment too soon. In the north, the First Canadian Army had renewed Operation *Veritable* with a drive by General Brian Horrocks' XXX Corps on Geldern, where it was expected to unite with Ninth Army. Operation *Grenade* had also reached its exploitation phase and, on February 27, General Simpson declared that phase operational, releasing all the reserve divisions, including the armor, to pursue and destroy all enemy forces west of the Rhine.

Only in XIX Corps' zone was there a question in the minds of Generals Simpson and McLain about committing the armor before they reached the Garzweiler defense zone. With room now available to insert another division between the 29th and 30th Infantry Divisions, should that unit be infantry or armor? Simpson, convinced that his Ninth Army had won the battle, ordered McLain to commit the 2nd Armored Division, with orders to race to the Rhine at Neuss. As we have seen, the concerns were unfounded as the "Old Hickory" Division took Garzweiler without undue difficulty before Major General Isaac D. White was able to unleash his 2nd Armored Division.[17]

There were no concerns elsewhere in Ninth Army about unleashing the armor. In Gillem's XIII Corps, the 5th Armored Division was already on its way, for the moment providing protection to the exposed flank of XIII Corps. Combat Command B (CCB) was the first element committed and launched Task Force Dickenson (consisting of Company A, 81st Tank Battalion, and Company A, 15th Armored Infantry Battalion, reinforced with Troop A of the 85th Reconnaissance Squadron) against Rheindahlen.[18] The plan was to cut communications with the German garrison holding Erkelenz. CCB was also to capture the towns of Wockerath, Terheeg, Mennekrath, Kaulhausen and Venrath, to cover XIII Corps' east flank. Colonel John T. Cole (West Point, 1917), commander of CCB, immediately moved out, supported by the 71st Armored Field Artillery Battalion.

A war correspondent later described a typical armored thrust at this stage of the war:

> From the air in a Piper Cub the tank drive was a thing of the sheerest military beauty: first came a long row of throbbing tanks moving like heavy dark beetles over the green cabbage fields of Germany in a wide swath—many, many tanks in a single row abreast. Then, a suitable distance behind, came another great echelon of tanks even broader, out of which groups would wheel from the brown mud tracks in the green fields to encircle and smash fire at some stubborn strong point. Behind this came miles of trucks, full of troops, maneuvering perfectly to mop up bypassed tough spots. Then came the field artillery to pound hard knots into submission. From the flanks sped clouds of tank destroyers, cutting across the landscape in wild swoops that hit the enemy and cut off communications with bewildering speed.[19]

The tanks fanned out and moved forward against heavy antitank fire coming from Holzweiler, where elements of the 11th Panzer Division were dug in. Six of General Oliver's tanks were hit and wheeled out of column. Maintenance men of the 81st Tank Battalion's Company B pulled into a field near Wey and, under fire from antitank guns and machine guns, managed to evacuate two of the disabled tanks for repair. The entire CCB then joined up around Mennekrath and prepared for a major push in the morning.

The morning's target was Rheindahlen, a key in the defenses of München-Gladbach. Task Force Anderson, with Companies B and C of the 81st Tank Battalion and the 15th Armored Infantry Battalion, drew the assignment of a frontal assault, while Task Force Dickenson was to wheel to the left flank and cut the railroad on the western edge of town. Colonel Cole ordered both task force commanders to move fast and hit hard, what in modern parlance would be termed "shock and awe." Task Force Anderson attacked between the towns of Rath and Herrath. Despite heavy artillery fire on both these towns, enemy antitank fire came from Rath, knocking out one of the tanks. The other tanks opened up and the enemy fire soon ceased. Dismounted infantry then came under mortar attack and found themselves stranded on the open plain. These men fought their way into Herrath and cleared the town of enemy troops.

Just behind the advance, 1st Lieutenant Harold L. Spiro (of B Company, 15th Armored Infantry Battalion) and his crew were working on freeing three half-tracks that had bogged down in the mud 200 yards north of Herrath when they observed a company of enemy infantry heading towards the town. Four self-propelled guns followed the infantry. Using the machine guns mounted on the stranded half-tracks, the Americans opened fire on the enemy column, scattering them and forcing the German armor to retreat, although two of the three American half-tracks were destroyed by return enemy fire. Spiro and his men withdrew into Herrath, where they found themselves facing a German Mark IV Panther tank. Both sides stopped as they spotted the other. Without a shot, the German crew jumped out of their tank and made feeble attempts to hide, then decided to surrender.

Meanwhile, the 71st Armored Field Artillery Battalion laid heavy fire on Rath to suppress the damaging antitank fire coming from there. A platoon of Company C, 15th Armored Infantry, went forward to clear the town. Minutes later the platoon returned to report they could find no enemy guns here. The attack on Rheindahlen resumed. Observers then saw a column, led by an American light tank, on a parallel route heading towards Rheindahlen. Early morning fog prevented accurate identification of the column, and fearing that it might be Task Force Dickenson, Colonel Anderson withheld fire. Both columns continued on their separate routes towards the 5th Armored Division's objective.

It wasn't until both columns reached the vicinity of Buchholz that this second column turned out to be German. It opened fire on the Americans and was identified as four 75mm self-propelled guns mounted on Mark IV chassis, with a single captured American light tank, repainted with German Army insignia. Hidden in nearby woods were two German antitank guns. Task Force Anderson had walked into a neatly laid trap, but the Germans had taken on more than they had bargained for. After the loss of two tanks, Task Force Anderson returned fire so accurately that all the enemy guns, including the captured American light tank, were destroyed. "If you were to tell me that a column of tanks was fired on by two German anti-tank guns from a distance of only 200 yards and four self-propelled guns from

400 yards, and only two tanks were hit, I'd call you a damned liar. But that's what actually happened," said Captain William L. Guthrie, commander of Company C, 81st Tank Battalion.[20]

Meanwhile, the rest of Task Force Anderson continued to advance and overran six German 170mm artillery guns, whose crews were still asleep when the Americans arrived. As the task force came upon Rheindahlen, however, it ran into a wall of fire from antitank guns and antiaircraft guns, used in a ground role and entrenched around the town. The Americans nevertheless pressed home their attacks. As Captain Weldon M. Wilson of Company B, 81st Tank Battalion, later explained, "If we had moved more slowly in that attack, most of our force would have been completely wiped out. It was speed that saved us."[21] Nevertheless, it was a close call for many. Private First Class John T. Tavoularis jumped off the tank on which he was riding only to be caught in enemy barbed wire and unable to move. The tank, not knowing Tavoularis was trapped behind it, began to back up. Other GIs turned away as the tank rolled over him, fearing he was being crushed under its treads. But luck was with Private Tavoularis that day. The soft ground merely allowed the tank to press him into it without injury. He was pulled out shaken, but unhurt.

Meanwhile, Task Force Dickenson found its way blocked by an extensive antitank ditch. Undeterred, Dickenson pulled his men back and went around to the east of Rath and then moved north on the highway. No serious opposition was encountered until the task force reached the outskirts of Rheindahlen, where enemy antitank guns and a stubborn Mark VI tank blocked its way. "Three of the Tiger tank's shells ripped into our tank," said Lieutenant Robert P. Lant, a platoon leader in Company A, 81st Tank Battalion. "The first two smashed out front sprockets and the third tore off our .50 caliber turret gun. But our 75mm gun was still okay, so we slammed about 12 shells back at the German tank."[22] The huge German war machine knocked out two more American tanks before it was itself knocked out. Altogether some 36 rounds of American tank fire had been needed to destroy the Tiger. An enemy infantry attack was then quickly dispersed by the task force's armor and infantry, and Colonel Cole called down five flights of P-47 Thunderbolt fighter-bombers from XXIX Tactical Air Command to finish off Rheindahlen. Enemy losses were totaled at 150 killed, 150 wounded and 147 captured. Losses to the 5th Armored Division were 10 men killed and 55 wounded in action.

* * *

General Anderson at XVI Corps was also eager to launch his armor, now that he had a bridgehead across the Roer. He ordered Brigadier General John M. Devine's 8th Armored Division to cross the river on February 27 and strike out north.[23] The weather favored the attack—although it was rainy, the ground was not too soft for armor.

The 8th Armored Division was activated April 1, 1942, at Fort Knox, Kentucky, and after the usual training and maneuvers it departed the United States on November 6, 1944. The division landed in France on January 5, 1945 and then fought with the 94th Infantry Division of XX Corps, Third Army, in the Saar-Moselle Triangle battles of January and February.[24] After moving north, the division took part in a diversionary attack east of the Roer, before participating in Operation *Grenade*. The division was tasked with the responsibility of clearing the area on the west bank of the Roer and pushing north to the city of Roermond. Supported by the entire divisional artillery and all heavy weapons of CCB, the division had assisted corps artillery in preparing a crossing for the Roer bridgehead.

Next came orders to prepare to cross the river south of Roermond, and then send a combat command on a reconnaissance to determine the strength of the enemy within the Roermond–Linne–St. Odilienberg triangle. Combat Command R (CCR) was given the assignment and strengthened with the addition of the 7th Armored Infantry Battalion. After artillery preparation by the 405th Armored Field Artillery Battalion, the attack was led off by Major George Artman's 58th Armored Infantry Battalion. Heavy mortar and small-arms fire met the advance, while roadblocks and mines slowed the attack of the supporting 80th Tank Battalion, under Major Austin E. Walker. Company C, 53rd Armored Engineer Battalion, cleared the roadblocks under enemy fire and cleared the Linne–Roermond Highway.

Captain Ralph J. Elias' Company B, 58th Armored Infantry Battalion, entered Spielmanshof only to have one platoon cut off and isolated. Radio contact with the platoon was lost and casualties mounted. Staff Sergeant William McClain and Private First Class Napoleon L. Bourget ran a dangerous 400-yard dash across fire-swept terrain to bring a new radio to the trapped platoon. Lieutenant Colonel A. P. Mossman, the assistant chief of staff, ordered in the 7th Armored Infantry Battalion to open a path to the trapped Americans. Contact was soon established and the battle continued. The lead tanks then came up against a 22-foot wide crater, which stopped their progress.

During a brief rest period in the Netherlands, the 130th Ordnance Maintenance Battalion and the 53rd Armored Engineer Battalion had combined their efforts to build a Treadway bridge-laying machine, in effect a bridge-laying tank. Six such prototypes were completed, each of which could carry a single-span bridge of 36 feet in length (or a double-span of 24 feet) and lay it over a water or trench obstacle without exposing the crew to enemy fire. One of these experimental models now made its debut at the 22-foot crater. Lieutenant Richard J. Symonds of Company C, 53rd Armored Engineer Battalion, drove his M-32 Tank Retriever into position, dropped his bridge, secured it and watched as tanks of the 80th Tank Battalion crossed over and knocked out a German pillbox.

These advances against the 176th Volks Grenadier Division and the *Para Lehr* (Training) Regiment of the 8th Parachute Division cracked the German defense.

By the end of the day, the area along the Roer had been cleared. CCR left any mopping up to the 15th Cavalry Group and moved to Huckelhoven across the river.[25] Upon arrival, they learned that the mission of the division was now to capture several important towns along the Roer's east bank and then be prepared to support a drive to the Rhine or support XIII Corps. General Devine immediately sent Combat Command A through the 35th Infantry Division, followed in march column by CCB and CCR. As Brigadier General Charles F. Colson, commander of CCA, passed XVI Corps headquarters at Sittard, he stopped in for an update from General Anderson. He was instructed to avoid the planned division assembly area, pass through the 137th Infantry Regiment and then drive on Wegberg, Germany. Colson dispatched Task Force Crittenden (commanded by Lt. Col. William S. Crittenden) to lead the way north.[26] Crittenden's orders from Colson were simple: "You're leading the Division. Enemy contact has been lost. Keep going east until you hit something. Use any and all available roads."[27]

*   *   *

With the bulk of Ninth Army now across the Roer and in full attack mode, the campaign became a race to secure a bridge over the Rhine. This scene would be repeated in most of the American and Allied armies now approaching that boundary. By March 1, 1945, the armor of Ninth Army was making advances of seven to 10 miles a day against scattered opposition. General White's 2nd Armored Division, now reinforced with the 331st Infantry Regiment of the 83rd Infantry Division, Company A, 739th Tank Battalion (Special Mine Exploder), and a flamethrower platoon of the same 739th Tank Battalion, was only seven miles from the Rhine. The advancing 29th Infantry Division was encountering civilians who shouted as they passed, "*Deutsch Soldatenweg!*" and "*Aller weg,*" or "German soldiers go away" and "everyone has gone away." The validity of these statements was strengthened by a report from Field Marshal Montgomery, who advised General Gerhardt that his intelligence didn't believe München-Gladbach would be defended. The key town fell to a two-battalion attack by Colonel Bingham's 116th Infantry after some skirmishing.[28]

For those who had fought their way across France the previous year, the pursuit phase of Operation *Grenade* reminded them of the glory days of the race across France, when they had chased the defeated Germans out of that country. As the divisions moved east and north, they entered towns where the trolley cars were still operating, and electric lights were still blazing in many places. Most villages in this area showed no scars of war, never having been shelled by either side. At times the only discordant note was the scream of the fighters of XXIX Tactical Air Command attacking retreating German columns.

There were exceptions, of course. The 84th Infantry Division was making good progress in its advance. A special grouping, Task Force Church (under the command

Lieutenant General William Hood Simpson (USMA 1909), Commanding General, Ninth U.S. Army, through its wartime career. (NARA 111-SC-204977)

Brigadier General James Edward Moore (USMA 1924), Chief of Staff of Ninth Army, throughout its wartime career. (NARA 111-SC-204979)

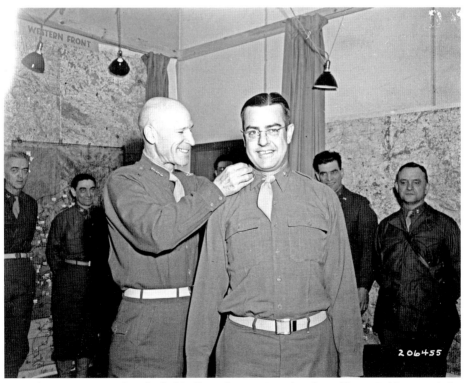

General Simpson presents his Chief of Staff, Ninth Army, Brigadier General James E. Moore, with the two stars of a Major General, April 14, 1945. (NARA 111-SC-206455)

Major General Alvan Cullon Gillen, Jr. commanded the XIII Corps under Ninth Army. October 1944. (NARA 111-SC-200168)

Major General John Benjamin Anderson (USMA 1914), Commanding General XVI Corps, in Texas, 1943. (NARA 111-SC-186822)

Major General Frank Augustus Keating, Commanding General 102nd Infantry Division, which served its entire combat career under Ninth Army. (NARA 111-SC-17962)

By direction of the President, Major General Raymond Stallings McLain, Commanding General, XIX Corps, receives the Distinguished Service Cross for exceptionally meritorious service from July 31, 1944 to October 1945, from General Simpson. (NARA 111-SC-203821)

Privates George Colfield of Washington, D.C., and Howard J. Davie of Baltimore and the 1317th Engineer General Service Regiment, protect a recently constructed Ninth Army bridge over the Rhine River, March 30, 1945. (NARA 111-SC-204770)

Company I, 23rd Infantry Regiment, 2nd Infantry Division, advance near Brest, France. Many GIs lost their lives when the Germans blew up their own pillboxes to prevent capture. (Real War Photos #A2426)

The 28th Infantry Regiment and supporting tanks, 8th Infantry Division, pass through a French town on their way to Avranches, France, July 31, 1944. (Real War Photos #A2721)

Snipers of the 7th U.S. Armored Division and 15th (Scottish) Infantry Division taking a break on the Holland front near Someren, Holland, February 11, 1944. (Real War Photos #A945)

Major General Lindsay McDonald Silvester (left), Commanding General 7th U.S. Armored Division, outlines the tactical situation north of Overloon, Holland, to British officers preparing to take over the area, October 7, 1944. (Real War Photos #A940A)

Infantrymen of the 84th Infantry Division and British tanks combine their firepower to drive Germans out of a building in Geilenkirchen, Germany, November 19, 1944. (Real War Photos #A3863)

Company B, 86th Chemical Mortar Battalion, supporting the 121st Infantry Regiment, 8th Infantry Division, Ninth Army, December 7, 1944. (Real War Photos #A2735)

An infantry patrol from Company L, 13th Infantry Regiment, 8th Infantry Division, flushing snipers out of Duren, Germany, February 24, 1945. (Real War Photos #A2720)

Soldiers of the 334th Infantry Regiment, 84th Infantry Division, Ninth Army, pass a road sign posted by the German 183rd Infantry Division. They are leaving Baesweiler on the way to Erkelenz, after pushing the 183rd Infantry Division out of the area, February 26, 1945. (Real War Photos #A3861)

Tanks and even a bicycle of the 2nd Armored Division, Ninth Army, move through the cleared streets of battered Krefeld, Germany, March 3, 1945. (Real War Photos #A641)

Vehicles of the 5th Armored Division, Ninth Army, roll through the narrow streets of Hüls, Krefeld, Germany, March 3, 1945. (Real War Photos #A887)

Vehicles of the 38th Cavalry Reconnaissance Group (Mechanized), 2nd Armored Division, Ninth Army, are parking in Altenahr, Germany, March 3, 1945. (Real War Photos #A630)

German civilians line the street of Ahlem, Germany, as tanks of the 2nd Armored Division roll through the town, April 2, 1945. (Real War Photos #A629)

A rifle squad, 10th Tank Battalion, 5th Armored Division, Ninth Army enters a farmyard near Seehausen, Germany, to check for hidden German soldiers, April 16, 1945. (Real War Photos #A885B)

Infantrymen of the 315th Infantry Regiment, 79th Infantry Division, Ninth Army, hurry across a dike of the Rhein-Herne Canal near Essen, Germany, in the drive to the Ruhr Pocket. (Real War Photos #A3794)

Two civil affairs officers of the 84th Infantry Division, Ninth Army, drive through the streets of newly captured Dülken, Germany. The loudspeaker on the vehicle is telling all civilians to report to a designated point for instructions. (Real War Photos #A3867)

German troops surround the 1st Battalion, 334th Infantry Regiment, 84th Infantry Division, XIII Corps, Ninth Army, while gathering their equipment at their assembly point north of Werben, Germany, on the west bank of the Elbe River. These are about 1,000 Germans who surrendered to the Americans on May 2, 1945, after being pushed back to the Ninth Army lines by Russian forces. (Real War Photos #A3870)

British Field Marshal Sir Bernard Law Montgomery, Viscount Montgomery of Alamein (1887–1976), commander of the 21st Army Group, under which Ninth Army served for much of the winter of 1944–45. (NARA 303-NT-325A-12)

General Sir Miles Christopher Dempsey, Commanding General, British 2nd Army, which fought alongside Ninth U.S. Army from October 1944 until the end of the war. (NARA 208-PU-50N-1)

Allied Supreme Commander Dwight David Eisenhower with General Henry Duncan Graham Crerar (left), Commanding General, First Canadian Army, which also fought alongside the Ninth U.S. Army during the campaigns in Northwest Europe, 1944–45. (NARA 208-PU-43D-1)

of the Assistant Division Commander, Brigadier General John H. Church)[29] led the way forward.[30] Many towns surrendered without a shot being fired. The commander of the 771st Tank Battalion, Lieutenant Colonel Jack C. Childers, remarked, "It was just a wild ride from one town to another."[31] But at the town of Steeg, the lead tank was knocked out by an antitank gun. Company A, 334th Infantry, dealt with the gun, but barely had the replacement lead tank started off when it too was knocked out. Clearly some serious opposition had arrived. In fact, as the Americans would soon discover, they now faced the determined 8th Parachute Division, which had been fighting the Canadians and had now turned around to defend the Rhine against attack from the south.

Church and his command group were about three miles behind the leading tanks. When the column stopped, the general wanted to see the problem for himself. He ordered his jeep driver to move up the column. Followed by other jeeps, carrying infantrymen and newspaper reporters, the general's vehicle moved ahead. They had barely begun when fire from the infantry in one of the other jeeps shot past the general's vehicle—they had spotted a German soldier taking aim at the task force commander, but had scared him off. Movement stopped, however, when faced with dug-in enemy infantry just north of Wegberg. As the jeeps turned back they ran a gauntlet of enemy fire from all sides. Church's jeep was hit and reeled off the road. His driver, Technician Fifth Grade Kyser Crockett, tried to keep the jeep moving despite having his arm blown off. The general's aide, 1st Lieutenant Norman D. Dobie, took over and steered the vehicle to a place of safety. Only then was it noticed that Church had been wounded in the face, knee and ankle. Refusing evacuation, he resumed command of his task force after medical treatment.

The 333rd Infantry moved up on the flank while Task Force Church continued its advance. An entire enemy artillery regiment was captured intact. In a nine-mile run, 54 enemy towns were captured. No fewer than 12 field guns, eight antitank guns, two assault guns, a motor vehicle and 15 horse-drawn wagons fell to the racing Americans. In just one day, February 27, 1,249 prisoners were taken. So swift was the American advance that most prisoners were merely waved to the rear. Wrote Staff Sergeant Ambrose Cerrito of Company C, 334th Infantry:

> Civilians were amazed. We caught them all completely by surprise. Food was on all the tables. People were still coming home from work. Everyone from three-year-olds up immediately began waving white handkerchiefs when they saw who we were. Apparently they were told we would kill them all. They were so scared that all they wanted was to move out and get away from us. The majority of them did not even take time to pick up a few belongings.[32]

But the fight at Steeg was far less easy. The paratroopers of the German 8th Parachute Division had emplaced antitank guns, tanks, mines and machine guns to protect their defenses at the villages surrounding Waldniel. A combined American force of infantry, mortars and mobile cannons forced the road junction at Steeg, only to hit another roadblock at Waldniel, where seven enemy tanks had been dug in to strengthen the defense. These were in turn protected by machine guns and mines. Once again a combined arms force pushed their way forward. It would take more than 12 hours to clear the area of Waldniel and vicinity.

During this fighting, the 125 men of Company G, 334th Infantry, reinforced with the second platoon of Company H's heavy machine guns, found themselves facing the small town of Berg along the main road to the next objective, Boisheim. They had to cross 300 yards of open ground to reach Berg, and as they began four machine guns opened fire. Newly commissioned from the enlisted ranks, 2nd Lieutenant Harold L. Howdieshell pushed his scouts into a ditch and began to toss grenades at the enemy. His aim was good and the machine guns fell silent. Just as he was about to throw another grenade a fifth machine gun, heretofore silent, opened fire and killed him. Other machine guns then opened up. Lieutenant Jack F. Schaper, leader of the 1st Platoon fell dead.

The company commander, Captain Charles E. Hiatt moved a platoon to out-flank the enemy. Prisoners began to come in and a house was captured from which the Americans could view most of the German defenses. Although it looked like a perfect defense, however, the guns destroyed by Lieutenant Howdieshell had left a gap. Fixing bayonets, Company G charged into the teeth of the enemy defenses and fought hand-to-hand. When it was all over only two enemy paratroopers had been captured, the rest lay dead in their positions. For its actions at Berg, Company G and the 2nd Platoon of Company H, 334th Infantry, received a Presidential Unit Citation.[33]

In the six days between the Roer and the Rhine, the 84th Infantry Division had advanced 20 miles (two-thirds in the last two days of the drive) and had captured 2,876 prisoners. The Rhine lay ahead.

*   *   *

With German resistance collapsing, the objective became to capture an intact bridge over the Rhine. Although all commanders knew that the Germans were ruthlessly efficient in blowing up bridges before the Allies were able to seize them, those same commanders believed it was worth a try. Even Eisenhower, who preferred a broad-front penetration of the German border, had mentioned to General Simpson that he was interested in getting an intact bridge across the Rhine in Ninth Army's zone.

General Mclain at XIX Corps ordered his 83rd Infantry and 2nd Armored Divisions to race for the town of Neuss, where four bridges spanned the river. General Macon's 83rd Infantry ("Thunderbolt") Division immediately fought through the night towards Neuss. The 329th Infantry Regiment, supported by the 322nd Field Artillery Battalion, pushed ahead as fast as they could, moving across generally open and flat terrain, opposed by enemy tanks and self-propelled guns. To speed their advance, these strong points were outflanked whenever possible. Strong perimeters defended by machine guns firing along prearranged zones slowed the advance, but did not stop it. In the dark, the American infantrymen moved through or around batteries of concrete-emplaced 88mm antiaircraft-antitank guns. Just before dawn broke on March 2, 1945, the lead elements reached Neuss. Two hours later, the 1st Battalion, 329th Infantry Regiment, advanced beyond the city towards the vital bridges. They could see the Rhine. Mobs of civilians crowded the streets, welcoming the Americans but slowing their advance, and a further delay was caused by hundreds of German soldiers surrendering.

While the Infantry struggled forward, the division artillery kept up a select fire on the bridges in order to keep the Germans off them and prevent demolition. The men of Company I moved out only to run into a last-ditch defense between them and the bridge they were targeting. Heavy machine guns and 20mm antiaircraft guns were keeping the infantry down. Company L and a platoon of Company A, 736th tank Battalion, moved to outflank the enemy. This attack overwhelmed the defenders, who came out of their trenches with hands raised. The western end of the bridge had been captured. But the satisfaction was short lived. Patrols sent onto the bridge reported that the eastern end had been blown out. Nearby, the 330th Infantry Regiment raced with tanks and tank destroyers from the 643rd Tank Destroyer Battalion, and engineers from the 308th Engineer (Combat) Battalion, for the bridge at Oberkassel, a suburb of Düsseldorf, only to see it blown as they approached.

Another bridge, at Krefeld-Uerdingen, lay in the zone of Gillem's XIII Corps. The 2nd Armored Division was 13 miles away and moving fast, but to get there the Americans had to cross the Nord Canal, a significant obstacle for the armor. But the "Hell on Wheels" Division found an intact bridge over the canal and raced ahead. By nightfall of March 1, the lead elements were within three miles of the bridge at Krefeld. At this point, Ninth Army's Operations Officer (G-3) Colonel Armistead D. Mead was at the headquarters of XIX Corps, reviewing the situation. In Simpson's name he ordered that the boundary between XIII Corps and XIX Corps be altered to allow the 2nd Armored Division to attack and capture the bridge at Krefeld.

Gillem protested, citing the poor terrain for armor that lay around the bridge. He felt that his own 84th Infantry and 102nd Infantry Divisions were better placed to seize a bridge in the area. To settle the dispute, General McLain and Colonel Mead went forward to see exactly what the situation was. They soon found that Gillem's divisions were being held up by heavy resistance in front of Krefeld. Mead overruled Gillem's objections and ordered the 2nd Armored Division to continue.

Meanwhile, unknown to McLain, Gillem or Mead, General Simpson and Field Marshal Montgomery were conferring about the difficulties that were facing the First Canadian Army, to the north. To assist the Canadians, Simpson offered to extend his zone along the Rhine, north to the town of Wesel, thus relieving the Canadians of some of the ground they would have to secure. The field marshal rejected the offer but did allow an expansion as far north as Rheinberg, 10 miles short of the town of Xanten, a major Canadian objective. These changes, however, made so late in the battle, had little effect on the outcome.

The changes in boundaries took some time to reach all of the affected commanders. Gillem, still convinced he was correct, told his 5th Armored Division to stop at the new boundary only if the 2nd Armored Division was already there. The 84th Infantry Division, unaware of any changes, was already planning to send its 334th Infantry and 771st Tank Battalion to bypass Krefeld and establish a bridgehead over the Rhine on its own. As it happened, the 5th Armored Division met the 2nd Armored Division at the outskirts of Krefeld on the afternoon of March 2. With no option, Gillem ordered his 5th Armored Division to remain inside the new Corps boundary. But, as he had predicted, the 2nd Armored Division found its way handicapped by numerous small streams, which delayed its advance.

The eager Americans were now attacking Krefeld from all sides. The 84th Infantry Division attacked from the north, intending to bypass the city itself and reach the bridge by a circuitous route. But when the leading force entered Krefeld they took a wrong turn and found themselves on a route which led directly into the heart of the city. German antitank guns opened fire and the advance forces were pinned down until nightfall. Meanwhile, CCB of the 2nd Armored Division, reinforced with two infantry battalions from the 95th Infantry Division's 379th Infantry Regiment, fought their way into Krefeld and tried to reach the bridge. German paratroopers defended the town stubbornly. The Americans pushed to within a few yards of the western end of the bridge, but could not get any further. A 13-foot hole blown on the western approach to the bridge halted the tanks, and without them the infantry could not push any further. Yet, after dark, a six-man patrol of engineers led by Captain George L. Youngblood slipped onto the bridge, crossed it and cut all visible wires. The patrol actually went all the way to the east bank before returning. Either they must have missed some wires, or the Germans replaced the ones they had cut, for at 0700 hours on March 4 the bridge was blown up. Not to be denied, McLain ordered the 95th Infantry Division (commanded by Major General Harry L. Twaddle) to drive on the road and rail bridges at Rheinhausen, six miles downstream from Krefeld.[34,35]

Initial resistance to the advance of the 95th was light. XIX Corps' orders to the division had given Twaddle two options. If the bridge could be seized intact, the division's 379th Infantry would remain attached to the 2nd Armored Division, which was to cross the bridge as soon as possible, forming a bridgehead across the Rhine. But if the bridge was destroyed when the division reached it, the 379th Infantry would rejoin the division, which would set up defenses on the west bank of the Rhine.

Before much planning could be done, it was learned from artillery observation pilots that the bridges had been destroyed. The 379th Infantry Regiment was returned to the 95th Infantry division and both it and the 2nd Armored Division prepared for a new attack. Both divisions began their attacks to seize the remaining territory on the west bank of the Rhine in their respective zones on March 4. By March 5, the zones had been cleared.

The reason for this light resistance was that the last line of defense planned by General Schlemm, commanding the First Parachute Army, had been pierced. With the approval of General Blaskowitz at Army Group H, a much smaller bridgehead was established at the confluence of the Ruhr and Rhine Rivers between Duisburg and Xanten. Hitler demanded this line be held to preserve the coal supply for the German Navy in the North Sea. But even this quickly fell apart when XIII Corps sent the 5th Armored Division racing into Orsoy on the Rhine, opposite one of the canals the Germans required for coal transportation. Meanwhile, at Moers and Homberg, the 84th Infantry Division found all bridges over the Rhine destroyed. Operation *Grenade* was over.

CHAPTER 9

The Wesel Pocket

The original objectives for Operation *Grenade* had been taken by March 5, 1945. But General Simpson remained unsatisfied. Like his fellow Allied commanders, he earnestly desired a bridge across the Rhine and the establishment of a firm bridge-head over that last major boundary before the heart of Germany could be reached. From there he would drive to the northeastern corner of the Ruhr industrial area, which he had been eyeing since planning Operation *Grenade*. With his staff, he had discussed what course to take should a bridge be captured intact. Alternately, they had discussed forcing a crossing over the Rhine by surprise, before the Germans could establish themselves in defenses across the river.

The plan that was settled upon envisioned a crossing between Düsseldorf and Uerdingen, then a sharp turn north to clear the east bank for additional crossings, before gaining open country along the northern edge of the Ruhr industrial area. That this plan would have worked was without doubt in the minds of the Ninth Army staff. The Germans had little with which to defend the area and were totally unprepared to oppose a crossing in strength. Excited about the prospects, Simpson took his plans to Montgomery at Twenty-First Army Group.

The Field Marshal refused, and the situation created a minor controversy which lasts to this day. From the American point of view, the refusal could only be based upon Montgomery's desire to launch a huge set-piece crossing of the Rhine on a broad front, with all the pomp and circumstance of air support, paratroopers and British leadership. The British point of view argues that launching Simpson's Ninth Army into the "industrial wilderness"[1] of the Ruhr would have swallowed it up, leaving it isolated and in danger across the Rhine. Montgomery never personally explained his decision, but evidence from the German General Staff, compiled after the war, clearly indicated that there would have been little resistance from the Germans had Simpson's plan been implemented. This is further reinforced by the surprise river crossing conducted at the southern end of the Allied line by Patton's Third Army under very similar circumstances.

There were still German troops west of the Rhine within Twenty-First Army Group's zone. Remnants of the formidable First Parachute Army still remained between Ninth Army and the First Canadian Army, and these showed no sign of intending to withdraw across the Rhine. Even if they had, Hitler had expressly forbidden any such withdrawal.

As described earlier, General Anderson's XVI Corps had crossed the Roer and turned to the north. Initially, the corps' progress had been relatively easy, much of the country through which it passed being undefended. Between February 28 and March 3, 1945, two major thrusts had been sent forward by XVI Corps. The first was a combat command of the 8th Armored Division under General Colson. The second was Task Force Byrne, a reinforced 320th Infantry Regiment from the 35th Infantry Division.

Colson's Combat Command A (CCA) crossed over the Hilfarth bridge in the zone of the 35th Infantry Division. Task Force Crittendon (commanded by Lieutenant Colonel Crittendon) led the way and soon passed through both the 35th and 84th Infantry Divisions. As it did so, Colson received the message from Brigadier General Devine urging him to "use any and all available roads."

In accordance with its orders, CCA continued to move forward during the night. At 0300 hours on February 28, 1945, the column halted on the outskirts of Wegberg, facing a strongly defended roadblock. Engineers of Company A, 53rd Armored Engineer Battalion, soon reduced the roadblock, while Troop A of the 88th Cavalry Reconnaissance Squadron became involved in a fight with its defenders. This fight lasted only the amount of time it took for the engineers to eliminate the roadblock, for the moment the road was cleared, the German troops withdrew into the darkness.

With enemy resistance eliminated, CCA rolled on through Wegberg toward the next objective. By 0530 hours they were again in action, forcing another roadblock on the outskirts of Merbeck. Sherman tanks of Company A, 18th Tank Battalion, moved off the road and flanked the German positions, knocking out their machine guns with direct fire. Again, the engineers came up and destroyed the roadblock, protected by the tanks and infantry of the 7th Armored Infantry Battalion. Shortly after dawn, Companies A and B, 7th Armored Infantry Battalion, were in Merbeck, mopping up enemy resistance despite strong artillery and mortar fire coming down on the village.

CCA was now turning to the northeast, aiming at the town of Tetelrath. The assault troops were reorganizing in Merbeck for this next advance, despite continued enemy artillery and mortar fire hitting the village. This fire continued as Company A, 7th Armored Infantry Battalion, advanced out of Merbeck. Soon the infantry-men were pinned down. In addition to artillery, small-arms fire from the front and flanks stopped the American advance. By careful advances, the company managed to reach an antitank ditch that crossed the road between the two villages. As they took cover, additional enemy small-arms fire was received from "practically every house on the south side of Tetelrath."[2]

To assist the infantry, three tanks from Company A, 18th Tank Battalion, came forward and tried to suppress the enemy fire and allow the infantry to advance.

This effort proved futile as high-velocity 88mm antitank guns opened fire and threatened the tanks themselves. Mortar fire continued to fall on the American spearhead. The self-propelled guns of the 398th Armored Field Artillery Battalion were brought forward and opened direct fire on the entrenched Germans. So confident were the Germans of their defenses that some, after surviving this direct fire, actually thumbed their noses at Lieutenant Michael P. Cokino's artillerymen. This act infuriated Corporal Thomas Colligan and Private First Class Samuel Coleman, who promptly turned one of their 105mm guns directly upon an enemy machine gun position, scoring a direct hit.

With his advance stalled by the determined enemy resistance, Crittendon ordered Company B, 7th Armored Infantry Battalion, to clear woods to the right of the road, to allow Company A to outflank the enemy. A short but bitter small-arms fight soon cleared the woods, but CCA still had to clear the road, which was heavily mined, covered by enemy machine guns and cut by the antitank ditch. Under the covering fire of all available tank and artillery guns, First Lieutenant Warren H. Baker led his platoon of Company A, 53rd Armored Engineers, forward. They were to clear the mines, either piling them to one side or holding them while the tanks and infantry rolled past. Then they had to breach the antitank ditch, after which the tanks and infantry could attack the enemy pillboxes directly and at close range. So thick were the enemy mines in this area that the 130th Armored Ordnance Maintenance Battalion had to be called up to finish removing them—dozens were buried under the road pavement.

The assault troops destroyed 15 pillboxes defending the road, many of which were so well camouflaged that only when they opened fire on the approaching Americans were they discovered. One platoon captured 30 enemy soldiers from one pillbox. By 1700 hours, CCA had cleared Tetelrath, capturing 125 enemy prisoners at a cost to themselves of 30 men and three tanks.

Even as CCA was clearing Tetelrath, General Anderson issued new orders to the 8th Armored Division. General Devine was ordered to continue his advance to the north and to be prepared to either assist XIII Corps on the right or to continue on to Venlo. In response, Devine ordered Colson to strike north for Amern-St. Georg.

Task Force Crittenden sent patrols forward and soon learned from Troop A, 88th Cavalry Reconnaissance Squadron (Mechanized), that two bridges remained intact across the Swalm River. These bridges could carry the heavy traffic of tanks and other armored vehicles. Beyond that was a heavily mined crossroads under enemy observation. Many enemy patrols had been encountered.

Crittenden organized a new task force, comprising Company A, 53rd Armored Engineers, and Troop A, 88th Cavalry, to seize the crossroads. While the cavalrymen protected them from enemy probes, the engineers removed 90 Regal and Teller mines from the crossroads. They then discovered an antitank ditch further along the road and a destroyed bridge past that. A Treadway bridge was quickly brought forward and laid across the ditch and a tank bulldozer was used to fill in other obstacles. The road to Amern-St. Georg was open.

Task Force Crittenden, followed by the rest of CCA, now crossed the Swalm. The town of Waldniel was quickly captured and before noon Amern-St. Georg was in American hands. As the town was secured, Task Force Crittenden was dissolved and replaced by Task Force Goodrich. Lieutenant Colonel Guinn B. Goodrich was given the 18th Tank Battalion (less Company A), Company C, 7th Armored Infantry Battalion, Company A, 53rd Armored Engineer Battalion, and Troop A, 88th Cavalry Reconnaissance Squadron. His orders were to strike north and seize the town of Lobberich.

After an hour's artillery barrage, Task Force Goodrich launched its attack early on the morning of March 2, 1945. A thrust from the south was briefly halted by a roadblock and another antitank ditch. In what was now standard procedure, two platoons of Company C, 7th Armored Infantry Battalion, formed a protective perimeter around the engineers, who worked swiftly to blow up the upright steel bars that had been embedded three feet deep in the roadway. Once a path had been blown, the tanks raced through it towards the town. An hour's fierce fighting was required to clear the town of the enemy, at which point the Americans found they had 125 prisoners and streets paved with money. Two of the shells of the 398th Armored Field Artillery Battalion had blown up the town bank, and the streets were littered with German paper currency!

Task Force Goodrich was then ordered to pass through the lines of the 35th Infantry Division and seize the town of Wachtendonk. Town after town fell to the racing task force. As they reached the town of Wankum, small-arms and mortar fire brought them to a halt. Concentrated fire from the tanks of the 18th Tank Battalion soon discouraged continued resistance, and the advance continued.

The town of Wachtendonk lay on the north bank of the Niers Canal. The only bridge across the canal had been destroyed by the Germans. Once again, covered by an artillery barrage, engineers threw a Treadway bridge over the canal and Task Force Goodrich continued its advance. By the evening of March 2, the town was cleared, although there remained holdouts in the surrounding countryside.

Colonel Edward A. Kimball's Combat Command B (CCB) had a similar experience. The task force rolled past the 35th Infantry Division and seized town after town. Ordered to bypass enemy resistance, CCB seized Arsbeck on its way to Ober Kruchten. Captain Charles C. Caserio's Company B, 53rd Armored Engineers, built bridges over streams covered by the guns of the 399th Armored Field Artillery Battalion. Ober Kruchten was captured before dark, and General Anderson ordered a halt. XVI Corps was about to be squeezed out of a front line zone by the rapid Ninth Army advance. The 8th Armored Division went into reserve until needed again.

* * *

The 35th Infantry Division had been equally busy during the last days of February and the first days of March. Between February 26 and 27 it had cleared its section of the Siegfried Line defenses, capturing 23 towns, while supported by the 784th Tank Battalion. When Anderson ordered two thrusts to the east and north, the division formed Task Force Byrne, under the command of Colonel Bernard A. Byrne, commander of the 320th Infantry Regiment. Formed on February 28, the Task Force's mission was to advance on Venlo, a critical Dutch town near the German border, about 20 miles to the north, which was also the target of the First Canadian Army. In addition to the 320th Infantry Regiment, Task Force Byrne included the 216th Field Artillery Battalion, the 275th Field Artillery Battalion, the 784th Tank Battalion (less Company A), Company C, 654th Tank Destroyer Battalion, Company C, 60th Engineer (Combat) Battalion, and Company C, 110th Medical Battalion.

The attack was led by Lieutenant Colonel Joseph D. Alexander's Third Battalion. The men mounted the tanks and raced past the Roer's Siegfried Line defenses. Combat engineers rode with each tank, and as each pillbox was encountered the engineers would dismount and, covered by riflemen, place demolitions to destroy each pillbox in turn. On the right, the 35th Reconnaissance Troop provided flank protection. Like the armored division nearby, the task force roared through town after town against little resistance. Before long it was within sight of the corps objective, Venlo. General Baade contacted Anderson and advised him that the 35th Infantry Division was in a position to take Venlo. Anderson's reply was succinct, "Take it."[3]

Like with the other divisions, the fighting could be fierce at times. Technician Fifth Grade Almon N. Conger, Jr., of the 134th Infantry Regiment's Medical Section, was normally a surgical technician. During one firefight he voluntarily left the relative safety of his assigned post and went forward to administer first aid to wounded soldiers. While he was doing so, he was himself hit. Disregarding his own injuries, he continued to treat the wounded, often putting his own body between them and the incoming enemy fire. The Washington State native survived to receive a Distinguished Service Cross.[4] In Company A of the same regiment, Private First Class Halbert E. Olson from Minnesota was about to throw an armed grenade into an enemy occupied cellar when it became entangled in his clothing. Realizing the terrible danger to those around him, he dove several paces away from his squad mates and threw his body over the grenade to prevent injury to anyone else. His Distinguished Service Cross was posthumously awarded.[5]

On March 2, Task Force Byrne entered Venlo to the cheers of crowds of jubilant Hollanders wearing their own orange freedom colors. But the race was not done yet. Wheeling to the east, the task force seized Straelen and dozens of other German towns, capturing hundreds of German prisoners and moving some 50 miles in just three days. To cap off a spectacular advance, the lead elements of the 35th Infantry Division launched a night attack on the town of Sevelen, where they found stacks of German propaganda leaflets addressed to the very same 35th Infantry Division, warning them that the Roer defenses were impregnable.

On March 3, 1945, at 1330 hours, elements of Company C, 134th Infantry Regiment, 35th Infantry Division, made contact with members of I (British) Corps' 52nd (Lowland) Infantry Division and 53rd (Welsh) Infantry Divisions near Geldern. The German forces west of the Rhine were now in what came to be called the Wesel Pocket. Mopping up continued for some days, including the dispatch of a large force to seize Lintfort, where huge coal mines lay. The fighting west of the Rhine was not over. The 137th Infantry Regiment came up against what they were soon calling "88 Alley," where the remnants of eight German divisions, including several paratrooper units, had been wedged together near Ossenberg. This grouping was brought together under the umbrella command of First Parachute Army. First organized as a training command early in 1944, this headquarters had fought in France and Holland before being pushed by the British towards Wesel.

While I (British) Corps established a north-south line between the Xanten Forest and Geldern, the Canadians were still fighting determined German paratroopers to clear the Xanten Forest itself. General Alfred Schlemm, commanding First Parachute Army, soon realized he had no choice but to fall back to an inner defense line. This

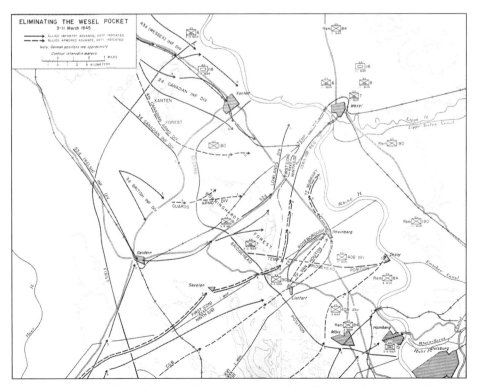

Eliminating the Wesel Pocket. (U.S. Army, Office of the Chief of Military History)

new line was 16 miles wide and anchored at the south on Orsoy. The area held by the Germans was relatively flat, with a circular-shaped ridge within the Xanten Forest and a wooded Boenninghardt Ridge the only tactical high ground in the zone. Within this area, the German general had about 50,000 troops with representatives from practically every division that had fought the British and Ninth Army east of the Roer. These included units from four different parachute divisions, the Panzer Lehr Division and the 116th Panzer Division. On the northern edge of his new perimeter, he had a fairly solid line, with much of his troops well organized. In this area his troops had been pushed back yard by yard by the British and Canadians and so they had retained their organization, if not their strength. To the south however, where the slashing columns of American task forces had cut through many of the combat and service units, there was far less organized resistance.

Schlemm's bridgehead was supported by two bridges that still crossed the Rhine behind First Parachute Army. These were the road and rail bridges at Wesel itself. Although located on the east bank, the city of Wesel lent its name to Schlemm's bridgehead. First Parachute Army needed to defend these bridges as they provided the only routes for supply, communications and reinforcements, as well as the only avenues of retreat. The Americans wanted the bridges for different reasons. They offered a way across the Rhine and their capture would also encircle First Parachute Army. Believing that an attack from the south against the more disorganized elements of First Parachute Army was more likely to succeed, General Simpson, with Montgomery's approval, launched XVI Corps against the Wesel bridges.

* * *

Schlemm had difficulties all around him. He had come from Italy in November 1944, to command the new First Parachute Army, which was then holding a position on the Western Front, from the junction of the Rhine and the Maas to Roermond, with four divisions. With the failure of the Ardennes counteroffensive and the obvious decision of the Allies to counterattack, his force was slowly built up. He and his commander (Colonel General Johannes Blaskowitz, commander of Army Group B) disagreed on where the Allied blow would fall. Despite reserves being kept away from his sector, Schlemm had built up an impressive line of defense to the northwest, facing the British and Canadians. Here, when General Crerar's First Canadian Army attacked through the dense Reichswald Forest, the Canadians were hit with a nightmare of water, ice, mud and an effective defense that slowed progress and cost them heavily in casualties. The Canadians' attack also finally convinced Schlemm's commanders that this was the main threat and they released some reserves to him.

Schlemm, who had fought at Anzio and created a defensive line from scratch to contain the Allies there, did much the same with his First Parachute Army. Within a few weeks he had built up his force to nine divisions, comprising three infantry, three parachute and three armored.[6] With this force he held a 20-mile-long line between the Maas and the Rhine and forced the British and Canadians to conduct what Eisenhower would later describe as some of the hardest fighting of the entire war. The young and indoctrinated parachutists, nearly all of whom had never even seen a parachute, continued to have faith that the German cause was still salvageable, and fought accordingly.

Schlemm's problems did not stem from his troops, but rather from his high command. As the First Canadian and Ninth U.S. Armies slowly closed in around his line of defense, orders came from Hitler that there was to be no retreat. Schlemm was ordered to establish a bridgehead west of the Rhine, from Krefeld to Wesel, and to hold that bridgehead at all costs. Schlemm later related:

> It was explained to me that this bridgehead was needed to maintain shipping traffic along the Rhine. This particular area was vital for the passage of coal from the mines of the Ruhr, since it was shipped along the river to the Lippe Canal, south of Wesel, and from there it was sent up the Dortmund-Emms Canal to the northern ports of Hamburg, Bremen and Wilhelmshaven. I could see the need for protecting this route, since it was the life-line upon which the German Navy relied to carry on its U-Boat warfare against the Allies.[7]

Despite Schlemm's best efforts, Krefeld fell to Ninth Army. This reduced Schlemm's bridgehead across the Rhine to 20 miles and his army was still under intense attacks from both north and south. It was then that a series of incredible orders began to reach him. The first ordered that under no circumstances was any bridge over the Rhine to be captured intact by the Allies. If a bridge was captured, the local army commander, in this case Schlemm, would answer with his head. No excuses or explanations were acceptable. But then, to make matters worse, no bridge over the Rhine was to be destroyed until the very last minute, in order to allow German troops and equipment to reinforce the defenses west of the Rhine as necessary. It was also necessary to evacuate as much industrial machinery as possible so as to maintain the German war effort. "Since I had nine bridges in my army sector," recalled Schlemm, "I could see my hopes for a long life rapidly dwindling."[8]

Schlemm moved his headquarters to Rheinberg, where he established wire communications with all the bridges in his sector. As Ninth Army approached Krefeld, he waited until what he thought was the last moment and then ordered the bridge there to be blown up. A local colonel refused, saying he needed the bridge for his own use. Schlemm literally shouted over the phone to blow the bridge immediately and, after some argument, during which the general threatened to personally shoot the colonel, it was destroyed.

Next, Schlemm was ordered to report to Hitler's headquarters, detailing the reason for every man and every piece of equipment that he wanted to evacuate across the Rhine. The fall of Krefeld and Homberg had eliminated the need to maintain his bridgehead, as the coal supply line was now cut by American artillery on the west bank of the Rhine. Schlemm's bridgehead was cluttered with abandoned vehicles, damaged tanks and armored vehicles, useless personnel, and artillery without ammunition, left by both First Parachute Army and the nearby Fifteenth Army. As a result, most of this equipment, which could have been salvaged had it been allowed to cross the Rhine, was abandoned by the roadside. Only in March would Hitler, at the repeated request of General Blaskowitz, allow a limited number of personnel and equipment to cross the Rhine. Even then, each man that crossed the Rhine had to have a certificate from his commander that he was too weak to continue fighting.

Meanwhile, Schlemm's troops were increasingly pushed into an overcrowded bridgehead and pounded relentlessly by the massed guns of the Allied artillery battalions. In this steadily shrinking area was crowded nine divisions, three corps headquarters and an army headquarters. One sugar refinery held the headquarters of three of the divisions, so tight was the remaining German-held area. Schlemm tried to argue some reason into his commanders' orders:

> It was only sheer luck that the bridge at Wesel had not yet been hit well enough to destroy it. I told General Blaskowitz that if the bridge was destroyed there would be no other escape route for my men trapped on the west bank of the Rhine. I also pointed out that if this force of fighting men was lost there would be no experienced troops left in this area to prevent an Allied crossing of the Rhine itself. I urged Blaskowitz to tell the Supreme Command at Berlin that if they did not believe my reports, the least they could do was to send a representative to Wesel and see the situation for themselves.[9]

Schlemm's argument worked. A representative from Berlin showed up, and Schlemm took him personally to the front and made sure he saw the foremost German positions, where the visiting lieutenant colonel came under enemy fire and was forced to hide in the dirt. His recommendation to Berlin was for an immediate withdrawal. On March 10, Schlemm pulled what remained of his First Parachute Army out of the Wesel Pocket.

*   *   *

Meanwhile, at Ninth Army, orders were to seize the Wesel bridges. General Anderson selected General Baade's 35th Infantry Division for the job. He attached Colonel Kimball's Combat Command B (CCB) of the 8th Armored Division and the 15th Cavalry Reconnaissance Group to it. Their mission was simply put—they were to capture the Wesel bridges and establish a bridgehead over the Rhine in that vicinity. Boundaries between corps, and even between the British Second and Ninth U.S. Armies, were to be ignored. Officially, Simpson had the boundary moved to the vicinity of Rheinberg, and later to Wesel itself.

Baade gave Kimball the mission of securing Lintfort and Rheinberg. Baade's intelligence picture was promising, and only minor opposition was expected. Rheinberg was supposed to be defended by about 300 disorganized and demoralized troops. Only a few self-propelled weapons and antitank guns were believed to be in the area. Leading the attack was Task Force Van Houten, commanded by Major John

H. Van Houten of the 36th Tank Battalion.[10] Troop B, 88th Cavalry Reconnaissance Squadron, would scout the best routes to reach Wesel.

On the left flank of CCB were two regiments of the 35th Infantry Division, while Colonel William S. Murray's 137th Infantry Regiment joined CCB. Further to the left, Colonel Byrne's 320th Infantry Regiment was soon in trouble. Two battalions came under intense fire from small arms, mortars, and artillery while approaching Hohe Busch, a small forest about half the distance to Rheinberg along the Sevelen–Rheinberg Highway. Return fire from the accompanying tanks and tank destroyers seemed to have no effect on the supposedly "disorganized and demoralized" enemy. A platoon of infantry did manage to enter a village just west of the forest, but it was soon forced out by encircling German troops.

Unaware that the infantry platoon had withdrawn, five medium and two light tanks of the 784th Tank battalion moved into the village. German hand-held anti-tank weapons soon knocked out one medium and both light tanks, and only the timely arrival of an infantry company spared the rest of them. The infantry went on to clear the village, but after dark the Germans put in a counterattack, which threatened to retake the town. One platoon was even surrounded in the village's hotel and suffered from hand grenades being thrown in through the windows.

The adjacent 137th Infantry had just as much trouble. Upon reaching a hill, the leading company came under heavy fire. Two platoons sought shelter in ditches or behind hedges along the road, while the other two sheltered in nearby houses. The company's forward artillery observer had lost his radio, so artillery support could not be called upon. Two German tanks then appeared and began firing on the trapped Americans. Captain Daniel Filburn, the company commander, and one of his platoon leaders, 2nd Lieutenant John H. Hartment, were killed. Without key leaders, and with the German tanks methodically blasting away at their positions, the infantrymen retreated. After reorganization and the attachment of tank destroyers, the company went back and held the village.

When another battalion of the 137th Infantry Regiment came under heavy fire, Major Harry F. Parker went to the nearby 88th Cavalry Reconnaissance Squadron and borrowed six half-tracks and some light tanks from the 8th Armored Division. He mounted Company G, 137th Infantry on the vehicles and sent the combined force racing into the village facing them. The village and a nearby hill were soon seized, along with more than 200 prisoners, and the swift loss of the village and hill persuaded other nearby defenders to withdraw.

General Baade, who still believed a swift rush could secure the Wesel bridges, now turned to Colonel Byrne's 320th Infantry Regiment and ordered it to strike north-wards for the key crossroads on the Geldern–Wesel highway behind Boenninghardt Ridge. CCB would take over the assignment of Rheinberg. After that, both CCB and the 137th Infantry Regiment would also strike for the bridges.

Byrne set out early on March 5, fully expecting to push aside a few defenders and reach his objective. But rear guards slowed the advance throughout the morning and just as the 1st Battalion, 320th Infantry, cleared the forest, a German force cut off the leading elements. It took the rest of the day to rescue the trapped platoon and to clear the Germans from fortified houses nearby. An attempt to outflank these defenses was halted at the cost of a company commander and two medium tanks.

Colonel Kimball's CCB encountered even heavier opposition. He sent one of his task forces, Task Force Roseborough, to take the town of Rheinberg.[11] Task Force Houten was to bypass the town and push on to the bridges. Once again this plan was based on the faulty intelligence of a weak defense. As Major Van Houten later explained: "We thought it was to be a road march."[12] It may have looked that way to Lieutenant Colonel Morgan G. Roseborough as his infantry force began its attack—the town of Lintfort was easily secured by mid-morning. But then, intending to move east towards the Rhine, Task Force Roseborough took a wrong turn in the town and found itself heading north, straight into a German ambush. Antitank guns quickly knocked out a tank and a half-track, while small-arms fire forced the infantry to dismount and move into the attack.

With Roseborough delayed by the ambush, Kimball ordered Van Houten to split his task force into three columns. One was to bypass Task Force Roseborough and drive up the main highway to Rheinberg. A second force was to use secondary roads to join the first column a thousand yards outside of Rheinberg, while the third was to use another highway and come into the town from the south. None of these columns managed to accomplish their assignments.

The column on the Rheinberg highway also ran into an ambush and lost four tanks to antitank fire and mines. The middle column never even reached the highway, as concealed enemy guns knocked out 12 of the column's 14 light tanks. The last column did manage to reach the highway leading into Rheinberg from the south, but was stopped outside the town by enemy infantry and lost two tanks to hand-held antitank weapons. Even Kimball, CCB's commander, found himself trapped inside a house by German machine gun and mortar fire. He escaped only after darkness silenced the enemy fire.

Captain David B. Kelly, Commander of Company B, 36th Tank Battalion, and the commander of the third column, had moved generally northeast onto the main highway to Rheinberg. Company B had no infantry support, and at Winterswinck heavy small-arms and antitank fire forced a halt. Enemy antitank teams had dug in 10 yards apart on the road in front of them and continued to inflict heavy damage on the American tanks. Kelly's tank was soon knocked out. Continuing to command on foot, he collected the crews of the knocked-out tanks and formed small infantry groups to try and displace the enemy antitank gunners. Weakly armed, these groups had little success. Meanwhile, Major Van Houten and Colonel Roseborough worked swiftly to gather infantry and additional armor support for Kelly. Company B, 49th Armored Infantry Battalion, commanded by Captain Clarence E. Smith, soon joined Kelly's band. While trying to reach Kelly, Van Houten's tank was hit and set on fire.

Captain Smith's Company B soon found itself under a "one-a-minute" barrage of 88mm antitank fire. Still, the advance resumed. Three 88mm guns were soon knocked out and two 20mm guns captured as well. But as the leading elements reached the northern edge of town, heavy automatic weapons fire pinned them down. In trying to find a way to renew Company B's attack, Captain Smith was killed instantly by enemy artillery fire and Second Lieutenant Benjamin R. Meech assumed command. After hours of bloody fighting, the town of Winterswick was cleared of the enemy. Company B, 36th Tank battalion, and Company B, 49th Armored Infantry Battalion, organized to resume their attack on Rheinberg.

In the renewed attack, the three leading tanks entered Rheinberg but were knocked out before they could make any progress. Nevertheless, this foothold was retained until CCB was relieved by the 3rd Battalion, 137th Infantry Regiment. Meanwhile, a mixed group, under the command of Captain Edward H. Look (the Operations Officer of the 49th Armored Infantry Battalion), had managed to reach the bank of the railroad station at Rheinberg. They had one remaining tank of the 1st Platoon, Company D, 36th Tank Battalion, under the command of Captain Arthur C. Erdman. As this last tank turned into the road to cross the tracks it was knocked out and set on fire. Erdman was thrown clear of the tank before it caught fire, but the others in the tank were killed. The remnants of Captain Look's small force withdrew to a nearby warehouse, where they remained surrounded until they were rescued at daylight.

The battle for Rheinberg would continue throughout the day and into the evening. The cost to CCB would be tallied at 199 casualties and 41 tanks. CCB lost all but 15 of its original 56 tanks. About 512 prisoners were taken and another 350 assumed killed, many identified as belonging to the 2nd Parachute Regiment. A total of 14 88mm antitank guns, 16 20mm antitank guns, four Mark IV tanks, a half-track, six trucks and a self-propelled gun had been destroyed or captured. After a brief rest, CCB was attached to the 137th Infantry Regiment of Lieutenant Colonel William S. Murray, but the overall battle was far from over.

* * *

Colonel Murray organized his force into three groups. Task Force Van Houten was joined by the 3rd Battalion, 137th Infantry. Task Force Roseborough remained unchanged and formed group two. Group three was Murray's own 137th Infantry, less the 3rd Battalion. The plan was to attack from Rheinberg to the northeast, using two groups forward and one in reserve. The path was to be from Rheinberg north to Grunthal, Broth and Buderich and then to the Wesel bridges and the Rhine. Groups one and two would lead the way as far as Grunthal, at which time group three would take the lead and move north of Wesel.

General Schlemm had been watching the progress of Anderson's XVI Corps closely. He quickly understood its objectives—to cut off his army from the Wesel bridges. He had seen this before, when he conducted rearguard actions in Russia and Italy. Still under orders not to withdraw, he had little choice but to establish a new defensive line. This line was held by just one corps headquarters, Schlemm having sent the other two across the Rhine. The new line included the town of Xanten and the Boenninghardt Ridge, but not much else. Under constant attack from Ninth Army to the south and II Canadian Corps from the north, even this line could not last long, but it did buy the Germans a few more days. It was not until March 9 that II Canadian Corps (Lt. Gen. G. G. Simonds), with the 4th Canadian Armored Division (Maj. Gen. C. Vokes), the 2nd Canadian Infantry Division (Maj. Gen. A. B. Matthews), and the 43rd (Wessex) Infantry Division (Maj. Gen. G. I. Thomas) managed to clear the Xanten area. Even then *General der Fallschirmtruppen* (Paratroopers) Eugen Meindl's II Parachute Corps managed to hold the Allies off while, unknown to the oncoming British, Canadians and Americans, the Germans were slowly evacuating their bridgehead. It wasn't until mid-morning on March 10 that air observation reported that both the Wesel bridges had been destroyed.

The British and Canadian Armies had captured 22,000 enemy troops and estimated that they had killed another 22,000. Ninth Army reported that it had captured 29,000 prisoners and estimated that it had inflicted an additional 16,000 killed or seriously wounded upon the Germans' First Parachute Army. This total of about 90,000 German casualties came from 19 different divisions. Against this, the British and Canadians reported 15,500 casualties in a month's fighting. Ninth Army reported casualties of 7,300 in the 17 days of fighting in Operation *Grenade*. Although this meant a four-to-one ratio of Allied casualties against German losses, no bridge had been captured across the Rhine.

It was also on March 10 that the German High Command decided upon a new commander in the West. Field Marshal von Rundstedt was "retired" (for the third time in the war) and replaced with Field Marshal Albert Kesselring. The 60-year-old new commander was, at this late stage of the war, one of the most successful Army Group commanders left to the Germans. Born in Bavaria, he joined the Austrian Army in 1904 and fought throughout World War I. Remaining in the Army after the war, he was a major general in 1932 and soon thereafter joined the *Luftwaffe*. He learned to fly and served as the *Luftwaffe's* Chief of Administration during a critical period in its development. By 1936, he was the *Luftwaffe* Chief of Staff. Later that same year, after some internal political maneuvering, Kesselring was sent out to the field as the Commander, Air Fleet 1. He led this force in the Polish Campaign of 1939 and against Belgium and Holland in 1940. He was made a field marshal on July 19, 1940, and fought in the Battle of Britain before moving to the Eastern Front. In November 1941, Kesselring was appointed to Supreme Command of the German Mediterranean Theater of Operations. In this position he commanded all German land and air forces within the Mediterranean. Here, he would fight the Allies in North Africa, Sicily and Italy for the next three years. His successful delaying tactics brought him to the favorable attention of Hitler, who was impressed by his ability to repeatedly delay the Allies' attempts to clear Italy and attack Germany from the south. By the end of the war, he would have the unique distinction of being the only one of Hitler's field marshals to have served continuously without ever being relieved of duty. In fact, as the Third Reich collapsed, in May 1945, Hitler would appoint Kesselring as his Supreme Commander in the south while giving Admiral Karl Doenitz the same command in the north, thereby identifying the officers he most trusted as his Third Reich came crashing down.

But that was still to come. On March 10, Task Force Murray suddenly found itself unopposed. A quick movement forward brought it to the edge of the demolished highway bridge at Wesel. The battle of the Wesel Pocket was over.

* * *

In 17 days Ninth Army had driven 53 miles, from the Roer at Jülich to the Rhine at Wesel. It had cleared 34 miles of the west bank of the Rhine at a cost of 7,300 casualties. It had forced a crossing of a flooded, defended river. In the course of the campaign, Ninth Army had made two distinct changes of direction and at the end a minor adjustment to reach Wesel. It had, for the first time, encountered millions of noncombatants, enemy civilians and impressed foreign workers from dozens of countries, as well as liberated prisoners of war. For the first time, the Americans encountered an enemy populace that had not fled the war zone. Millions of these unfortunates were now wandering the battle zone and rear areas with no place to go, no food, no prospects and no health care.

So swiftly had Ninth Army advanced that, by March 4, only five of the army's twelve assigned divisions were still in contact with the enemy. The others were garrisoning captured towns and villages and preparing for the next operation. General Simpson and his staff were concentrating now on a surprise Rhine crossing. Two plans were eventually completed, with both envisioning a crossing somewhere between Düsseldorf and Mundelheim. The intermediate objective of both plans was the seizure of the city of Hamm, a rail center at the northeastern corner of the Ruhr Industrial Area. The two plans differed only in the routes by which the different corps of Ninth Army would move once they were put into effect, but the refusal (again) of Montgomery to approve these plans changed Ninth Army's role in the future Rhine crossing.

Disappointed over the decision not to force a crossing, Simpson immediately set about preparing for the next offensive. The army command post moved forward to München-Gladbach on March 10 and began preparing to cross the Rhine. Military government and civil affairs units soon found themselves fully engaged in dealing with the civilian, foreign-worker and prisoner-of-war issues. Soon the army headquarters was a plethora of uniforms of different nations and organizations. Both the United States Navy and the Royal Navy appeared. British Army, French Army,

Canadian Army, Royal Air Force, Belgian, Netherlands and United Nations Relief and Rehabilitation Administration personnel all appeared in anticipation of the coming offensive.

Simpson ordered that rest centers be established for the troops that could be spared from the front. Existing rest centers were enlarged and made available to all Ninth Army troops, and entertainment centers were established further to the rear. At its height, this program, under the command of Lieutenant Colonel George W. Bailey, Jr., accommodated 5,000 soldiers on a "hotel service" basis. It included hotel rooms with beds and linens, individually served meals, recreational rooms staffed by the American Red Cross and a wide variety of other options for leisure hours, including movies and other entertainment. During Ninth Army's campaigns, more than 120,000 soldiers made use of these facilities.

Ninth Army was also burdened, as mentioned above, with health and sanitation problems. Most of the towns and cities it had conquered had been largely destroyed. No electricity, running water or sewage systems remained intact. Food was non-existent, as were medical facilities. Ninth Army efforts to restore all these vital services and to provide food and medical care were begun immediately and were generally successful. Farmers were ordered to return to their farms to produce food, joined by unemployed city laborers. Measures to prevent epidemics were implemented and an outbreak of typhus, with 180 cases, was addressed at once. Mass disinfection with DDT powder and the isolation of the typhus cases soon removed this threat. Some 10,000 displaced persons were evacuated to the Netherlands, Belgium and France, while an additional 15,000 were cared for in 16 camps established within Ninth Army's area. Meanwhile, plans to bring the war into Germany continued.

Operation *Flashpoint*

By March 11, 1945, Ninth Army had closed up to the Rhine throughout its sector. To its north, the British Second and First Canadian Armies had done the same. All eyes now turned to look across the river. A few days earlier, on March 7, First Army had managed to seize an intact bridge across the Rhine at the town of Remagen and already had a bridgehead on the opposite bank. Further south, Third Army was crossing the Moselle River and closing up to the Rhine in its sector of the Allied front. Below Third Army, General Patch's Seventh Army had already reached the Rhine and was waiting for clearance to force a crossing, much like the Ninth. Adjacent to Patch, Marshal Jean de Lattre de Tassigny's First French Army was also poised to cross the river.[1]

Much like the plans for the cross-Channel invasion of June 1944, the planning for the Rhine crossing had originated, at least in Ninth Army's case, some six months earlier. While current operational planning had always taken precedence, Ninth Army staff had continually updated and re-worked plans to force a Rhine crossing and plunge into the heart of Germany. Many arrangements had to be completed before such a crossing could be attempted. Without a bridge, the attack would be an assault river crossing against a defended east bank. Engineer troops had to be trained to use specialized equipment. Crossing sites had to be identified and scouted, which Ninth Army had to do repeatedly, since it had moved several times and therefore had new sites available depending upon its final location in the Allied line. Intelligence of enemy defenses and map coverage were both necessary. Assembling the forces required for the attack would take time and was always subject to change due to emergencies elsewhere.

And then there was the river itself. In 1944, the Rhine varied from about 900 to 1,500 feet in width. At low water, the maximum depth was about 10 feet, with a river bottom of sand and gravel. The banks were usually also of sand and gravel, with many stone revetments projecting into the river, which was bordered by two continuous systems of dikes, constructed of earth and sometimes reinforced. The velocity of the surface of the river averaged about five feet per second, increasing to eight feet per second at the highest navigable water period.

It wasn't until November 1944 that Ninth Army staff began to make concrete plans for the crossing. With the Rhine in tantalizingly close proximity, a basic plan was drawn up for an army of three corps, comprising nine infantry divisions and three armored divisions. One corps would demonstrate near Düsseldorf and near Uerdingen. A second corps would launch three infantry divisions at a crossing at Rheinberg and strike for the industrial area, but would not fully penetrate that region at this time. The main effort was to be made by the third corps, at Xanten and Rees, with three infantry and two armored divisions. This force would make a wide encirclement of the Ruhr after seizing Wesel. The plan assumed offensives by the British and Canadians to the north. Interestingly, much of this early basic plan would later be used.

Aware of the magnitude of the coming task, Ninth Army's Engineer Officer, Brigadier General Richard U. Nicholas, had met on October 18 with the Chief Engineer of the European Theater of Operations and the engineers of all American armies then operational in the theater. Preliminary decisions included the stockpiling of river-crossing equipment and supplies necessary for such an operation. A special section of Ninth Army's engineer depot was established to store this equipment. In addition, an engineer combat group was established at Viée, Belgium, at the Maas river, for training purposes. This group also provided training for all the engineer units of Ninth Army, including the building of floating bridges, ferrying, construction of protective booms, bridge maintenance and the operation of storm boats, outboard motors, and assault boats. Particular attention was given to the maintenance of floating Bailey bridges, since few engineers had been trained in this type of bridging. Laying communications across the river was another aspect.

On November 15, 1944, the United States Navy arrived to assist. Although most of the threat of a German attack by sea had been eliminated by this time, the Navy had maintained a small contingent at the port of Cherbourg to protect against raids from the German-held Channel Islands and the Biscay ports that remained in German hands. The detachment was under the command of Vice Admiral Alan G. Kirk.[2] When General Bradley's Twelfth Army Group engineers came to him for assistance, he initiated Operation *Delaware*, under the command of Commander William J. Whiteside. His Task Group 122.5 was to provide landing support craft for army units as they approached the Rhine. Initially, each of Bradley's armies would receive 24 Landing Craft, Vehicle, Personnel, (LCVP), which would be carried forward on tank transporters, but it was soon pointed out that these were too small to carry an M4 Sherman Tank. To rectify the situation, an additional 45 Landing Craft, Medium (LCM) were added to the equipment list. Too big for tank transporters, these would move along the Albert Canal as far as the Meuse River, south of Maastricht, where they would be mounted on army trailers and trucked forward.

Task Group 122.5 was subdivided into three task units. Each of Bradley's armies would be assisted by one of these units. Task Unit 122.5.3 was assigned to Ninth

Army and ordered to be prepared to initiate crossings near Rheinberg, beginning on March 23, 1945.

Meanwhile, others became involved in the planning. On December 6, 1944, representatives of Major General Matthew B. Ridgway's XVIII (Airborne) Corps had met with Ninth Army staffers to discuss the possible employment of the airborne units under its command in a future Rhine crossing.[3] Although planning seemed to be progressing well, the sudden call for XVIII (Airborne) Corps to participate in the Battle of the Bulge had halted the process. It wasn't until January 19, 1945, that another planning conference was held, by Twenty-First Army Group. In this conference, which included representatives from the British Second, First Canadian, and Ninth U.S. Armies, the details were mostly technical and dealt with the distribution and use of specialized equipment, but one aspect did disturb General Simpson. It seemed that there was a disagreement about which crossing sites would be made available to his army. From the conference held on January 19, it was clear that the British Second Army intended to use crossing sites, specifically at Rheinberg and at Rees, that Simpson had planned to use for his men. General Moore quickly pointed out that the bridges at Wesel and the road nets in that area were the minimum required for the support of American operations east of the Rhine and that these must be assigned to Ninth Army for the plan to succeed.

The staff of Lieutenant General Sir Miles C. Dempsey's British Second Army disagreed. They felt that the Wesel crossings were needed by them to sustain their own offensive. While acknowledging that the bridges at Wesel would have to be constructed by Ninth Army's engineers, they would still need to have priority over them. This controversy now brought up the issue of assigning zones of operation for the various armies of Twenty-First Army Group.

The matter was settled on January 21, when Montgomery issued his directive dealing with the plans and instructions for the Rhine crossing. After reading this directive, Simpson and his staff were "flabbergasted!"[4] Ninth Army had no role in the coming crossing. Field Marshal Montgomery had allocated "one American corps of two infantry divisions" to British Second Army. No mention was made of Ninth Army, nor any of its corps commands.[5]

Ninth Army's initial reaction was one of confusion. Who was supposed to support the one American corps assigned to the British Second Army? Who would build the necessary bridges that the British themselves admitted they did not have the engineering capacity to build? What use, if any, was to be made of the vast stockpile of bridging equipment within Ninth Army? What were Ninth Army's 12 divisions and two other corps supposed to do while the British crossed the Rhine?

Additional conferences were quickly scheduled to iron out these and many other issues. It was pointed out that the Americans had the bridge-building capacity the British lacked. It was also mentioned that the limited number of British and Canadian combat divisions could only secure a limited bridgehead across the Rhine and that the Americans would be required to provide enough troops to seize all the proposed crossing sites. Finally, the British and Canadians lacked sufficient combat divisions to launch any major exploitation of the bridgeheads once established across the Rhine. This required that at some time Ninth Army would have to be passed through the British Second Army over these limited and narrow bridgeheads, a dubious solution at best. A lengthy discussion of these and other problems began in late January between Ninth Army and the British Second Army.

The result of these discussions was an agreement to divide the Xanten crossing site, which would allow for a two-corps American effort north and south of Wesel. The front of the British Second Army would be correspondingly reduced between Xanten and Emmerich. The finalized plan allowed for a three-army Rhine crossing simultaneously, Ninth Army to the south, British Second Army in the center, and First Canadian Army to the north. Once again Montgomery rejected the plan, but he saw the necessity of additional crossings and an American force to ensure success of the planned Rhine crossing.

As a result, while the British Second Army retained the Wesel crossing site, Ninth Army was authorized, on February 4, to cross with two American Corps at the Rheinberg crossing site formerly assigned to the British. Further, the new plan assigned the Wesel crossing sites and the route to the east and the Ruhr, to Ninth Army, once the British had secured the bridgehead. Additional divisions were to be brought from the Mediterranean Theater of Operations to strengthen the British and Canadian forces. The number and use of airborne forces remained incomplete, although they were expected to attack Wesel from the rear. The overall offensive was named Operation *Plunder*, while Ninth Army's part in the attack was termed Operation *Flashpoint*.

*   *   *

Operation *Flashpoint* planned for one American corps to hold the west bank of the Rhine from Düsseldorf north to Duisburg. A second corps would attack in a narrow zone of operations between the northern edge of the Ruhr and the Lippe River. The third corps was to be assembled in reserve for a strike north of the Lippe to the east and committed as soon as the Wesel bridgehead had been established, the bridges required there built, and the town's streets opened to traffic.

To the north of Ninth Army, the British Second Army would attack with two corps at Xanten and Rees. A third corps would be held in reserve for crossing as soon as possible. XVIII (Airborne) Corps would assist the British Second Army with a drop behind Wesel and support the British advance until such time as the corps headquarters was relieved and its units distributed to the British Second and Ninth U.S. Armies. Simpson would be responsible for the logistical support of the American units within XVIII (Airborne) Corps. Further north, the Second Canadian Army would cross in the Emmerich area.

Not all issues had been resolved. The matter of supply routes and supply depots remained questionable. It wasn't until Twenty-First Army Group issued a final directive, on February 21, that most matters seemed to have been addressed. This confirmed the crossing sites for all the armies, including Simpson's Ninth, and set a provisional target of March 31 as the assault date. The directive went on to state that no crossing would be attempted until the entire area west of the Rhine and north of Düsseldorf was cleared of the enemy. A boundary was established between Ninth Army and the British Second Army along the Venlo-Geldern-Wesel Road, and that road assigned to Ninth Army to allow it to move the vital bridging equipment forward. This was complicated by instructions that while Ninth Army was to build the main bridges at Venlo, use of those bridges was restricted to the British Second Army.

In the directive, Ninth Army was also to create a bridgehead at Rheinberg and then extend that bridgehead to the south and east far enough to ensure its maintenance using only its own forces. Ninth Army also had the responsibility to protect the bridges at Wesel, as well as its own at Rheinberg. Ninth Army was also to install a total of four bridges at Wesel in the British sector.[6] The fact that the Americans were to build and protect the British bridges at Wesel was unusual but necessary, due to the lack of sufficient British resources. Simpson also responded to another British request by assigning Brigadier General Nicholas the task of ensuring Ninth Army engineers were made available upon request by the British, to maintain the roads and bridges in the British sector.

With the final directive in hand, Simpson made his army assignments. General Anderson's XVI Corps would plan the one-corps assault-crossing of the Rhine. This assignment carried the stipulation that Anderson's corps might not be the actual corps making the attack, but, since it was currently in reserve, it had the time and resources to undertake the required planning. It was further believed that the planning for the race to the Rhine placed Anderson's corps in the best position to make the river crossing. The operation was to be planned for two infantry divisions, one armored division and supporting troops.

Once across the Rhine, the assault corps was to establish an initial bridgehead and then expand that bridgehead to the line Walsum–Kirchhellen. It was also to assist in the seizure of Wesel from the south and southeast and to seize any intact crossings over the Lippe River Canal. Anderson and his staff completed a plan on February 19 and submitted it to Ninth Army, where developments and changes were constantly incorporated. In the month between the plan's completion and its execution, numerous adjustments were made based upon the needs of the British Second and First Allied Airborne Armies. The rapid advance of the Allies once across the Roer moved the assault date up to March 24. Finally, the airborne phase, originally planned for three airborne divisions, was reduced to two due to lack of airlift resources—the 6th British Airborne Division (Major General E. L. Bols) and the 17th U.S. Airborne Division (Major General William M. Miley).

The assault troops were designated as the 30th Infantry Division and the 79th Infantry Division, veterans of France, Luxembourg and Germany. These two units were withdrawn from the front and assembled at Echt, on the Maas, for specialized training. By March 8, both were back along the west bank of the Rhine awaiting the command to attack. Here, they continued training with the 1153rd and 1148th Engineer Combat Groups, which would be the engineers conducting the river crossing. Both groups, assigned to XVI Corps, worked with the infantrymen day and night to ensure success.

As the Roer crossing had once again demonstrated, armored support was needed as soon as possible after forcing a river crossing. To expedite this, a company of Duplex Drive (DD) Tanks from the 736th Tank battalion was assigned to the early assault waves.[7] Ninth Army's Ordnance Officer, Colonel Claude A. Black, found that the tanks, supplied by the British, were not in operable condition when Ninth Army received them. It took two months to obtain the necessary parts and manuals in order to make them operational for the crossing.

Another tank battalion, the 747th Tank Battalion, was given the job of operating the Navy's assault landing craft. These included the Landing Vehicle, Tracked (LVT) and amphibious cargo and personnel carriers, known as "alligators." Here again, much maintenance work was required before these vehicles were combat ready. Training of the tank crewmen continued even as maintenance was being performed, so as not to cause delay.

Ninth Army also found that there was a shortage of operators for the motor-driven assault boats. The entire army was canvassed for men with experience in operating outboard motors and some 284 men were identified and given special training by XVI Corps, to which they were assigned. That training, carried out on the Maas, identified many shortages and deficiencies, which Ninth Army worked to correct. One such problem was getting tanks across the river. As mentioned, it was believed that an LCM would be adequate to carry a Sherman tank, based upon the measurements of the two pieces of equipment. However, when the 743rd Tank Battalion conducted tests it was discovered that the clearance and freeboard were too small in actual practice to drive the tanks on or off the landing craft. Ninth Army's solution was to substitute light tanks for the larger M4 Sherman tanks, which would be floated across the river by reinforced Bailey bridge rafts powered by five outboard motors.

As always in his planning, Simpson looked for ways to lower the expected casualty rate. Ninth Army staff approached a special unit, the 23rd Headquarters Special Troops, whose specialty was deception. Equipped with inflated rubber tanks, vehicles and artillery guns, this group added sound effects to make their deceptions realistic and convincing. They were asked to put on a "performance" near Uerdingen in the hopes that the enemy would believe it was the area of Ninth Army's main effort. To further deceive the enemy, General Gillem's XIII Corps was assigned to conduct a demonstration in the Düsseldorf–Uerdingen zone. Although no XIII Corps unit was to actually cross the river, it was to act as if a crossing was planned.

The movement of supporting artillery was concealed by moving only at night and maintaining former positions as if the guns were still in place. Radio silence was imposed on all units not in contact with the enemy. Engineer supplies were concealed with utmost care and false engineer equipment depots were displayed within XIII Corps' zone. Engineers in XIII Corps also openly constructed approach roads to the Rhine to further deceive the enemy. Patrols were more intense in XIII Corps than elsewhere. The medical facilities set up in anticipation of casualties were ordered to conceal their Red Cross markings until the day of the assault, while a factory was set up in a populated area to manufacture dummy assault boats. The assault troops in XVI Corps were ordered to remove their identifying shoulder patch identifications until just 12 hours before the attack. Movement in XVI Corps was done at night and all daylight movement was held to a minimum, while maximum camouflage discipline was imposed. Meanwhile, General McLain's XIX Corps conducted river-crossing training along the Erft River and canal, and later sent the 83rd Infantry Division to replace the 30th and 79th Infantry Divisions at the Maas when they moved forward to the Rhine.

Much of this extensive effort at deception worked. Several dummy engineer parks were attacked by enemy aircraft, but not one actual engineer park was attacked. Later interrogations of prisoners revealed that neither of the two assault divisions, the 30th and 79th Infantry Divisions, had been identified by the enemy as being in the area. Nor did the enemy have a clear picture of Ninth Army's order of battle. As late as April 1, German intelligence still believed that the main Ninth Army crossing would come at Uerdingen and retained elements of three divisions at that location.[8] It would not be until Ninth Army's XVI Corps had reached the Ruhr itself that these German units would be re-deployed east.

Problems continued to arise even as the assault was launched. At the last moment it was learned that the netting for use in the antisubmarine booms at the Rhine bridge sites had been shipped incomplete—there were no floats to hold up the netting. Ninth Army engineers quickly improvised floats from 55-gallon steel drums and installed the netting. Without enough drums available, captured enemy stocks were searched and a sufficient supply located. Ninth Army also had to prepare to supply the 17th Airborne Division once it came under its control. Although the unit's initial supply was the responsibility of the First Allied Airborne Army, the division would soon be within Ninth Army's zone of responsibility. A depot was therefore established with food, gasoline, ammunition and special items of signal and engineer equipment. Fearing high casualties among the airborne troops, Ninth Army set up a special medical facility, including a battalion headquarters, a field hospital platoon, a collecting company, an ambulance platoon, and an evacuation hospital for the use of the 17th Airborne Division.

* * *

Across the Rhine the Germans prepared as best they could for the coming assault. Clearly, an Allied river crossing somewhere along the lower Rhine was coming, and soon. The only question that remained was where and when it would strike. Determined to do their best, the Germans set about preparing a defense. German General Staff officers studied reports and data and decided that the main Allied assault would come somewhere between Emmerich and Dinslaken, seven miles southeast of Wesel. Colonel General Johannes Blaskowitz, the commander of Army Group H, assigned this sector to the stronger of his two subordinate armies, General Schlemm's First Parachute Army. The sector downstream from Emmerich went to *General der Infanterie* Guenther Blumentritt's Twenty-Fifth Army. General Blaskowitz and his fellow commanders anticipated an Allied airborne landing in conjunction with the assault crossing, and this was expected in the general area 10 miles northeast of Wesel in order to ease an Allied bridgehead in that area.

Schlemm's First Parachute Army, which soon found itself in the direct path of the Allied assault, had three corps, two of which had three *ad hoc* divisions each, while the third corps had two standard divisions. Opposite the British near Rees stood the strongest corps, II Parachute Corps, with about 12,000 combat troops, but its only reserve was a replacement training division. Army Group H's only reserve was XLVII Panzer Corps, a veteran of many battles on different fronts of earlier in war, with remnants of a panzer grenadier division and a panzer division. Total tanks within XLVII Panzer Corps came to 35. In total, Army Group H had barely 200 tanks and assault guns, and its main strength lay in its reasonable artillery contingent. In addition to the guns of a *volks* artillery corps and a *volkswerfer* (mortar) brigade, Blaskowitz increased firepower by withdrawing nearly all mobile antiaircraft guns from the Netherlands and using them to supplement the artillery and mortars defending Wesel, primarily intended to thwart the expected airborne attack. Allied intelligence officers would later estimate that there were over 300 heavy and light antiaircraft guns assigned for this purpose. The Germans had no time to build concrete fortifications, so all fortifications east of the Rhine were of the field variety. There existed a solid forward line along the river and the railroad that parallels the river, but there was little in-depth fortification. These plans were submitted to Kesselring and approved on March 14.

Kesselring knew that his chances to successfully defend the Rhine were slim. He had no reserves to back up his troops and he was aware that German morale was questionable (varying as one commentator put it, "from suspicion to callous resignation") and that his officer corps "lacked confidence and wondered just what were the demands of duty."[9] He had available to him barely 85,000 men in Army Group H, less than one Allied Corps. Things continued to get worse. On March 21, Allied aircraft bombed the headquarters building of the First Parachute Army, severely wounding General Schlemm. There was no immediate replacement available, so Schlemm, running a high fever and in no condition to lead an army, retained command until March 28, when General Blumentritt arrived to take over.

As the days passed, the Germans became increasingly nervous about the coming attack. An Allied smoke screen, covering their movements on the west bank, drew an increased rate of artillery fire from the Germans. On March 20, General Blaskowitz ordered the highest state of alert among the troops defending the Rhine. German planes, individually or in small groups, took advantage of periods when Allied aircraft were elsewhere and strafed what Allied concentrations they could find. German aircraft also concentrated on knocking the Americans' light observation planes out of the sky to hinder Allied artillery fire. Just about every Allied patrol that crossed the river was received by German small-arms or mortar fire. Most German patrols that crossed the river to gather intelligence disappeared, the members usually winding up in an Allied prisoner-of-war camp.

Things on the Allied side of the Rhine had, by mid-afternoon on March 23, reached a state of readiness. Montgomery waited only for a weather report to determine if conditions were suitable for the airborne phase of Operation *Plunder*. When the forecast was favorable, he ordered the operation to proceed. At 1800 hours that same day, the Allied artillery's harassing fire slowly increased in intensity near Rees. Three hours later, it had reached bombardment status as the leading assault waves of Lieutenant General Sir Brian Horrocks' XXX (British) Corps entered the river southeast of Rees. Seven minutes, later the first assault craft of the 51st (Highland) Infantry Division (General Rennie) touched down on the east bank of the Rhine against sporadic opposition.[10] Although this sector was defended by veteran paratroopers of *General der Fallschirmtruppen* Eugen Meindl's II Parachute Corps, they were kept down by the intense artillery fire protecting the assault waves. Mud slowed the advance of the amphibious vehicles and some of the DD tanks became stuck, but the advance formed an initial bridgehead. By dawn, the village of Speldrop, a mile northwest of the crossing site, was taken, although its ownership was still disputed by the German 8th Parachute Division.

General Blaskowitz did not believe this was the main assault, but nevertheless ordered his 15th Panzer Grenadier Division from reserve to counterattack, hoping to destroy this bridgehead before others could be secured. This fit nicely into Montgomery's plan, which intended the landings at Rees to draw off German reserves from other landing sites.

An hour after the landings at Rees, the 1st Commando Brigade (Brigadier Derek Mills-Roberts) of General Ritchie's XII (British) Corps crossed two miles downstream of Wesel after heavy bombing by the Royal Air Force. By dawn, the Commandos controlled most of the town, with the exception of a few holdouts scattered about the city who were systemically rooted out. The XII (British) Corps attack continued until 0200 hours on March 24, when Ninth Army began its own assault. The 15th (Scottish) Infantry Division (Major General C. M. Barber) crossed opposite Xanten with two infantry brigades. In the sector defended by the German 84th Infantry Division, things went as planned and initial objectives were secured. On the sector defended by the 7th Parachute Division, however, the British had a harder time and it was not until full daylight that the initial objectives could be reached.

*   *   *

Operation *Flashpoint* began at the same time as the 15th (Scottish) Division's assault at Xanten. General Anderson launched his river crossing with his veteran 30th and 79th Infantry Divisions, supported by the 8th Armored Division. In reserve were the 35th and 75th Infantry Divisions. In addition, Anderson had his usual XVI Corps Artillery (Brigadier General Charles C. Brown) and Ninth Army's 34th Field Artillery Brigade (Brigadier John F. Uncles) with 13 battalions of medium, heavy and super-heavy guns in support. General Gillem's XIII Corps Artillery (Brigadier General George D. Shea), with another 11 artillery battalions, was also supporting XVI Corps. All were veterans of one or more recent campaigns. A tank destroyer group with six battalions, six separate tank battalions, three engineer combat groups, two antiaircraft artillery groups, a smoke generator battalion, a chemical (4.2in. mortar) battalion and dozens of smaller units were available. In addition, General Simpson still held XIII and XIX Corps in reserve with six more veteran divisions. The XXIX Tactical Air command was also available, although some of its strength was detached to support Operation *Varsity*, the airborne phase of the attack.

Despite this overwhelming force, it still fell to the frontline infantryman, tanker and engineer to win the battle. Facing XVI Corps across the Rhine were two corps of the First Parachute Army. LXXXVI Corps, of *General der Infanterie* Erich Straube held Wesel and a line from the Lippe to Dinslaken. The German 180th Infantry Division faced the 30th U.S. Infantry Division and part of the 79th Infantry Division. The weakest defenders, LXIII Corps, under *General der Infanterie* Erich Abraham, covered the remaining two miles south as far as Duisburg. It contained an *ad hoc* formation known as the Hamburg Division and the 2nd Parachute Division.

As Ninth Army prepared to initiate Operation *Flashpoint*, the Supreme Allied Commander, General Eisenhower, came for a visit. Together with General Simpson he mingled with the assault troops and found them "remarkably eager to finish the job."[11] The evening provided a three-quarter moon and a west wind, which kept the smoke screen flowing towards the enemy. At 0100 hours on the morning of March 24, General Anderson's XVI Corps Artillery opened fire with 2,070 pieces manned by 40,000 artillerymen of Ninth Army. The earth shook and the sound was deafening. Every minute, for an hour, more than a thousand shells, ranging in weight from 25 to 325 pounds of explosives, detonated on the east bank of the Rhine. In total, more than 65,000 rounds were fired. Behind the German lines, Allied aircraft pounded airfields within range of the crossing sites.

Under cover of this cacophony of sound and fury, the infantrymen and engineers of Ninth Army's 1153rd Engineer Combat Group moved up the assault boats and took their places on the west bank of the Rhine. Other engineers began to move the vital bridging equipment into place for installation as soon as the east bank could be cleared of the enemy. All three infantry regiments of General Hobbs' 30th Infantry Division would cross at the same time. The 119th Infantry was on the left, just southeast of Buederich, near where the Lippe and Rhine met. The 117th Infantry crossed in the center at the village of Wallach, while the 120th Infantry crossed two miles southeast near the big bend in the Rhine at Rheinberg. Each regiment used one battalion in the assault, organized into four waves, with two-minute intervals between waves. Occasional German mortar fire fell as the infantrymen and engineers waited for the signal to begin, but few casualties resulted. Machine guns fired tracers toward the east bank to guide the assault boats, while colored aircraft landing lights would show the path for the follow-up troops.

The 30th Infantry Division had adopted the nickname "Old Hickory" from its origins in Andrew Jackson's home state of Tennessee. By the end of 1944 they were calling themselves the "Workhorse of the Western Front" since they had fought in every major battle since Normandy—the Mortain Counterattack, France, Aachen, the Siegfried Line and the Battle of the Bulge. Once again they were in the lead, storming the Rhine, the last natural barrier before Germany.

Facing them across the river was a dike and then open ground for about two miles. Then came two railroad embankments, which crossed their sector running southeast, about 1,000 yards apart. Further east, the country became more rugged, with more woods and other terrain that would benefit the defenders. Seven miles beyond the Rhine lay an *Autobahn*, running north and south. Seven miles further east lay the Dorsten–Osterfeld highway, but there was a concerning lack of good east–west roads to carry Allied traffic toward the enemy. One road paralleled the Lippe Canal and another fair road entered the division zone some 10 miles east of the river, but that was all. Most roads in the area ran north to south.

Air support would come, as usual, from the XXIX Tactical Air Command. The 366th Fighter-Bomber Group was assigned to the support of the 30th Infantry Division, while the follow-up 79th Infantry Division was assigned the 373rd Fighter-Bomber Group. Other aircraft would fly deep penetration missions to harass enemy reinforcements and communications.

As the assault hour approached, the west bank of the Rhine, normally quiet and vacant except for outposts, suddenly became quite crowded. Assault troops moved up, carrying their heavy assault boats and storm boats the final 300 yards down to the water's edge. Massive trucks carrying the Navy's assault craft crawled up to the crossing sites and began unloading. The engineers set about building the pontoon bridges they were to install. Enemy artillery and mortar fire did little to delay these proceedings. At 0200 hours the actual assault began.

The American artillery fire moved deeper into Germany, while tracer bullets fired over the heads of the assault troops showed them proper direction. As was to be expected, occasional errors marred the perfection of the assault. Company G, 120th Infantry, had one wave of its boats land accidentally on a spit of land almost 1,000 yards away from the rest of the second battalion. In the zone of the 119th Infantry Regiment, two power-driven assault boats were knocked out by enemy fire. Apart from these incidents, though, the assault went off almost exactly as planned. Even the planned rush across the river of some bulldozers to smooth out the east banks of the river turned out to be unnecessary, although the bulldozers crossed successfully.

The 2nd Battalion, 119th Infantry, seized the dike and the locks at the mouth of the Lippe Canal within half an hour of landing. Nearby, the 1st Battalion, 117th Infantry, took the riverside town of Ork and 150 prisoners in less than two hours against modest opposition. One of the 117th Infantry's company commanders would later remark, "There was no real fight to it, the artillery had done the job for us."[12] The 2nd Battalion, 120th Infantry, after recovering Company G, stormed the town of Mehrum and moved a mile beyond before daylight. As the assault troops moved east, support battalions began to cross the river and move up.

The Germans were stunned by the power and force of the attack. The first few hundred prisoners who entered Ninth Army prisoner-of-war cages six hours later were "still in a stunned or dazed condition from the artillery pounding to which they had been subjected. 'Hellish' – 'terrifying' – was all some could say at first. One officer prisoner of war apologized for his seemingly incoherent answers, saying his head still felt thick and numb from the recent ordeal."[13]

It was left to the 3rd Battalion, 120th Infantry Regiment, to make the most spectacular advance of the operation. The battalion landed on the east bank by 0400 hours and started out from Mehrum towards Gotterswickerhamm, two miles due east along the river bank. Here, opposition led by a fanatical Nazi lieutenant held up the advance until he was killed by Captain Harold P. Plummer of Company K. Immediately upon the death of their leader, the rest of the garrison, about 100 men, surrendered. By noon, the battalion was at Mollen, along one of the railroad embankments crossing the division's front.

Tanks came up in support, but could not play a role until the two railroad embankments were seized, for the underpasses were covered by German antitank weapons. The 3rd Battalion attacked and knocked out the first line of defense. Then the assault turned to securing the underpasses. These were defended stoutly by small-arms fire and antitank weapons. Three enemy armored vehicles were also defending the embankments. Nevertheless, the 3rd Battalion, now aided by the 2nd Battalion, 119th Infantry, overcame these defenses before lunchtime. Nearby, the 117th Infantry encountered the same type of opposition and also cleared its area by noon. Engineers quickly moved up to fill in the massive craters the Germans had dug to delay the advance of American tanks, and the advance rolled east. By afternoon on the first day, there was no longer an organized defense facing the Workhorse Division.

The 79th Infantry Division was assigned the right flank of XVI Corps. It, too, would attack in a column of battalions using two infantry regiments. Supported by the 1148th Engineer Combat Group, the 89th Chemical Mortar Battalion, the 74th Chemical Smoke Generator Company, the 809th Tank Destroyer Battalion and artillery of the 8th Armored Division,[14] the 313th Infantry Regiment would attack on the right and the 315th Infantry Regiment on the left. That the assault was imminent was highlighted when Generals Eisenhower, Simpson and Anderson visited the division on March 24.

Considering that the "Cross of Lorraine" Division's history included Normandy, Cherbourg, Brittany, France, and other hard-fought battles, the 79th Infantry Division's own history calls the Rhine River crossing "easy."[15] Less than 30 casualties were incurred during the attack and these included men who suffered from exposure after their boats overturned while crossing the river. Another man broke his wrist when he stepped out of his assault boat. Indeed, even the overturned boat was accidental. Captain John E. Potts, the Operations officer of the 315th Infantry Regiment, found himself in an assault boat meant to carry 12 men, but 20 had crammed themselves inside. The boat began taking on water, and when another vessel came alongside to help, the wave created by the approach swamped the boat, throwing the men into the Rhine. Captain Potts found himself swimming around in the river until he hailed a nearby boat. He was pulled into that boat and had to explain to Lieutenant Colonel Earl F. Holton, his battalion commander, why he was swimming the Rhine when he was supposed to be across the river leading the attack!

Behind the advancing infantry, the Navy's boats began to rush supplies and equipment across the river without difficulty. Engineers began working on the bridges called for in the assault plan. Royal Air Force balloons were raised to deter enemy aircraft and antiaircraft units moved into position for the same purpose. More than 700 enemy prisoners were sent to the rear. By mid-afternoon, all three infantry regiments were across the river and advancing as planned. Supported by the 149th and 187th Engineer (Combat) Battalions, they destroyed the enemy's 588th Infantry Regiment and moved east against light opposition. Other than the occasional harassing artillery fire, some strafing attacks by enemy aircraft and a brief enemy stand in front of the 313th Infantry Regiment at a fortified factory, little stood in the way of Ninth Army on the east bank of the Rhine.

* * *

Behind XVI Corps, Ninth Army was busy as well. Troops were pouring across the river as engineers struggled to get the approaches to the crossings in shape for such heavy traffic. After the "swimming" DD Tanks had crossed the river, follow-up armored and infantry support was ferried over by landing craft. The essential DUKW amphibious trucks brought over tons of supplies necessary for the continued advance, and U.S. Navy crews kept their boats in operation without let-up. Only one Landing Craft, Medium (LCM) and two Landing Craft, Vehicle, Personnel (LCVP) were lost during the operation.

By noon the engineers had built and had in operation two Bailey rafts and several Treadway rafts within the 30th Infantry Division's zone. Tanks were crossing on these rafts before daylight. In the 79th Infantry Division's zone, enemy artillery fire delayed things for a short while, but ferries were quickly in operation, and by the next morning one medium tank was being ferried across the river every 10 minutes. But even as all this labor and fighting continued, all eyes suddenly turned to the skies above. Operation *Varsity* was about to begin.

CHAPTER 11

Operation *Varsity*

The situation of the Allied airborne forces after Normandy had become one of searching for a role. Time and again plans were made for an airborne attack to advance the Allied armies, only to have the ground troops reach their objectives before it could be mounted. Literally dozens of plans were proposed, most never getting past the suggestion stage, before events on the ground had made the participation of airborne forces unnecessary. When a major airborne operation was finally mounted, by Montgomery's Twenty-First Army Group, at Arnhem, it failed to accomplish all of the missions assigned to it, primarily because planners overestimated the ability of the airborne forces to accomplish their goals without the rapid arrival of ground support, while also underestimating the enemy.

But Montgomery still believed that airborne attacks had a useful place in the campaign in Northwest Europe. Because of this, he included an airborne attack in the overall plan for Operation *Plunder*—the airborne phase was known as Operation *Varsity*. It had first been planned in November 1944, when it appeared that the Allies were approaching the Rhine, but had been put on hold while the Battle of the Bulge played out. Simply put, an airborne corps of three (later reduced to two) divisions was to be dropped east of the Rhine to enhance the river crossings of Twenty-First Army Group, which included General Simpson's Ninth Army.[1]

For of a variety of reasons, including limited transportation, combat losses and other factors, the two divisions chosen for Operation *Varsity* were the 6th British Airborne Division and the 17th U.S. Airborne Division. The original third division, Major General Elbridge G. Chapman's inexperienced 13th U.S. Airborne Division, was accordingly dropped from the troop list. The 6th British Airborne Division had been formed in May 1943 and spent the rest of that year training and organizing. It participated in the Normandy landings, where it distinguished itself in holding the left flank of the British invasion beaches. It was to remain in Normandy far longer than its American counterparts and thus took longer to recover and reorganize. Operation *Varsity* would be its first airborne combat operation since the invasion.[2]

The 17th Airborne Division was formed at Camp Mackall, North Carolina, with a cadre from the 101st Airborne Division. After training, it participated in the Carolina Airborne-Troop Carrier Command Maneuvers in December 1943, before moving to the Tennessee Maneuvers in February 1944. After additional training in Tennessee and Massachusetts, it departed Boston in August 1944, and landed in England for final training and preparation for airborne operations. The division was rushed to France on Christmas Eve 1944, to participate in the ongoing Battle of the Bulge. It fought as ground troops in that campaign and on into Belgium before returning to France to prepare for Operation *Varsity*.

The division commander was Major General William Maynadler ("Bud") Miley. Born into a military family on December 26, 1897, in Fort Mason, California, he was commissioned into the infantry from West Point in 1918, where he earned the Best Gymnast Award. Miley served at a number of posts in the interwar years, including as professor of military science and tactics at Mississippi State College, instructor at West Point, and as an infantry officer in the Philippines. His moment came in October 1940, when he was appointed as the commander of the new and experimental 501st Parachute Battalion at Fort Bragg, Georgia. One of his troopers recalled, "He could do a standing backflip, things like that. He was the perfect choice to command the 501. We were a wild, hell-for-leather outfit, but we were a bit ragged militarily."[3] Here, he became an advocate of the airborne concept and soon took command of the 503rd Parachute Infantry Regiment from General William "Father of the Airborne" Lee when the latter was seriously injured in a jump accident. Miley remained with the airborne branch, serving as commander of the 1st Parachute Brigade in 1942 and receiving a promotion to brigadier general in June of that year. Miley was the Assistant Division Commander of the 82nd Infantry Division in August 1942, when that unit was converted to an airborne division. In March 1943, he was promoted to major general and given command of the new 17th Airborne Division, which he led throughout the war.

Montgomery was convinced that the German military had made serious mistakes west of the Rhine and that this was the time to take full advantage of those mistakes. He believed that the offensive in the Ardennes had been an error, wasting reserves that could have prolonged the German defense in the west in an attack to reach an unattainable goal. To add to the errors, instead of withdrawing behind the Rhine (the traditional and historic defense line of western Germany) the Germans had decided to fight west of the river in order to protect their industrial area, the Ruhr, which lay just east of the river. He concluded, "After all that had gone before, the crippling losses sustained by the enemy in the Rhineland brought the end of the war to a matter of weeks."[4]

So convinced was Montgomery of the need for a full-power assault, that in the initial stages of the planning two airborne operations were envisaged.[5] In addition to Operation *Varsity*, planners had created Operation *Choker II*. The latter plan would have placed the 82nd Airborne and 101st Airborne Divisions under General Ridgway's XVIII (Airborne) Corps, making the main effort on or about April 10, 1945. Operation *Choker II* would have assisted General Patch's Seventh Army in its Rhine crossing at the southern end of the Allied line. Operation *Varsity*, also under XVIII (Airborne) Corps, would launch on or about April 1. A shortage of aircraft and gliders forced *Varsity* to be reduced to two rather than three divisions. For much the same reasons (a shortage of aircraft and the speed of the ground advance), Operation *Choker II* was subsequently cancelled.

Montgomery was a firm believer in the use of "maximum weight and impetus at our disposal,"[6] what in the next century would be termed "Shock and Awe." To this end, he naturally wanted to include the available airborne forces to strengthen his attack to its maximum weight. He ordered that the airborne assault be tasked with the strengthening of the bridgehead established by the ground troops and to rapidly deepen that bridgehead by landing ahead of them. After linking up with the British Second and Ninth U.S. Armies, the airborne troops would reinforce the ground assault.[7]

*　　*　　*

Airborne troops of World War II had special needs and capabilities. In order to be air-transportable, airborne divisions carried lighter equipment, and had few vehicles and lighter artillery support available to them, at least until they merged with ground forces. They also carried fewer combat troops on their organizational charts. This deficit had been recognized during airborne operations in North Africa, Sicily and Italy. As a result, during the Normandy attack the 82nd and 101st Airborne Divisions had each been reinforced with an additional airborne infantry regiment. This had proved successful, but with the Germans on the run at this stage of the war, the airborne divisions reverted to the officially authorized tables of organization—two parachute regiments and one glider regiment, three 75mm pack howitzer artillery battalions, one 105mm artillery battalion, a combat engineer battalion and other support troops. The most recent table of organization and equipment (December 1944) authorized an airborne division 768 officers, 51 Warrant Officers and 12,160 enlisted men. Standard infantry divisions had three infantry regiments, four artillery battalions of 105mm and 155mm guns and a total of 14,253 officers and men.

Command and control of airborne units was another problem that had arisen before Normandy. Eisenhower had been concerned about the control, management, re-supply and reinforcement of the specialized airborne contingents. He specifically wanted a headquarters that commanded not only the airborne troops, but also the troop carrier aircraft squadrons that would carry them into battle and supply them in combat. Complicated by the fact that the U.S. Army Air Forces were a separate part of the U.S. Army at this stage of the war, this presented some problems. There were concerns of Air Corps officers being placed in command of airborne troops, and vice versa.

Convinced of the need for a combined troop carrier-airborne command, Eisenhower approached the U.S. Army Chief of Staff, General Marshal and made his proposal. After much discussion on just which commander would be responsible for which aspect of an airborne operation, the decision was made to create what came to be known as the First Allied Airborne Army. Such an army would control both the ground and air operations of any airborne offensive, but once the troops were on the ground and the aircraft no longer needed, each would revert to the local commander of the appropriate service. To operate under such an army at the tactical level, two corps commands were also authorized.

Lieutenant General Lewis H. Brereton, the commander of the Ninth U.S. Army Air Force, was named as commander of the First Allied Airborne Army. General Ridgway was given a new corps command, XVIII (Airborne) Corps, and assigned to that army. Until such time as both new headquarters could be organized and established, the Ninth Army and General Simpson would control the training and administration of the airborne troops. Knowing that Ridgway was to command XVIII (Airborne) Corps, Simpson gave him interim command of the airborne troops assigned to Ninth Army. At the time, XVIII (Airborne) Corps controlled the 17th, 82nd, and 101st Airborne Divisions, as well as several smaller independent airborne units. His second-in-command was Major General Richard N. Gale, who had commanded the 6th British Airborne Division in Normandy. The British I (Airborne) Corps, under the command of Lieutenant General Frederick A. H. "Boy" Browning, would control the British 1st and 6th Airborne Divisions and smaller independent units.

In March 1945, the First Allied Airborne Army staff renewed planning for what would become known as Operation *Varsity*. The staff was no stranger to planning airborne operations—in the preceding months it had planned no less than six different operations, none of which were executed—and *Varsity* was soon taking shape.

Major General Paul L. Williams' IX Troop Carrier Command would carry the airborne troops across the Rhine, using some of the new C-46 transport aircraft. Tactical command would rest with Ridgway's XVIII (Airborne) Corps, which was to link up with British Second and Ninth U.S. Armies once established across the Rhine. The immediate task was to seize and hold the high ground five miles north of Wesel in order to assist the ground troops in establishing their bridgehead. Unlike with previous operations, the airborne assault would not begin until after the ground troops had crossed the Rhine. British troops would be flown from 11 airfields in East Anglia, in 699 aircraft and 429 gliders. The 17th Airborne Division would depart from France and Belgium in 903 aircraft and 897 gliders and would meet the British over Brussels. From there, protected by 1,253 fighters of the Eighth U.S. Army Air Force, the combined stream of planes would head for Wesel. Distant cover was provided by the Fifteenth U.S. Army Air Force flying from Italy, which bombed Berlin as a diversion. The British Second Tactical Air Force added 900 fighters to the protective screen and the Ninth U.S. Army Air Force sent up 676 additional fighters.

Barely 200 German fighters rose to meet this overwhelming armada, and not one reached the troop carriers as they delivered their cargo. German antiaircraft defenses were another matter. Having been under an intensive bombing campaign for the past two years, by both the United States Army Air Force and the Royal Air Force, the Germans had developed an extensive antiaircraft defense. This was especially true in the area of the Ruhr, a major manufacturing zone. These antiaircraft defenses shot down 53 Allied aircraft and damaged another 440 troop carriers during *Varsity*, but their impact on the operation was minimal and most parachute and glider landings went essentially as planned. That is not to say there weren't some errors and mix-ups, but nothing that seriously affected the operation.

The landings began around 1000 hours and lasted until 1300 hours. They were followed by 240 heavy bombers of the Eighth Air Force, which dropped 582 tons of supplies to the men on the ground. So successful was this re-supply, and so swift was the organization implemented on the ground, that a second re-supply effort scheduled for the following morning was considered unnecessary and was cancelled. Indeed, things went so well that Eisenhower would later call *Varsity* "the most successful airborne operation carried out to date."[8] Another expert believed it to be "the highest state of development attained by troop-carrier and airborne units."[9]

*   *   *

The first American unit to drop was the veteran 507th Parachute Infantry Combat Team at 0948 hours on the morning of March 24, 1945. The regiment and its attached 464th Parachute Artillery Battalion (Lieutenant Colonel Edward S. Branigan) were commanded by Colonel Edson D. Raff, a veteran officer who had made his first combat jump in North Africa and who had succeeded to command when the regiment's first commander was captured during the Normandy battles.[10] Fighting as an attached regiment of the 82nd Airborne Division in Normandy, the regiment had been scattered over miles of territory and spent the first few days just trying to reach its intended drop zones. In Operation *Varsity*, only the First Battalion missed its drop zone (due to haze over the area), but not nearly as badly as in the cross-Channel attacks 10 months earlier. Colonel Raff landed with Lieutenant Colonel Paul F. Smith's First Battalion about a mile from the intended drop zone, about two miles northwest of the town of Diersfordt, and immediately gathered some men and attacked a German defensive position designed to protect the intended drop zone, capturing five enemy artillery pieces in the process. The battalion then went on to the drop zone, which it cleared, capturing 300 prisoners. Raff's Second Battalion, under Lieutenant Colonel Charles Timmes, landed on its correct drop zone and soon made contact with British ground units that had already crossed the Rhine.

Private George J. Peters, of Company G, 507th Parachute Infantry Regiment, had joined the paratroops from Cranston, Rhode Island, and soon found himself serving as a radio operator. With 10 other paratroopers he landed in a field near Flueren, east of the Rhine. Some 75 yards away, a German machine gun covered by several riflemen opened fire and immediately pinned the group down. The position of the men was critical—several were still trying to rid themselves of their parachutes as direct enemy fire came at them across the field. The machine gun kept the men from getting to their equipment bundles, which held their weapons and other supplies. Seeing the danger, Private Peters rose to his feet and, armed only with his M-1 Garand rifle and some grenades, began a one-man assault against the enemy force. His attack immediately drew the enemy's fire off his buddies. About halfway to his objective Peters, while firing his rifle, was hit and knocked to the ground by a burst of machine gun fire. Without hesitation, he rose to his feet and struggled forward. Again he was hit and knocked to the ground. Unable to rise again, he crawled forward despite his mortal wounds and tossed grenades into the enemy position, knocking out the gun, killing the crew and driving off the supporting riflemen. For his self-sacrifice in saving the members of his squad, Private George J. Peters was awarded a posthumous Medal of Honor.[11]

By 1400 hours, Colonel Raff had assembled his regiment and reported that all of his assigned objectives had been secured. One of his companies had even knocked out a German tank with a 57mm recoilless rifle, the first successful use of this new weapon by paratroops.[12] A group of about 200 paratroopers from the First Battalion, under their battalion commander, had also been mis-dropped northwest of the drop zone. Colonel Smith and his rump battalion nevertheless found themselves in a good position to attack one of the division's main objectives, the castle of Schloss Diersfordt. During the attack, they met with the rest of the regiment. Raff withdrew all but Lieutenant Colonel Allen W. Taylor's Third Battalion, the designated assault force, and took the growing number of prisoners to the division assembly area. There he reported that his regiment had destroyed five tanks, captured 1,000 prisoners and captured several pieces of artillery.

General Miley had jumped with his staff and knew the moment he landed that he was nowhere near his intended drop zone. As he lay on the ground under German machine gun fire, he looked in vain for his staff. They were not anywhere near him, but his search found three privates and a machine gun equipment bundle in the same field. Calling to the soldiers to meet him at the equipment bundle, he quickly had the gun firing at the enemy. Soon thereafter, he had established his command post at the village of Flueren.

Colonel James W. Coutts loaded his 513th Parachute Infantry Regiment and attached 466th Parachute Field Artillery Battalion (under Lieutenant Colonel

Kenneth Booth) into 72 C-46 transport aircraft. They faced a more difficult landing when all of their transport pilots missed their drop zone "X" and instead dropped the combat team onto the British glider troops' landing zones near Hamminkeln (it was the worst drop of the entire operation). In contrast, Colonel Booth's attached battalion landed correctly and immediately set up its guns, but found themselves without infantry support because of the bad drop of the 513th. Under heavy fire, Booth sought out Colonel Coutts by radio and explained his predicament. Coutts rounded up what men he could find and set out to reach the 466th Parachute Field Artillery, but the Germans resisted his advance.

The 513th Parachute Infantry had landed in a strongly fortified area and was immediately engaged in fierce combat. As the men fought, British gliders began to land in their area. Soon both Americans and British were attacking together to eliminate the German strong points. One unit, Company E, had landed well to the west of Hamminkeln, near railroad tracks that ran along the edge of the Diersfordter Forest. As they marched to rejoin their regiment, they came under fire from a group of Germans in a cluster of concrete buildings besides the railroad tracks. An attempt to knock out the enemy resulted in the Americans being pinned down by machine gun and artillery fire. Private First Class Stuart S. Stryker, of Portland, Oregon, was a platoon runner with Company E. He saw the assault platoon pinned down under severe enemy fire, unable to return fire or retreat. He voluntarily left his place of comparative safety and, armed with an M-1 carbine, ran to the head of the company. Standing in full view of the enemy, he yelled to the men of Company E to follow him in a charge against the Germans. Inspired by his fearlessness, the men rose and followed Stryker into a hail of bullets. As he came within 25 yards of the enemy post, Stryker was killed but his gallant leadership had encouraged his buddies to eliminate the enemy post and free the trapped platoon. A total of 200 prisoners were taken and three captured American bomber pilots were freed. For his self-sacrifice, Stryker received a posthumous Medal of Honor.[13]

Several times Colonel Coutts outmaneuvered the Germans on the way to his designated drop zone, but on occasion the Germans could not be outmaneuvered and fought strongly. When this happened Coutts and Booth conferred on the radio, which resulted in a unique situation. Several times the 466th Parachute Field Artillery found themselves firing towards the 513th Parachute Infantry. In fact, they were firing at the Germans facing the paratroopers as they fought their way towards the guns. Coutts later recalled that it "worked very well and must have seemed very confusing to the Krauts."[14] By mid-afternoon, the combat team had been reunited and all of its objectives taken. Although he had taken heavy casualties, Coutts could report that he had captured 1,500 Germans and destroyed several heavy guns, including two 88m antiaircraft/antitank guns and some armored vehicles.

One battalion commander, Lieutenant Colonel Allen Miller of the Second Battalion, 513th Parachute Infantry, jumped out of his burning aircraft only to land in a pigpen. There was so much enemy fire coming at him that he felt he was back on the rifle range, as a target. Dropping his parachute, Miller drew his pistol and crawled to a shed. Peering around the corner, he saw a German machine gun crew firing on other parachutists. Miller shot all four German machine gunners before running for the main farmhouse. There he uncovered several more machine guns firing on his battalion. Miller rolled a thermite grenade into one room and a grenade into another, eliminating the machine guns and crews. Then he ran out into the fields and gathered his battalion.

Colonel James R. ("Bob") Pierce commanded the 194th Combat Team, which consisted of his own 194th Glider Infantry Regiment and Lieutenant Colonel Joseph W. Keating's 681st Glider Field Artillery Battalion, with its three batteries of 75mm howitzers. Lieutenant Colonel John W. Paddock's 155th Antiaircraft Artillery Battalion and Lieutenant Colonel Paul F. Oswald's 680th Glider Artillery battalion were in the same lift group, as were engineers and vehicles. This group had a rough trip to the target area, with the gliders bouncing around in the air currents and heavy turbulence. It was so difficult to control the gliders that the pilots had to rotate positions every 15 minutes. Troops became airsick and several gliders crashed on the journey, killing those aboard. In total, 21 gliders were lost or had to abort their missions.

Colonel Pierce's men landed on Landing Zone "X" and Landing Zone "S" in good formation, despite the losses in the air. This was the first time that a glider landing had been attempted without first having paratroops land and clear the ground of enemy defenses. For the first time in the European theater, a glider combat team was landing on its own.[15] The combat team landed in the midst of German artillery units, which were still firing on the British and American ground troops crossing the Rhine. As a result, enemy fire on the two landing zones was heavy, but Pierce's men immediately rose to the challenge and assembled their units and artillery under heavy fire amid the wreckage of their gliders. Although some units of the Third Battalion and some artillery and ammunition failed to arrive, Pierce declared by noon that he had accomplished his initial mission. In doing so he had captured 42 artillery pieces, 10 tanks, two mobile-antiaircraft vehicles, and five self-propelled guns, not to mention 1,000 prisoners.

The divisional support artillery battalion was Colonel Oswald's 680th Glider Field Artillery Battalion, newly equipped with 105mm snub-nose howitzers. Coming down on Landing Zone "S," Oswald found that three of his guns were missing. Wrestling with the remaining guns, they were set up while 900 rounds of artillery ammunition was recovered from the wrecked and burning gliders on the landing zone. All of this was accomplished under what was described as a "withering" crossfire from the enemy surrounding the zone. Unable to complete their task due to the constant German fire, the artillerymen took up their personal weapons and cleared the area around the landing zone of enemy resistance, capturing 150 Germans and two nearby batteries of German artillery. For this action, the 680th Glider Field Artillery Battalion was awarded a Presidential Unit Citation.[16] Oswald lost 19 men killed and 56 wounded in the landing and subsequent battle.

Unknown to Generals Ridgway or Miley, the 17th Airborne Division had some high-ranking reinforcements on March 24. Knowing that this would probably be the last combat parachute drop of the European theater, Brigadier General Josiah T. Dalby (commander of the Airborne Training Center at Camp Mackall, North Carolina) and Brigadier General Ridgley M. Gaither(commander of the Parachute School at Fort Benning) managed to climb unnoticed into a C-47 transport carrying paratroopers of the 466th Parachute Field Artillery Battalion and made the drop with the rest of that unit. Finding themselves with only a handful of men, matters were made worse for the two generals when a battery of German 20mm antiaircraft guns opened fire on the small group. Undeterred, Dalby organized a group of paratroopers, British and American glider pilots, and anyone else he could find, and led an attack that overran the enemy battery.

In all, Operation *Varsity* put 9,577 American airborne troops on the ground in one morning. Of these, 4,964 were parachutists and 4,613 were glider-borne troops. Some 900 aircraft and 900 gliders were used to deliver this force to its target. All of this was closely watched by Generals Eisenhower, Simpson, Anderson, Ridgway and other senior commanders from the west bank of the Rhine. General Bradley, who felt that the entire operation was unnecessary, viewed the affair from an aircraft.

The British operation went much the same as did the American drop—10 of the troop carriers were knocked down by antiaircraft fire, but only after they had discharged their paratroopers, and another 70 aircraft were damaged. The 6th British Airborne Division was to drop near the village of Hamminkein and seize the high ground and bridges in that area. Brigadier James Hill's 3rd Parachute Brigade and Brigadier J. H. N. Poett's 5th Parachute Brigade were to land first, followed by Brigadier R. H. Bellamy's 6th Airlanding Brigade. In addition to the air support, they were able to call upon the nearby XII (British) Corps for artillery support.

The 8th Battalion, Parachute Regiment, led the 3rd Parachute Brigade into battle. Followed by the 9th Battalion and the 1st Canadian Parachute Battalion, whose commander, Lieutenant Colonel J. A. Nicklin was killed while caught in a tree by his parachute. The Brigade quickly seized its objectives, although the 8th Battalion remained isolated throughout the day. The 5th Parachute Brigade had a tougher time, dropping into mortar fire and airbursts from antiaircraft guns. Every farm and house was an enemy pillbox, but the 7th, 12th and 13th Battalions, Parachute Regiment, quickly cleared the area and seized all their objectives.

The 6th Airlanding Brigade had difficulties as well. The dust and fog created by the earlier bombardment and fighting caused many gliders to become easy targets for the Germans, who shot down several. The glider pilots had problems finding their landing zones, and many landed in the wrong place, but specially organized groups successfully seized the important bridges by *coup de main*. Many British paratroopers soon found themselves fighting alongside their American counterparts from the 513th Parachute Regiment, who had also been dropped in the wrong place. A German tank-infantry force was overcome and the town of Ringenberg captured.

For a short time, the situation was very confused, so much so that Major General Bols, who dropped within 100 yards of his planned command post at the Köpenhof Farm, had to fight his way there, killing one enemy soldier as he did so. By 1500 hours that afternoon, physical contact had been made with the 15th (Scottish) Infantry Division of the British Second Army. That night, a strong German tank-infantry counterattack was beaten off, but one of the bridges across the Issel River had to be blown up to prevent its recapture.

During the battle, Corporal Frederick George Topham was a medical aid man assigned to the 1st Canadian Parachute Battalion. He was soon busy, working on the wounded Canadians around him, when he heard a cry from a wounded man lying out in the open. Treating an injured man, Topham watched as two other medical orderlies went out into the field. The first man reached the wounded soldier, only to be shot and killed. As the second man reached him, he, too, was shot and killed.

Topham could stand it no longer. He ran out into the field to the wounded trooper. After completing his first aid to the wounded man, all the while under enemy fire, he was preparing to move him to the rear when he was himself shot in the nose. The bleeding was intense and he was in severe pain, but after carrying the wounded man to safety in nearby woods, Topham returned to the battle and continued to treat other wounded men for some two hours while the battle raged about him. He refused all attempts to treat his wounds and continued to bring in wounded men from under the noses of the enemy. Only when all the wounded had been recovered did he stop long enough to have his serious wound dealt with. After initial treatment, he was ordered to be evacuated, but Topham refused and begged to be allowed to return to duty as soon as his wounds were seen by a physician. As he walked back to the rear he came upon a vehicle that had been hit by enemy fire and was burning fiercely. Enemy mortar shells continued to drop in the area, and a nearby officer ordered all Canadians not to approach the blazing Bren Gun Carrier, fearing an explosion. Learning that there were men trapped in the vehicle, Topham, ignoring the orders, went to it and rescued three wounded paratroopers, one at a time, under mortar fire. Although one of the men subsequently died, the other two survived. For his actions on March 24 east of the Rhine, Topham received the highest award given in the British military forces, the Victoria Cross.[17]

Of all the airborne operations mounted by Allied forces in World War II, Operation *Varsity* was the most successful—all of the planned objectives were achieved. The British 6th Airborne Division secured the left flank of General Anderson's XVI Corps, thereby protecting Ninth Army's flank. Both airborne divisions captured vital bridges, which enabled the attack to continue uninterrupted after the bridgehead had been achieved. The 17th U.S. Airborne Division secured the right flank, and cleared Diersfordt Castle and surrounding villages, many of which had been fortified. The accuracy of the airborne drop was better than any previous drop, with most of the paratroopers and gliders landing within two miles of their intended zones. The organization of the glider pilots into *ad hoc* units, and the pre-assault infantry training, contributed to the operation's success. Use of new technology, such as the C-46 transport aircraft and the 57mm antitank guns, proved effective if not perfect.

General Ridgway believed that the operation was not only a success, but necessary. He believed that "the airborne drop was of such depth that all enemy artillery and rear defensive positions were included and destroyed, reducing in one day a position that might have taken many days to reduce by ground attack alone."[18] Another historian of the campaigns of World War II wrote that *Varsity* "unquestionably aided British ground troops" but qualified this with the comment that "although the objectives assigned the divisions were legitimate, they were objectives that ground troops alone under existing circumstances should have been able to take without undue difficulty and probably with considerably fewer casualties."[19]

The ground troops of XVI Corps reported 41 killed during their river crossing. British ground forces losses are unknown, but were probably higher, since they employed greater numbers. Casualties for the 6th British Airborne Division were 248 killed and 738 wounded, plus 98 Glider Pilot Regiment members killed and 77 wounded. This accounts for 12 percent of the total British force. The 17th U.S. Airborne Division lost 393 killed and 834 wounded, with 41 pilots of the 9th Troop Carrier Command killed and 153 wounded, or 13 percent losses. The highest loss ratio for individual units was in the Glider Pilot Regiment, with a 27 percent loss rate.

For this, the last major physical barrier between the Allies and the interior of Germany had been breached. The heart of the German industrial area, the Ruhr, now lay open to Ninth Army, attacking from the north and west, while First Army would come in from the south and west. Germany's last chance to prolong the war in the west had been lost. World War II in Europe would end barely six weeks after the conclusion of Operation *Varsity*.

CHAPTER 12

Battle for the Ruhr

Operation *Varsity* had been the last major crossing to place the Allied armies on the east bank of the Rhine. Now began the powerful and rapid exploitation into the heart of Germany. Not that it would be easy, for Hitler still was determined to hold onto the Ruhr at all costs in order to keep his flagging war effort going.

The problems began on the first day after *Varsity* ended. Strong and determined defense by the 7th Parachute Division (Lieutenant General Wolfgang Erdmann) held back the advance of the right flank of the British and Canadian forces. Those defenses, on high ground commanding the crossing sites, prevented British engineers from completing the essential bridges over the Rhine to allow reinforcements and supplies to move to the front. Other German paratroopers cut off small groups of British and Canadians at the town of Rees and it was not until the following day that they were driven off by a Canadian counterattack.

But the Allied airborne attack had seriously disrupted the overall defenses of the German II Parachute Corps (*General der Fallschirmtruppen* Eugen Meindl). Its 84th Infantry Division had collapsed under the combined air and ground attack and there were no replacements available. A counterattack by the 15th Panzer Grenadier Division (Major General Eberhardt Rodt) against the British at Rees failed. More serious was the situation south of the Lippe River, where Ninth Army's XVI Corps was close to breaking through the last of the German defenses in the area. So serious was this threat that General Blaskowitz, commanding Army Group H facing the crossing sites, re-directed his sole remaining reserve from the airborne landings to a strike against General Anderson's corps. XLVII Panzer Corps (*General der Panzertruppen* Heinrich Freiherr von Luettwitz) was ordered to send its 116th Panzer Division against the 30th Infantry Division of XVI Corps.

There was no end to the problems facing German commanders at this stage of the war. For General von Luettwitz, this order meant obtaining more fuel for his tanks and armored vehicles (something not easily done in Germany at this time), then detouring around the Allied airhead zone, and finally moving only at night to avoid allied air power. For the 116th Panzer Division it became a race against time.

While von Luettwitz was trying to execute his new orders, General Hobbs of the 30th Infantry Division issued his own. Like many of the American commanders, he had a strong idea that a breakout was imminent and intended to force one as soon as possible. He delayed his morning attack on March 25 to allow the remainder of his divisional artillery to cross the Rhine and set up in support of his infantry regiments. At 0900 hours he sent his infantry to the east to seize high ground marked by an incomplete highway. Opposition, from the remnants of the German 180th Infantry Division, was spotty. Encouraged by the lack of organized resistance, Hobbs ordered his two assault regiments to become task forces, each built around an infantry regiment, a tank battalion and a tank destroyer battalion.[1] The 117th Infantry's task force was to drive nine miles to a road and rail center at Dorsten. The 120th Infantry's task force moved six miles to Kirchhellen, where they would cut the main highway between that town and Dorsten, leading into the Ruhr.

But like von Luettwitz, Hobbs had problems fulfilling his orders. The first problem was the terrain, which led for some five miles through thick stretches of wooded areas, any one of which could hold a concealed enemy force. These woods were crossed by narrow dirt trails and roads, neither conducive to a rapid military movement. The second problem was the roads, which were not strategically placed for American purposes. Finally, the need to organize into task forces, as ordered by General Hobbs, took time. The 120th Infantry, the first to move, was delayed until late afternoon, only to run into enemy antiaircraft guns in a ground role, as well as armored vehicles, artillery pieces and even forest fires. By nightfall, prisoners were reporting that the "Old Hickory" Division was no longer facing a defeated 180th Infantry Division reinforced with home guards, but that the prisoners were coming from the 60th Panzer Grenadier Regiment of the 116th Panzer Division. General von Luettwitz had won the race.

The 117th Infantry, delayed even longer, had barely left its line of departure before encountering the newly arrived defenders. The 30th Infantry Division had fought the 116th Panzer Division before, in Normandy, and knew what kind of opponent they were now facing. General Hobbs briefly reconsidered his attack orders, but late that evening ordered the attack to continue. The Americans dug in for the night.

Meanwhile, just south of the 30th, General Wyche's 79th Infantry Division was also encountering problems. After crossing the Rhine at Rheinburg, the division had seized Dinslaken, bypassed the industrial city of Duisburg, and then turned south to cross the Rhine-Herne Canal to protect XVI Corps' right flank. The intelligence officer of the 1st Battalion, 313th Infantry Regiment, tried to negotiate the surrender of Duisburg, but the German command refused. Its reduction was left to follow-up units.

Hobbs' attack went well initially. Although German resistance, now reinforced with elements of the 2nd Parachute Division, continued to be strong, General Anderson introduced a task force of General Baade's 35th Infantry Division, in turn boosting the offensive strength of his XVI Corps.[2] Baade's "Sante Fe" division would turn south to support the 79th as the battle moved east. Meanwhile, the 30th pushed east steadily, despite the increasingly difficult roads, trails, and enemy defenses.

It fell to the 120th Infantry Regiment, commanded by Colonel Branner P. Purdue, to make the most progress. It did not seem likely as they began their attack. First they had to fight off a counterattack by tanks and panzer grenadiers of the 116th Panzer Division near Kirchhellen. Then they began a slow yard-by-yard advance until evening, when they reached a wood that overlooked an enemy airfield. From that field, enemy guns were firing at the attacking 117th Infantry Regiment nearby. One company commander of the 117th reported, "We got into a lot of trouble on the objective. As we got to the edge of the woods we got fire from AA emplacements on the hill. There were tanks in Besten and tanks in the woods. The enemy was dug in and digging in on the high ground. There were no enemy on the objective, but those that faced us were looking right down our throats."[3]

Colonel Purdue waited until full darkness, then called forward his reserve 1st Battalion. Heavy German artillery along the lines of approach repeatedly delayed the attack but Purdue sent his men forward, running downhill against the enemy while the German artillery fire was directed against the empty foxholes the attackers had just vacated. The airfield was cleared in under an hour without a single casualty. Despite these successes, though, no actual breakthrough had been achieved. The presence of the 116th Panzer Division had stymied the efforts of General Hobbs, and although the advance continued, gains were limited. By the evening of March 26, the full complement of the German division had arrived, including its tanks and supporting artillery. In the time bought by the panzer division, XLVII Panzer Corps brought up a reinforcing unit, the 190th Infantry Division (Lieutenant General Ernst Hammer). Though it was understrength, especially in supporting arms, it was experienced, having fought in Holland against the allied airborne operation at Arnhem.

Hobbs continued his attacks, pressured by General Simpson, who was eager to force a breakthrough and gain the maneuvering room his Ninth Army needed to fully deploy its growing strength. General Anderson's own Corps had two more divisions waiting and the full XIX Corps was behind them. In the hopes of expediting a breakthrough, Anderson ordered forward his 8th Armored Division.

Simpson's anxiety for an early breakthrough stemmed not so much from the delays the Germans were imposing on XVI Corps as from the problems Ninth Army was having in getting its supplies and follow-up forces forward. When the German II Parachute Corps delayed the enlargement of the British and Canadian bridgehead near Xanten and Rees, it also delayed the establishment of vital bridges needed to get supplies and troops forward for the Allied forces. That, in turn, prevented the bridgehead from being expanded sufficiently to allow additional troops to join the battle. Without these bridges, the British were required to share the American bridges at Wesel, where a Treadway bridge and a 25-ton pontoon bridge had been built.

An agreement gave Ninth Army five hours per day to use these bridges, while the British had the remaining 19 hours. That offered insufficient time for Ninth Army to create an adequate buildup for a push to the Ruhr.

Another problem was that the delays in the British sector had slowed the movement of the XVIII (Airborne) Corps to the north, delaying additional Ninth Army troops from crossing and entering the battle. Until General Ridgway's Corps cleared its present zone, no additional Ninth Army troops could be brought up against the German defenders. For Simpson, it was frustrating to have to watch his units make costly frontal attacks knowing that if there had been sufficient room to deploy the additional units waiting just across the Rhine, he could have brought this additional power to bear, cracking the enemy defenses more swiftly and at less cost.

Already Ninth Army engineers had built several bridges that could support additional combat troops across the Rhine, but there was no room on the front for those troops. The commitment of the 8th Armored Division was certain to add to an already congested situation. Conversely, unless that division could force a breakthrough, there was no room for maneuvering additional units in the Ninth Army bridgehead. Simpson called a meeting of his corps commanders on the afternoon of March 27 and decided to take the risk. Brigadier General Devine's tanks and armored infantrymen would have to make a penetration regardless of the risks of congestion. Simpson also ordered General McLain to be prepared to concentrate his XIX Corps within the bridgehead and be prepared to exploit any breakthrough.

General Ridgway objected to the proposal. While he agreed that to avoid the area around Wesel was sound, he doubted that the already crowded roads north of the Lippe River could support any large part of Ninth Army. He believed that his XVIII (Airborne) Corps could yet advance and within two days provide enough room for more of Ninth Army to get into action across the Rhine. Simpson eventually agreed to delay his order, while at the same time appealing to General Dempsey and Field Marshal Montgomery for the earliest possible permission to fully utilize the bridges at Wesel for Ninth Army's needs. If this permission could be granted, he would be able to use both XIX Corps and XIII Corps across the river with XVI Corps.

To ease the arrival of the 8th Armored Division, the infantrymen of the 30th Infantry Division attacked again in an attempt to open a route for the armor through the enemy defenses. Once again, dense forests and miserable roads and trails, combined with strong German resistance, frustrated any such effort. When General Devine's 8th Armored Division surged forward, his tanks and infantry were hit with the same difficulties. The first day's advance secured barely three miles.

However, March 28 proved General Ridgway correct. This was the day that the 513th Parachute Infantry Regiment, combined with Churchill tanks of the British 6th Guards Armored Brigade, pushed 17 miles beyond Dorsten.[4] That action outflanked General Luettwitz's XLVII Panzer Corps, forcing a withdrawal. This was also the day when Montgomery revised his orders to expand Ninth Army's access to the bridges at Wesel and expanded the corridor across the Rhine allocated to Ninth Army. As of the morning of March 30, Ninth Army would have nearly unrestricted use of the Wesel crossings. This allowed it to begin moving forces north of the Lippe even before getting full control of the bridges. Beginning March 31, the situation would be reversed, with Ninth Army having control of the Wesel Bridges for nineteen hours each day and the British for five. With that, Operation *Plunder* was over. Of the seven Allied Armies on the Western Front, five were now over the Rhine and prepared to exploit an advance deep into Germany.[5] All eyes turned now to the German industrial heartland, the Ruhr.

Before the first Allied soldier set foot on the west coast of France, planners had considered how to crush Germany once across the Rhine. Two main target areas were identified as crucial to ending Germany's resistance. These were Germany's major industrial areas, from which much of the country's weapons, armor and ammunition flowed to the front-line troops. To the south, in the zone of Twelfth Army Group, lay the Saar industrial area. In the north lay the more extensive industrial area known as the Ruhr. This latter area was a small rectangle of 35 miles along the east bank of the Rhine, from Wesel to Düsseldorf, extending some 60 miles east into Germany. Within this vast pocket were some 2,500 factories and scores of iron and coal mines, all supporting the German war effort. In between these two industrial areas was the extensive series of forests known as the Ardennes.

When the Allies overran France, it was natural that two thrusts would be directed around the Ardennes, one to the north by Montgomery's Twenty-First Army Group (now including Ninth Army), and the other to the south under Bradley's Twelfth Army Group. In part, this distribution had contributed to the success of the German counteroffensive in December 1944, which resulted in the Battle of the Bulge, but before the attack materialized, Montgomery had already been pushing Eisenhower to abandon the southern prong and concentrate all efforts on reaching the Ruhr. In part, this was one reason Ninth Army had been given to the Field Marshal. Eisenhower stuck to the original plan, but allowed Twenty-First Army Group to conduct a massive airborne operation intended to get it closer to the Ruhr faster than otherwise expected.

By the end of March 1945, all of this was moot. All Allied forces were across the Rhine, or about to be across. Both planned thrusts could and would now be executed. Indeed, by the end of March the situation was entirely changed. The Allies were across the Rhine in strength. In Italy, the Anglo-Americans were already engaged in secret negotiations with SS officers prepared to surrender all Axis forces in Italy. To the east, Russian forces were about to encircle Berlin. German front-line divisions were barely able to maintain a semblance of organization. Heavy weapons were being driven directly from factories to the front, so close were the Allies to the German sources of production. Tactically, Field Marshal Walter Model's Army Group B, defending the Rhine, was now outflanked to the south by Bradley's Twelfth Army

Group and to the north by Twenty-First Army Group. All German attempts to halt or destroy these two bridgeheads had failed decisively, but the fighting continued. To "encourage" his troops, Hitler issued another one of his "no retreat under pain of death" orders.

The 8th Armored ("Thundering Herd") Division began to cross the Rhine at noon on March 27, 1945. Reinforced by the 290th Infantry Regiment of the 75th Infantry Division, the tanks of the division's Combat Command A attacked to seize crossings over the Rhein–Herne–Emscher–Zweigkanal and secure the road between Hamm and Soext. Almost immediately, two tanks were lost to mud and marshy ground, and recovery tanks were unable to reach them due to the wide expanse of the marsh. Eventually the 130th Ordnance Maintenance Battalion would have to lay a corduroy road over the marsh, while under fire, to retrieve the tanks.

Meanwhile, the advance slowed under increasing antitank fire from antiaircraft guns used in a ground role. Each gun position could only be reduced by the actions of the armored infantry, who attacked under the covering fire of their tanks. German artillery was active and knocked out some vehicles of the supporting 398th Field Artillery Battalion. Under these difficult conditions, the attack moved slowly forward.

To the south, First Army, which had seized an intact bridge at the German town of Remagen in mid-march, forming a strong bridgehead, awaited the Rhine crossing of Twenty-first Army Group. Once that had been accomplished, First Army was free to exploit that bridgehead and move east. This inactivity while awaiting Montgomery's crossing in the north had deceived (however unintentionally) Field Marshal Model, who believed the army was stymied and that the main Allied effort would come in the north. To meet such an attack, Model strengthened his northern flank at the expense of the southern. He prepared a strong defense along the Sieg River and tried to concentrate forces for a planned counterattack against Ninth Army. All of these plans came to nothing when First Army broke out of its bridgehead on March 25. The attack by First Army crushed several of the defending German forces. The sudden collapse opened the way for rapid exploitation, with some units being given the simple yet direct order "Just go like hell!" The Americans began a race against isolated pockets of resistance, surging ever eastward.

Ninth Army was equally prepared to exploit its bridgehead, now that men and supplies could be sent across the river almost at will. On March 29, General Simpson issued his orders for the breakout. General Anderson's XVI Corps was to move southeast and build up an attack force along the Rhein–Herne Canal, along the northern fringe of the Ruhr industrial area. Its mission here, with four infantry divisions assigned, was to protect Ninth Army's northern flank.[6] General McLain's XIX Corps would move north of the Lippe and provide the main effort to encircle the Ruhr. McLain would take two armored and three infantry divisions and strike for the town of Hamm, at the northeastern tip of the Ruhr, and there link up with First Army.[7] General Gillem's XIII Corps was ordered to cross the Rhine at Wesel and seize the city of Münster with three infantry and one armored divisions.[8] Once Münster had been taken, XIII Corps was to maintain contact with the British Second Army to the north, while continuing to move east. The objective was to seize that critical maneuvering room so desperately needed by Ninth Army. Simpson also ordered that all enemy airfields were top priority targets, and that any captured with useable runways were to be immediately reported to Ninth Army HQ. Meanwhile, Ninth Army's 55th Antiaircraft Brigade was given the responsibility of protecting the Rhine bridges from enemy paratroopers, air attacks, floating mines, swimming saboteurs and river craft attacks. General Ridgway's XVIII (Airborne) Corps was to pass the 6th British Airborne Division to the British Second Army and the 17th Airborne Division to General Gillem.

Action started immediately, with the 2nd Armored Division and its attached 377th Infantry Regiment of the 95th Infantry Division moving across the Rhine into the already congested bridgehead early on March 28. This force was to bypass Wesel and cross the Lippe before beginning its eastward attack. Meanwhile, the 8th Armored Division continued on its mission to reach the Lippe to the south and seize Dorsten, which XIX Corps desired as a bridge site. Once taken, the division was to continue east, clearing the banks of the Lippe as it went. Both the 8th Armored and 30th Infantry Divisions would then come under XIX Corps control.

General Devine had originally intended to bypass Dorsten, and his plan had received tentative approval from General Anderson. He intended to isolate Dorsten and let follow-up units clear it. However, late on March 28 Anderson informed Devine that General Simpson wanted the town taken, so that it could be used as a bridge site.[9] As a result, Devine had to change direction some 180 degrees to the north and attack without much chance to reconnoiter his objective. Both CCA and CCR would have to conform to the new orders.

Combat Command A led the attack with the 7th Armored Infantry Battalion. The soldiers moved over unfamiliar terrain in the dark, but they found a railroad which ran south from Dorsten and followed it to their attack positions. Early on the morning of March 29, the attack began with 15 battalions of artillery dropping one hundred shells per minute on the unfortunate town. Yet despite this massive preparation, when the Americans attacked they received heavy fire from antitank guns and artillery, from the north and northeast. Several German Mark IV and Mark V heavy tanks were dug in on high ground to the north of the town. Still, by mid-morning the town had been taken. When Devine reported his success, Anderson complimented him on doing a difficult job well.

The antiaircraft guns, which the Germans were now using against tanks and infantry, were dominant throughout the area. The Ruhr had been attacked from the air for years, and it had a thick line of antiaircraft defenses, which were now turned against the oncoming Americans. As Major Robert Logan, commanding the 405th Armored Field Artillery Battalion put it, "These Krauts had been in the same positions two or three years. They had flower beds in bloom around their emplacements. The gunners were experienced and well-trained, but they had numerous youngsters 16 years old as ammunition passers."[10]

March 29 also saw the 79th Infantry Division secure its position along the Rhein–Herne Canal, with posts overlooking the Ruhr Valley. Patrols received heavy fire from the nearest city, Duisburg, and were forced to retire. The nearby 35th Infantry Division seized the city of Gladbeck and by March 31 it was within two miles of Recklinghausen. On the same day the 75th Infantry Division passed through the 8th Armored Division and took up the lead pushing east.

General McLain's XIX Corps led off with the veteran 2nd Armored Division, which enjoyed the rare experience of rolling forward against minimal opposition. In fact, so disorganized were the Germans at this point that Lieutenant Colonel Wheeler Merriam, commanding the 2nd Armored Division's 82nd Reconnaissance Battalion, saw a German train passing him as he halted to report his position to division headquarters. General White, commanding the 2nd Armored Division, immediately called down the firepower of the 92nd Armored Artillery Battalion, which quickly cut the train in half. One observer commented: "… the stunned prisoners believed that the enemy was still on the west bank. They had no idea that the American were on the east bank, much less that they had gained so much territory."[11]

The Germans were still fighting, however. When CCB found an intact bridge over the Dortmund-Ems Canal, Company B, 17th Armored Engineer Battalion, was sent forward to secure the bridge and make sure any demolitions were neutralized. But just as they arrived, the enemy blew the bridge, wounding several engineers. Undeterred, Brigadier General Sidney R. Hinds continued looking until his scouts found two underpasses that were blocked by oil drums, debris and dirt, defended by German infantry, artillery and antiaircraft guns. The combat command secured these underpasses and resumed its journey east. At Herbern, a company of enemy infantry barred the way until the 3rd Battalion, 41st Armored Infantry, and the 1st Battalion, 67th Armored Regiment, attacked and cleared the way. The German defenders, officer school candidates, were pushed aside by the armor, infantry and supporting fire until 50 were killed and the remaining 90 surrendered. Conversely, at the town of Ahlen the civilian government came forward to surrender the town, which was housing over 3,000 German wounded. The German police guided the 2nd Armored Division through the town while the local population cheered their advance.

While taking a break to eat and refuel, one of the prisoner-of-war interrogators with CCB called ahead to the next town on their route and demand its surrender. After threatening to level the town if so much as one shot was fired at them next morning, the enemy refused to surrender, but the following morning, when Combat Command B entered the town, they found that the German military had abandoned it and fled east. In another instance, a military police platoon was having dinner at the railroad station outside Ahlen when a German troop train pulled into the station. The military police opened fire on the train, and the Germans fired back. Batteries of the 92nd Armored Field Artillery opened fire on the train as well, while the Germans replied with 20mm cannons, but they soon surrendered. Aboard the train, the military police found a million antipersonnel mines.

Behind the leading 2nd Armored Division, General Simpson had sent the 83rd Infantry Division. Mounted on trucks from corps artillery units and captured vehicles (which earned them the nickname of the "Rag-Tag Circus"), General Macon's men raced alongside, behind and sometimes ahead of the armored forces. These Normandy veterans "chased the Germans up and down hills and mountains, across canals and rivers; raced through, around and after them towards the Russians."[12] By the end of March 31, 1945, the combined armor-infantry team had raced 40 miles from their original line of departure.

This massive breakthrough totally disrupted the German defenses. The American advance separated Army Group H from its own First Parachute Army. It further left adrift General Luettwitz's XLVII Panzer Corps and *General der Infanterie* Erich Abraham's LXIII Corps, both of which appealed to Field Marshal Model for directions. Instructed to form a new line facing north behind the Rhein-Herne Canal and behind the Lippe River, these two corps, under the *ad hoc* command *Gruppe von Luettwitz*, would form the northern line of defense for the Ruhr. As a result, the defenses around the Ruhr began to take shape by April 1, 1945. In the north and northeast (the sector facing Ninth Army), *Gruppe von Luettwitz* was holding a front from Lippstadt, along the Möhne Reservoir, to Hamm. Beyond that lay the German Fifteenth Army and then Fifth Panzer Army.

As March 31, 1945, drew to a close, General Simpson received a call from Major General J. Lawton ("Lightning Joe") Collins, commanding VII Corps in First Army. He had sent his own 3rd Armored Division forward, as had Simpson with his 2nd Armored Division. But when General Maurice Rose's 3rd Armored Division reached the vicinity of Paderborn, they ran into a strong defense bolstered by SS troops. General Rose had been killed and the 3rd Armored needed help—enemy attacks were already striking at the division's rear areas. It was feared that this was the beginning of a major German attempt to break out of the encirclement in the Ruhr.

General Collins asked for a combat command to be sent from Ninth Army toward Lippstadt, a halfway point between Beckum and Paderborn. Collins, in turn, would send a combat command of the 3rd Armored Division there as well, completing the encirclement of the Ruhr and cutting off any German escape attempts. Simpson, as usual, immediately agreed. Orders were sent to General White to divert a combat command as per Collins' request.

These orders were sent on to General Hinds, who received them at 0150 hours on April 1. Ordered to change direction, Hinds sent one of his columns toward Lippstadt well before dawn, the movement going slowly at night but picking up speed with daylight. Just as the Americans approached Lippstadt, they encountered a German column believed to be trying to break out of the encirclement. Lieutenant Colonel Arthur J. Anderson, commanding 3rd Battalion, 41st Armored Infantry Regiment, asked Hinds for reinforcements. Told that he was his own reinforcement, Anderson gave battle. Behind him, Hinds "held his breath" and awaited developments. While he waited, General McLain, XIX Corps commander, appeared to verify that Combat Command B had reached its objective, but McLain wanted to personally check the information before forwarding it on to General Simpson. Hinds used his last remaining tank and armored car to escort McLain to safety. The report was correct, and by mid-afternoon of April 1, 1945, Easter Sunday, the men of the 2nd and 3rd Armored Divisions met at Lippstadt, sealing off the Ruhr pocket.

Celebrations were brief. Immediately, the 30th Infantry Division came up to relieve the 2nd Armored Division. General White's men again turned east, moving through the legendary Teutoburger Wald to enter upon the German plain beyond. By this time the men of the 2nd Armored Division, indeed the entire Ninth Army, were convinced that their ultimate objective was the German capital city of Berlin. Meanwhile, Brigadier General John H. Collier and his Combat Command A had been pushing east without respite. They were to cross the Dortmund–Ems Canal, cut communications to Hamm, and then attack eastward to Berlin. But once at the canal there were no bridges. Undeterred, men from the attached Company G, 377th Infantry Regiment, 95th Infantry Division, found an abandoned barge and used it as a temporary bridge. Enemy machine guns contested the crossing, but the heavy weapons of CCA protected the infantry as they made their bridgehead across the canal. Engineers quickly built a Treadway bridge for the tanks and vehicles, and once again the 2nd Armored Division was off for Berlin.

Behind them, they left an encircled Ruhr industrial area. Within that pocket, measuring roughly 55 miles from north to south and 75 miles east to west were the headquarters and supporting troops of the German Army Group B, all of the Fifth Panzer Army and two corps of the First Parachute Army—a total of seven corps and 19 divisions. Intelligence officers estimated they had trapped at least 150,000 enemy soldiers, a figure that would soon be revised considerably upwards.[13]

Outside the pocket, German commanders tried desperately to break in and rescue those troops. New units were created, others drawn from reserve, but in fact most of these existed on paper only. The attack, such as it was, struck mostly within the sector of the 1st and 104th Infantry Divisions, First Army, and was repulsed after some hard fighting. At the end of April 1 the Germans in the Ruhr pocket were encircled by three American armies with little hope of escape.[14]

Meanwhile, Simpson had divided responsibilities. In addition to securing his half of the Ruhr Pocket, he was ordered by Montgomery to, "hold a secure right flank facing the Ruhr as far east as Paderborn" and "to assist 12th Army Group in mopping up the Ruhr."[15] But he was also responsible for the continued advance to

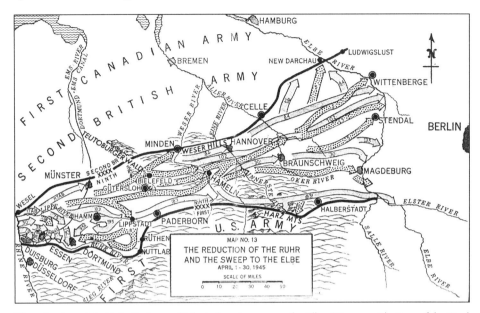

The reduction of the Ruhr Pocket and Ninth Army's sweep to the Elbe. (*Conquer. The Story of the Ninth Army, 1944–1945*, Infantry Journal Press)

the Elbe River alongside the Field Marshal's Twenty-First Army Group. In effect, Ninth Army was attacking in two directions, east and south.

Simpson gave responsibility for the drive to the Elbe to General Gillem's XIII Corps and most of General McLain's XIX Corps. The remaining elements of XIX Corps and General Anderson's XVI Corps were detailed to the reduction of the Ruhr, in conjunction with First Army. For the next two weeks, between April 1 and April 14, Ninth Army would be attacking constantly, and always in opposite directions. It was a diverse scope of attacks, in one case driving deep into a defended urban area and in the other racing against crumbling opposition across open fields and defended towns. Simpson visited First Army headquarters on April 2 to ensure the coordination of the two forces within the pocket. Ninth Army, by virtue of its position, drew the densely-populated, heavily built-up industrial section north of the Ruhr River, while First Army took on the rugged terrain of the southern portion below the same river.

Simpson's plan was for a converging attack by two corps towards the heart of the Ruhr. XVI Corps was to attack south to the Ruhr River from its positions along the Rhein–Herne Canal. XIX Corps troops would strike simultaneously from Hamm and Lippstadt and drive southwest to the army boundary. First Army forces would attack north and northwest to meet with Ninth Army along the Ruhr River. Once the pocket had been sufficiently reduced, Anderson's XVI Corps would take over the remaining front while XIX Corps turned its full attentions east. To strengthen

Anderson's corps, the 8th Armored Division was transferred to it from XIX Corps. In place of it, the 95th Infantry Division, less one regiment attached to the 2nd Armored Division, joined XIX Corps. At this point, XIX Corps had assigned units fighting 125 miles apart. Its attack into the pocket would be conducted by the 8th Armored Division and the 95th Infantry Division. The 15th Cavalry Group would screen the corps flank between Hamm and the Dortmund–Ems Canal as well as the east flank of XVI Corps.

XVI Corps had already been fighting in the Ruhr since it had crossed the Rhine. Using the 79th, 35th and 75th Infantry Divisions, it had made initial probes into the area late in March. Reinforced by Ninth Army's 34th Field Artillery Brigade, with 21 non-divisional field artillery battalions, massive artillery support was available for the reduction of the Ruhr. In effect, there was no start date for the reduction of the pocket. It had begun as soon as Ninth Army crossed the Rhine, and continued unabated for the next two weeks. In a battlefield of industrial, urban, suburban and rural areas, infantry was best suited for the assault. Strongpoints had to be isolated and systematically reduced by foot soldiers, tank destroyers, tanks and artillery. Cities like Essen, with a population of 668,000, and Dortmund, with 550,000 people, presented problems rarely encountered previously by American forces. Resistance was sporadic but determined.

One of the leading American forces was the 95th Infantry Division under General Twaddle. Twaddle's first objective in this Ruhr battle was Hamm. Originally the location chosen for the junction of First and Ninth Armies, the town had been left behind when it became necessary to expedite the juncture at Paderborn. Now Colonel Samuel L. Metcalf's 378th Infantry Regiment was assigned the task. Colonel Metcalf planned a holding attack and patrol actions to keep the defenders occupied while he outflanked them on the left, where a railroad led towards the town. After relieving the 331st Infantry Regiment, 83rd Infantry Division, the 378th Infantry moved into the small bridgehead over the Lippe River and Lippe-Seiten Canal. Metcalf attacked with his 3rd Battalion while his 1st Battalion made a show of strength in front of the town. The 2nd Battalion held the vital bridgehead.

Even before the Americans could launch their attack, the 1st Battalion was struck by a strong counterattack. Lieutenant Colonel Ewel E. Eubank, commanding the battalion, found himself facing a tank-supported infantry attack including a truck filled with demolitions intended to blow up the underpass from which the Americans had initiated their bridgehead. Thick fog and early morning darkness allowed the soldiers of the 116th Panzer Division to get within 100 yards of the underpass before Company C saw them and opened fire. The attack pressed on, knocking out one squad defending the underpass. But Private First Class George A. Hyatt fired a bazooka at the lead vehicle carrying the demolitions at the same moment that the truck hit a mine protecting the underpass. The tremendous explosion destroyed the other German vehicles and killed most of the attackers. Several 1st Battalion troops were also injured by the blast. It cost Company C 22 casualties, but the Germans had not blown up the underpass.

Defending Hamm were elements of the 116th Panzer Division and some 200 SS troops, reinforced with the Hamm police force. The 378th Infantry attacked as planned and after fierce fighting took the town. Supported by artillery, the German lines were broken after three days of fighting that cost the Americans numerous casualties. Included in the success was nearly one thousand German boxcars loaded with food, ammunition and other supplies.

Near Recklinghausen, the 8th Armored Division had also come up against the 116th Panzer Division. The city had been strongly fortified and the enemy reinforced by the 60th and 156th Panzer Reconnaissance Battalions. Commanded by what the Americans would call, "a fanatical Nazi leader who had exacted from his men an oath to die rather than surrender"[16] the German positions were stoutly defended. After six days of vicious fighting the Americans managed to push the Germans south of the Ruhr River and out of Ninth Army's area of operations.

Withdrawals such as these were not always good for the civilian population. In the village of Esbeck, the local militia, or *Volkssturm*, units began to withdraw as the Americans came near. As the last of them departed, the villagers began to hang out white flags to prevent further damage to the town from the oncoming Americans. But before the first American arrived, a party of SS troops passed through, saw the white flags, pulled out a 70-year-old villager and shot him in reprisal.[17]

The attack proceeded into city after city, each with bombed-out buildings, blocked streets and twisted lampposts already red with rust. One American soldier remembered a ruined street where a building had stood, the only remaining sign of it a twisted metal drainpipe that reached up to a third floor that no longer existed and there, incredibly, supported a bathtub with a loofah still visible hanging over the side. Empty window frames and walls standing alone and unsupported were commonplace. Bits and pieces of the civilian lives that had once inhabited these shells abounded. Most who ventured into this abyss forever remembered the incredible stench of sewer gases, feces and urine, not to mention gunpowder and the smell of death from the hundreds of dead buried within the ruins.

It was during these ongoing attacks to clear the Ruhr Pocket that General Simpson learned that his Ninth Army had been returned to the control of the American Twelfth Army Group. Under General Bradley, First, Third, Ninth and Fifteenth Armies would now operate as a combined army group. The rest of the Battle for the Ruhr would be entirely an American affair, under American control.

But Simpson was sick of this type of fighting. He was wasting his men against urban areas that by all rights should have surrendered once they had been surrounded. To expedite the fighting, on April 7 he turned to General Twaddle and his 95th Infantry Division. Under Twaddle, a task force was formed consisting of his own infantry division, the 8th Armored Division, the 15th Cavalry Group and a regiment of the 17th Airborne Division.[18] Under the operational control of General Anderson at XVI Corps, Task Force Twaddle was to cut straight into the heart of the Ruhr Pocket. That same day, the task force seized the town of Gelsenkirchen, north of Essen. Then it took Hamm, the largest rail center in the country. Facing strong resistance from General Siegfried von Waldenburg's 116th Panzer Division, Task Force Twaddle pushed deeper into the pocket.

The symbol of the German war machine, the Krupp factories in Essen, fell to the 194th Glider Infantry Regiment. Ever mindful of the political winds, the approaching paratroopers were greeted with welcome signs and civilians standing to greet them with bottles of wine and other gifts as they entered the city. Rather than fighting, the Americans engaged in an impromptu street party. Nearby, the men of the 79th Infantry Division went in search of the head of the Krupp dynasty, Alfred Krupp. A search of his office found only a caretaker present, who directed the Americans to his home, where Krupp, whose family had produced arms from Napoleon to Hitler, meekly surrendered.

Not all cities in the Ruhr Pocket surrendered as easily as did Essen. The city of Dortmund required the full attention of Task Force Twaddle, plus the 75th Infantry Division, before it fell. Defended by determined SS troops, regular German Army troops and German Air Force antiaircraft crews, the city launched several counter attacks, which caused the Americans serious concerns. In one instance, a platoon of Military Police under Major Charles LeCraw was cut off within the city. One of the policemen volunteered to change into civilian clothes and infiltrate past the German lines to bring help. Knowing that if he was captured in civilian clothes he could be shot as a spy, the American, reported only as Private First Class Weiss, managed to accomplish his mission and bring help.

The bloody fighting continued unabated. On April 12, near the town of Drabenderhone, Company C, 386th Infantry, 97th Infantry Division, found itself pinned down in front of dug-in German defenses. Private First Class Joe R. Hastings, of Magnolia, Ohio, was a machine gun squad leader in the company. Seeing his buddies pinned down under rifle, machine gun, mortar and 20mm antiaircraft gun fire, he raced forward under this same fire over 350 yards of open terrain until he reached a suitable firing position. From here he killed the crew of a 20mm gun and knocked out a nearby machine gun. Then he drove several enemy riflemen from their positions. His actions allowed the First Platoon to reorganize and renew their attack, after removing the wounded to safety. Seeing that, to his right, the Third Platoon was also pinned down by heavy 40mm guns and machine guns, Hastings then raced over 150 yards and led the platoon's attack, during which he knocked out the 40mm gun and two more machine guns. For his gallantry he was awarded a posthumous Medal of Honor.[19]

General Simpson called for more support to speed Ninth Army's attack. Calling upon the British, he was given a squadron of the Fife and Forfar Yeomanry Regiment.

This battalion, from the specialized 79th British Armored Division, was armed with Churchill tanks that towed a trailer of liquid napalm. The short cannon within the Churchill tanks was able to send a blowtorch of flame some 70 or 80 yards forward of the tank itself. The terror inspired by this weapon often caused otherwise stalwart defenders to surrender upon sight of the first flame. More and more, this fearsome weapon had to be used in the heavily defended urban areas of the Ruhr Pocket.

While Simpson was trying to finish off Dortmund, the defenders saw that their days were numbered, but rather than surrender, they launched a fierce counter attack with several hundred infantry and some of their largest tanks, the 60-ton Tiger. They struck against the 8th Armored Division, but the Americans fended off the Germans, knocking out several of the attacking tanks, and by evening the battle was drawing to a close. A nearby airfield, defended by SS troops, changed hands seven times during the attack.

The Battle for Dortmund ended with a whimper, rather than a bang. Snipers and Hitler Youth continued resistance for days after the Germans surrendered the city. Booby-traps were liberally sprinkled throughout the town and enemy artillery and SS troops continued to harass the Americans long after the battle "officially" ended.

The collapse of the resistance at Dortmund seemed to mark the end of organized resistance within the Ruhr Pocket. Senior German Generals began openly talking about surrender. Clearly further resistance was futile and pointless. Yet a few, like the commander of the 180th Infantry Division, refused to consider surrender. Despite the opposition, two leading German commanders, Generals Bayerlein and von Waldenburg, began to work towards a surrender. First, because of recent casualties caused by American artillery, they notified American commanders of the location of a prisoner-of-war camp containing Americans at the town of Hemer. An American Major, recently captured, was sent to the nearest American formation, the 99th Infantry Division, and told to advise them of the camp. He was also authorized to tell the American commander that the 116th Panzer Division was interested in surrendering. As events developed, this unit would surrender to the 7th Armored Division.

Despite the hesitation of some of their leaders, the average German soldier had no interest in further fighting. Knowing they were surrounded, with no hope of rescue and with their homes being overrun everywhere by the enemy, many German soldiers decided to surrender. Indeed, Major General Walter Lauer, commanding the 99th Infantry Division, would soon get a call from one of his battalion commanders in which he said, "The whole damned German Army is flowing right down the valley toward my position."[20] Racing to the scene, General Lauer arrived in time to see thousands of German troops, unarmed and with hands raised, surrendering.

Not long after, it was not just the ordinary soldier surrendering. The 194th glider Infantry captured former German Chancellor Fritz von Papen. Not far behind were General Bayerlein, commanding LIII Corps, General Luettwitz of XLVII Corps,

General von Waldenburg of the 116th Panzer Division, General Denkert of the 3rd Panzer Grenadier Division, and commanders of many other German formations that had been resisting within the Ruhr Pocket. Indeed, there were such numbers giving up that many had to search for someone to take their surrender, since the Americans were too busy clearing the area and had little time for such niceties. One German officer, however, refused to surrender. Field Marshal Walter Model, the seniormost German commander within the Ruhr Pocket, chose suicide rather than surrender. With that, the Battle for the Ruhr Pocket was over.

By April 18, 1945, the Americans had rounded up 317,000 German soldiers, more than had surrendered at Stalingrad in February 1943, and more than had surrendered to the Allies at the end of the North African campaign. Thousands more, of whom no records had been kept, had died in the fighting, along with untold thousands of civilians. The battle cost Ninth Army 341 men killed in action, 121 missing in action and somewhat more than 2,000 wounded. First Army losses were estimated as three times as high. Clearly, Simpson's efforts to reduce his losses in a battle he couldn't avoid had been successful.

In clearing the Ruhr Pocket, Ninth Army's XVI Corps expended 259,061 artillery rounds. Garrisoning the Ruhr was assigned to Ninth Army's 55th Antiaircraft Brigade, the 17th Airborne Division, and the 75th, 79th and 95th Infantry Divisions. General Anderson's corps closed its operations there on April 16 and prepared to join the rest of Ninth Army to the east, where the battles were still raging.

CHAPTER 13

On to Berlin

When Allied troops crossed the Rhine in March 1945, they were only some 275 miles from the German capital of Berlin. Russian troops in a bridgehead recently established over the Oder River, in Eastern Germany, were barely 30 miles from that same city. The only logical conclusion to draw from this was that the Soviet Armies would reach the German capital well before the Americans and British could get much closer. This situation posed a problem for Eisenhower.

Months before, while planning future operations, Eisenhower had decided that once his armies crossed the Rhine and secured the Ruhr industrial area, they would direct their main force to seize Berlin.[1] Although not a strategic target, it was considered the symbolic final objective of the long and difficult campaign to defeat Germany. The original plans had been for Montgomery's Twenty-First Army Group, with General Simpson's Ninth Army still attached to it, to make that main effort. If by some chance the Russians had already seized Berlin, then Twenty-First Army Group would be directed against the north German ports. General Bradley's Twelfth Army Group would clear central Germany towards Leipzig, while General Jacob Devers' Sixth Army Group would seize the industrial southern portion of Germany.

With Russian forces more than 200 miles closer to Berlin than his own troops, Eisenhower felt justified in implementing his alternative plans for the future advances of his combined forces. He decided to strengthen Bradley's army group with Ninth Army and direct the combined force into central Germany, against the critical oil plants that continued to supply the essential fuel for the German war effort. Bradley's armies were also to strike east until they made contact with the Soviet Army, thereby cutting Germany in two and easing its final conquest. Montgomery's forces would, as planned, move north to seize the northern ports and seal off the Baltic region, allowing for the eventual clearing of Norway and Denmark, where it was feared fanatical German units might continue to resist. Devers' Sixth Army Group would strike south and east against a "National Redoubt," at which the Nazis were reportedly determined to make a final stand.

Eisenhower also saw no reason to lose American lives on what had, by this time, become merely a prestige target with little military significance. He believed and had stated earlier that Germany had two "hearts," one industrial (the Ruhr) and the other political (Berlin). He firmly believed that if the industrial heart died, the political heart would follow quickly. With his forces now busy clearing the industrial heart of Germany, his interest in Berlin waned.[2] To be sure, he asked for the thoughts of his senior commander, Bradley, whose forces would have to make the push to Berlin. Bradley, in his well-known reply, estimated it would cost 100,000 Allied casualties to take Berlin, and added that it was, "A pretty stiff price for a prestige objective."[3]

Initially, all of this was unknown to the field commanders. Indeed, Montgomery did not learn of the change of plan until after he had issued an order directing his Twenty-First Army Group (then including Ninth Army), on to Berlin. Once advised of the new plan, the British protested the decision, but the American Chiefs of Staff supported Eisenhower's decision. They deferred to the commander on the scene, and refused to intervene. The British Prime Minister, Winston Churchill, took the matter up with President Roosevelt, who likewise declined to intervene. Although few knew it at the time, Ninth Army would therefore not strike for Berlin.

Once again part of Bradley's Twelfth Army Group, Simpson was directed to move the greater portion of his army not engaged in the Ruhr to the east, aiming for the Elbe River in the area of the German city of Magdeburg. There, a major highway network led directly to Berlin, barely 55 miles away. From this assignment, Simpson and many of his subordinates naturally believed that Ninth Army's ultimate objective was in fact the German capital. Indeed, supporting this conclusion was Bradley's additional order that, once across the Elbe, Ninth Army was to be prepared to either advance on Berlin or move to the northeast in support of British forces.[4]

Simpson received these new instructions just as his leading elements were approaching the Weser River, which lay about midway between the Rhine and the Elbe. It was the last major water obstacle before the Elbe and Berlin. At the request of Simpson, Bradley authorized Ninth Army to "jump" the Weser in order to avoid allowing the Germans enough time to build up a defensive line along the river. Meanwhile, he ordered First Army to catch up while Third Army marked time near Ohrdruf.

General Gillem's XIII Corps reached the Weser with the 5th Armored Division and the 84th Infantry Division before daylight on April 5. Arriving at the river near Minden, almost due west of the city of Hannover, they immediately began to seek a crossing, while British troops occupied Minden. Behind them, the 2nd Armored Division was delayed for a few hours by resistance from the German First Parachute Army in the Teutoburger Wald, but arrived at the Weser at the town of Hamelin (of Pied Piper fame) later that morning. Behind them, the 30th Infantry Division finished clearing the Teutoburger Wald and moved up. Simpson also sent the 102nd Infantry Division forward as soon as it could clear the rear-area congestion. The 83rd Infantry Division, recently relieved from fighting in the Ruhr, was to follow.

Ninth Army was advancing north of the Harz Mountains, connecting with First Army south of those mountains. The terrain was a series of low, rolling hills, which gave easy access to Magdeburg on the Elbe. Within the army's zone lay some of Germany's largest cities, including Hannover, Brunswick and Magdeburg itself. Very little in the way of enemy forces defended this zone. A hastily constituted new German army, the Eleventh Army under *General der Infanterie* Otto Hitzfeld, was assigned to plug the gap, but its few units were widely scattered. Hitler ordered the formation of another new army, the Twelfth Army (*General der Panzertruppen* Walter Wenck), but it was largely a paper command and its mission was to attack to relieve the already doomed defenders of the Ruhr Pocket, not to defend the Weser River line.

Along the Weser, initial efforts to seize an intact bridge had failed. While XIII Corps sought a crossing, General McLain brought up his XIX Corps to General Gillem's right, but attempts to cross were stymied. The 335th Infantry, 84th Infantry Division, attempted to cross a battalion near the town of Barkausen, but as they approached the bank, enemy artillery fire directed from across the river prevented them from crossing. "All hell broke loose when the 1st Battalion detrucked (sic). The enemy had a number of 20mm and 88mm guns and heavy mortars emplaced north and south of the ridge line on the east bank of the river. Observation was perfect. They picked off engineer trucks and other vehicles like ducks on a pond. The ridge line and eastern bank were infested with snipers."[5]

McLain's XIX Corps had better luck. Like XIII Corps, the 2nd Armored Division faced the Teutoburger Wald (where in A.D. 9 three veteran Roman legions had been decimated by German tribes in a classic military ambush)[6]. Undeterred, Combat Command A attacked. General Collier divided his command into three task forces, one for each pass, and surprise was total. Task Force Warren was assigned to secure the northernmost pass, and set out at last light.[7] Capture of this pass would prevent the enemy from defending the narrow defile, while at the same time block any escape attempts from those enemy troops trapped in the Ruhr Pocket.

Task Force Warren raced down an autobahn as fast as its tanks could move, bypassing an enemy strong point in the village of Brackwede. Despite the many enemy vehicles encountered along the highway, the Americans held their fire in order to deceive the Germans and allow themselves to advance without resistance. They passed civilian cars, some with women in them. In other cases, German soldiers tried to hitch a ride on the American vehicles until they suddenly realized that they were not friendly troops. At one section of the road, the American column passed under the overpass while a three-vehicle German reconnaissance patrol went by overhead. After full darkness, the leading element came upon a German roadblock, at which the three leading scouts were told by a German sergeant to be on the lookout for Americans who were reportedly headed in their direction. The German sergeant was then killed by those very Americans whom he had mistaken for friends.

Two hours after the advance began, it was finally halted near Wilhelmsdorf, when German antitank fire stopped the column. It took most of the night for the infantrymen to clear the roadblock, and by daylight Task Force Warren reached the foothills of the Teutoburger Wald. The town of Lamershagen put up a fierce resistance until infantrymen cleared it in a bitter house-to-house fight. Behind Task Force Warren, Task Force Zeiena awaited clearance to leapfrog ahead to secure crossings over the Weser.

By now the Germans were alerted and fighting back. At the town of Oerlinghausen, German paratroopers armed with 20mm antiaircraft guns and machine guns held up the advance for more than a day until Company I, 377th Infantry Regiment, marched three miles around their flanks and, together with the task force, attacked the village from two sides. The next day the Germans launched two counterattacks, which drove the Americans out of the contested town. It wasn't until the task force managed to cut the enemy supply and communications lines that the remaining Germans retreated. On April 4, Combat Command A reached the Weser. As CCA's reconnaissance elements approached a large bridge over the river, at Hamelin, the enemy blew it up in their faces. A nearby railroad bridge went the same way.

General Collier immediately ordered his attached 119th Infantry Regiment, 30th Infantry Division, to cross in assault boats and establish a bridgehead on the east bank, which it quickly accomplished against modest resistance. Combat engineers

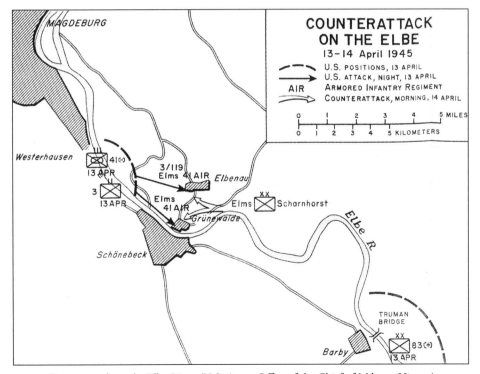

Counterattack on the Elbe River. (U.S. Army, Office of the Chief of Military History)

then built a 384-foot bridge across the river and Combat Command A crossed the Weser on April 5, establishing a bridgehead three miles deep and four miles long. It was followed by the 30th Infantry Division.

Meanwhile, XIII Corps had not given up on getting across the Weser. Stymied in their first attempt at Dehme, the 84th Infantry Division moved west, near to the town of Barkhausen. It was not the best site, since the approaches to any bridge built there would have to cover soft ground, difficult for heavy military traffic. But from an assault standpoint it was the best available, since the enemy did not have direct observation over the site and could only place fire on the area from the flanks. Once across, the infantry would be protected even from this fire by the hills of the Weser Gebirge. The 1st Battalion, 335th Infantry, was to be the assault force. Using assault boats, it was to cross and establish a defensive perimeter on the east bank until the rest of the regiment crossed and a bridge was built. The follow-up force, the 3rd Battalion of the same regiment, would also cross in assault boats and then strike south to enlarge the bridgehead.

The 1st Battalion began its crossing of the Weser at 0500 hours on April 6. Under cover of darkness, the battalion sent Companies A and C across in assault boats, manned by men of the 309th Engineer (Combat) Battalion. Surprise was perfect—not a shot was fired as the first wave of troops landed on the east bank. It wasn't until 30 minutes later that the first German reaction, a 20mm antiaircraft gun, began to fire occasional rounds into the bridgehead. It was plain from the random nature of this enemy fire that the gunners had no idea exactly where, or perhaps even if, the Americans had crossed the river.

The assault battalions quickly moved out to their objectives, taking full advantage of the element of surprise. The first town in their path was Lerbeck. Corporal Burley A. Nichols was leading the advance when a German sentry shouted, "Halt." Afraid to fire his rifle and alert the rest of the enemy in town, Nichols hit the sentry with his own rifle, breaking its butt. Another sentry quickly appeared and Nichols repeated his actions, using the rifle the first German had dropped to the ground. Nearby, Private First Class Richard E. Ehmann fell to the ground as an enemy machine gun opened fire on him. A German concussion grenade then landed near his right hand. Thinking quickly, Ehmann flipped the grenade away, hearing a scream as the grenade exploded next to the enemy soldier who had thrown it. With that, Lerbeck was in American hands. The entire 1st Battalion was across the river less than an hour after the first boats entered the Weser. Nor did the success end there—the entire 3rd Battalion came across without a single casualty as well, although more and heavier German fire had begun to come against the bridgehead by then.

It was now the turn of the regiment's 2nd Battalion to cross. By this time, it was full daylight and German railroad guns on the east bank, north of the bridgehead, were getting the range. The 2nd Platoon, Company C, 638th Tank Destroyer Battalion, was ordered to move north to deal with the threat. After firing 30 rounds they had knocked out both enemy guns and blown up 15 railroad cars of ammunition, along with other supplies and a fuel depot. Enemy machine gunners, meanwhile, were pinned down by American machine guns set up to protect the bridgehead. Many of them quickly surrendered once the Americans advanced upon their positions. The 2nd Battalion, 335th Infantry, also completed its crossing without a single casualty.

The first counterattack came against the 1st Battalion as it advanced beyond Lerbeck. Three German tanks, a self-propelled gun and about 40 infantrymen attacked Company A as it moved along the road to Nemmen. The Americans took shelter in the houses while the self-propelled gun shelled those buildings. The German infantry attacked, but suffered several casualties and withdrew. Without infantry support, the German armor then also withdrew. The 1st Battalion secured Nemmen, posted sentries and quickly fell asleep, the first time they had been able to in more than two days. While they slept, the 171st Engineer (Combat) Battalion completed an infantry bridge across the Weser. Nearby, the 22nd Armored Engineer Battalion built a Treadway bridge for heavier military traffic. In order to improve the approaches, the engineers had to truck in tons of bricks and rubble to strengthen the access to the bridges. Both were ready for traffic before darkness on April 6.

The relatively easy crossing of the Weser by Ninth Army was largely the result of the lack of defenders. In the original German plans, XLVII Panzer Corps had been assigned to defend the Weser in this sector, but it no longer existed, having been trapped within the Ruhr Pocket. The only other major force in the area, *General der Infanterie* Guenther Blumentritt's First Parachute Army, had been driven off to the north by Twenty-First Army Group's advance. The last remaining force was *Wehrkreis* VI, the German home defense system, which was technically now a part of General Hitzfeld's Eleventh Army.

The attack of Ninth Army across the Weser severed communications between the senior German commands on their western front. General Blaskowitz's Army Group H, including the First Parachute Army, could no longer communicate with Field Marshal Albert Kesselring, commanding the Western Front. The German High Command now placed Army Group H as the senior command in charge of the occupied Netherlands and directly responsible to the High Command in Berlin. To defend the line of the Weser, already breached by Ninth Army, a new force called Army Blumentritt was created. General Blumentritt, formerly the commander of the First Parachute Army, was to assume control of any troops and staff available from *Wehkreise* VI and *Wehkreise* XI, plus some naval troops stationed near Bremen. This paper command was expected to hold the Weser River line.[8]

Meanwhile, General White was determined that his 2nd Armored Division would be in at the kill when the Americans seized Berlin. After the bridges were blown up in their faces at Hamelin, Combat Command A crossed over a new bridgehead at the town of Ohr, which had been established by the 119th Infantry Regiment, 30th Infantry Division. Crossing on April 5, CCA was ordered to clear Eldgasen, which took them until the following morning. Then they raced ahead 18 miles to the Leine River, north of Sarstedt. When the tanks and infantry from Company E, 119th Infantry, captured a bridge over the river, someone spotted a burning fuse attached to 1,200 pounds of explosives. Sergeant Wilhelm O. Jordan jumped from his tank and instinctively pulled the fuse out of the explosives. The sensitive detonating cap exploded in his hands and cost him two fingers, but a bridge had been secured across the river. The town of Sarstedt fell soon thereafter.

Brigadier General Sidney R. Hinds' Combat Command B was also rushing forward. After clearing the Teutoburger Wald, CCB headed full speed for the Weser. After a brief stop to refuel and replenish supplies, the command pushed into Bad Pyrmont and overcame initial resistance. Air reconnaissance could identify no organized enemy resistance in front of Hinds, but reported that all bridges along the planned route had already been destroyed. Hinds therefore redirected his command to Ohr and crossed over the bridges built there by the 119th Infantry and Combat Command A. Next day CCB also raced forward and reached the Leine River. They crossed at Gronau in mid-morning and moved east to Bartelde, then turned north to capture a pass through the Diekholzen Forest. The 1st Battalion, 41st Armored Infantry, isolated the town of Hildesheim. But the 67th Armored Regiment was held up by infantry armed with the antitank launchers known as "*panzerfausts*" for several hours. Finally pushing these enemy troops aside, the advance continued to and over the Innerste River south of Hildesheim. Here, 1st Lieutenant Arthur Hadley brought up his "talking tank," actually a tank with a loudspeaker mounted on it. Hadley, a Yale graduate, was a psychological warfare officer who had already talked several German towns into surrender. At Hildesheim he moved his tank to the edge of town and announced that a hundred allied dive bombers would level the town if it did not immediately surrender. The ploy seemed to work and Germans began surrendering until a flight of German planes appeared overhead. Their rare appearance stiffened German morale and Hadley was forced to leave his prisoners and fight his way back to CCB. The 1st Battalion, 67th Armored Regiment, would soon secure the town.

Behind the spearheads, infantry mopped up as they, too, advanced on the Elbe. The 102nd Infantry ("Ozark") Division had spent some time guarding the west bank of the Rhine, but in early April it rejoined XIII Corps and pushed east. It had the responsibility of maintaining physical contact with Twenty-First Army Group, now heading north and east and therefore moving away from Ninth Army. The 1st Battalion, 407th Infantry, was alerted on April 5 to be prepared to secure the city of Münster, where rioting had broken out. Another unit, the 3rd Battalion, 405th Infantry, had been assigned the job of securing Ninth Army's command post. As the division advanced, it quickly became clear that "the Germans were ahead of and behind us as well as on both flanks."[9] Nevertheless, the Americans moved forward, reacting to the opposition whenever encountered.

The term "mopping up" sounds straightforward, but it came with its own dangers. When Company D, 405th Infantry, was ambushed as it motored along a road, Corporal William E. Dennis took command and maintained fire against the enemy until all the wounded had been safely evacuated.[10] Technical Sergeant Harold T. Klausmeyer, Jr., of Company G, 406th Infantry, deliberately drew the enemy's fire so that his squad members could advance and knock out a machine gun holding up the advance. He again exposed himself to the enemy's fire as he rescued his wounded squad leader.[11] When his patrol of the 102nd Cavalry Reconnaissance Troop was pinned down by enemy fire and his squad leader killed, Corporal Aarol W. Irish directed its defense until all ammunition was exhausted, then played dead as the Germans overran his vehicle. After they left he personally evacuated his wounded buddies, despite his own serious injuries.[12] Thanks to bravery like this, the advance continued unchecked.

The 406th Infantry soon found itself facing a long, mountainous ridge known locally as the "*Wesergebirge.*" This ridge, with its steep, densely wooded slopes, offered good defensive positions for hundreds of enemy troops, who had been pushed aside by the earlier passage of the 5th Armored and 84th Infantry Divisions. Many of these Germans were from an officer candidate unit, others from the Hitler Youth. Battle groups were formed and they prepared to defend the *Wesergebirge*, taking advantage of defenses probably prepared for the defense of the nearby city of Hannover. Beginning on April 8, the 406th Regimental Combat Team fought to clear this ridge. Despite being well behind the "front line," the battle was fierce.

The opening shots were fired when an advance party of the division HQ, seeking new quarters, was ambushed at the entrance to Steinbergen Pass. Small-arms fire killed Technical Sergeant Emerson Potticher and wounded several others in the group. Some of the group were captured and taken to an enemy command post. Later in the day, Lieutenant Colonel Kenneth W. Rees, the division's senior ordnance officer, was also wounded and captured at the same roadblock. Earlier, when the 102nd Infantry Division relieved the 84th Infantry Division of responsibility for the ridge, intelligence officers believed there would be no serious opposition.

The 406th Infantry crossed the Weser and launched its attack at noon on April 9. Believing they faced only a small force, the Intelligence and Reconnaissance Platoon, reinforced with a platoon of Company G, set out to investigate the ridge. As they passed the 335th Infantry, 84th Infantry Division, they were warned that the enemy was dug-in and well-armed, so they left their vehicles and advanced on foot. They had not gone far before they came under heavy small-arms fire. Tanks from Company B, 701st Tank Battalion, came up in support. Captain Joseph Seldon, commanding the tanks, remembered:

> Germans hiding in the houses on both sides of the road ambushed the tanks. Both were hit simultaneously by Panzerfausts. The crews escaped, except one man who was killed by a sniper. The infantry boys really went to work then. They dragged the sniper from the house he was hiding in and polished him off. He was a fanatical fellow who kept attempting to break loose all the time. They also took about thirty-two PWs from that one section of town.[13]

The "Ozarks" were soon calling the area "*Panzerfaust* Valley," as more and more defenders stubbornly refused to surrender, but fought on with fierce determination. Companies F and G moved deeper into the zone, with Company B's tanks still accompanying them. A self-propelled gun and several armored half-tracks tried to counterattack, but the Americans ambushed them, bringing up three 105mm assault guns, which knocked out the enemy armor. The battalion commander later interviewed several of the prisoners captured in the attack. He commented on the Germans:

> …they were youngsters, sixteen and seventeen years old, who had only been in the army two or three months. Their fathers were all high-ranking Wehrmacht officers and because of this they were selected to attend the Officers' Candidate School, which was in the castle just north of Schaumberg. They were totally imbued with the military traditions of their families and were determined to resist to the end.[14]

Fighting like this continued for the next two days. As the German position weakened, the enemy commander realized he had to surrender. He sent an American prisoner, Lieutenant Colonel Rees, to the 406th Infantry Regiment, together with a German officer, to propose surrender. The Germans were instructed to assemble all of their troops and to stack all weapons and equipment in the courtyard of their headquarters castle. A dozen officers and 1,400 enlisted men were taken into custody. About 600 were killed in the battle and another 1,000 were believed to have escaped. The advance of XIII Corps, now with the 84th and 102nd Infantry Divisions and 11th Cavalry Group attached, could continue unhindered.

The fanatical defenders overcome by the 102nd Infantry Division were the exception rather than the rule. Generally, Ninth Army met units made up of hastily organized "battle groups," service troops, antiaircraft troops without guns, replacement and training units and some hastily created "divisions" that existed largely in name only. The Germans were fighting with any forces that could be scraped together. Ninth Army came upon several units that had special medical needs, "stomach" and "ear" battalions in which men with those problems had been assembled, given weapons and a few officers to lead them, and then thrown in the path of the rampaging Ninth Army. Hastily organized home guard units, or *Volkssturm*, did not even have uniforms, but instead wore armbands indicating their "military" status. These groups of old men and boys more often than not faded away after the first shots were fired, although some did in fact stand and defend their towns, usually when SS troops were behind them. Ninth Army quickly adopted the policy of disarming these civilians in "uniform" and returning them to their civilian occupations to prevent overwhelming the prisoner-of-war camps.

Behind the lines, Ninth Army was relieved to see that the German Air Force, which had continued to attack Allied bridges over the Rhine, had given up that fruitless task and had now turned its limited efforts against the leading American columns racing to the Elbe. To put an end to this harassment, Ninth Army made overrunning enemy airfields a priority task, and XXIX Tactical Air Command made those same airfields its main target. Nevertheless, the German Air Force, such as it was at this point in the war, did manage to continue pinprick attacks, flying from hidden airfields and even off concrete highways, and hiding aircraft in the woods alongside those roads.

Ninth Army headquarters moved across the Rhine on April 4, and established a new HQ at the small town of Haltern, to better maintain communications with its own fast moving columns. A week later it would again advance, this time to the town of Gütersloh. Each move (and there would be several more in the weeks to come) required a massive operation by the Army's signal troops, to establish secure and complete communications between the army's front and rear units. It took an average of three days to establish the required switchboard and telephone-carrier facilities for each new headquarters. The signal corps men attached to Ninth Army HQ found themselves constantly tearing down or setting up a new communications system, without a break, for the next month.

The constant moves by headquarters were the result of the race east. All of Ninth Army was rushing headlong to the Elbe, where many of the senior commanders believed they would be directed to seize the German capitol. General Simpson later remembered, "My people were keyed up. We'd been the first to the Rhine and now we were going to be the first to Berlin. All along we thought of just one thing—capturing Berlin, going through and meeting the Russians on the other side."[15] Simpson had already planned exactly how his army would drive on Berlin. After reaching the vicinity of Hildesheim he "planned to get an armored and infantry division set up on the autobahn running just above Magdeburg on the Elbe to Potsdam, where we'll be ready to close in on Berlin."[16] Then his entire Ninth Army would follow to capture Berlin. As he told his staff, "Damn, I want to get to Berlin and all you people, right down to the last private, I think, want it, too."[17]

Simpson was not wrong in his belief. General White, commanding the 2nd Armored Division, had planned on striking for Berlin even before his division had crossed the Rhine. His Operations Officer, Colonel Briard P. Johnson, had actually drawn up a plan on maps. It basically followed Simpson's outline, and division headquarters had prepared maps and overlays for the operation. Phase lines had been indicated, and White believed that his division could reach the German capitol in 48 hours once across the Elbe.

Nor was White alone in this belief. Covering his flanks was General Macon's 83rd Infantry Division. The "rag-tag circus" troops were determined to keep moving east at the fastest pace possible. To avoid accidental air attack by XXIX Tactical Air Command, each vehicle was hastily painted with a white star and a coat of olive green paint. The division had even managed to acquire a German plane and, even more unusual, found someone to fly it. This, too, received a hastily applied coat of olive green, a white star and the stenciling "83rd Infantry Division" as it flew over enemy and friendly troops seeking a faster way forward. So thick was the collection of enemy vehicles within the 83rd Infantry Division column that, on at least one occasion, a German staff car filled with senior officers joined it, thinking it was friendly, only to learn to their dismay that it was not.

Not to be outdone was General Oliver's 5th Armored Division. Its Combat Command A crossed the Weser on April 9, following Combat Command Reserve. Led by Troop A, 85th reconnaissance Squadron, CCR seized two bridges over the Weser–Elbe Canal at Sehnde. The combat command then raced east, capturing bridges as it went. Not all the bridges were fully intact however. At one location, Sergeant June R. McCloud of Troop A raced with his squad to the bridge at Didderse. He radioed back, "Hello, Able 31 to Able 5. I'm at the bridge. It's intact. Wait. I'm going to cross." But just as he approached, the enemy exploded demolition charges on the bridge. McCloud radioed back, "Hello, Able 5. They just blew the bridge! Stand by. I'm going to take a look." Some minutes later, McCloud came back on the radio. "Hello, Able 5. Bridge is okay. All of the charge didn't go off. I'm cutting the rest of the wires."[18] And another bridge fell to the charging Americans.

The 5th Armored Division continued. At one bridge site, German defenders halted the column. Platoons led by Lieutenant Mouse P. Maurer and Lieutenant Joseph Clifton faced heavy small-arms and antitank fire, which stopped their advance. They could see German engineers placing demolition charges on the bridge. Immediately, Staff Sergeant John N. Schaeffer of the 34th Tank Battalion moved his tanks forward and opened fire on the engineers, while the assault gun platoon of the 46th Armored Infantry Battalion joined him. The Germans withdrew and another bridge was seized intact. Brigadier General Eugene A. Regnier's CCA raced east.

The next objective was the bridge at the town of Tangermunde, where the Americans ran into serious resistance from antitank teams. Leading the attack was Lieutenant Colonel Richard H. Jones' 34th Tank Battalion. Two of his tank commanders, Sergeant Charles H. Householder and Sergeant Leonard B. Haymaker, returned the fire with cannon and machine guns. Blasting basement windows and doors, the Americans fought their way into the town. Sergeant Householder fell to sniper fire and his tank was knocked out by a *panzerfaust*, so Sergeant Haymaker took the lead, before his tank was also knocked out and set ablaze. Seeing that his crew could not escape under the enemy fire, Haymaker charged the enemy with his Thompson sub-machine gun covering his crew as they escaped, but he was killed while saving them.

Medics racing to aid the wounded men were fired on by the Germans, and several were killed and wounded as they tried to pull men to safety. Private Robert G. Milliman pulled two men from Householder's tank. After carrying one to safety, he returned for the other only to be killed by enemy sniper fire. A platoon commander moved forward to an intersection where they discovered a crowd of German infantrymen with *panzerfausts*. Private First Class Luther A. Parham, firing the tank's turret mounted machine gun, killed or wounded 75 German soldiers, relieving much of the pressure on the Americans.

Meanwhile, Lieutenant Colonel William H. Burton, Jr., commanding the 46th Armored Infantry Battalion, sent in his Company C to remove the enemy. They began to clear the town, building by building, until they came to an intersection where enemy sniper and *panzerfaust* fire stopped them. A platoon leader, Lieutenant Edgar D. Swihart, worked his way forward to a house, from which most of the enemy fire was coming. Covered by Staff Sergeant Raymond J. Caplette, both men managed to get to within 50 yards of the building. From there, Caplette fired a bazooka into the house, after which Swihart rushed in and eliminated the remaining German soldiers.

Meanwhile, others were trying to keep the Germans from blowing up the vital bridge over the Elbe at Tangermunde. Captain Henry P. Halsell was the CCA air officer and remembered:

> The 47th Field Artillery Battalion was across the road from me and the 71st Field Artillery Battalion was behind me. The 557th Field Artillery's 155mm self-propelled guns were going into position further back. The weather was beautiful, with the sun shining brightly. The Artillery was firing every 30 seconds and I could see the time fire burst over the bridge site and the red dust of brick rise from the town after each volley.[19]

This attempt to keep the Germans from placing and detonating demolition charges failed, however, and the bridge at Tangermude, which would have placed the 5th Armored Division only 53 miles from Berlin, fell into the river.

It was left to General White's 2nd Armored Division to win the race across the Elbe. After destroying some 67 large antiaircraft guns, emplaced to defend the Hermann Goering Steel Works southwest of Braunschweig, the division raced 20 miles, led by CCB under General Hinds. The command pressed ahead without regard to overtaking fleeing German columns, pushing them aside without taking prisoners. Blasts from the cannon of the leading tanks quickly cleared hastily built roadblocks. In one instance, Major James F. Hollingworth, facing a roadblock, lined up his 34 tanks and gave a rare order in the 20th century: "Charge." The defenders of the roadblock melted away. By late afternoon on April 11, 1945, the leading element of Lieutenant Colonel Merriam's 82nd Reconnaissance Battalion reached the outskirts of Magdeburg. They were halted not so much by enemy fire, but by crowds of German civilians who had no idea the war was upon them and who were casually walking the streets, shopping and greeting each other. A few shots fired into the air dispersed the crowds, and 1st Lieutenant Harold Douglass led a platoon through the town to the airport. There, the Americans shot up 25 enemy planes on the ground and two more that were attempting to land.

But the Germans were not through. Local forces regrouped and opened fire on the Americans. Antiaircraft guns and *panzerfausts* knocked out two American half-tracks and two jeeps. Lieutenant Douglass called for help and the 1st Battalion, 67th Armored Regiment, raced in, but was stopped at the west edge of town. The reconnaissance men had to retreat to save themselves but, after advancing 52 miles in 13 hours, the 2nd Armored Division was at Magdeburg.

Not far away, Colonel Disney's Combat Command B attacked and made good progress until it reached Anderluch, where it ran into a column of 1,700 German soldiers. The Germans quickly surrendered and the column proceeded until about 2000 hours that night, when a message was sent by Disney to division headquarters. It read simply, "We're on the Elbe."[20] He was soon joined by the 83rd Infantry Division and the 5th Armored Division. Ninth Army was in position for the final drive on Berlin.

When Major Hollingsworth topped a ridge overlooking the town of Schönebeck, he saw a bridge standing and in use by the Germans. They were evacuating their own armor over it. Intent on capturing an intact bridge over the Elbe, Hollingsworth tried a decoy. He sent one of his tank companies to attach itself to the rear of the enemy column in the hope that it could cross the bridge undetected and seize it before the Germans could destroy the bridge—but the Germans spotted the Americans and opened fire immediately. With the approaches heavily mined and covered by small-arms fire, the Americans were stymied. The following morning, the Germans, having withdrawn all they could, blew the bridge up. Undeterred, General Hinds had already tasked the 17th Armored Engineer Battalion to locate a crossing site and build a bridge there. Meanwhile, the rest of the 2nd Armored Division surrounded Magdeburg and attempted to negotiate a surrender with the military commander and the mayor. All offers were rejected and the attack was renewed. Heavy opposition from infantry and antitank guns on the east bank slowed the advance.

While the battle to isolate Magdeburg continued, Combat Command B tried to find a suitable site to force a river crossing. An old wagon ferry site in Westerhausen, north of Schönebeck, was chosen because it was also a good site to build a bridge. Using DUKWs, the essential amphibious trucks, the 1st and 3rd Battalions, 41st Armored Infantry Regiment, reached the east bank of the Elbe at 2300 hours on April 12, 1945. The 3rd Battalion, 119th Infantry Regiment, 30th Infantry Division, followed across as a reserve. All three battalions were unopposed and set up a strongly held bridgehead, as engineers set to work on a bridge behind them. An excited General White phoned General Simpson and reported, "We're across."[21]

The Germans knew it too, and they immediately prepared to eliminate the threat to their capitol. Before dawn, German artillery was shelling the bridging site. The fire was heavy and accurate. American artillery tried to knock out the enemy guns, while smoke pots were set to try and hide the site from enemy observation. Three times the engineers started work, and three times German artillery stopped them. On the fourth attempt, the engineers reached to within 25 feet of the east bank when German fire knocked out part of the bridge and again stopped work.

The men on the east bank were exhausted, having been moving and fighting for days on end without rest. Now, with no antitank support available to them, they were ordered to retire to the west bank. Generals White and Hinds had learned that the 83rd Infantry Division had established its own bridgehead downstream, at the town of Barby. The 2nd Armored Division could use that crossing to get tanks and men across the Elbe, but before the advanced battalions could move back, a German counterattack, supported by tanks and self-propelled guns, struck the bridgehead. The outer perimeter, which had no antitank defenses, was quickly overrun. The Germans took prisoners and placed them in front of their armored vehicles as human shields, then advanced on the rest of the bridgehead. Colonel Disney, commanding the east bank force, went down wounded, and Lieutenant Colonel Francis H. Barnes took command. A final perimeter was established and General White, still believing that a bridge was near completion, delayed ordering a retreat. Colonel Barnes reported in person to White that the situation was serious and getting worse. Without antitank guns or tanks, the men on the east bank could not hold. Reports soon arrived that the 3rd Battalion, 41st Armored Infantry, had been wiped out. Artillery slowed the German advance but a request for air support was denied. Allied planes were not available because their airstrips had been left so far behind the racing allied spearheads that they could not reach them in time.

The 17th Armored Engineer Battalion continued working on a bridge, while nearby the 82nd Engineer (Combat) Battalion tried to install a ferry to get tanks and guns over the river. German artillery fire denied both efforts. Finally, at about 1330 hours, Hinds gave the withdrawal order. White had already given permission, and the bridgehead was evacuated in an orderly manner. First the riflemen came out, carried by the three remaining DUKWs and covered by the machine gunners and bazooka men. Two of the three DUKWs were lost, leaving just the one to continue the evacuation, and some soldiers preferred to swim the river.

First Lieutenant Louis W. Perry and 60 men of the 3rd Battalion, 119th Infantry, were trapped in a basement on the east bank. Spotted by an aerial observer of the 78th Armored Artillery Battalion, they came out at night under the cover of an artillery barrage and smoke screen. One infantry company stayed on the east bank, protecting the ferry site, and would not be withdrawn until the 2nd Armored Division left the west bank of the Elbe.

Meanwhile, General Macon's 83rd Infantry Division had been keeping pace with the leading armored elements of Ninth Army. The division's history explains how an infantry division could keep up with a motorized armored formation: "We pressed into service every conceivable means of transportation we encountered. If it had wheels, we used it. It was not unusual to see thirty or more riflemen clinging to a single tank, or to see two or three men on one motorcycle, or a whole platoon riding down the street in a dilapidated German jalopy."[22] In moving this way, they picked up yet another nickname, the "83rd Armored Division."

During the race to the Elbe, the 330th Infantry Regiment had cleared the heavily defended Harz Mountains, bringing in some 60,000 enemy prisoners of war. But it was at the town of Barby, on the Elbe, that the division made its greatest impact. Here, the Germans defended the town and a house-to-house battle was required to clear it. On April 13, 1945, the 329th and 331st Infantry Regiments crossed the river in assault boats screened by smoke, supported by the 736th Tank Battalion and 643rd Tank Destroyer Battalion. The armored units were ferried across the river by the 308th Engineer (Combat) Battalion and a firm bridgehead was soon established. Colonel Edwin B. Crabill, commander of the 329th Infantry Regiment, strode up and down the bridgehead shouting, "Don't waste the opportunity of a lifetime, you're on your way to Berlin."[23] The site was covered by the 453rd Antiaircraft Artillery Battalion and the 113th Cavalry Group. Bridges were soon built by the 295th Engineer (Combat) Battalion and the 992nd Bridge Company.

As they had done upstream, the Germans reacted swiftly to the encroachment on the east bank of the Elbe. Artillery bombarded the sites and the few remaining aircraft of the German Air Force struck repeatedly. Swimming saboteurs and mines floated down the river were other methods aimed at destroying the crucial bridges over the Elbe. None succeeded. The 83rd Infantry Division christened its bridge over the Elbe the "Truman Bridge," in honor of the new President of America. Despite heavy and continuing attacks on the bridge, it remained standing. The Americans had crossed to stay.

General White sent CCB to the 83rd Infantry Division's crossing site, where it was attached to the division, crossed the river, and helped the infantry hold and enlarge the bridgehead. Meanwhile, Simpson at Ninth Army had prepared his plans for the army's advance on Berlin. Led by the 2nd Armored Division, which was to be flanked by the 30th Infantry Division to the north and the 83rd Infantry Division to the south, XIX Corps was to attack towards Berlin, followed by XIII Corps. The 35th Infantry Division was to secure the crossing sites at Magdeburg while the corps attacked on April 15. Many of Ninth Army's leaders were confident that the attack would reach Berlin within 24 hours.

CHAPTER 14

To the End

General Simpson and all the senior commanders within Ninth Army were poised for the final drive on the German capital city. Everything was in place for the final "end the war" push. By April 12, 1945, Ninth Army had both XIX Corps and XIII Corps on the Elbe, with a strong bridgehead at Barby. The 5th Armored Division, at Tangermunde, was barely 53 miles from Berlin after rushing over 200 miles in 13 days. General Anderson's XVI Corps was still back in the Ruhr, mopping up and establishing a military government system for that area. German forces were weak, unorganized and with the lowest morale yet seen in the war. Ninth Army, on the other hand, was now a fully professional, experienced, well-armed and well-equipped force, ready to make the last dash to Berlin.

The American soldiers were calling the advance "the rat race," reminiscent of the race across France the previous summer. As happened then, units ran off maps and had to ask local civilians for directions. Supplies could not keep up with the rapidly advancing troops, and rest was out of the question. Officers took to encouraging their men with the expression "Would you trade sleep for blood? Get up and get going!"[1] To the north, the 84th Infantry Division of XIII Corps cleared Hannover and then contacted the British Second Army near Celle. The 102nd Infantry Division followed in the wake of the 5th Armored Division and cleaned up isolated pockets of resistance. The 30th Infantry Division found itself engaged at Braunschweig and fought hard to knock out more than 60 88mm antiaircraft guns.

XXIX Tactical Air command found itself in new circumstances as well. Its airfields remained west of the Rhine, making it difficult to cover the wide-ranging spearheads of Ninth Army. Captured German airfields at Münster, Gütersloh, Paderborn and Braunschweig were so badly damaged by Allied attacks that they were useless for American aircraft. A few airstrips were established, but these could not be used for anything but emergency landings as they had no facilities, fuel or ammunition depots. This problem restricted the operations of XXIX TAC, despite its fighters and fighter-bombers carrying wing or belly tanks of additional fuel. The planes could still reach the front lines, but the time they could spend over those lines was extremely limited. Emergency refueling airstrips at Münster and Gütersloh could refuel individual planes in emergencies but did not have the supply to handle full squadrons on a regular basis. When the situation improved, as the American airstrips were moved across the Rhine, the closeness of the Russian Armies and Air Force so limited the operational areas over which XXIX TAC could conduct operations, that there were simply no more targets available.

In contrast, German air operations increased significantly, intended to knock out Ninth Army's bridgeheads over the Elbe. All attacks against the Rhine bridges ceased as the full attention of the German Air Force now centered on the Elbe. For a full week, German aircraft repeatedly attacked the American crossings. Ninth Army reported a total of 421 air attacks against its bridgeheads and claimed they had knocked down about 30 percent of the attacking aircraft. It was only when the advancing Allied armies overran the last of the German airfields that the attacks dwindled away.

On the ground, Ninth Army units expanded their grip on the west bank of the Elbe, with the 35th, 84th and 102nd Infantry Divisions clearing the bank in both directions. The city of Magdeburg remained a thorn in Simpson's side, as it refused to surrender despite several pleas by American commanders. Ninth Army could not fully consolidate its gains and establish a firm base for the advance on Berlin with Magdeburg still in enemy hands. Simpson planned a heavy attack against the city, using the full resources of XXIX TAC, after which XIX Corps artillery would pound the city, followed by a ground attack by the 30th Infantry and 2nd Armored Divisions.

The day before this massive attack was to begin, Simpson was called to meet with General Bradley at Twelfth Army Group headquarters, at Wiesbaden, Germany. He flew there on April 15, a sunny Sunday morning. Bradley had promised he had something very important to talk about with Simpson, something too important to be discussed over the phone. Convinced that this was the order to advance on Berlin, Simpson eagerly awaited the news. Bradley met him at the airfield. "We shook hands," recalled Simpson, "and then and there he told me the news. Brad said, 'you must stop on the Elbe. You are not to advance any farther in the direction of Berlin. I'm sorry, Simp, but there it is.'"[2] A shocked Simpson replied, "where in the hell did you get this?" Bradley merely replied, "From Ike." So surprised was Simpson that he could not remember much of the ensuing conversation. "All I remember is that I was heartbroken, and I got back on the plane in a kind of daze. All I could think of was, how am I going to tell my staff, my corps commanders, and my troops? Above all, how am I going to tell my troops?"[3]

Returning to his headquarters, Simpson passed on the bad news to his staff and corps commanders. Then he went up to the Elbe, where General Hinds was still trying to get more troops across the river. As soon as he saw Simpson, Hinds knew something was wrong. "I thought," recalled General Hinds, "that maybe the old man didn't like the way we were crossing the river. He asked how I was getting along."

Hinds replied, "I guess we're all right now, general. We had two good withdrawals. There was no excitement and no panic and our Barby crossings are going good."[4] Simpson replied, "Fine. Keep some of your men on the east bank if you want to. But they are not to go any farther. Sid, this is as far as we're going." So shocked was Hinds that he replied in an insubordinate manner, saying, "No sir, that's not right. We're going to Berlin." It took a moment for Simpson to control his own emotions before he could reply to Hinds, saying simply, "We're not going to Berlin, Sid. This is the end of the war for us."[5]

Simpson was wrong about this being the end of the war. There remained the problem of Magdeburg, which had to be cleared. As planned, XIX Corps and XXIX Tactical Air Command partnered to eliminate this last hold-out garrison along the Elbe in Ninth Army's zone. Beginning April 16, XXIX TAC bombed and strafed all remaining German airfields, which were crowded with the remnants of the German Air Force. Claims were made for 147 German planes destroyed and another 85 damaged. Hangers, buildings, barracks and runways were blown up or cratered to finally eliminate the German air threat. The air partner of Ninth Army also participated in the reduction of the stubborn Magdeburg garrison. A huge air attack planned by Simpson included the medium bombers of Ninth Air Force, with 11 groups of medium bombers added to the fighter-bombers of XXIX TAC. The fighter-bombers would attack the city both before and immediately after the medium bombers unloaded their deadly cargos on the city. The first fighter-bomber attack was designed to keep antiaircraft gunners pinned down as the medium bombers made their approach, while the following attack was intended to keep the defenders pinned down as the infantry began their own assault.

The air assault began soon after noon on April 17. Some 775 tons of bombs were dropped on the city and XIX Corps artillery fired antiaircraft suppression missions as well. So effective was this fire that not one of the 360 American aircraft involved was shot down by German antiaircraft fire. As soon as the medium bombers finished their attack, and while the fighter-bombers returned for their final run, the 30th Infantry Division began its advance on Magdeburg from the north, while the 2nd Armored Division attacked from the south and west.

The Battle of Magdeburg raged for the next 24 hours. Initially, General Hobbs and his 30th Infantry Division viewed Magdeburg as a relatively easy objective and allocated only the 120th Infantry Regiment to the attack. Like others before them, a group led by the regimental intelligence officer drove up to an enemy roadblock to demand the city's surrender. They were blindfolded and taken deep into the city, later determining that they had been taken to an island in the middle of the Elbe where the German garrison commander had his headquarters. After all this, they were told that the garrison commander did not have the authority to surrender. The Americans sensed that most German troops did in fact want to surrender, but the intransigence of the garrison commander and the presence of SS troops at critical locations within the city precluded any such attempt.

This incident changed Hobbs' mind. He added his 117th Infantry Regiment to the attack.[6] The American infantry found that although the air attacks had been impressive, they had largely struck the center of the city which had already been thoroughly bombed. Few, if any, bombs had fallen on the outskirts of town where the enemy ground defenses were positioned. The enemy defended from hastily built roadblocks, antitank ditches and buildings. Each point was usually built around machine guns and antitank guns, and snipers also took their toll. The close-quarter fighting precluded artillery support, but the advance continued at the pace of an infantryman. Tanks of the 743rd Tank Battalion and tank destroyers from the 823rd Tank Destroyer Battalion were of some assistance, but again the close-quarters of city fighting limited their contribution. The most effective supporting weapons were the infantry's own mortars. As darkness fell, the 30th Infantry Division halted its attack until daylight.

Combat Command A of the 2nd Armored Division also attacked from the other side of the city. The troops soon found that if they promised not to destroy a civilian's home, they would be only too happy to point out the German defenses in their area. With civilians pointing out the enemy positions for the tanks and tank destroyers to knock them out, the advance progressed well. The armored division's attack also stopped as darkness fell, but renewed the next morning and CCA quickly cleared the remaining portion of its sector. After a few more days of mopping up, the 2nd Armored Division was relieved and sent back to the area around Braunschweig for rest and reorganization.

The 30th Infantry Division also renewed its attack and pushed steadily down to the edge of the Elbe. Just as the leading infantrymen arrived, at the very last moment, the Germans blew up the bridge. Now the Americans had to deal with thousands of civilians, who often got in the way of the advancing troops. As one account described it, "the street fighting had become a policeman's headache."[7] Like the 2nd Armored Division, the 30th Infantry Division's fighting in Europe was over.

Just as the fighting for Magdeburg was winding down, Bradley came to visit Ninth Army headquarters. As the generals discussed the ongoing battle, Simpson's phone rang. He listened to the voice on the other end, then turned to Bradley and said, "It looks as if we may get the bridge in Magdeburg after all. What'll we do then, Brad?"[8] Bradley was well aware of the answer Simpson wanted to hear—the bridge at Magdeburg led directly to the autobahn that in turn led directly to Berlin—but he replied, "Hell's bells, we don't want any more bridgeheads on the Elbe. If you get it you'll have to throw a battalion across it, I guess. But let's hope the other fellows blow it up before you're stuck with it."[9] Disappointed, Simpson replaced the receiver. Moments later he received a second call. The bridge at Magdeburg was no more. Ninth Army's advance was at an end.

There were still pockets of resistance within Ninth Army's zone, and attention was paid to these now that the army was halted in place. Supplies began to catch up with the advanced units and other administrative matters could now be addressed. XIX Corps still had a bitter fight going on between the 330th Infantry Regiment of the 83rd Infantry Division and Germans holding out in the Harz Forest. On April 20, the 8th Armored Division came up from the Ruhr and attacked enemy forces still holding out in the mountains of the Halberstadt area, taking the town of Blankenburg. General Gillem's XIII Corps spent a week knocking out thousands of Germans in the rear areas who were trying to organize a counterattack against the rear elements of Ninth Army. They had attacked supply columns, cut communication wires and generally made a nuisance of themselves before XIII Corps took them on and eliminated the threat. In one instance, a group of between 500-600 German soldiers, with 18 armored vehicles and two tanks, seized the town of Jubar, where they captured 13 American trucks and 47 American soldiers. The following day, April 18, a larger enemy force with perhaps 20 tanks and several self-propelled guns attacked near the town of Lindhof and had to be stopped. XIII Corps dealt with all these threats as soon as they were identified. Using the 335th Infantry Regiment, 84th Infantry Division, and the 407th Infantry Regiment, 102nd Infantry Division, supported by Combat Command B of the 5th Armored Division and the 11th Cavalry Group, Gillem cleared one pocket of resistance after another. By April 22, the only remaining enemy force behind Ninth Army's lines was trapped in the Klötze forest, where they were subjected to a severe and constant pounding by XIII Corps artillery. Gillem personally oversaw this operation, even to the point of adjusting artillery fire on the forest from his bedroom window. Finally, a regiment of the 29th Infantry Division went in and mopped up the remnants in the forest.

Along the Elbe front, little changed. Patrols were sent out in the hope of contacting the approaching Russian forces. Several units were relieved and sent to the rear to assume military government duties. On April 20, a new order from Twelfth Army Group extended the zone of Ninth Army along the Elbe another 30 miles to the northeast, from Celle to Ludwigslust. This job fell to XIII Corps, which made the last offensive move of Ninth Army, clearing the area of German holdouts with the 5th Armored Division, and the 29th and 84th Infantry Divisions, supported by the 34th Field Artillery Brigade. The job was done in two days against varied resistance. The 5th Armored Division contacted the British Second Army on the Elbe at Neu Darchau and Dannenberg on April 22, 1945.

With no advance to be conducted, logistical and administrative matters now became the focus of Ninth Army headquarters. Transportation continued to be a problem, with two forward corps needing support and a third corps (XVI) to the rear requiring support for the welfare of tens of thousands of civilians, ex-prisoners of war and combat troops needing a variety of goods and services. Ninth Army began to supply the forward elements by air, particularly with gasoline and ammunition delivered at forward airfields. Although affected by weather, this temporary measure prevented serious shortfalls. Another use of available air transport was for the evacuation of the wounded. Using Douglas C-47 cargo planes flying from advanced airfields, the wounded and sick were flown out to Communications Zone hospitals, eliminating the need for rough trips in ambulances over hundreds of miles of road. An "advanced section hospital" was established at Rheydt to hold patients until air transport became available. Later, additional sites were established. During the month of April, 11,085 patients were air evacuated by Ninth Army to army hospitals in the Communications Zone.

Once again, Ninth Army had to address the issue of cemeteries for its casualties. Still under the restriction of not burying any American war dead on German soil, Ninth Army established three new cemeteries at Margraten in the Netherlands. The dead had to be transported across much of western Germany to reach the new locations, yet another strain on an already overtaxed transportation system. The army's 43 truck companies were widely dispersed, some to the corps, others to armored divisions, leaving only 18 truck companies directly under Ninth Army control. Another 16 ten-ton truck companies were on loan from the Communications Zone. The situation required that every truck was running day and night to meet the army's needs. Maintenance was ignored, and drivers had fewer and fewer rest periods. Yet the army maintained its supply level and never hesitated due to shortages.

One other task the trucks were given was the evacuation of prisoners of war. In the first two weeks of April, 10,464 prisoners were taken in by Ninth Army. These had to be removed from the combat zone as soon as possible. As a result, every truck convoy bringing up supplies was to take back as many prisoners as it could carry. In many cases, there were "potential" prisoners of war wandering behind the lines who had yet to be officially "captured." Many American units had no time to process prisoners, so many groups of Germans simply wandered along the roads until some officer directed a truck convoy to load them up and take them to a collecting point in the rear. Oftentimes, a single military policeman in a jeep would guard hundreds of German POWs as they marched west.

One driver, never identified, came up with a method to get more POWs to the rear quickly. He loaded his truck to capacity and then moved forward, stopping suddenly. The inertia of the stop pushed the prisoners forward just a little bit more, allowing for additional prisoners to be hurriedly loaded into the truck before it set off for the prisoner-of war enclosures. None of this seemed to disturb the prisoners, most of whom were only too happy to get out of the combat zone as quickly as possible.

Other more mundane but nevertheless essential tasks occupied Ninth Army in the last days of April. Railroads and bridges from the Rhine to the Elbe had to be repaired, expanded and enlarged in order to keep supplies moving forward and the detritus of war moving to the rear. Similar attention was paid to the German road net, with the autobahns being repaired as quickly as the engineers could get to them. In Ninth Army's zone alone, this required the construction of 22 new bridges within the first 25 miles. Yet, by the end of April, this was a major supply road net. By May the route was open all the way to Magdeburg.

One of the most crucial issues faced by all the Allied armies at this point was the issue of allied prisoners of war. Thousands had been liberated from prison camps within Ninth Army's zone. These included Americans, British, Belgian, Italian, French, Polish, Yugoslav, Romanian, New Zealander, Australian, South African, Serb, Czech, Greek, Indian, Dutch and Canadian personnel. Having been housed in unsanitary and poorly ventilated buildings, sleeping closely packed in unheated barracks, many were ill and suffering from a variety of diseases. As each location was liberated, Ninth Army medics took immediate measures to clean up the camp. Clean water, medical supplies, and food were swiftly brought in to strengthen the prisoners. With this immediate care, most saw quick improvement. As soon as possible, these prisoners were transported to the rear for processing back to their native countries. At Hildesheim, using a former German airfield, which had buildings capable of holding 10,000 men, XIX Corps converted the place to a temporary holding facility and evacuation center. After repairing the heating, lighting, sewer and water facilities, four Red Cross Clubmobiles were moved into the camp site. A quartermaster bath unit followed, and engineer units worked 24 hours a day to maintain and upgrade the camp. Medical supplies, blood plasma, DDT powder and 20,000 blankets were flown in from the Communications Zone. Within three days, 600 American and 9,400 British prisoners had been funneled into the Hildesheim camp. Each man received a hot shower, was dusted with DDT, and examined by medical officers. Red Cross bags containing soap, towel, comb, toothbrush, razor and blades was provided to every man. Once cleared for travel, the men were organized into groups of 22 each, given quarters with clean blankets and fed. Chaplains were in attendance. A Special Service company even arranged dances with the Red Cross girls. Motion pictures were shown. As American and British planes landed on the nearby runways, the men were loaded in groups after the gasoline, food and medical supplies were unloaded. As the system became more routine, it was not unusual for men who had arrived at the camp by 0900 hours one morning to be on a plane by 1400 hours that same day.

Feeding everyone in Ninth Army's zone was a Herculean task. In April, Ninth Army itself numbered 485,000 U.S. troops. In addition to these, there were 204,379 Allied prisoners of war within its responsibility. To this was added some 124,618 German prisoners of war and 924,500 displaced persons. Feeding this total of 1,738,500 people each day took every ounce of ingenuity the Ninth Army staff could muster. Despite Supreme Allied Headquarters policy that the responsibility for feeding displaced persons was that of the German government, in fact there was no German government in Ninth Army's zone, or anywhere else for that matter. When liberating camps with six or eight thousand hungry people, Ninth Army could not turn them away. Instead, using German stocks when available, they fed as many of these people as possible while trying to get them to a more suitable location. An international agreement had stipulated that each nationality had a distinct menu, which again was taken from available German stockpiles. When there were no stockpiles, German prisoners of war received one-half the normal K or C ration of an American soldier. Displaced persons received two-thirds of a ration. This was at a time when even American soldiers were short on food because of the distance between their units and the nearest supply bases. In fact, on April 18, May 8 and May 10, no food supplies reached Ninth Army's troops, and they were forced to resort to emergency supplies.

To add to Ninth Army's burdens at this time, XVIII (Airborne) Corps, the 82nd Airborne Division, 8th Infantry Division, and 7th Armored Division were assigned to Ninth Army for administration and supply purposes. The corps was under the tactical direction of the Twenty-First Army Group, which, being British, could not supply the American units with their food, ammunition and other supplies.

The long-awaited meeting with the Russian Army finally came for Ninth Army on the last day of April, when the 125th Cavalry Squadron of the 113th Cavalry Group, patrolling out of the 83rd Infantry Division's 30-mile bridgehead at Barby, sighted Russian forces near Zerbst. At 1330 hours on April 30, 1945, troops of the Ninth Army shook hands with those of the 121st Rifle Division of the Red Army.

The approach of the Red Army increased the flow of Germans seeking to surrender to the Americans. In the three days of May 2–4, more than 100,000 Germans surrendered to Ninth Army. Some came in planes, often with girlfriends, wives or family. Some swam the Elbe to reach the American side. In one case, the German Twelfth Army, with elements of the German Ninth Army attached, offered to surrender 65,000 troops (including 6,000 wounded) and 100,000 civilians to the 102nd Infantry Division. In accordance with Allied policy, General Simpson refused the offer, particularly since both German forces had fought on the Eastern Front. However, any individual soldier who could cross the Elbe at his own risk would be received as a prisoner of war on the American side. Civilians were excluded. This resulted in some unbelievable sights, with Germans crossing the river by swimming, over destroyed bridges, or in boats, rafts and anything else that would float. But by May 6, 1945, with the Red Army closing on the Elbe, all such surrenders ceased.

Ninth Army's battle casualties from April 1 to May 9 were 1,358 killed in action, 5,572 wounded in action and 878 missing in action. German prisoners of war taken in the same period numbered 584,450. Ninth Army had pushed some 230 miles from the Rhine to the Elbe and cleared 13,000 square miles of enemy territory. It would now be concerned with the military government of its portion of Germany.

That phase of Ninth Army's history would be short-lived. By June 15, 1945, it had turned over its zone of occupation to Seventh Army and had prepared to move back to the United States before going on to the Pacific, where the war still raged. Its nine months and 10 days of active operations in Europe were complete. General Simpson flew to Washington on June 20, 1945, to learn the role of Ninth Army in its new war. After consulting with the War Department, he flew to China to meet with Lieutenant General Albert C. Wedemeyer, the Commander of the U.S. forces in the China Theater. He was soon joined by General Moore, who had assumed command of Ninth Army in Simpson's absence. The two men observed operations in China to decide if Ninth Army had a role in that campaign. Later, at a meeting with Wedemeyer and the Chinese leader, Generalissimo Chiang Kai-Shek, Simpson and Moore learned that both men desired to see Ninth Army in the China Theater. Plans were issued in which Simpson would be assigned as the Commanding General, Field Forces, China Theater and as Deputy Theater Commander. In this role he would command two army groups, one in the north of China under Lieutenant General Lucian K. Truscott (who had commanded Fifth Army in Italy), and a second to the south under the command of Major General Robert B. McClure (who already commanded the Chinese Combat Command in that area).

Meanwhile, Ninth Army, under the temporary command of Brigadier General Roy V. Rickard, the Army's Assistant Chief of Staff G-4, moved to Deauville, France, in preparation for the journey home. The main body of the headquarters staff sailed for home on the army transport *John Ericsson* on July 27. They arrived in New York on August 6, 1945. Personnel were given 30 days leave and ordered to reassemble at Fort Bragg, North Carolina. Key staff members were ordered to go to Washington, D.C., to meet with the just returned General Simpson and be briefed on their new assignment. It was as this group assembled in Washington that news came of the Japanese surrender. Ninth Army's China mission was cancelled.

Instead, the headquarters staff was to assemble at Fort Bragg. There, on October 10, 1945, Ninth Army was officially inactivated. It had fought for nine months and 10 days, during which it had taken Brest, received the surrender of 20,000 German troops at Beaugency, fought in five countries (France, Belgium, Luxembourg, the Netherlands, and Germany, including at one time fighting in all five simultaneously), battled through the Siegfried Line, made an assault crossing of the Roer and Rhine Rivers, encircled the Ruhr industrial area with First Army, driven 230 miles into Germany, was the first to reach the Elbe and the first to establish a bridgehead across that river, occupied 30,000 square miles of Germany, liberated 600,000 allied prisoners of war and more than 1,250,000 displaced persons, captured 758,923 enemy prisoners of war, and ended its war within 50 miles of Berlin. As General Simpson said when he issued his last address to his troops, "Your exploits will rank among the greatest of military achievements."[10]

Upon the deactivation of Ninth Army, Lieutenant General Simpson was assigned command of Second Army, headquartered at Memphis, Tennessee. With General Moore still acting as his chief of staff, he oversaw the transfer of Second Army headquarters to Baltimore, Maryland, in June 1946. In November of that same year, Simpson retired. He settled in San Antonio, Texas, among several other retired American generals of World War II, and was promoted to full general on the retired list in 1954. He passed away on August 15, 1980, at the age of 92, and is buried with his wife in Arlington National Cemetery.

Ninth U.S. Army Command Staff

Lieutenant General William H. Simpson, Commanding General

Major General James E. Moore, Chief of Staff

Colonel George A. Millener, Deputy Chief of Staff

Colonel Art B. Miller, Jr., Secretary of the General Staff

Colonel Daniel H. Hundley, Assistant Chief of Staff, G-1[1]

Colonel Harold D. Kehm, Assistant Chief of Staff, G-2[2]

Brigadier General Armistead D. Mead, Jr., Assistant Chief of Staff, G-3

Brigadier General Roy V. Rickard, Assistant Chief of Staff, G-4

Colonel Carl A. Krage, Assistant Chief of Staff, G-5

Brigadier General Richard U. Nicholas, Engineer Officer

Colonel John A. Klein, Adjutant General

Colonel John G. Murphy, Antiaircraft Officer

Colonel Lawrence H. Hanley, Artillery Officer

Colonel Claude A. Black, Armor Officer

Colonel William E. Goe, Quartermaster

Colonel Joe J. Miller, Signal Officer

Colonel William E. Shamora, Surgeon

Lieutenant Colonel Kenneth K. Kelley, Special Services Officer

Brief Chronology of Ninth U.S. Army

September 1943: Fourth U.S. Army separated from Western Defense Command and designated a training command under Major General William H. Simpson.

October 13, 1943: Newly promoted Lieutenant General William H. Simpson assumes command of Fourth Army at San Jose, California.

November 1, 1943: Headquarters, Fourth Army, moved to the Presidio of Monterey, California and becomes operational as a training command.

January 1944: Fourth Army headquarters moves to Fort Sam Houston, Texas and takes over the training command responsibilities of Third Army.

March–May 1944: Headquarters, Fourth Army, receives additional staff to form an additional army headquarters with the intent of allowing General Simpson's headquarters to eventually move to the European Theater of Operations.

May 5, 1944: Headquarters, Fourth Army is divided into two army headquarters, Fourth Army and Eighth Army.

May 11, 1944: General Simpson, with key Eighth Army staff, leaves for the ETO, arriving May 12, 1944.

Late May 1944: Headquarters, Eighth Army is redesignated headquarters, Ninth Army at the request of General Dwight D. Eisenhower, SHAEF commander, to differentiate it from the British Eighth Army, also under SHAEF command.

June 22, 1944: Main body of headquarters, Ninth Army, sails for England aboard *Queen Elizabeth*.

September 5, 1944:	Ninth Army becomes operational and takes command of all Allied Forces in the Brittany Peninsula, relieving Third Army.
September 1944:	Engages in the Battle of Brittany.
October 2, 1944:	Moves to Arlon, Belgium.
October 22, 1944:	Moves to Maastricht, Netherlands.
November 16, 1944:	November Offensive begins; army reaches Roer River.
December 16, 1944:	Battle of the Bulge begins.
December 20, 1944:	Ninth Army placed under command, Twenty-First Army Group.
December 21, 1945:	Army assumes responsibility for northern First Army zone to release additional troops for ongoing Battle of the Bulge.
January–February 1945:	Battles for the Roer River Dams.
March 2, 1945:	Reaches the Rhine at Neuss.
March 3, 1945:	Krefeld cleared by XIII Corps, Ninth Army.
March 10, 1945:	Headquarters opens at München-Gladbach, Germany.
March 24, 1945:	Crosses the Rhine into Germany.
April 1, 1945:	Contacts the First Army at Lippstadt, encircling the Ruhr Valley and industrial sites.
April 4, 1945:	Returns to control of Twelfth Army Group. Army reaches the Weser River.
April 11, 1945:	Advanced units (XIX Corps) reach the Elbe River. Hannover cleared by XIII Corps. Essen cleared by XVI Corps.
April 13, 1945:	Elements of Ninth Army (83rd Infantry Division) establish a bridgehead across the Elbe.
April 14, 1945:	Ruhr Pocket cleared. Bridgehead of the 2nd Armored Division across the Elbe River is withdrawn.
April 21–25:	West bank of the Elbe cleared by Ninth Army forces.
April 30, 1945:	113th Cavalry Group, Ninth Army, contacts Russian forces.
May 9, 1945:	Hostilities in Europe cease. Ninth Army reaches its peak troop strength of more than 650,000 officers and men under command.

May 25–June 15, 1945:   Ninth Army units are gradually relieved by British and Russian troops.

June 15, 1945:   Area of occupation and remaining troops pass to control of Seventh Army.

July 28, 1945:   Headquarters sails from Le Havre for the United States aboard the *John Ericsson*.

August 6, 1945:   Headquarters arrives in New York and moves to Camp Shanks, New York.

September 4, 1945:   Headquarters opened at Fort Bragg, North Carolina.

October 10, 1945:   Headquarters, Ninth U.S. Army, inactivated.

APPENDIX C

Major Combat Units of Ninth Army

UNIT	Call Sign	Dates Assigned
2nd Infantry Division	("Ivanhoe")	Sept 1944–Oct 1944
2nd Armored Division	("Powerhouse")	Nov–Dec 1944, Feb–June 1945
3rd Armored Division	("Omaha")	May–June 1945
5th Armored Division	("Volcano")	Jan–June 1945
6th Armored Division	("Bamboo")	Sept 1944, May–June 1945
7th Armored Division	("Workshop")	Nov–Dec 1944, May–June 1945
8th Infantry Division	("Granite")	Sept–Oct 1944, Dec–Jan 1944–45, Feb–June 1945
8th Armored Division	("Tornado")	Feb–June 1945
9th Infantry Division	("Notorious")	May 1945
9th Armored Division	("Combat")	Sept–Oct 1944
10th Armored Division	("Crown")	Sept–Oct 1944
11th Armored Division	("Batman")	Sept–Dec 1944[1]
12th Armored Division	("Wishbone")	Sept–Dec 1944
17th Airborne Division	("Commodore")	Mar–April 1945
26th Infantry Division	("Council")	Sept 1944
29th Infantry Division	("Latitude")	Sept 1944, Oct 1944–June 1945
30th Infantry Division	("Custom")	Oct–Dec 1944, Feb–May 1945
35th Infantry Division	("Justice")	Feb–May 1945
44th Infantry Division	("Fleet")	Sept–Oct 1944
69th Infantry Division	("Tracer")	May–June 1945
70th Infantry Division	("Wyandotte")	May–June 1945
75th Infantry Division	("Diamond")	Dec 1944, Feb–June 1945
76th Infantry Division	("Triangle")	May–June 1945
78th Infantry Division	("Discus")	Nov 1944–Jan 1945, May–June 1945

79th Infantry Division	("Bishop")	Feb–June 1945
82nd Airborne Division	("Champion")	May–June 1945
83rd Infantry Division	("Blackstone")	Sept–Oct 1944, Feb–June 1945
84th Infantry Division	("Checkmate")	Sept, Nov–Dec 1944, Feb–June 1945
87th Infantry Division	("Half Year")	May–June 1945
89th Infantry Division	("Tuxedo")	May–June 1945
94th Infantry Division	("Cedar")	Sept–Oct 1944
95th Infantry Division	("Cement")	Sept–Oct 1944, Feb–June 1945
99th Infantry Division	("Dauntless")	Sept–Oct 1944
102nd Infantry Division	("Domino")	Sept 1944–June 1945[2]
104th Infantry Division	("Cranbury")	Sept–Dec 1944, Jan 1945, May–June 1945
7th (British) Armored Division		Feb 1945
51st (British) Highland Division		Dec 1944

Corps Assigned

III Corps ("Century") VII Corps ("Jayhawk")
VIII Corps ("Monarch") XIII Corps ("Control")
XVI Corps ("Colfax") XVIII (Airborne) Corps ("Macadam")
XIX Corps ("Armor") XXI Corps ("Cotter Key")

Endnotes

Chapter 1

1   Harry James Maloncy (1009–1971) later commanded the 94th Infantry Division in Northwest Europe. Mark Wayne Clark (1896–1984) later commanded Fifth Army in Italy and Fifteenth Army Group in the Mediterranean. Lesley James McNair (1883–1944) was killed in action by a "friendly" bombing incident while observing operations in Normandy during the July breakout battles. Tragically, his son, Colonel Douglas C. McNair, was killed a week later while serving as Chief of Staff to the 77th Infantry Division on Guam.

2   For a brief summary of the tasks a field army is responsible for, see Appendix A.

3   The Sixth, Eighth and Tenth Armies operated in the Pacific, Fifth Army operated in the Mediterranean and First, Third, Seventh, Ninth and Fifteenth Armies operated in Europe. Second and Fourth Armies remained in the United States.

4   Walter Krueger (1881–1967) commanded Sixth Army in New Guinea and the Philippines and was scheduled to lead the invasion of Japan. For details see Nathan N. Prefer, *Leyte 1944, The Soldier's Battle*. (Havertown, PA: Casemate Publishers, 2012).

5   Editorial Committee, Ninth Army, *Conquer: The Story of the Ninth Army, 1944–1945* (Washington: Infantry Journal Press, 1947), p. 16.

6   William Henry Harrison Morris (1890–1971) later voluntarily took a reduction in rank to command the 10th Armored Division in the European Theater of Operations.

7   The same class as future generals Jacob Devers and George S. Patton.

8   After the war, General Simpson commanded Second Army until his retirement in November 30, 1946. He was promoted to full general on the retired list in 1954 by special Act of Congress (Public Law 83-508). He died on August 15, 1980, aged 92. He is buried in Arlington National Cemetery.

9   John A. English, *Patton's Peers: The Forgotten Allied Army Commanders of the Western Front, 1944–1945* (Mechanicsburg, PA: Stackpole Books, 2009), p. 138.

10   Quoted in Thomas E. Ricks, *The Generals: American Military Command From World War II to Today* (New York: Penguin Press, 2012), p. 107.

11   Thomas R. Stone, "General William Hood Simpson: Unsung commander of the US Ninth Army," in *Parameters*, Vol. XI, No. 2, 1981, pp. 44–52.

12   Ricks, *The Generals*, pp. 107–108.

13   Ibid., p. 108.

14   Ibid.

15   Captain Harry C. Butcher, USNR. *My Three Years With Eisenhower* (New York: Simon and Schuster, 1946), p. 741.

16   D. K. R. Crosswell. *Beetle: The Life of General Walter Bedell Smith* (Lexington, KY: University Press of Kentucky, 2010), p. 759. "Lee" refers to Lieutenant General John Clifford Hodges Lee, Chief of the Services of Supply, European Theater of Operations.

17   Ibid., p. 768.

18   Dwight D. Eisenhower, *Crusade in Europe* (New York: Avon Books, 1968), p. 398.

19   Letter, Eisenhower to Simpson, March 26, 1945, in Alfred D. Chandler, Jr., ed., *The Papers of Dwight David Eisenhower: The War Years: IV* (Baltimore: John Hopkins Press, 1970), pp. 2545–2546.

20   Ibid., p. 2466.

21   Ibid., p. 2467.

22   Eisenhower to Marshall, March 26, 1945, in Joseph Patrick Hobbs, *Dear General: Eisenhower's Wartime Letters to Marshall* (Baltimore: John Hopkins Press, 1971), p. 219.

23   There was also another American Eighth Army, fighting in the Pacific under Lieutenant General Robert L. Eichelberger.

24   Generals Collins (VII Corps), Middleton (VIII Corps) and Cortlett (XIX Corps), among others.

25   Chester Hanson Diary, as quoted in Thomas R. Stone, Ph. D. Dissertation, Rice University, 1974, p. 24.

26   Commanded by Lieutenant General Alexander M. ("Sandy") Patch.

27   Mentioned in this context were Generals Leonard ("Gee") Townsend Gerow (1888–1972), commanding V Corps; Charles Harrison Corlett (1889–1971), commanding XIX Corps; and Joseph Lawton Collins (1896–1987), commanding VII Corps.

28   General Gerow would eventually receive command of Fifteenth Army near the end of the European campaign.

29   Quoted in English, *Patton's Peers*, p. 141.

30   Roger Hesketh. *Fortitude: The D-Day Deception Campaign* (Woodstock and New York: The Overlook Press, 2000), p. 249.

31   John Lesesne DeWitt (1880–1962). Born in Nebraska and attended Princeton University for two years before participating in the Spanish-American War. Commissioned into the infantry in 1898 and served in the AEF during World War I. Quartermaster General of the Army 1930–1934. Commanded various infantry formations until promoted to major general in December 1936. Commanded Philippine Division. Commandant of the Army War College. Promoted to lieutenant general in December 1939. Commander Fourth Army December 1939–September 1943. Commander Western Defense Command. Commandant of the Army and Navy Staff College September 1943. Retired November 1945. General on the retired list July 1954.

32   Alvan Cullon Gillem, Jr. (1888–1973) attended the University of Arizona and University of the South before gaining a commission in the infantry after enlisted service. He served in the Philippines, Montana, Siberia and Hawaii before graduating from the Army War College in 1926. Promoted to major general in July 1941, he commanded II Armored Corps, Desert Training Center, Armored Force and then XIII Corps from November 1943.

Chapter 2

1   Troy Houston Middleton (1889–1976) was born in Hazelhurst, Mississippi. Bachelor of Science from Mississippi Agricultural and Mechanical College 1909. Enlisted service 1910–12. Commissioned in the infantry in 1912. Served in France during World War I. Graduated Command and General Staff School, Army War College. Commanded 45th Infantry Division 1942–44. Commander VIII Corps 1944–45. Retired as a lieutenant general August 1945.

2   Richard Emmel Nugent (1902–79) was born in Altoona, Pennsylvania, and commissioned into the infantry from West Point in 1924. Transferred to the Air Corps 1930. Graduated Command and General Staff School 1939. War Department General Staff 1942–44. Commander, XXIX Tactical Air Command 1944–45. Retired as a lieutenant general August 1951.

3   *Combat History of the Second Infantry Division in World War II* (Nashville, TN: Battery Press, 1979), p. 50.

4   James Alward Van Fleet (1892–1992). Born in New Jersey and commissioned into the infantry from West Point in 1915. Wounded in France during World War I. Commanded the 8th Infantry Regiment, 4th Infantry Division, during Normandy invasion. Promoted to brigadier general and Assistant Division Commander, 2nd Infantry Division. Later commanded 90th Infantry Division and III Corps. Commanding General Eighth Army Korea 1951–53. Retired as a general in 1953.

5   General Van Fleet's task force was temporarily merged with the existing Task Force A, which included the 50th Armored Infantry Battalion, a company of the 68th Tank Battalion and the 603rd Tank Destroyer Battalion as well as a battery of the 777th Automatic Antiaircraft Battalion, all loaned from the 6th Armored Division. The 15th Cavalry Group and a combat engineer battalion were also included in the combined task force.

6   Martin Blumenson, *Breakout and Pursuit: U.S. Army in World War II. European Theater of Operations* (Washington, D. C.: Government Printing Office, 1984), p. 641. Blumenson states that the German forces were from the 353rd Division. However, *Combat History of the Second Infantry Division*, p. 55, describes the opposition as "mainly units of the 266th Infantry Division and naval personnel with a seasoning of tough fighters from the 2nd Parachute Division."

7   War Department General Order Number 37, May 11, 1945.

8   The "bazooka" was an antitank rocket launcher officially known as Launcher, Rocket, AT (antitank) M1. It was named after a comic musical instrument used by radio comedian Bob Burns.

9   Jonathan Gawne, *The Battle For Brest: The Americans in Brittany—1944* (Paris: Histoire & Collections, 2002), p. 53. Gawne claims that Deatherage used a German bazooka.

10 Presidential Unit Citation (Army), Streamer embroidered HILL 154 BREST (3rd Battalion, 38th Infantry cited) War Department General Order 15, 1945.

11 Bofors Guns were Swedish designed light antiaircraft weapons that were widely used by the Allies. The multiple mounts fired a two-pound 40mm shell at 120 rounds per minute with a range of about 10,800 yards.

12 Task Force S had a variable composition but the main units were the 116th Infantry Regiment, the 2nd and 5th Ranger Infantry Battalions, the 224th Field Artillery Battalion and elements of the 86th Cavalry Reconnaissance Squadron. It also made use of 200 Russian deserters from the German Army.

13 Ninth Army General Order Number 36, 1944.

14 Department of the Army Order 43, World War II Streamer Embroidered "Brest" (50th Armored Infantry Battalion cited).

15 Donald Armpriester Stroh (1892–1953). Born in Harrisburg, Pennsylvania, Stroh graduated with his Bachelor of Science Degree from Michigan Agricultural College in 1915. He was commissioned into the cavalry in 1917 and served as an intelligence officer and aide between the wars. He served as an observer in England, as Assistant Division Commander of the 9th Infantry Division, and as Commanding General, 8th Infantry Division. He was promoted to major general in August 1944, a month after he took command of the Golden Arrow Division. He retired in November 1947.

16 Gawne, *The Battle For Brest*, p. 88.

17 General Order Number 89, 1944, First U.S. Army.

18 The effect upon General Stroh can only be imagined. In November, while his division was fighting in the Hürtgen Forest, he was relieved of command, without prejudice. The official reason was that he was exhausted and needed a rest. He would return to battle near the end of the war as commander of the 106th Infantry Division.

19 Wesson received a posthumous Distinguished Service Cross. See General Order Number 6, 1945, First U.S. Army.

20 The Thompson M1928 Machine Pistol fired a .45 caliber bullet at the rate of 675 rounds per minute. It weighed 10.7 pounds empty and could accept ammunition magazines of 20, 30, 50

or 100 rounds. Its maximum effective range was about 219 yards. Although highly rated for its volume and power of fire, it was heavy and expensive to produce.

21   General Order Number 90, 1944, First U.S. Army.

22   Presidential Unit Citation (Army), Streamer embroidered BREST FRANCE (3rd Battalion, 23rd Infantry cited). War Department General Order Number 15, 1945.

23   Presidential Unit Citation (Army), Streamer embroidered BREST FRANCE (3rd Battalion, 9th Infantry cited). War Department General Order Number 15, 1945.

24   War Department General Order Number 24, April 6, 1945.

25   See *Combat History of the Second Infantry Division in World War II*, Second Infantry Division, 1946, p. 60.

26   War Department General Order Number 31, April 17, 1945.

27   General Order Number 93, 1944, First U.S. Army.

28   Blumenson, *Breakout and Pursuit*, p. 647.

29   War Department General Order Number 31, April 17, 1945.

30   Some sources credit this to Pfc. Ervin D. Lammley of the Intelligence Section, 3rd Battalion, 121st Infantry.

31   There is some dispute who uttered these words. Some witnesses say it was Lieutenant Dunham who first used the words, but General Canham always after claimed that honor.

32   During his captivity, Ramcke was promoted to lieutenant general of paratroops and awarded the Diamonds to his Knight's Cross. He also escaped from prison camp in Mississippi to post a letter to the United States Congress, which in turn began an investigation into the treatment of German prisoners of war in the U.S.

Chapter 3

1   *Conquer*, p. 35.

2   This is the same General Malony mentioned in previous chapters. Harry James Malony was born August 24, 1889, in Lakemont, New York. After being commissioned in the infantry from West Point in 1912, he served with the American Expeditionary Force in France during World War I. He graduated from the Command and General Staff School in 1926 before serving as a professor of military science and tactics at the University of Oklahoma. Malony graduated from the Army War College and then taught there for four years. He was a member of the Atlantic Bases Board until promoted to brigadier general in January 1941 and major general in August 1942. He organized and trained the 94th Infantry Division and led it throughout its combat career.

3   At war's end, Major General Herman F. Kramer's 66th Infantry Division, which replaced the 94th Infantry Division in containing the pockets in Brittany, would count in excess of 50,000 German prisoners of war who surrendered at that time.

4   For its performance between September 4 and September 16, 1944, the Intelligence and Reconnaissance Platoon, 329th Infantry Regiment received a Unit Citation. See General Orders, 83rd Infantry Division, November 2, 1945.

5   In many respects, the arrangements of General Malony in integrating the FFI into his division mirror what was intended years later in Korea, when the Army established the KATUSA, Korean Augmentation to the U.S. Army, in which South Korean soldiers were added to U.S. Army combat units.

6   In fact, the 94th Infantry Division moved to Third Army's XX Corps and fought in the Saar-Moselle Campaign. For details, see Nathan N. Prefer, *Patton's Ghost Corps: Cracking the Siegfried Line* (Novato, CA: Presidio Press, 1998). As noted above, it was replaced at Brittany in January 1945, by the 66th Infantry Division.

7   General Order Number 49, Third U.S. Army 1945.

8   John Millikin was born January 7, 1888, in Danville, Indiana. He was commissioned into the cavalry from West Point in 1910. He served in the Mexican Punitive Expedition, taught at St. John's College and served in the American Expeditionary Force. He graduated from the Command and General Staff School and the Army War College before becoming a brigadier general in October 1940. Millikin commanded the 6th Cavalry Brigade before being promoted to major general and given command of the 83rd Infantry Division. He then commanded the 33rd Infantry Division before commanding the III Corps. Later he would command the 13th Armored Division in Germany.

9   Quoted in Thomas R. Stone, "He had the guts to say NO: A military biography of General William H. Simpson," Dissertation, Rice College, 1974, p. 30.

10 The "Red Ball Express" was so named because signs with large painted red circles marked the routes.

11 Alfred D. Chandler, ed., *The Papers of Dwight David Eisenhower: The War Years. Vol. III* (Baltimore and London: John Hopkins Press, 1970), p. 1609.

12 Omar N. Bradley and Clay Blair, *A General's Life: An Autobiography by General of the Army Omar N. Bradley* (New York: Simon and Schuster, 1983), p. 395.

13 Stone, Dissertation, p. 120.

14 General Sir Miles Christopher Dempsey, GBE, KCB, DSO, MC, was born in Cheshire and educated at the Royal Military College at Sandhurst. He was commissioned into the Royal Berkshire Regiment and saw combat in the World War I in France, where he was wounded. After receiving several awards for gallantry, he was a company commander at the age of 19. Badly gassed in 1918, he spent the rest of the war in Iraq. Between the wars he attended the Staff College at Camberley and served two years on the War Office staff. When World War II commenced, he went to France with the British Expeditionary Force, where he commanded an infantry brigade. Dempsey then commanded the 46th Infantry Division and came to the attention of Montgomery, who marked him for higher command. When Montgomery went to North Africa, he insisted on Dempsey as one of his corps commanders. When the now Field Marshal Montgomery returned to England to command the British forces for the cross-channel invasion, he brought Dempsey with him. He was made commander of the British Second Army, the main British invasion force.

15 The 113th Cavalry Group (113th and 125th Cavalry Squadrons) was reinforced with a light tank battalion, a combat engineer company and a tank destroyer company. It defended between Gangelt to Maeseyck, a distance of about 21,000 yards.

16 Ninth Army History, p. 69.

17 Ibid, p. 70.

18 Major General Leland Stanford Hobbs had been born February 24, 1892, in Gloucester, Massachusetts. After being commissioned into the infantry from West Point in 1915, in the same class as Eisenhower and Bradley, he served with Patton in the Mexican Punitive Expedition, before becoming a staff officer. He instructed at West Point before graduating from the Command and General Staff School in 1934 and the Army War College in 1935. After serving on the staff of Third Army, he had the unique (for Army officers) distinction of graduating from the Naval War College in 1940. Now a brigadier general, he served with the 80th Infantry Division until promoted to major general in September 1943, and assigned the command of the 30th Infantry Division. He brought the division ashore at Omaha Beach on June 10 and led it through some difficult fighting, particularly at St. Lo and Mortain, where the division stopped a serious German counterattack that threatened to cut off the advanced American corps. The division had then moved east and engaged in the reduction of the German city of Aachen, which cost it severely in terms of casualties.

19 Frank Augustus Keating was born in New York City on February 4, 1895, and was commissioned into the infantry of the New Jersey National Guard in 1917. He saw service as a National Guard

instructor in the Philippines and Hawaii. He commanded the 15th Infantry Regiment from 1939–41, before becoming Chief of Staff of the 2nd Infantry Division. Promoted to brigadier general in July 1942, he served as the commander of amphibious training in Massachusetts before taking command of the 102nd Infantry Division. He was promoted to major general in January 1945 and retained command of the 102nd Infantry Division throughout the war.

20 The 176th, 183rd, 246th and 49th Infantry Divisions and the 3rd Panzergrenadier Division.

21 Quoted in Charles B. MacDonald, *The Siegfried Line Campaign: U.S. Army in World War II. European Theater of Operations* (Washington, D. C.: Government Printing Office, 1984), p. 401.

22 General Sir Brian Gwynne Horrocks was born in India, the son of an army doctor. After graduating from the Royal Military Academy at Sandhurst he was commissioned into the Middlesex Regiment. In World War I he was wounded and captured in 1914, spending the war as a prisoner. He spent his time learning German, French and Russian while in prison camp. Upon repatriation, he volunteered to serve in Russia on a British Military Mission. Again, he was captured and made a prisoner of war. He would spend the next 15 years at the rank of captain. He attended the Staff College at Camberley and then served on the War Office staff. Returning to Camberley, he was there when the World War II erupted and took command of a battalion in France. He was soon promoted to brigadier general, serving under General Montgomery. For the two years after Dunkirk, he served in England, commanding a division. When Montgomery went to North Africa, he sent for Horrocks, who was given a corps command before being wounded. In August 1944, when Field Marshal Montgomery became dissatisfied with the commander of XXX Corps, he replaced him with Horrocks. He would retain that command until the end of the war.

Chapter 4

1 XXIX Tactical Air Command consisted of the 36th, 48th, 373rd and 404th Fighter-Bomber Groups and the 363rd Tactical Reconnaissance Group.

2 Robert L. Hewitt, *Workhorse of the Western Front: The Story of the 30th Infantry Division* (Washington, D. C.: Infantry Journal Press, 1946) p. 147.

3 War Department General Order Number 95, October 30, 1945.

4 General Willis D. Crittenberger commanded IV Corps in Italy, General Harmon XXI Corps in Germany, and General Edward Brooks VI Corps in southern France and Germany.

5 Donald E. Houston, *Hell on Wheels: The 2d Armored Division* (Novato, CA: Presidio Press, 1977), p. 301.

6 Ibid.

7 These included the 207th and 506th General Headquarters Tank Battalions equipped with Mark VI Tiger Royal Tanks.

8 Houston, *Hell on Wheels*, p. 305.

9 American Army World War II armored "Combat Commands" were a combined arms team, which varied with each mission. Generally speaking, they consisted of a tank battalion, an armored infantry battalion, a company of combat engineers, a tank destroyer company, and support units. It was a highly flexible and non-standard organization.

10 29th Division G-2-G-3 Journal, November 16, 1944, as quoted in MacDonald, *The Siegfried Line Campaign*, p. 525.

11 Ninth U.S. Army Operations Report, IV, 41, quoted in Ibid., p. 528.

12 29th Div. G-2-G-3 Journal, November 16, 1944, Ibid., p. 529.

13 Ibid., November 17, 1944, p. 534.

14 There remained a small enclave on a triangle of land between the Roer and Inde Rivers, which the division later cleared, but it had no impact on the rest of the campaign.

Chapter 5

1 English, *Patton's Peers*, p. 144.

2 Stephen T. Taaffee, *Marshall and His Generals: U.S. Army Commanders in World War II* (Lawrence, Kansas: University Press of Kansas, 2011), p. 251.

3 Gillem was unusual in that although he was not a West Pointer, he rose to corps command, something very few non-West Point World War II Army officers achieved. He went on to command VII Corps and Third Army after the war before retiring in August 1950.

4 Theodore Draper, *The 84th Division in the Battle of Germany* (New York: The Viking Press, 1946), p. 22.

5 Major General Sir Gwilyn Ivor Thomas was a graduate of the Royal Military Academy at Sandhurst and a veteran of World War I. A Royal Artillery officer, he had been twice wounded and received the Military Cross and Bar, as well as the Distinguished Service Order. He had been in command of the Wessex Division since March of 1942 and led it from Normandy to Germany.

6 The squadrons were the 113th and 125th Cavalry Reconnaissance Squadrons.

7 Bolling was born in Philadelphia, on August 28, 1895. He attended the United States Naval Academy at Annapolis 1915–16 before being commissioned into the Officers Reserve Corps in 1917. He served with the 3rd Infantry Division in France during the Aisne-Marne, Champagne-Marne, St. Mihiel and Argonne campaigns. Between the wars he graduated from the Command and General Staff School and Army War College. He was promoted to brigadier general in August 1942 and assigned as the Assistant Division Commander of the 8th Infantry Division, then the 84th Infantry Division. When the division commander (Major General Roscoe B. Woodruff) was promoted to a corps command, Bolling assumed leadership of the division in June 1944, but was not immediately promoted, although Brigadier General William A. McCulloch, a veteran of Guadalcanal and Bougainville, was appointed Assistant Division Commander. Bolling led the division overseas and was its commander throughout its combat career. He would be promoted to major general in January 1945.

8 The Sixth Panzer Army was in fact across from XIII Corps, but it was destined for the coming Ardennes counteroffensive, and would not be involved in fighting on the Roer plain.

9 Quoted in Taaffee, *Marshall and His Generals*, pp. 251–252.

10 Draper, *The 84th Division in the Battle of Germany*, p. 34.

11 Ibid., p. 38.

12 Ibid, p. 43.

13 There were 32 men of Lieutenant Carpenter's 1st Platoon, 18 men of the 2nd Platoon, six from his 3rd Platoon and four from Company K Headquarters. Lieutenant Garlington had 35 men of Company I's 3rd Platoon and five men from the company mortar section, for a total of 100 enlisted men and two officers.

14 Ibid, p. 58.

15 Ibid, p. 62.

16 Presidential Unit Citation (Army), streamer embroidered SIEGFRIED LINE (Company K, 335th Infantry cited); War Department General Order 92, 1945.

17 General Order Number 71, Ninth Army, 1945.

18 Major Allan H. Mick, *With the 102nd Infantry Division Through Germany* (Washington: Infantry Journal Press, 1947), p. 69.

19 Ibid.

20 Ibid.

21 Ibid., p. 82.

22 General Order Number 5, Ninth Army, 1945.

23 Ibid.

24 Combat Interview cited in Ninth U.S. Army Operations Report IV, p. 328.

Chapter 6

1   After the war, General Moore served on the staff of the Secretary of the Army, commanded the 10th Infantry Division, was commandant of the Army War College and the Chief of Staff of SHAPE, 1959–63. He died on January 28, 1986.

2   English, *Patton's Peers*, p. 147. A similar statement is made in Taafe, op. cit. "G-3" refers to the general staff of an army.

3   Major General E. N. Harmon, with Milton MacKaye and William Ross MacKaye, *Combat Commander: Autobiography of a Soldier* (Englewood Cliffs, NJ: Prentice-Hall, 1970).

4   This Army was originally titled the 6th Panzer Army but later in the campaign became the 6th SS Panzer Army for largely political reasons.

5   For details on Seventh Army's operations see Nathan N. Prefer, *Eisenhower's Thorn on the Rhine: The Battles for Colmar, 1944–1945* (Havertown, PA: Casemate Publishers, 2015).

6   Hugh M. Cole, *The Ardennes: The Battle of the Bulge. United States Army in World War II. The European Theater of Operations* (Washington, D. C.: Center of Military History, 1988), pp. 332–333.

7   Ibid.

8   David Irving, *The War Between the Generals: Inside the Allied High Command* (New York: Congdon & Lattes, 1981), p. 358.

9   Ibid., p. 359.

10 Cole, *The Ardennes*, p. 333, agrees that Simpson offered both the 7th Armored and 30th Infantry Divisions before the order to transfer the 7th Armored to First Army ever reached him. There are variations on the exact sequence, but all agree that Simpson was quick to help on his own initiative.

11 The 5th Armored Division, although assigned to VII Corps from December 23, 1944, was held in Twenty-First Army Group reserve.

12 Mark M. Boatner III, *The Biographical Dictionary of World War II* (Novato, CA: Presidio Press, 1996), pp. 372–373.

13 Russell F. Weigley, *Eisenhower's Lieutenants: The Campaigns of France and Germany, 1944–1945* (Bloomington, IA: Indiana University Press, 1981), p. 563.

14 General Leese would succeed Montgomery in command of the British Eighth Army on Montgomery's recommendation.

15 Omar N. Bradley and Clay Blair, *A General's Life: An Autobiography by General of the Army Omar N. Bradley* (New York: Simon and Schuster, 1983), p. 165.

16 Ibid.

17 Ibid.

18 Martin Blumenson, *The Patton Papers, 1940–1945* (New York: DeCapo Press, 1996), p. 608.

19 Irving, *The War Between the Generals*, p. 124.

20 Interview of Simpson with Lt. Col. Thomas R. Stone, April 22, 1971, in William Hood Simpson Papers, United States Army Military History Institute, as quoted in English, *Patton's Peers*, p. 150.

21 The 25-pounder field gun-howitzer was the standard field gun of the British Army in World War II. It was used as divisional artillery and had a maximum range of 12,500 yards. It fired a 25-pound shell of 3.45 inches caliber at a muzzle velocity of between 1,470 to 1,747 feet per second.

22 The 11th Cavalry Group consisted of the 36th and 44th Cavalry Reconnaissance Squadrons.

23 Quoted in Mick, *With the 102nd Infantry Division Through Germany*, p. 91.

24 Ibid.

25 Ibid., p. 92.

26 Ibid.

27 Ibid., p. 93.

28 The 17th Cavalry Reconnaissance Squadron was a part of the 15th Cavalry Group.
29 *Conquer*, p. 135.

Chapter 7

1 General Sir Neil Methuen Ritchie, GBE, KCB, DSO, MC (1897–1983) was born in British Guiana and graduated from the Royal Military College at Sandhurst in 1914. Assigned to the Black Watch Regiment, he fought in France during World War I and was wounded. Fighting in Mesopotamia and Palestine brought him the Military Cross and a Distinguished Service Order. A captain for the next 14 years, he attended the Staff College at Camberley and served as a staff officer. In 1939, now a colonel, he was serving at the War Office when he was appointed Chief of Staff of II (British) Corps at Dunkirk. He commanded the reforming 51st Highland Division and, after additional staff duty, was appointed Commander of the British Eighth Army in North Africa. After one successful offensive, several defeats cost him that command. Given command of the 52nd (Lowland) Division in England, he received command of the XII Corps in December 1943. He retained this command throughout the Northwest European campaigns and was promoted general at the war's end.
2 Henry Duncan Graham ("Harry") Crerar had fought in World War I and graduated from the Royal Military College. By World War II he was Chief of the Canadian General Staff and had commanded I Canadian Corps in Great Britain. It was he who lobbied for Canadian participation in the Dieppe Raid and the Italian Campaign. His personal relations with both Montgomery and his own two corps commanders were less than friendly.
3 General Parker was born in Wytheville, Virginia, on July 27, 1891. He attended George Washington University from 1909–11. He accepted a commission in the field artillery in 1913 and was assigned to the Panama Canal Zone during World War I. Parker graduated from the Command and General Staff School in 1925 and the Army War College in 1937. After commanding the Field Artillery Replacement Training Center at Fort Bragg, North Carolina, he was promoted to brigadier general in October 1941, and major general in June 1942. He assumed command of the 78th Infantry Division in 1942 and retained that command until the end of the war.
4 Other divisions received by Ninth Army in February included the 30th Infantry, 35th Infantry, 75th Infantry, 83rd Infantry, 84th Infantry and 95th Infantry Divisions. The 7th (British) Armored Division was also attached to Ninth Army in February 1945.
5 XIX Corps had under command the 29th, 30th and 83rd Infantry Divisions and the 2nd Armored Division. XIII Corps had under command the 84th and 102nd Infantry Divisions and the 5th Armored Division in reserve. XVI Corps had under command the 35th and 79th Infantry Divisions and the 8th Armored Division in reserve.
6 These were, respectively, the 75th and 95th Infantry Divisions.
7 Ninth U.S. Army Letter of Instructions 13, February 6, 1945.
8 Ninth U.S. Army Letter of Instructions 10, January 28, 1945, quoted in *Conquer*, pp. 147–151.
9 Rick Atkinson, *The Guns at Last Light: The War in Western Europe, 1944–1945* (New York: Henry Holt and Company, 2013), p. 538.
10 See Nathan N. Prefer, *Patton's Ghost Corps: Cracking the Siegfried Line* (Novato, CA: Presidio Press, 1998).
11 A World War II U.S. Treadway bridge was a floating bridge. It was built on a series of rafts or pontoons, with two tracks laid across it spaced to allow vehicles and armored vehicles to cross over water obstacles. Depending upon the model of bridge, it could accommodate as much as a 25-ton vehicle.
12 Draper, *The 84th Division in the Battle of Germany*, p. 144.
13 Ibid.

14 Ibid., p. 143.
15 Ibid., p. 145.
16 Ibid.
17 Ibid.
18 Mick, *With the 102nd Infantry Division Through Germany*, p. 122.
19 Ibid., p. 141.
20 Ibid., p. 142.
21 MacDonald, *The Siegfried Line Campaign*, p. 155.
22 General Order Number 142, 1945, Ninth Army.
23 General Order Number 290, 1945, Ninth Army.
24 Mick, op. cit. p. 139.
25 Hewitt, *Workhorse of the Western Front*, p. 219.
26 Draper, *The 84th Division in the Battle of Germany*, p. 149.
27 Ibid., p. 153.
28 The 3rd Battalion, 334th Infantry Regiment, received a Presidential Unit Citation for its stand at Baal. See Presidential Unit Citation (Army) embroidered Roer-Rhine Rivers (1st and 3rd Battalions, Company G and Cannon Company, 334th Infantry Regiment cited) in War Department General Order Number 68, 1945 and War Department General Order Number 11, 1946.

Chapter 8

1 Quoted in Hewitt, *Workhorse of the Western Front*, p. 223.
2 Mick, *With the 102nd Infantry Division Through Germany*, p. 143.
3 General Order Number 206, 1945, Ninth U.S. Army.
4 General Order Number 199, 1945, Ninth U.S. Army.
5 General Order Number 191, 1945, Ninth U.S. army.
6 Mick, *With the 102nd Infantry Division Through Germany*, p. 159.
7 The World War II Bailey Bridge, invented by Sir Donald Bailey of the Military Engineering Experimental Establishment of the Royal Army, was composed of steel lattice panel girders held together by high-tensile pins at their four corners. Girders could be doubled or tripled up to add strength and length. It was capable of more than one level and the roadway was supported by lateral transoms. It could be launched on rollers into a water obstacle and was first used during the North African campaign.
8 Draper, *The 84th Division in the Battle of Germany*, pp. 158–159. Fort Benning was the location of the U.S. Army's Infantry School. "Doughboys" was slang for the American soldier and "Jerries" slang for Germans.
9 Born in Fort Wayne, Indiana, Paul William Baade was commissioned into the infantry from West Point in 1911 and served in France during World War I. He graduated from both the Command and General Staff School in 1924 and the Army War College in 1929, before serving as a staff officer and regimental commander. He was promoted to brigadier general and appointed Assistant Division Commander of the 35th Infantry Division in 1942, and later appointed the division's commanding officer with the rank of major general (one of his predecessors in command of the 35th Infantry Division had been Simpson). Baade would retain that command throughout the division's combat career.
10 Drawn from the National Guards of Kansas, Missouri and Nebraska, the 35th Infantry Division was called into Federal service on December 23, 1940, and underwent the usual training and maneuvers. It left New York on May 12, 1944 and arrived in France over Omaha Beach on July

6, 1944. It fought in the hedgerow country of Normandy, at St. Lo, and at Hill 122. At Mortain, it was the relieving force that reached trapped elements of the 30th Infantry Division who had halted a major German counterattack. It fought its way across France and crossed the Saar River in mid-December. The division was then assigned to relieve Bastogne, after which it was given a brief rest period at Metz. It moved up to the Roer and joined Ninth Army early in February 1945, relieving the British 52nd (Lowland) Infantry Division.

11 Lunsford Errett Oliver was born in Nemaha, Nebraska and commissioned into the Corps of Engineers from West Point in 1913. He served on engineering projects until graduating from the Command and General Staff School in 1928 and the Army War College in 1938. Oliver taught at the Command and General Staff School until assigned to I Armored Corps in 1940. After promotion to brigadier general in February 1942, he served as Assistant Division Commander of the 1st Armored Division and, upon promotion to major general in November 1942, took command of the 5th Armored Division, which he led throughout the war.

12 The 5th Armored Division was activated at Fort Knox, Kentucky, on October 1, 1941, and participated in the standard Army training and maneuvers. It arrived in France on July 25, 1944, at Utah Beach, and fought in Normandy, Northern France, and Belgium. It was the first Allied unit to enter Germany when its 85th Cavalry Reconnaissance Squadron crossed the German border near Stalzenburg on September 11, 1944. It fought in the Hürtgen Forest and was held in reserve during the Battle of the Bulge. The division crossed the Roer on February 25 and assembled at the town of Hottorf.

13 Hewitt, *Workhorse of the Western Front*, p. 227.

14 Ibid., pp. 227–228.

15 Ibid., p. 228.

16 See Prefer, *Patton's Ghost Corps*.

17 In January 1945, Major General Harmon had been promoted to a corps command and replaced by Major General Isaac D. White. White (1901–1990) was born in Petersborough, New Hampshire, and commissioned into the cavalry from Norwich University in 1922. He graduated from the Command and General Staff School in 1939 and was assigned to the 2nd Armored Division in August 1940. He served in the division as a battalion commander, combat command commander and division commander during the war.

18 Contemporary American Task Forces were usually named after the senior commander, which often changed due to casualties, assignments and other factors.

19 Vic Hillery, *Paths of Armor: The Fifth Armored Division in World War II* (Nashville, TN: The Battery Press, 1985), p. 225.

20 Ibid., p. 228.

21 Ibid., p. 229.

22 Ibid., p. 230.

23 General Devine was born in Providence, Rhode Island, and commissioned into the field artillery from West Point in 1917. He served in the occupying forces in Europe in 1918 and then earned his Master of Science Degree from Yale in 1922. He taught at West Point and graduated from the Command and General Staff School in 1938. He taught military science and tactics at Yale for two years before being assigned to the 1st Armored Division in 1940. He served in a number of staff appointments until promotion to brigadier general in May 1942. Devine commanded troops in the 6th Armored Division and artillery in the 90th Infantry Division before receiving appointment as commander of the 8th Armored Division in 1944. He would be promoted to major general in May 1945.

24 See Prefer, *Patton's Ghost Corps*.

25 The 15th Cavalry Group consisted of the 15th and 17th Cavalry Reconnaissance Squadrons.

26   Task Force Crittenden included Company A, 18th Tank Battalion, Companies A and B, 7th Armored Infantry Battalion, Troop A, 88th Cavalry Reconnaissance Squadron (Mech.), and the 1st Platoon, Company A, 809th Tank Destroyer Battalion.

27   Capt. Charles R. Leach, in *Tornado's Wake: A History of the 8th Armored Division* (Nashville, TN: Battery Press, 1992), pp. 104–105. "Tornado" was the 8th Armored Division's radio call sign.

28   Joseph Balkoski, *The Last Roll Call: The 29th Infantry Division Victorious, 1945* (Mechanicsburg, PA: Stackpole Books, 2015), p. 139.

29   John Huston Church (1892–1953) was born in Glen Iron, Pennsylvania, and attended New York University before being commissioned into the infantry in 1917. He saw service in World War I, serving with the Maryland National Guard and in the Philippines. He graduated from the Command and General Staff School in 1937 and then had a series of positions in staff and command assignments.

30   Task Force Church's major units were: 334th Infantry Regiment; 771st Tank Battalion; 84th Reconnaissance Troop; 326th Field Artillery Battalion; Company A, 637th Tank Destroyer Battalion; Company B, 309th Engineer (Combat) Battalion; Company B, 309th Medical Battalion; and Battery D, 537th Automatic Antiaircraft Artillery Battalion.

31   Draper, *The 84th Division in the Battle of Germany*, p. 164.

32   Ibid., p. 167.

33   War Department General Order 68, 1945 and War Department General Order 11, 1946. Streamer ROER-RHINE Rivers (1st and 3rd Battalions, Company G and Cannon Company, 334th Infantry Regiment cited.).

34   The 95th Infantry Division had been activated at Camp Swift, Texas, on July 15, 1942, and after the usual training and maneuvers had left the United States from Boston on August 10, 1944. It arrived in France on September 15 and fought in the Moselle River bridgehead and at Metz with Third Army. It later crossed into Germany through the Maginot Line in November 1944. It fought to cross the Saar River and at Saarlautern. It was then pulled into reserve for a rest and transferred to Ninth Army on February 5, 1945.

35   Harry L. Twaddle had been born in Clarksfield, Ohio, and received his engineering degree from Syracuse University in 1910. He was commissioned into the infantry in 1912 and served in Alaska during World War I. He instructed at the Infantry School before graduating from the Command and General Staff School in 1923 and the Army War College in 1925. Service on the War Department General Staff followed. Major General Twaddle took command of the 95th Infantry Division in March 1942 and led it throughout its combat career.

Chapter 9

1   Chester Wilmot, *The Struggle for Europe* (New York: Harper & Brothers, 1952), p. 677.

2   Ibid., p. 105.

3   35th Infantry Division History, Chapter XII.

4   Ninth U.S. Army General Order Number 129, 1945. See also 134th Infantry Regiment Web site, www.coulthartom/134/

5   Ninth U.S. Army General Order Number 117, 1945. See also 134th Infantry Regiment Web site.

6   These were: the 84th, 180th and 190th Infantry Divisions; the Panzer Lehr, 15th Panzer Grenadier and 116th Panzer Divisions; and the 6th, 7th and 8th Parachute Divisions.

7   Quoted in Milton Shulman, *Defeat in the West* (London: Secker & Warburg, 1986), p. 297.

8   Ibid., p. 298.

9   Ibid., pp. 299–300.

10 Task Force Houten consisted of: the 36th Tank Battalion (less Company C); Company A, 49th Armored Infantry Battalion; 1st Platoon, Company B, 809th Tank Destroyer Battalion; and 1st Platoon, Company B, 53rd Armored Engineer Battalion.

11 Task Force Roseborough consisted of: the 49th Armored Infantry Battalion (less Company A); Company C, 36th Tank Battalion; 2nd Platoon, Company B, 809th Tank Destroyer Battalion; and 2nd Platoon, Company B, 53rd Armored Engineer Battalion.

12 MacDonald, *The Siegfried Line Campaign*, p. 182.

Chapter 10

1 For details see Prefer, *Eisenhower's Thorn*, p. 277.

2 Alan Goodrich Kirk was born in Philadelphia in 1888 and graduated from the United States Naval Academy in 1909. He was commissioned in 1911, after the usual two years as a midshipman. He graduated from the Naval War College in 1929 and commanded the U.S. Naval Task Force on D-Day, June 6, 1944.

3 Matthew Bunker Ridgway was born March 3, 1895, at Fort Monroe, Virginia. He was commissioned into the infantry from West Point in 1917 and then served as instructor and head of athletics at the Military Academy. He graduated from the Command and General Staff School in 1935 and the Army War College in 1937. After serving with the War Plans Division of the War Department, he was promoted to brigadier general in January 1942. Ridgway served as Assistant Division Commander of the 82nd Infantry Division (later the 82nd Airborne Division) before promotion to major general and appointment as commander of that division. He led the 82nd in Sicily and Normandy before being promoted to command the specialized XVIII (Airborne) Corps in August 1944.

4 Ninth Army History, p. 209.

5 Ibid.

6 These were: two Class 40 floating bridges; one semi-permanent Class 70 bridge; one Class 36 floating bridge; and a Class 70 raft ferry.

7 Duplex Drive tanks had been used at Normandy on D-Day. They were standard Sherman tanks whose hulls had been waterproofed and which were fitted with special canvas walls that provided enough displacement to float the vehicle. They were fitted with a propeller drive in addition to the normal land propulsion to enable them to "swim" across water obstacles.

8 The 2nd Parachute Division, 176th Infantry Division and 183rd Infantry Division.

9 Quoted in MacDonald, *The Last Offensive* (Washington: Center of Military History, 1984), p. 301.

10 Major General T. G. Rennie was killed in action during the day's fighting.

11 Eisenhower, *Crusade in Europe*, p. 389.

12 Hewitt, *Workhorse of the Western Front*, p. 239, quoting 1st Lieutenant Whitney O. Refvem.

13 Ninth Army History, p. 243.

14 These were the 215th, 280th and 695th Field Artillery Battalions.

15 79th Infantry Division History, p. 126.

Chapter 11

1 The 13th U.S. Airborne Division was to have been included in this operation. Its objective was to seize dominating high ground east of Wesel, but Montgomery felt this assault would be too difficult and cancelled this portion of the operation. John R. Galvin. *Air Assault: The Development of Airmobile warfare* (New York: Hawthorn Books, 1969), p. 238.

2   The 6th (British) Airborne Division consisted of the 3rd and 5th Parachute Brigades and the 6th Airlanding Brigade.

3   Clay Blair, *Ridgway's Paratroopers: The American Airborne in World War II* (New York: Doubleday & Company, 1956), p. 37.

4   Field Marshal the Viscount Montgomery of Alamein, K. G., G. C. B., D. S. O., *Normandy to the Baltic* (London: Hutchinson & Co., 1946), p. 196.

5   There was even a third operation under consideration (Operation *Eclipse,* the airborne occupation of Berlin), should the Germans suddenly surrender.

6   Montgomery, *Normandy to the Baltic*, p. 201.

7   There was considerable reluctance to execute this operation on the part of General Ridgway, who preferred to remain with First Army and join the race to Berlin. He was also displeased to be told by General Dempsey, commanding the British Second Army, that his XVIII (Airborne) Corps, with the 13th Airborne and 17th Airborne Divisions, were to remain with the British Second Army for an extended period after crossing the Rhine. See Clay Blair, *Ridgway's Paratroopers: The American Airborne in World War II* (Garden City, NY: Doubleday & Company, 1985), p. 525.

8   John R. Galvin, *Air Assault* (New York: Hawthorn Books, 1969) p. 247.

9   Ibid.

10   Lieutenant Colonel George V. Millett, Jr.

11   War Department General Order Number 16, February 8, 1946.

12   The 57mm recoilless rifle was a late-war development for use as an antitank weapon by the infantry. Known as the M18, it weighed 45 pounds and was just over five feet in length. It could be fired from the shoulder or from a tripod. It fired several types of ammunition, including high explosive and antitank rockets. The M18 was often packed for parachute delivery in the M10 Paracrate, with 14 rounds of ammunition. It was more powerful and had a longer range than the standard bazooka. A few of the newer 75mm recoilless rifles were also with the 17th Airborne Division.

13   War Department General Order Number 117, December 11, 1945.

14   Quoted in Blair, *Ridgway's Paratroopers*, p. 550.

15   This was the first planned landing on an uncleared landing zone. At Arnhem, the First Airlanding Brigade landed on uncleared landing zones, but that was not intentional, the plan being to have those zones cleared earlier by the paratroopers of the 1st British Airborne Division, something they were unable to do.

16   Presidential Unit Citation (Army), Streamer embroidered WESEL.

17   John Frayn Turner, *VCs of the Second World War* (South Yorkshire, UK: Pen & Sword Books, 2004), pp. 293–294.

18   Quoted in Stephen L. Wright, *The Last Drop: Operation Varsity, March 24–25, 1945* (Mechanicsburg, PA: Stackpole Books, 2008), p. 289.

19   Charles B. McDonald, quoted in Wright, Ibid.

Chapter 12

1   The 117th Infantry task force comprised that regiment with Lieutenant Colonel Hunt's 744th Light Tank Battalion and companies of the 823rd Tank Destroyer Battalion. The 120th Infantry Regiment task force comprised that regiment with the 743rd Tank Battalion and other companies of the 823rd Tank Destroyer Battalion.

2   This was Task Force Miltonberger (named after the Assistant Division Commander, Brigadier General Butler Buchanan Miltonberger) which consisted of the 134th Infantry Regiment, 127th Field Artillery Battalion, Company A, 60th Engineer (Combat) Battalion, Company A, 654th Tank Destroyer Battalion and Company A, 784th Tank Battalion.

3　Quoted in Hewitt, *Workhorse of the Western Front*, p. 247.

4　This was the day on which Technical Sergeant Hedrick of the 194th Glider Infantry earned his Medal of Honor, previously described.

5　At this point, March 31, 1945, only the First French Army and the Second Canadian Army were not across the Rhine, although Canadian units were crossing within the British zone.

6　The 29th, 35th, 75th and 79th Infantry Divisions.

7　The 30th, 83rd and 95th Infantry Divisions, and 2nd and 8th Armored Divisions.

8　The 17th Airborne, 84th Infantry, 102nd Infantry and 5th Armored Divisions.

9　XVI Corps Letter of Instructions Number 44, March 28, 1945.

10　Quoted in Leach, in *Tornado's Wake*, p. 141.

11　Houston, *Hell on Wheels*, p. 403.

12　C. D. Philos, Major, *The Thunderbolt Across Europe: A History of the 83rd Infantry Division, 1942–1945* (Nashville, TN: Battery Press, 1997), p. 85.

13　These early figures did not take into consideration more than 100,000 antiaircraft personnel within the pocket, raising the final total to nearly one-third of a million enemy troops.

14　In addition to First and Ninth Armies, the newly activated Fifteenth Army held the west bank of the Rhine along the Ruhr pocket.

15　Ninth Army History, p. 270.

16　Leach, in *Tornado's Wake*, p. 144.

17　Derek S. Zumbro, *Battle for the Ruhr: The German Army's Final Defeat in the West* (Lawrence, KS: University Press of Kansas, 2006), p. 307.

18　The 194th Glider Infantry Regiment of the 17th Airborne Division. The remainder of the division was assigned to XVI Corps.

19　War Department General Order Number 101, November 8, 1945. Pfc. Hastings was killed in action four days after this attack.

20　Major General Walter E. Lauer, *Battle Babies: the Story of the 99th Infantry Division in World War II* (Nashville: Battery Press, 1985) p. 269.

Chapter 13

1　SHAEF Planning Draft of Post-Neptune Courses of Action after the Capture of the Lodgment Area, Main Objectives and Axes of Advance, I, 3 May 44, SHAEF SGS Post OVERLORD Planning, 381, I.

2　This theme appears in several of General Eisenhower's letters and also in conversations with his chief of staff, Major General Walter Bedell Smith.

3　Bradley, *A Soldier's Story*, pp. 531–537.

4　Twelfth Army Group Letter of Instructions 20, April 4, 1945.

5　Draper, *The 84th Division in the Battle of Germany*, p. 209.

6　Including, for those who were superstitious, the XIX Legion.

7　Task Force Warren included Company D, 66th Armored Regiment, Company E, 377th Infantry Regiment (attached from the 95th Infantry Division), Battery A, 65th Armored Field Artillery Battalion, and a section from Company A, 702nd Tank Destroyer Battalion.

8　Originally, the commander was the German paratroop leader, General Kurt Student, but after four days, Student exchanged commands with General Blumentritt, at the same time as the name change.

9　Mick, *With the 102nd Infantry Division Through Germany*, p. 189

10　Ibid. Corporal Dennis received a Silver Star.

11　Ibid. Technical Sergeant Klausmeyer received a Silver Star.

12　Ibid. Pfc. Irish received a Silver Star.

13 Ibid., p. 192.

14 Ibid., p. 193.

15 Quoted in Cornelius Ryan, *The Last Battle* (New York: Simon and Schuster, 1966), pp. 283–284.

16 Ibid., p. 284.

17 Ibid.

18 Sequence quoted in Fifth Armored Division Association, *Paths of Armor: The Fifth Armored Division in World War II* (Nashville: Battery Press, 1950), p. 299.

19 Ibid., p. 304.

20 Houston, *Hell on Wheels*, p. 417.

21 Ryan, *The Last Battle*, p. 284.

22 83rd Infantry Division History, p. 86.

23 Quoted in MacDonald, *The Siegfried Line Campaign*, p. 387.

Chapter 14

1   *Conquer*, p. 300.

2   Quoted in Ryan, *The Last Battle*, p. 331.

3   Ibid.

4   Ibid.

5   Ibid., p. 332.

6   It should be recalled that the division's third regiment, the 119th Infantry, was still attached to the 2nd Armored Division.

7   Hewitt, *Workhorse of the Western Front*, p. 266.

8   Ryan, *The Last Battle*, p. 388.

9   Ibid.

10 *Conquer*, p. 365.

Appendix A

1   United States Army staff positions were, and are, abbreviated as follows: G-1 = Personnel; G-2 – Intelligence; G-3 = Operations; G-4 = Supply; G-5 = Civil Affairs and Military Government. Higher headquarters, including army level headquarters, also had special staffs for duties such as adjutant general, artillery, antiaircraft artillery, chemical warfare, engineer, medical, ordnance and other such responsibilities as shown.

2   On March 3, 1945, Colonel Kehm replaced Colonel Charles P. Bixel, the sole cavalryman on Ninth Army's staff, who was relieved of his post on February 22, 1945.

Appendix C

1   Administrative assignment to United Kingdom Base Section under Ninth U.S. Army.

2   The 102nd Infantry Division was the only major combat unit that served throughout the European campaign within the Ninth U.S. Army.

Bibliography

Adams, John A., *General Jacob Devers* (Bloomington, IA: Indiana University Press, 2015).

Alanbrooke, Field Marshal Lord, *War Diaries, 1939–1945* (Los Angeles, CA: University of California Press, 2001).

Allen, Peter, *One More River* (New York: Charles Scribner's, 1980).

Ambrose, Stephen E., *The Supreme Commander: The War Years of General Dwight D. Eisenhower* (Garden City, NY: Doubleday, 1970).

_____, *The Supreme Command* (New York: Doubleday, 1970).

Ancell, R. Manning with Miller, Christine M., *The Biographical Dictionary of World War II Generals and Flag Officers: The U.S. Armed Forces* (Westport, CT: Greenwood Press, 1996).

Atkinson, Rick, *The Guns at Last Light: The War in Western Europe, 1944–1945* (New York: Henry Holt and Company, 2013).

Atwell, Lester, *Private* (New York: Simon & Schuster, 1958).

Balkoski, Joseph, *From Beachhead to Brittany* (Harrisburg, PA: Stackpole Books, 2008).

_____, *From Brittany to the Reich* (Baltimore: Old Orchard Press, 2010).

Beck, Alfred M., et al, *The Corps of Engineers: The War Against Germany. U.S. Army in World War II* (Washington, D. C.: Center of Military History, 1985).

Berlin, Robert H., *U.S. Army World War II Corps Commander* (Fort Leavenworth, KS: Combat Studies Institute, 1989).

Blair, Clay, *Ridgway's Paratroopers: The American Airborne in World War II* (New York: Doubleday & Co., 1985).

Bland, Larry I. and Stevens, Sharon R., eds., *The Papers of George Catlett Marshall, Vol. 4* (Baltimore: John Hopkins Press, 1996).

Blumenson, Martin, *The Patton Papers, 1940–1945* (New York: De Capo Press, 1996).

_____, *Breakout and Pursuit: European Theater of Operations: United States Army in World War II* (Washington, D. C.: Office of the Chief of Military History, 1961).

Boatner, Mark M., III, *The Biographical Dictionary of World War II* (Novato, CA: Presidio Press, 1990).

Bradham, Randolph, *To The Last Man: The Battle for Normandy's Cotentin Peninsula and Brittany* (South Yorkshire, UK: Pen and Sword Books, 2008).

Bradley, Omar N., *A Soldier's Story* (New York: Henry Holt and Company, 1951).

Bradley, Omar N. and Clay Blair, *A General's Life: An Autobiography by General of the Army Omar N. Bradley* (New York: Simon and Schuster, 1983).

Briggs, Richard A., *The Battle of the Ruhr Pocket: A Combat Narration* (West Point, KY: 1957).

Butcher, Harry C., *My Three Years with Eisenhower* (New York: Simon and Schuster, 1946).

Byrnes, Lawrence G., *History of the 94th Infantry Division in World War II* (Nashville, TN: Battery Press, 1982).

Calhoun, Mark T., *General Lesley J. McNair. Unsung Architect of the U.S. Army* (Lawrence, KS: University Press of Kansas, 2015).

Callahan, Raymond, *Churchill and His Generals* (Lawrence, KS: University Press of Kansas, 2007).

Castagna, Capt. E., *The History of the 771st Tank Battalion* (Berkeley, CA: 1946).

Chandler, Alfred D., Jr., ed., *The Papers of Dwight David Eisenhower, Vol. IV, The War Years* (Baltimore: John Hopkins Press, 1970).

Churchill, Winston S., *The Second World War* (6 Volumes) (London: Cassell, 1948–54).

Clark, Lloyd, *Crossing the Rhine* (New York: Atlantic Monthly Press, 2008).

Clark, Mark, *Calculated Risk* (New York: Harper, 1950).

Cole, Hugh M., *The Ardennes: Battle of the Bulge. The European Theater of Operations. U.S. Army in World War II* (Washington, D. C.: Chief of Military History, 1964).

Collins, J. Lawton., *Lightning Joe, An Autobiography* (Baton Rouge, LA: Louisiana University Press, 1979).

_____, *Combat History of the 8th Infantry Division* (Nashville, TN: Battery Press, 1984).

Cooper, Matthew, *The German Army 1933–1945* (London: MacDonald & Jane's, 1978).

Copp, Terry, *Cinderella Army: The Canadians in Northwest Europe, 1944–1945* (Toronto: University of Toronto Press, 2006).

Crabhill, Buckshot, *The Ragtag Circus from Omaha Beach to the Elbe* (New York: Vantage, 1969).

Crosswell, D. K. R. Beetle, *The Life of General Walter Bedell Smith* (Lexington, KY: University Press of Kentucky, 2010).

De Guingand, Francis, *Operation Victory* (London: Hodder and Stoughton, 1947).

_____, *Generals at War* (London: Hodder and Stoughton, 1964).

Dean, Gardner A., *One Hundred and Eighty Days, XIII Corps* (Hannover: Richard Peterson, 1945).

D'Este, Carlo, *Patton. A Genius for War* (New York: Harper Collins, 1995).

_____, *Eisenhower: A Soldier's Life* (New York: Henry Holt, 2002).

De Guingand, Francis. *Operation Victory* (New York: Scribner's Sons, 1947).

Devlin, Gerard M., *Paratrooper!* (New York: St. Martin's Press, 1979).

Doubler, Michael D., *Closing with the Enemy* (Lawrence, KS: University Press of Kansas, 1994).

Draper, Lieutenant Theodore, *The 84th Infantry Division in the Battle of Germany, November 1944–May 1945* (Nashville, TN: Battery Press, 1985).

Eisenhower, David, *Eisenhower at War, 1943–1945* (New York: Random House, 1986).

Eisenhower, Dwight D., *Crusade in Europe* (Garden City, NY: Doubleday, 1948).

Ellis, Major L. F., C.V.O., C.B.E., D.S.O., M.C. with Lt. Col. A. E. Warhurst, *Victory in the West: Vol. II. The Defeat of Germany* (London: Imperial War Museum. H. M. Stationary Office, 1968).

Elstob, Peter, *The Battle of the Reichswald* (London: MacDonald, 1971).

English, John A., *Patton's Peers. The Forgotten Allied Field Army Commanders of the Western Front, 1944–1945* (Mechanicsburg, PA: Stackpole Books, 2009).

Essame, Major General Hubert, *The Battle for Germany* (London: Batsford, 1969).

Ewing, Joseph H., *29 Let's Go* (Washington, D. C.: Infantry Journal Press, 1948).

Forty, George, *U.S. Army Handbook, 1939–1945* (Gloucestershire, UK: Sutton Publishing, 1995).

Fuermann, George M. and Cranz, F. Edward, *Ninety-Fifth Infantry Division History 1918–1946* (Nashville, TN: Battery Press, 1988).

Galvin, John R., *Air Assault, the Development of Airmobile Warfare* (New York: Hawthorn Books, Inc. 1969).

Gavin, James M., *On to Berlin: The Battles of an Airborne Commander* (New York: Viking Press, 1978).

Gawne, Jonathan, *The Americans in Brittany, 1944: The Battle for Brest* (Paris: Histoire & Collections, 2002).

Greenfield, Kent Roberts, ed., *Command Decisions* (New York: Harcourt, Brace, 1959).

Griesbach, Lt. Marc F., ed., *Combat History of the Eighth Infantry Division in World War II* (Nashville, TN: Battery Press. 1988).

Hamilton, Nigel, *Monty: Final Years of the Field-Marshal, 1944–1945* (New York: McGraw-Hill, 1986).

_____, *Monty: Master of the Battlefield, 1942–1944* (London: Hamish Hamilton, 1986).

_____, *Monty: The Field Marshall, 1944–1976* (London: Hamish Hamilton, 1986).

Harmon, E. N., *Combat Commander* (Englewood Cliffs, NJ: 1970).

Hayhow, Ernie, *The Thunderbolt across Europe: A History of the 83rd Infantry Division, 1942–1945* (Munich: F. Bruckermann, 1945(.

Hewitt, Robert L., *Workhorse of the Western Front: The Story of the 30th Infantry Division* (Washington, D. C.: Infantry Journal Press, 1946).

_____, *History of the XVI Corps: From its Activation to the End of the War in Europe* (Washington, D. C.: Infantry Journal Press, 1947).

Hillery, V. and Hurley, E., *Paths of Armor: The Fifth Armored Division in World War II* (Nashville, TN: Battery Press, 1985).

Hobbs, Joseph P., *Dear General: Eisenhower's Wartime Letters to Marshall* (Baltimore: John Hopkins Press, 1971).

Hoegh, Leo A. and Doyle, Howard J., *Timberwolf Tracks: The History of the 10th Infantry Division 1942–1945* (Washington, D. C.: Infantry Journal Press, 1946).

Houston, Donald E., *Hell on Wheels, The 2nd Armored Division* (Novato, CA: Presidio Press, 1977).

Horrocks, Sir Brian, *Corps Commander* (New York: Scribner, 1977).

_____, *A Full Life* (London: Collins, Ltd. 1960).

Huston, J. A., *Biography of a Battalion* (Gering, Nebraska: Courier Press, 1950).

Huston, James A., *Out of the Blue: US Army Airborne Operations in World War II* (West Lafayette, IN: Purdue University Studies, 1972).

Hutnick, Joseph J. and Kobrick, L., eds., *We Ripened Fast: the Unofficial History of the 76th Infantry Division* (Privately Published, n.d).

Irving, David, *The War Between the Generals: Inside the Allied High Command* (New York: Congdon and Lettés, 1981).

Irwin, John P., *Another River, Another Town: A Teenage Tank Gunner Comes of Age in Combat – 1945* (New York: Random House, 2002).

Jacobsen, Hans A., ed., *Decisive Battles of World War II* (London: A. Deutsch, 1965).

Jewell, Brian, *Over the Rhine: The Last Days of War in Europe* (Tunbridge Wells, UK: Spellmount, 1985).

Jordan, Kenneth N., Sr., *Yesterday's Heroes: 433 Men of World War II Awarded the Medal of Honor, 1941–1945* (Atglen, PA: Schiffer Publishing, 1996).

Keegan, John, ed., *Churchill's Generals* (New York: Grove Weidenfeld, 1991).

Kesselring, Field Marshal Albrecht, *Memoirs of Field-Marshal Kesselring* (London: William Kimber, 1953).

Kessler, Leo, *The Battle of the Ruhr Pocket* (Chelsea, MN: Scarborough House, 1990).

Lauer, Walter E., *Battle Babies: The Story of the 99th Infantry Division in World War II* (Nashville, TN: Battery Press, 1950).

Leach, Capt. Charles R., *In Tornado's Wake: A History of the 8th Armored Division* (Nashville, TN: Battery Press, 1992).

Leinbaugh, Harold P., and Campbell, John D., *The Men of Company K* (New York: Morrow, 1985).

_____, *Lightning: The History of the 78th Infantry Division* (Washington, D. C.: Infantry Journal Press, 1947).

Linderman, Gerald F., *The World Within War: America's Combat Experience in World War II* (New York: Free Press, 1997).

MacDonald, Charles B., *The Last Offensive: The European Theater of Operations. U.S. Army in World War II* (Washington, D. C.: Center of Military History, 1984).

_____, *The Siegfried Line Campaign: The European Theater of Operations. U.S. Army in World War II* (Washington, D. C.: Center of Military History, 1984).

_____, The *Mighty Endeavor: American Armed Forces in the European Theater in World War II* (New York: Oxford University Press, 1969).

_____, *A Time for Trumpets: The Untold Story of the Battle of the Bulge* (New York: William Morrow and Company, 1984).

_____, *The Battle of the Huertgen Forest* (New York: Jove, 1983).

_____, *Company Commander* (New York: Bantam Books: 1947, 1978).

Mansoor, Peter R., *The GI Offensive in Europe: The Triumph of American Infantry Divisions, 1941–1945* (Lawrence, KS: University Press of Kansas, 1999).

McKee, Alexander., *The Race for the Rhine Bridges* (London: Souvenir, 1971).

McManus, John C., *The Deadly Brotherhood* (Novato, CA: Presidio Press, 1998).

Mick, Major Allan H., *With the 102nd Infantry Division through Germany* (Washington: Infantry Journal Press, 1947).

Mitchell, George C., *Matthew B. Ridgway: Soldier, Statesman, Scholar, Citizen* (Mechanicsburg, PA: Stackpole Books, 2002).

Montgomery, Bernard L., *The Memoirs of Field-Marshal the Viscount Montgomery of Alamein, K. G.* (Cleveland: World, 1958).

_____, *Normandy to the Baltic* (Boston: Houghton Mifflin, 1946).

Nance, William Stuart, *Sabers Though the Reich: World War II Corps Cavalry from Normandy to the Elbe* (Lexington, KY: University Press of Kentucky, 2017).

Neillands, Robin, *The Battle for the Rhine: The Battle of the Bulge and the Ardennes Campaign, 1944* (Woodstock, NY: Overlook Press, 2005).

Ninth Army Editorial Committee, *CONQUER: The Story of Ninth Army 1944–1945* (Washington: Infantry Journal Press, 1947).

_____, *Ninth United States Army Operations, World War II* (4th Information and Historical Service, n. p., 1945).

Ninth U.S. Army, *Ninth Army Engineer Operations in the Rhine River Crossings* (N. p. 1945).

Nordyke, Phil, *The Combat History of the 82nd Airborne Division in World War II* (St. Paul, MN: Zenith Press, 2005).

North, John, *Northwest Europe 1944–1945: The Achievement of 21st Army Group* (London: Her Majesty's Stationary Office, 1953).

Pamp, Frederick E., *Normandy to the Elbe: XIX Corps* (n. p., 1945).

Patton, George S., *War as I Knew It* (Boston: Houghton Mifflin, 1975).

Pay, D. R., *Thunder from Heaven: Story of the 17th Airborne Division, 1943–1945* (Birmingham: Mich Books, 1947).

Pogue, Forrest C., *The Supreme Command: U.S. Army in World War II* (Washington, D. C.: Government Printing Office, 1954).

_____, *George C. Marshall: Organizer of Victory (*New York: Viking Press, 1973).

_____ , *George C. Marshall* (3 vols) (New York: Viking Press, 1963–73).

_____, "The Decision to Halt at the Elbe," in Kent Roberts Greenfield, ed., *Command Decisions* (Washington, D. C.: Office of the Chief of Military History, 1960).

Prefer, Nathan N., *Patton's Ghost Corps: Cracking the Siegfried Line* (Novato, CA: Presidio Press, 1998).

_____, *Eisenhower's Thorn on the Rhine: The Battles for Colmar, 1944–1945* (Havertown, PA: Casemate Publishers, 2015).

Price, Frank James, *Troy H. Middleton: A Biography* (Baton Rouge: Louisiana State University Press, 1974).

Ridgway Matthew, *Soldier: The Memoirs of Matthew B. Ridgway* (New York: Harpers, 1956).

Ryan, Cornelius, *The Last Battle* (New York: Pocket Books, 1985).

Shulman, Milton, *Defeat in the West* (London: Secker & Warburg, 1947).

Smart, Nick, *Biographical Dictionary of British Generals of the Second World War* (South Yorkshire, UK: Pen and Sword, 2005).

Smith, Walter Bedell, *Eisenhower's Six great Decisions: Europe, 1944–1945* (New York: Longmans Green, 1956).

Standifer, Leon C., *Not in Vain: A Rifleman Remembers World War II* (Baton Rouge, LA: Louisiana State University Press, 1992).

Stanton, Shelby L., *Order of Battle, U.S. Army, World War II* (Novato, CA: Presidio Press, 1984).

Stock, James W., *Rhine Crossings* (New York: 1973).

Sylvan, William C., and Smith, Francis G., Jr., Greenwood, John T., ed., *Normandy to Victory: The War Diary of General Courtney H. Hodges and the First U.S. Army* (Lexington, KY: University Press of Kentucky, 2008).

Taaffe, Stephen R., *Marshall and his Generals: U.S. Army Commanders in World War II* (Lawrence, KS: University Press of Kansas, 2011).

_____, *The Cross of Lorraine: A Combat History of the 79th Infantry Division, June 1942–December 1945* (Nashville, TN: Battery Press, 1986).

_____, *The 35th Infantry Division in World War II* (Nashville, TN: Battery Press, 1988).

Thompson, R. W., *Battle for the Rhineland* (London: Hutchinson, 1958).

Toland, John, *The Last Hundred Days* (New York: Random House, 1966).

Truscott, Lucian K., Jr., *Command Missions: A Personal Story* (New York: Dutton, 1954).

United States Senate, Committee on Veterans' Affairs, *Medal of Honor Recipients, 1863–1978* (Washington, D. C.: Government Printing Office, 1979).

Warner, Philip, *Horrocks: The General Who Led from the Front* (London: Hamish Hamilton, 1964).

Weigley, Russell F., *Eisenhower's Lieutenants: The Campaigns of France and Germany, 1944–1945* (Bloomington, IN: Indiana University Press, 1981).

Whitaker, W. Denis and Whitaker, S., *Rhineland: The Battle to End the War* (New York: St. Martin's Press, 1989).

Williams, Mary H. (comp.), *Chronology 1941–1945. United States Army in World War II* (Washington, D. C.: Department of the Army, 1960).

Winton, Harold R., *Corps Commanders of the Bulge* (Lawrence, KS: University Press of Kansas, 2007).

Wishnevsky, Stephen T., *Courtney Hicks Hodges* (Jefferson, NC: McFarland, 2006).

Wright, Stephen L., *The Last Drop: Operation Varsity, March 24–25, 1945* (Mechanicsburg, PA: Stackpole Books, 2008).

Yeide, Harry, *The Tank Killers: A History of America's World War II Tank Destroyer Force* (Philadelphia: Casemate Publishers, 2007).

_____, *Steel Victory: The Heroic Story of America's Independent Tank Battalions at War in Europe* (New York: Ballantine books, 2005).

_____, *The Infantry's Armor: The U.S. Army's Separate Tank Battalions in World War II* (Mechanicsburg, PA: Stackpole books, 2010).

_____, *Steeds of Steel: A History of American Mechanized Cavalry in World War II* (Minneapolis, MN: Zenith Press, 2008).

Zaloga, Steven, *Operation Cobra 1944: Breakout from Normandy* (Westport, CT: Praeger, 2004).

Zumbro, Derek S., *Battle for the Ruhr* (Lawrence, KS: University Press of Kansas, 2006).

_____, *XIX Corps in Action from the Siegfried Line to Victory* (Germany: 62nd engineer Topographic Company, 1945).

Articles, Theses, etc.

"Battle for Brest" in *Life*. 17. (October 16, 1944), pp. 38–39.

"Battle of the Ruhr, The" in *The Cavalry Journal*, 55 (1945), pp. 13–15.

"Big Simp of the Ninth" in *Newsweek*, XXIV (27 November 1944), p. 33.

"Biography of Lieutenant General William H. Simpson" Public Relations Office, Headquarters, Second Army, Tennessee, October 11, 1945

Blumenson, Martin, "The Decision to Take Brest" in *Army* (March 1960), pp. 45–51.

_____, "To the Last Stone: The Siege of St. Malo" in *Army* (August 1970), pp. 38–48.

Brett, Thomas J., "The U.S. North Flank" in *The Cavalry Journal* 54, (1945), pp. 24–25.

"British-American Contact" in *The Cavalry Journal*, 55, (1946), pp. 3–7.

Chase, Francis Jr., "The Rhine was 1000 Miles Wide" in *Saturday Evening Post*, 217 (May 5, 1945) 20, p. 106.

Citino, Robert M., "Death in the West" in *World War II*, (May/June 2015), pp. 34–43.

Donaldson, Chase, "From the Roer to the Rhine" in *The Cavalry Journal*, 54 (1945), pp. 22–23.

Dziuban, Stanley W., "Rhine River Flood Prediction Service" in *The Military Engineer*, XXXVII (1945), pp. 348–353.

"Envelopment of the Ruhr" in *Army and Navy Journal*, LXXXII (1945), pp. 1113 & 1128.

"Fall of Geilenkirchen, The: An Important Siegfried Strongpoint Captured in a Combined action by British and American Forces" in *The Illustrated London News*, 115 (1944), pp. 620–621.

Ganz, A. Harding, "Questionable Objective: The Brittany Ports, 1944" in *Journal of Military History* 1 (January 1995), pp. 77–95.

"German Tactics in a Delaying Defense" in *Military Review* XXV (1945), pp. 85–87.

Grim, Seton H., "A Combat Battalion on the Rhine" in *The Military Engineer*, XXXVII (1945), pp. 497–500.

MacMillan, Henry J., "The Bridging of the Roer" in *Infantry Journal*, LVII (1945), pp. 50–51.

Martin, Ralph G., "Roer to the Rhine" in *Yank*, III (April 6, 1945), pp. 2–4.

Neff, John C., "Race to the Rhine" in *Infantry Journal* LXI (1947), pp. 36–40.

"People of the Week: Lieut. Gen. William H. Simpson" in *The United States News*, XVII (1944), pp. 62 & 64.

Pogue, Forrest C., "Why Eisenhower's Forces Stopped at the Elbe" in *World Politics*, IV. (1952), pp. 356–368.

Prefer, Nathan N., "Too High a Price: The Brittany Campaign, 1944" in *World War II Quarterly*, Spring 2016.

———, "Cracking the Geilenkirchen Salient" in *World War II History*, October 2016.

Ravenhill, C., "The Influence of Logistics on Operations in Northwest Europe, 1944–1945" in *Journal of the Royal Service Institution*, 91. (1946), pp. 495–502.

Sebree, Edmund B., "Research Memorandum Leadership at Higher Levels of Command as Viewed by Senior and Experienced Combat Commanders" Presidio of Monterey, California, U.S. Army Leadership Human Research Unit, 1961.

Simpson, Lt. Gen. William H., "Rehearsal for the Rhine: An Account of the Ninth United States Army Operation 'Grenade'" in *Military Review* 25 (1945), pp. 20–28.

———, "Partners in Battle: A Ground Force Commander's Appraisal of Air Power" in *Air Force*, XXVIII (1945), pp. 4–6& 34.

———, "Rehearsal for the Rhine" in *Military Review*, XXV (1945), pp. 20–28.

Stone, Thomas R., "*He Had the Guts to Say No: A Military Biography of General William Hood Simpson*" Ph.D. Dissertation, Rice University, 1974.

———, "William H. Simpson: A General's General" Unpublished Master's Thesis, Rice University, 1971.

———, "General William Hood Simpson: Unsung Commander of the US Ninth Army" in *Parameters* 11, No. 2 (June 1981): pp. 44–45.

"Why Ike Didn't Capture Berlin: An Untold Story" in *U.S. News and World Report*, April 26, 1971, pp. 70–73.

Index